THE
COLLAPSE
OF
HISTORY

OVERTURES TO BIBLICAL THEOLOGY

Reconstructing
Old Testament
Theology

THE
COLLAPSE
OF
HISTORY

Leo G. Perdue

FORTRESS PRESS   Minneapolis

THE COLLAPSE OF HISTORY
Reconstructing Old Testament Theology

Library of Congress Cataloging-in-Publication Data

Perdue, Leo G.
    The collapse of history : reconstructing Old Testament theology /
Leo G. Perdue.
        p.   cm.—(Overtures to biblical theology)
    Includes bibliographical references and index.
    ISBN 0-8006-1563-8 (alk. paper)
    1. Bible. O.T.—Theology—History of doctrines—2. 2. Bible.
O.T.—Theology. I. Title. II. Series.
BS1192.5.P47   1994
230—dc20   94-2824
                                                          CIP

The paper used in this publication meets the minimum requirements of American National Standard for Information Sciences—Permanence of Paper for Printed Library Materials, ANSI Z329.48-1984. ∞™

Manufactured in the U.S.A.   AF 1–1563

98   97   96   95   94   1   2   3   4   5   6   7   8   9   10

Contents

Editor's Foreword

It is no secret that the fortunes of Old Testament theology in recent time have been lean indeed. Old Testament theology seems largely to have reached a plateau (or stalemate) with the work of Walther Eichrodt and Gerhard von Rad, and most scholarly efforts since then have continued to replicate their models. Or more precisely, it is Eichrodt who has been replicated. His concentration on a single theme as an organizing principle has been imitated by other scholars with reference to themes other than his accent on covenant. With his most distinctive approach, von Rad has dominated much of the subsequent discussion, so that his influence has been enormous, although there has been no effective development out of his work.

Since the great work of Eichrodt and von Rad in the 1930s through the 1950s, Old Testament theology has not claimed the energy and attention of many scholars. Indeed, in a reaction against a theological propensity in interpretation dominated for an extended period by Karl Barth, scholarship has moved away from any normative notion of theology in Bible study and has returned to a greater interest in the history of Israelite religion. All of this is a commonplace in the field.

The work of Leo Perdue is a most important effort to redefine and rehabilitate the task of theological interpretation that has recently languished. Perdue shows why the task can be resumed in a fresh way. The title of the book, *The Collapse of History*, permits Perdue to identify both the key assumption and the crucial problem of the regnant categories of Old Testament interpretation. With the rise of historical criticism, Old Testament study has been cast primarily in historical categories. Not only was the embrace of historical categories an intentional move of scholars to circumvent the authoritarian control of religious interpretation (so Gabler) but that embrace readily resonated with the larger assumptions of an Enlightenment perspective that valued objectivity, positivism, and scientific precision about the text. Thus Old Testament study has been in the grip of historical categories, as has all of Western intellectual history over the past two centuries. (A continuing evidence of this tendency is the propensity to trace the developmental "stages" of everything.) It has become clear that even von Rad, for all his imaginative work, finally could not escape the grip of "history," which left his credo-theology with an irresolvable dilemma. Perdue shrewdly traces the influence and demise of the "historical-theological" program of von Rad and Wright.

The major contribution of Perdue's work, however, is not simply to present yet one more obituary of that movement of interpretation. It is, rather, to show in a comprehensive way, as none has done before Perdue, that Old Testament theology has not come to a halt or to a practice of thin, predictable imitation but has rather, with considerable vitality and power, moved in new directions. The clue is that the new efforts are no longer mesmerized by or beholden to the issues of "history" but have emerged in the different categories of constructive imagination, not caged in by "facticity." To be sure, as long as the models of Eichrodt and von Rad are normative, the new efforts do not seem to be "biblical theology." That is, they do not meet our preconceived notions of what the task is. But as Perdue makes clear, Eichrodt and von Rad operate in a context and with a set of epistemological assumptions that no longer pertain, so that these works now belong no longer to the "current scene" but to "the history of the discipline." When one reads Eichrodt or von Rad, powerful and compelling as they are, one also senses how dated the formulations have become.

As successors to these works, a variety of perspectives and methods that are focused variously on creation, canon, liberation, narrative, and imagination have emerged. It is now obvious that sociological analysis and literary criticism have become the dominant methods of scholarship, in large measure displacing the influence of the older historical criticism. Perdue demonstrates, however, that these new, emerging practices are not simply methods of scholarship; they are modes of doing theology, thus marking a departure from the older patterns and modes, which inevitably produces a different content for the discipline. These newer methods, moreover, have already produced a significant body of interpretative material. When Perdue provides an inventory of those materials, one is impressed by how much has been done that is both current and compelling.

It does not trouble Perdue at all that we now have available a half dozen alternative approaches to Old Testament theology. The older historical model had established a kind of hegemony about how to do the work. With "the collapse," however, it is not likely that any single perspective will be able again to establish such dominance. Rather, the work of Old Testament theology will feature alternative methods that are not in competition as though one of them needed to prevail, but with each capable of learning from and being influenced by the others. I suggest that what these newer approaches all have in common, against the older view, is a hermeneutical awareness that theological interpretation is inevitably and inherently constructive. That is, the text does not provide a single theological program, nor is interpretation a description of what is "there."

Our newer awareness of the work of interpretation minimizes the importance of facticity. Rather than a settled "message," the text provides the materials out of which different readers and interpreters will fashion different presentations. Such hermeneutical maneuverability is of course against the positivism of mono-meaning. Thus theological interpretation is likely to be evocative and pervasively unresolved rather than a practice of interpretative closure. Perdue has noticed that Paul Ricoeur shows up at a variety of places in the new, emerging modes of theological interpretation. While Ricoeur is not the only such influence, his frequent appearance in scholarly work suggests that theological interpretation is especially a practice of imaginative speech that only belatedly can be made propositional and systematic, or historical in any conventional sense.

Perdue makes clear that we are in a quite new situation for doing Old Testament theology, but that new situation is not one of stagnation or stalemate. It is, rather, an opportunity for enormously imaginative work. In moving into such modes of interpretation, Old Testament scholarship plays its part in the larger cultural transition away from positivism into a world of multifaceted imaginative possibility. Perdue has marked this transition in a way that is enormously helpful.

Finally, Perdue completes his review with a demanding proposal for a way ahead. In an irenic posture that takes account of and appreciates various disciplines (including the older modes of historical criticism), Perdue proposes that Old Testament theology must embrace both careful critical work and imaginative interpretation, that is, it must be both descriptive and constructive. The interpreter must care both for the history of interpretation and for the large cultural context of contemporary work. (The outcome is an echo of Gadamer's "fusion of horizons.") Commitment to "the power of imagination" does not nullify historical studies but insists (*a*) that we move beyond history to a contemporary horizon and (*b*) that we recognize that even our "historical studies" are themselves imaginative and constructive.

Perdue has served us well in noting the dramatic shifts in the nature of biblical theology and in providing categories for understanding what is in fact happening in the field. Our coming work is not in a context of Barthian confessionalism that sought magisterial (canonical?) norms. Nor is it in Enlightenment positivism which wants to find "truth" in "fact" and which assumes that "the describer" can be neutral and uninvolved. Rather, our fresh work is in reading texts always toward contemporary horizons, recognizing that reality is "linguistic" and well as "historical." I anticipate that Perdue's book will serve to emancipate and legitimate work that yearns to escape the old options of description on the one hand and conceptualization on the other.

Walter Brueggemann

Preface

The reawakening of significant interest in biblical theology in recent years has led to vigorous debate about methodology, purpose, and objectives in articulating the understanding of God, humanity, and the world. What has stimulated the debate about methodology has been the tension between historical-critical strategies of interpretation originating in the Enlightenment and more recent ones with different epistemologies that, collectively, are placed under the general rubric of postmodernism. Social-scientific study of the Bible, liberation and feminist theologies, the Bible as Scripture, the variety of developing methods in literary criticism, narrative theology, and the phenomenology of imagination offer new and engaging approaches to understanding and articulating biblical theology.

Questions regarding the purpose and objectives of biblical theology also continue to be discussed. What is the relationship of biblical theology to the history of Israelite religion and early Christianity? Is the purpose of the biblical theologian to describe the theology or theologies of the biblical books and writers, that is, to set forth a historical theology; or is the purpose to construct a biblical theology that engages the present world, that is, to shape a contemporary hermeneutic? Should the purpose be to set forth the distinctive theologies of various books and corpora of literature in the Bible or to select a central theme and then compose a systematic rendering of biblical faith? Should the biblical theologian make value judgments about particular biblical understandings, either by reference to her or his own faith and religious community or to other, varying views within the biblical text?

The enormous pluralism that characterizes contemporary biblical study and the ways of doing biblical theology in the present makes the debate particularly interesting. This reality of pluralism is grounded in the fragmentation of cultures and their undergirding epistemologies throughout global communities. The emergence of a broad consensus about biblical theology appears to be most unlikely, at least for any reasonable prognostication. Pluralism, however, should not become a license for legitimating every presentation of biblical theology. Open conversation that frankly engages the variety of approaches to biblical theology and its many particular presentations needs to proceed along the lines of common criteria of evaluation.

This book attempts to trace the variety of approaches to Old Testament theology that have appeared since World War II. Earlier surveys have tended to limit their inquiry to more traditional, even classical biblical theologies and thus often have ignored the many new approaches that have recently developed. These approaches and, in most instances, their major representatives are examined in this volume and evaluated with a view toward enhancing conversation. The proposal is made that historical-critical approaches that lead to biblical theology and the newer methods for the study of the Bible do not necessarily result in irresolvable conflict.

This volume was conceived at the University of Chicago during my sabbatical year in 1987–88 where I was a Senior Research Fellow in the Institute for the Advanced Study of Religion and Scholar-in-Residence at Disciples Divinity House. I wish to thank Bernard McGinn, Naomi Shenstone Donnelley Professor of Historical Theology at the Divinity School and at that time the Director of the Institute for the Advanced Study of Religion, for leading a stimulating seminar for fellows and for supplying a supportive environment for my research and thinking. I also acknowledge with appreciation the hospitality afforded me by my congenial host for the academic year, W. Clark Gilpin, Dean of the Divinity School and Associate Professor of History of Christianity and of Theology, who during my sabbatical year was Dean of the Disciples Divinity House at Chicago. In addition to being an engaging conversation partner, Dean Gilpin provided me with a comfortable room in which to live and invited me to participate in the intellectual life of Disciples House. I also am indebted to Professor Mary Knutsen, currently Associate Professor of Theology at Luther Northwestern, for the many stimulating conversations we had about theology when we were faculty colleagues at Phillips Graduate Seminary during the late 1980s. Professor Knutsen was kind enough to offer critical readings of this work in the early stages of its formation.

Finally, I wish to acknowledge the many contributions to my theological formation by James L. Crenshaw, currently Professor of Old Testament, Duke Divinity School. Professor Crenshaw was my *Doktorvater* during my graduate studies at Vanderbilt, and he has been a valued conversation partner in the areas of wisdom studies and Old Testament theology and cherished friend for a quarter of a century. His intellect, grace, wit, and passion for truth have earned my deep admiration and respect. I wish to dedicate this volume to him in gratitude for many past conversations and in anticipation of many future ones.

Abbreviations

AB	Anchor Bible
ATD	Das Alte Testament Deutsch
BA	*Biblical Archaeologist*
BASOR	*Bulletin of the American Schools of Oriental Research*
BETL	Bibliotheca ephemeridum theologicarum lovaniensium
BHT	Beiträge zur historischen Theologie
BKAT	Biblisher Kommentar: Altes Testament
BZAW	Beihefte zur *ZAW*
CBQ	*Catholic Biblical Quarterly*
EvT	*Evangelische Theologie*
HBT	*Horizons in Biblical Theology*
IB	*Interpreter's Bible*
ICC	International Critical Commentary
IDB	G. A. Buttrick (ed.), *Interpreter's Dictionary of the Bible*
Int	*Interpretation*
JAAR	*Journal of the American Academy of Religion*
JBL	*Journal of Biblical Literature*
JR	*Journal of Religion*
JSOT	*Journal for the Study of the Old Testament*
JSOTSup	Journal for the Study of the Old Testament—Supplement Series
JTS	*Journal of Theological Studies*
KD	*Kerygma und Dogma*

NCB	New Century Bible
NICOT	New International Commentary on the Old Testament
OTL	Old Testament Library
RevExp	*Review and Expositor*
RSR	*Recherches de science religieuse*
SBLDS	SBL Dissertation Series
SBT	Studies in Biblical Theology
SIAW	*Studies in Ancient Israelite Wisdom*, ed. James L. Crenshaw
SVT	*Supplements Vetus Testamentum*
TLZ	*Theologische Literaturzeitung*
TQ	*Theologische Quartalschrift*
TS	*Theological Studies*
TToday	*Theology Today*
VT	*Vetus Testamentum*
WMANT	Wissenschaftliche Monographien zum Alten und Neuen Testament
ZAW	*Zeitschrift für die alttestamentliche Wissenschaft*

INTRODUCTION

CHAPTER 1

The Present Status
of Old Testament
Theology

*History above all is a cemetery and field
of the dead.*   —K. G. Steck
God created man, because he loves stories.   —Elie Wiesel
The past is not dead; it is not even past.   — William Faulkner
*If thinking wants to think God, then
it must endeavor to tell stories.*   —Eberhard Jüngel

These quotations are juxtaposed metaphors whose interactions
may provide some insight into the current fragmentation of Old
Testament theology. Some description of the present status of Old
Testament theology is necessary if additional clarity is to be
achieved about present and future tasks, methods, and goals.[1] It is
also necessary, because many of us who have attempted to do Old
Testament theology have become inarticulate of late. Words, gram-
mar, and syntax that produce the theological construction of reality
are increasingly elusive, due to both the destabilization of tradi-

1. Important surveys of Old Testament theology include F. F. Bruce, "The
Theology and Interpretation of the Old Testament," *Tradition and Interpretation*
(ed. George Wishart Anderson; Oxford: Clarendon, 1979) 385–416; John J.
Collins, "Is a Critical Biblical Theology Possible?" *The Hebrew Bible and Its
Interpreters* (ed. William Henry Propp et al.; Winona Lake, Ind.: Eisenbrauns,
1990) 1–17; George Coats, "Theology of the Hebrew Bible," *The Hebrew Bible
and Its Modern Interpreters* (ed. Douglas A. Knight and Gene M. Tucker;
Philadelphia and Chico, Calif.: Fortress Press and Scholars Press, 1985) 239–62;
Gerhard Hasel, *Old Testament Theology: Basic Issues in the Current Debate* (4th
rev. ed.; Grand Rapids: Eerdmans, 1991); John H. Hayes and Frederick Prussner,
Old Testament Theology: Its History and Development (Atlanta: John Knox, 1985);
Jesper Høgenhaven, *Problems and Prospects of Old Testament Theology* (The
Biblical Seminar; Sheffield: JSOT, 1987); Hans-Joachim Kraus, *Die biblische
Theologie* (Neukirchen-Vluyn: Neukirchener Verlag, 1970); H. Graf Reventlow,
Problems of Old Testament Theology in the Twentieth Century (Philadelphia:
Fortress, 1985); and James D. Smart, *The Past, Present, and Future of Biblical
Theology* (Philadelphia: Westminster, 1979).

tional paradigms that have allowed theological discourse to take place since the Enlightenment and the emergence of several new ones with often competing yet quite different claims.[2]

Traditional paradigms and their theological worlds, centered in and constructed by history and historical method, have come under serious assault, leaving many of us who were educated in historical exegesis in a state of disorientation and confusion that produces a variety of scholarly psychoses. I have chosen to call this destabilization of the dominant paradigm of historical criticism "the collapse of history." By "the collapse of history" I do not mean to argue or even imply that history and historical method are now passé, impossible, or insignificant for modern Old Testament scholarship and Old Testament theology, although many voices are now being heard that argue that the modern period, in which historical criticism has been nurtured for a quarter of a millennium, is coming to an end and that we have entered or are in transition to a postmodern world with significantly different epistemologies and sociopolitical arrangements.[3] Neither do I mean to suggest that history and historical-critical method will not continue to contribute in important ways to Old Testament theology, although even some sympathetic practitioners, not to mention ardent critics, have argued as much. But I do mean that for at least a generation now active revolt against the domination of history and historical method for Old Testament study in general and Old Testament theology in particular has been under way and in large measure has seceded from the epistemological rule of this once unchallenged strategy of interpretation.[4] With the rise of new methods for studying the Bi-

2. For a discussion of the collapse of the biblical theology movement, a largely American phenomenon, see Brevard Childs, *Biblical Theology in Crisis* (Philadelphia: Westminster, 1970).

3. Important discussions of postmodernism include Frederic B. Burnham, ed., *Postmodern Theology: Christian Faith in a Pluralist World* (San Francisco: Harper & Row, 1989); Edgar V. McKnight, *Postmodern Use of the Bible: The Emergence of Reader-oriented Criticism* (Nashville: Abingdon, 1988); Stephen Moore, "The 'Post-' Age Stamp: Does It Stick? Biblical Studies and the Postmodernism Debate," *JAAR* 57 (1989) 543–59; Alan M. Olson, "Postmodernity and Faith," *JAAR* 58 (1990) 37–53; Carl A. Rascke, "Fire and Roses: Toward Authentic Post-Modern Religious Thinking," *JAAR* 58 (1990) 671–89; Robert P. Scharlemann, ed., *Theology at the End of the Century: A Dialogue on the Postmodern* (Charlottesville, Va.: University of Virginia Press, 1990); and Huston Smith, "Postmodernism's Impact on the Study of Religion," *JAAR* 58 (1990) 653–70.

4. E.g., James Luther Mays argued in 1980: "Currently there is a restlessness in many quarters at the dominance of biblical interpretation by historical criticism— in newer literary criticism, in structuralism, in the hermeneutics of Paul Ricoeur, to mention only several." What these methods share is a concern primarily with

ble, nurtured within a newly emerging sociopolitical ethos in the contemporary world, there are new configurations of biblical study and Old Testament theology that either break with or seek to transform significantly the epistemological undergirding of historical criticism that is oriented to the construction of a largely uniform (e.g., "biblical" or "Christian" or "Western" or "modern") worldview. Indeed, pluralism, whether a problem to be addressed or an enrichment to be affirmed, is understood increasingly as fundamental to the very nature of knowledge and the methodologies that develop to understand the world or worlds in which humans exist.

In spite of the turmoil in contemporary biblical study and the larger epistemological framework for knowing and persuading and in spite of the appearance of many recent descriptions of Old Testament theology, what I find surprisingly lacking is a serious analysis of new methods for biblical study and their contributions to Old Testament theology.[5] Most surveys have been content to continue to discuss the classical approaches to Old Testament theology and often take little, if any, notice of new, vital, and radically different approaches that are grounded in different epistemologies and that pose often different, unconventional questions.

Many scholars, including some who have written descriptions of ways of doing Old Testament theology and even some who have written recent Old Testament theologies, have ignored the voices of discontent that are directed against Enlightenment strategies for knowing, historical criticism, and traditional biblical theology that builds on this methodology. These critical and, until recently, marginalized voices include liberation and narrative theologians, canon and literary scholars, phenomenologists and linguists, and feminists from First and Third World countries. Indeed, some biblical scholars continue to write and to speak as though the destabilized language of traditional approaches somehow will continue to convince and convict, perhaps hoping that new methods and their impact on theological discourse may eventually disappear.[6]

Other scholars have abandoned what usually has been regarded

---

the text rather than with the history behind the text ("What Is Written: A Response to Brevard Childs's *Introduction to the Old Testament as Scripture*," HBT 2 [1980] 151–63).

5. See Phyllis Trible, "Five Loaves and Two Fishes: Feminist Hermeneutics and Biblical Theology," *TS* 50 (1989) 279–95.

6. See, e.g., Horst Dietrich Preuss, *Theologie des Alten Testaments* (2 vols.; Stuttgart: Kohlhammer, 1991–92); and Høgenhaven, *Problems and Prospects of Old Testament Theology*. I am currently translating Preuss's *Theologie des Alten Testaments* for the OTL, published by Westminster/John Knox.

as the subject matter of Old Testament theology—that is, God—in order to focus their attention on other matters, including the social and anthropological description of human beings.[7] Theology becomes, in this case, a part of social knowledge, even ideology. It is an easier task to speak about the human than it is about the transcendent. Still others pursue the microscopic examination of historical fragments themselves, eschewing larger constructions of meaning, especially theological and ethical ones, as abstract, or speculative, or outside the domain of legitimate biblical scholarship. This retreat into historical analysis, conceived by the rubrics of positivism and shaped by the history of religions, leaves to contemporary theologians, pastors, and pundits, who often are not thoroughly trained in the complexities of biblical study, the task of engaging biblical theology in conversation with contemporary hermeneutics and constructive theology.

Even among those who consider themselves to be biblical theologians open to new methodologies and hermeneutical issues that originate in the contemporary world, many have bidden farewell to conversation involving dialogue, debate, and argumentation about the tasks and methods of theology, stressing that it is the quality of interpretation, not the method leading to its creation, that is the pressing concern. After all, it is argued, the text itself is various, questions are diverse, methods are many, and their application leads to meanings that are multivalent. Thus, in this age of multiculturism and diversity, we should celebrate our pluralism and rejoice over our differences.[8] Yet this too only contributes to increased fragmentation and may even lead to the danger of making theology primarily a matter of private taste. Subsequently, conversation is becoming more difficult, even among specialists. Serious efforts at criteriology need to be undertaken in order to find established procedures for evaluating theological interpretations and approaches, much in the fashion of some contemporary theologians. The establishment of a carefully proposed and rigorously applied criteriology would not result in only one way of doing Old Testament theology. However, appropriate criteria, carefully applied, could evaluate and assess the quality of an interpretation in important ways and remove it from the realm of subjective pref-

7. For a recent survey of this field, see Norman K. Gottwald, ed., *Scientific Criticism of the Hebrew Bible and Its Social World: The Hebrew Monarchy, Semeia* 37 (1986).
8. See James Sanders, *Canon and Community* (Guides to Biblical Scholarship; Philadelphia: Fortress, 1984) 15.

erence and preposterous claims. But even before criteriology may be established, an introduction to the issues and approaches, especially current ones, needs to provide an entrée into this vital yet very diverse discipline.

All of this is not to say that the field of biblical theology—and I shall proceed in this narrative with the assumption that there is a field of scholarly discourse that justifies this nomenclature—is stagnant or declining. Indeed, the reverse is true: biblical theology today is a vibrant, living organism of interest to both the academy and the church. But there are multiple paradigms competing for attention, often with disparate claims, objectives, and methods with different philosophical and theological orientations and assumptions. The variety of expression and the lack of clear ways of proceeding have silenced the voices of many raised in a simpler time to practice a more traditional, if not also confessional, approach. We are the ones who have fallen silent. But for the most part, biblical theology today has not become a silent statue but rather a "tower of Babel" with articulations that command no consensus, either clash with or ignore different approaches, and command no overwhelming following. Coming to some basic understanding of new approaches and content is essential if conversation between biblical theologians and ultimately between biblical and contemporary theologians is to occur with rigorous and engaging vitality.

REASONS FOR THE COLLAPSE OF HISTORY

It is difficult to point to a single cause behind the collapse of history as the dominant paradigm for Old Testament theology that has led to the present disarray. It has been due in part to the challenge of the appropriateness of historical-critical method, at times grounded in philosophical positivism, for even descriptive theological discourse. During the past generation, other methods for Old Testament study have developed that have different philosophical underpinnings which even may eschew the historical enterprise, although this is not always, or even necessarily, the case. These include, for example, new criticism, the canonical approach, history of religions, phenomenology, and some expressions of feminist hermeneutics. At times, exponents of newer paradigms argue that these approaches make more accessible theological meaning which, in their judgment, resides in and is shaped by, not some objective history behind ancient texts, but rather the community of believers, the order and continuation of creation, the interaction of canon and community, the experience of the interpreter, the narrative world created through the interaction of the implied audience with the "voice" of the text and the text itself, or the imagination of writer or audience or text. For example, theologians of imagination and new critics may argue that theological discourse, including that of biblical theology, does not issue simply from the historian's "reproductive imagination," to use the language of Paul Ricoeur, but also from the fiction writer's "productive imagination."[9] In any case, for proponents of newer approaches history as the theme, the center of meaning, and the frame for theological discourse has lost its once proud position of dominance.

The fragmentation of theological discourse resulting from the collapse of history is also due in part to the diverse character of contemporary theology which shares a common heuristic world with biblical scholarship. In 1981, Lonnie Kliever used the metaphor of "the shattered spectrum" to describe the state of contemporary theology.[10] Theology has become even more diverse in the following decade. Liberation, process, hope, creation, feminism, metaphor, story, and imagination have emerged to reconceive the strategies and questions of contemporary theology, and these in turn have impacted directly and indirectly biblical theology. No commanding contemporary theology has yet appeared to form a consensus—say, in the manner of old liberalism or neoorthodoxy in times that are past. Subsequently, the current disarray of contemporary theology has contributed significantly to the present diversity of ways to approach Old Testament theology.

A third, more existential factor has contributed to the disarray in biblical theology resulting from the collapse of history. This is the loss of confidence in the epistemological claims of the Enlightenment to be grounded in objectivity and critical, rational inquiry. Patriarchy, colonialism, the Holocaust, the deterioration of the biosphere, and the threat of nuclear war are the real and potentially destructive by-products of the technology of modern civilization. As Gibson Winter has warned, in the modern age it is those who control capital and technology who inherit the earth, and the drive

---

9. Paul Ricoeur, "The Metaphorical Process," *Semeia* 4 (1975) 75–106; and idem, "The Narrative Function," *Semeia* 13 (1978) 177–202. See the discussion of Ricoeur and Brueggemann below, in Part Four.

10. Lonnie Kliever, *The Shattered Spectrum: A Survey of Contemporary Theology* (Atlanta: John Knox, 1981). For a cogent and clear survey of American contemporary theology, see Deanne William Ferm, *Contemporary American Theologies: A Critical Survey* (rev. ed.; San Francisco: Harper & Row, 1990).

for power over nature and nations has brought modern civilization and life itself to the brink of annihilation. We now find ourselves threatened by the very technology and its by-products we once hailed as our savior or comforter. According to Winter, we must develop a new paradigm for the construction of reality in the modern world, one that will make creation, not an object for human dominion, but a sustaining place for human dwelling. This paradigm should see history, not as the mastery of the weak by the strong, but as the movement toward a viable world in which all nations and peoples share, celebrate, and live in peace and justice.[11] To make biblical study and Old Testament theology no more than a discipline of antiquarian interest removes them from the vital interests of contemporary society and its search for meaning and values.

Fourth, the collapse of history has resulted from an increasing number of biblical theologians rejecting the descriptive approach[12] in favor of a reflective, critical, constructive, or systematic strategy. A purely descriptive approach, which is epistemologically questionable in and of itself, results in the fragmentation of theology into a variety of disconnected and often contradictory ideas. Indeed, the descriptive approach is capable of presenting multiple theologies of the two Testaments, but not a single theology. This is due to the fact that the canon is a library of books written over many centuries by many different authors and redactors whose theologies are rather diverse.

The descriptive approach also does not attempt to engage present culture, leaving that task to those contemporary theologians (e.g., Paul Tillich) who see modern culture as an important consideration in theological discourse. This refusal results in part from the academy's general tendency to disengage the biblical text and the scholarly enterprise from contemporary theology. Lessing's "ugly ditch" between past and present, separating descriptive analysis from modern application, is one that has widened considerably in certain circles of biblical interpretation since the 1960s. An increasing number of biblical scholars, however, are not satisfied only to describe the contents of Old Testament theology; rather, they insist that questions of modern culture should be addressed to the text. If

11. Gibson Winter, *Liberating Creation: Foundations of Religious Social Ethics* (New York: Crossroad, 1981).
12. See the classic statement for the descriptive approach by Krister Stendahl, "Biblical Theology, Contemporary," *IDB* 1:419f.

we are to overcome, or at least narrow, this separation between past and present and to awaken the text to life, we need to engage in discourse that allows scholars and communities of faith to engage in conversation and continue to articulate new theological understandings.

Perhaps all of the above reasons could be subsumed under the argument in some contemporary circles that we either have entered into a postmodern world that has followed and supplanted the reign of the Enlightenment or at least are in a period where the epistemologies and worldviews issuing from the Age of Reason are contested by numerous rivals. Postmodernism is an especially amorphous and elusive expression, for it is used to refer to almost any way of knowing or not knowing in recent years that differs from or is critical of Enlightenment thinking. Thus postmodernism may include such diverse entities as Third World liberation movements, reader-response criticism, and deconstructionism. If there is a unifying factor in postmodernism, it is, ironically, an affirmation of pluralism in ways of knowing and being in the world. Thus perspectives on reality as well as reality itself (one should say "realities") are a kaleidoscope that is constantly changing.[13] Of course, the *Geist der Aufklärung* (spirit of the Enlightenment), especially reason that issued forth in scientific method, provided the epistemological basis for historical criticism. Subsequently, a methodology for critical inquiry and theological analysis grounded in an intellectual age whose culture and cultural products are under serious criticism has a much more difficult time of it in making persuasive arguments. Whether this represents a crisis in epistemology that will lead to an abandonment of historical-critical method remains to be seen, but I suggest that reports of the death of this approach, to borrow from Mark Twain, "have been greatly exaggerated."

Finally, the collapse of history, at least theologically speaking, results from the failure of the paradigm to do what all models must continue to do to enable silent lips to speak: comprehend salient theological features implicit and explicit in the biblical text, adequately articulate the Christian faith, acknowledge and cope with anomalies that defy the logic of a theological system, and construct a convincing, dynamic theological hypothesis that responds to and then correlates with human experience. A careful and rigorous ap-

13. The metaphor of kaleidoscope is used by Huston Smith, "Postmodernism's Impact on the Study of Religion," 660–61.

plication of criteriology must weigh the merits of any theological presentation, whether of biblical, historical, or contemporary theology. In any intellectual inquiry, no theology, or, for that matter, no ideology, should be exempted from the close examination of rational investigation and judicious criticism. Here I speak as an unrepentant rationalist. Simply to argue that all theology is ideology and thus exempt from critical evaluation, since all linguistic and historical constructions are concerned with power and self-interest, leads to potentially dangerous consequences, as the demonic Nazi period should have taught us.[14]

It is the collapse of the historical paradigm as the singular approach for doing Old Testament theology that is the central problem in present theological discussion, but it is also the cause for new and critical reflection about how we approach and carry out the task. With the current, vigorous debate that has emerged, new paradigms of theological discourse have taken shape. If no compelling consensus has yet to appear on the horizon, at least new conversation is under way.[15] What is at stake is nothing less than the vitality of theological interpretation, both biblical and contemporary, and, some would say, authentic and faithful life in the modern, if not the postmodern, world.[16]

DESCRIPTION OF THE PRESENT TASK

The following narrative is designed to provide a basic introduction to recent and emerging approaches to Old Testament theology. It seeks to allow one a more informed entrée into the modern conversation. Subsumed under this overarching goal are three objectives. The first objective is to review critically the various ways of doing Old Testament theology since World War II, with particular emphasis on the present period. Several recent efforts seek to accomplish this task, but these have sometimes failed to explore many contemporary approaches that are blazing new paths for contemporary biblical theology. While there is in general a tendency to

14. See Jack Forstman, *Christian Faith in Dark Times: Theological Conflicts in the Shadow of Hitler* (Louisville, Ky.: Westminster-John Knox, 1992).
15. The series Overtures to Biblical Theology has been specifically conceived to bring together exegesis and contemporary hermeneutics in a variety of ways.
16. This is not to suggest that there are not strong efforts to integrate Old Testament theology into a system that allows for diversity. The work of Ronald Clements, e.g., points to an integration of literary, historical, cultic, and intellectual dimensions, collectively called "the dimensions of faith" (*Old Testament Theology* [London: Marshall, Morgan & Scott, 1978] 1–52).

trace with great thoroughness German scholarship, not enough consideration has been given to important work done outside the Continent. Furthermore, these studies often fail to be attentive to two important relationships that biblical theology has with other interpretative enterprises. First, there is the important connection between methodology in biblical exegesis and the way the theological task is conceived. Thus, with the continuing developments in exegetical interpretation, new ways of going about the theological task are continually developed and improved. Second, the paradigms for doing biblical theology are normally shaped or at least influenced by interaction with contemporary theology. Hence the developments in contemporary theology that impact dramatically biblical theology need to be identified.

The second objective of this narrative is to illustrate the various ways of conceiving Old Testament theology by giving specific consideration to the Book of Jeremiah. This will result, first of all, in providing concrete specificity for the abstract discussion of theological paradigms. This focus on Jeremiah also will result in pointing to some new directions in presenting the theology of this prophetic book. Jeremiah is receiving a considerable amount of interest in modern scholarship.[17] However, with some notable exceptions, little has been done in presenting the theology of this prophetic book since the 1950s, when some effort was made to give Jeremiah, and especially the prose tradition, a neoorthodox cast. It is surprising that classical liberalism has tended to color many of the theological presentations of the Book of Jeremiah even in the present.[18] This narrative will evaluate the past theological presentations of the Book of Jeremiah and outline new formulations that result

17. Walter Brueggemann, *To Pluck Up, To Tear Down: A Commentary on the Book of Jeremiah 1-25* (International Theological Commentary; Grand Rapids: Eerdmans, 1988); idem, *To Build, To Plant: A Commentary on Jeremiah 26-52* (International Theological Commentary; Grand Rapids: Eerdmans, 1991); Robert P. Carroll, *Jeremiah* (OTL; Philadelphia: Westminster, 1986); Ronald Clements, *Jeremiah* (Interpretation; Atlanta: John Knox, 1988); William Holladay, *Jeremiah* (2 vols.; Hermeneia; Philadelphia: Fortress, 1986, 1989); Douglas R. Jones, *Jeremiah* (NCB; Grand Rapids: Eerdmans, 1992); William McKane, *Jeremiah* (ICC; Edinburgh: T. & T. Clark, 1986); and J. A. Thompson, *The Book of Jeremiah* (NICOT; Grand Rapids: Eerdmans, 1980). For a survey of issues and interpretations prior to 1983, see Leo G. Perdue and Brian W. Kovacs, eds., *A Prophet to the Nations: Essays in Jeremiah Studies* (Winona Lake, Ind.: Eisenbrauns, 1984).

18. Perdue, "Jeremiah in Modern Research," Perdue and Kovacs, *A Prophet to the Nations*, 1-32.

from the application of recent paradigms. Of course, there are obvious limitations in using only one biblical book for illustration, since larger issues of canon (Old Testament and New Testament), systematic formulation, and the relationship between Old Testament theology and the history of Israelite religion cannot be addressed as comprehensively as possible. Nevertheless the approaches to Jeremiah represented by new and developing methodologies should at least be instructive for those seeking an entrée into the modern discussion.

The third objective is to select examples of recent approaches to biblical study and the doing of Old Testament theology that, as a whole, focus attention more on the text and its language with an explicit view to move into contemporary theology than on the history of Israelite religion residing behind the text. This dichotomy between biblical theology as a discipline within theology as a whole and biblical theology understood within the rubric of the history of Israelite religion has produced much of the tension and controversy in biblical theology for two centuries. It is intriguing to note, however, that the agenda for biblical theology set out in Johann Philipp Gabler's famous inaugural address at the University of Altdorf in 1787 often has not been carried out by those doing biblical theology.[19] According to Gabler, an important differentiation should be made between dogmatic (systematic) theology and biblical theology. Prior to Gabler, biblical theology was a handmaiden of dogmatics. This meant that the Bible set forth the divine, universal, eternal truths that dogmatic theology was to arrange in systematic order. In opposing this view, Gabler argued that biblical theology was a historical enterprise that sought to portray the theology of the biblical authors. The appropriate method to follow was historical criticism. For Gabler, a distinction should be made between "true" biblical theology that is the limited, conditional theology of the biblical writers and "pure" biblical theology that reveals the eternal theological truths of divine revelation. Dogmatic or systematic theology was concerned to shape a coherent theology that applied theological truths of "pure" biblical theology to the contemporary world. Thus Gabler tried to mediate between biblical theology as a historical exercise to reconstruct the history of Israelite religious

---

19. For the text of the speech, see Otto Merk, *Biblische Theologie des Neuen Testaments in ihrer Anfangszeit* (Marburger Theologische Studien 9; Marburg: Elwert, 1972) 273–84.

ideas and biblical theology as a tool of systematic theology that was to incorporate the salient, universal ideas of the Bible into a systematic form addressing current situations.[20]

This volume seeks to indicate that, while there are major tensions between various approaches to Old Testament theology and the two major ways it has been conceived (to use Gabler's terms, as "pure" or "true" biblical theology), there are significant points of contact and even commonality that should allow fruitful discourse to occur. But how to engage the historical paradigm in conversation with paradigms not grounded in history is the primary question. The concluding two chapters will make some suggestions as to how this conversation, and subsequently Old Testament theology itself, may proceed.

This volume is divided into four major parts. Part One, "Old Testament Theology: Redemption and History," outlines in three movements the continuum of "history" as the focus, content, and methodology for doing Old Testament theology. Chapter 2, "History as Event," focuses on the biblical theology movement in North America that combines a largely positivistic historiography and the archaeological work of the Albright school with neo-orthodoxy. Chapter 3, "History as Tradition: The German School," outlines the work of Gerhard von Rad. This approach brings together the understanding of history set forth by German idealism, traditiohistorical method, and neoorthodoxy. Chapter 4, "History as Liberation: Social Science and Radical Theology," examines the work of Norman Gottwald. Significant features of this approach are neo-Marxist historiography, social-scientific methodology, and an emphasis on human liberation from oppressive sociopolitical systems.

Part Two, "Old Testament Theology: Cosmology and Anthropology," traces one recent shift away from the domination of history in Old Testament theology. Chapter 5, "History and Creation: Myth and Wisdom," examines the recent emergence of creation as a central concern of Old Testament theology in the present. The major features of this approach include both methods from phenomenology and history of religions and the modern focus on creation by leading contemporary theologians.

Part Three, "Old Testament Theology: Scripture and Metaphor,"

20. For a recent discussion of Gabler's proposal, see Ben C. Ollenburger, "Biblical Theology: Situating the Discipline," *Understanding the Word: Essays in Honor of Bernhard W. Anderson* (ed. James Butler et al.; JSOT 37; Sheffield: JSOT, 1985) 37–62.

outlines two recent approaches to Old Testament theology that involve the movement from history to the text and its implied audience. Chapter 6, "From History to Scripture: Canon and Community," concentrates on a second shift from history, in this case to the received canon of the Hebrew Bible. Chapter 7, "From History to Metaphor: Literary Criticism and Feminist Hermeneutics," considers the approach of rhetorical criticism, metaphorical theology, and feminist hermeneutics to Old Testament theology.

Part Four is "Old Testament Theology: Story and Imagination." Chapter 8, "From History to Fiction: Biblical Story and Narrative Theology," examines the important role that imagination plays in both narrative history and narrative fiction and seeks to demonstrate the common ground held by these two types of literary genres. Chapter 9, "From History to Imagination: Between Memory and Vision," examines the nature and role of imagination in historiography and theology and suggests that this approach demonstrates how history and theology may engage in meaningful conversation. Chapter 10, "The Future of Old Testament Theology," makes observations about the present state of Old Testament theology, sets forth some criteria to use in evaluating various formulations, and suggests a proposal for proceeding with the task in the future.

The argument will be made that in addition to distinctive features of approaches to biblical study and Old Testament theology there are also important, common features shared by historical criticism and literary analysis that should avoid polarizing the discussion for all but the extreme historicists and the most radical of postmodernists. The extremists are not interested in discussion, in any event. It will be suggested that these many, diverse methods have their contribution to make to Old Testament theology and to the ongoing conversations in contemporary hermeneutics. But at the same time, they should be brought together in critical dialogue. The reconstruction of theological discourse in the present awaits those who have not only ears to hear and eyes to see but also tongues to speak and minds to imagine.

PART ONE

Old Testament Theology: Redemption and History

CHAPTER 2

History as Event:
The Biblical Theology
Movement in America

OLD TESTAMENT THEOLOGY
AND HISTORICAL CRITICISM

One thing is clear from reviewing Old Testament theology since its origins in the late nineteenth century. The focus, content, and method for doing Old Testament theology derive in the main from new and developing methodologies for biblical study. Coming to classical form in the latter part of the nineteenth century under the influence of first romanticism and then positivism, historical criticism has continued to be the dominant paradigm for biblical studies, including much Old Testament theology. Its questions and goals have continued to focus on history qua history, that is, the determination of what "really happened" and "why." Source criticism, textual criticism, biblical archaeology, traditions history, and even form criticism are used by the historian to reconstruct the history and thought of ancient Israel, Judaism, and early Christianity.

The process of positivistic historiography includes the following steps: ascertainment (the establishment of a corpus of facts), explanation (the construction of an argument that organizes the data of history and explains why something happened), correlation (the establishment of relationships with other facts and construction of schemes and patterns), and impact (how these events influenced other occurrences).[1] While there are other philosophical constructions (e.g., neo-Marxism, or the conflict model, used by Norman Gottwald), the dominant one in Old Testament circles has continued to be positivism. Choosing to be descriptive and scientific (at

---

1. Edgar Krentz, *The Historical-Critical Method* (Guides to Biblical Scholarship; Philadelphia: Fortress, 1975).

least in a nineteenth-century sense) in its research models and agendas and eschewing normative judgments because of a professed objectivity, Old Testament historiography has attempted to be self-critical by recognizing that the knowledge of the past is limited by incomplete sources, the fallibility of the interpreters, and the subjectivity of the historian involved in the selection of what is considered to be significant data. The methods that have developed over the years and that have been successfully wedded to the earlier paradigm include text, literary (source), form, and tradition criticisms; archaeology; comparative religions; sociology; and anthropology.[2]

With the goal of research being the presentation of history qua event, the Bible is, at least in the first and primary instance, not Sacred Scripture expressing and witnessing to the faith of believing communities; rather, it is one of many sources, including literary texts and cultural artifacts, for reconstructing the social, economic, political, and religious life of ancient Israel. The major implication is that Judaism and Christianity must be understood within the ongoing history of the world, not as separate from or unique to that process. Any claim of "salvation history," that is, that God has acted in and through these historical communities, derives from the subjective faith of the believer, not from the evidence of the data. Nevertheless, for theologies that place great stock in history—for example, classical liberalism and Wolfhart Pannenberg's earlier work—the marriage of historical research and Christian faith lasted for nearly a century. When scholars discovered that events in the Bible did not happen or were inaccurately portrayed, the ideas could still be affirmed as true theologically.

Even in the attempt to write history, historical method has been the subject of rigorous criticism from a variety of perspectives. These criticisms have pointed to the limitations of positivism in the tasks of historiography, although I shall not attempt to debate these issues at this juncture.[3] But when it comes to doing Old Testament

---

2. The method has developed on the basis of the three principles of Ernst Troeltsch ("Über historische und dogmatische Methode in der Theologie," *Zur religiösen Lage, Religionsphilosophie und Ethik* [2d ed.; Aalen: Scientia Verlag, 1962]): the principle of criticism (history only achieves probability and must continue open to new evidence and reevaluation), the principle of analogy (contemporary experience and occurrences become the bases for establishing probability in the past), and the principle of correlation (the connection of data and causality). For a detailed discussion, see Krentz, *Historical-Critical Method*, 55–72.

3. See Walter Wink, *The Bible in Human Transformation: Toward a New*

theology and engaging in intelligent discourse about contemporary hermeneutics, the problems are especially acute, as we shall see.

THE RISE OF NEOORTHODOXY

Following World War II, neoorthodoxy became the dominant contemporary theology in North America and Europe. This theology had already blossomed in Europe in the period between the two world wars, especially in the writings of Karl Barth and Emil Brunner. The battle over the Bible in Europe was largely over by the end of the nineteenth century, and the horrors of trench warfare in World War I quickly ended the unchallenged reign of classical liberal theology. Although assuming different shapes among the Reformation traditions of Presbyterians and Lutherans, the guiding themes of neoorthodoxy were the sovereignty and providence of God, redemption through encounter with the Word, the eschatological act of redemption in Jesus Christ, the centrality of Christ as Lord and Redeemer, the depravity of human nature, justification by faith, and sola scriptura—that is, the return to the normative rule of the Bible. Redemptive history and special revelation, in sharp contrast to natural theology, were the mainstays of neoorthodoxy.

Neoorthodoxy considered the rediscovery of the Bible, like the finding of the lost coin, to be a cause for great celebration. The modern church needed to hear afresh what had been lost or forgotten. The proclamation of the message of the Bible and the community's confessional response to its affirmations and claims were at the center of the life of faith. Much of the loss of the vitality of the message of the Bible was thought to derive from the obsession of biblical scholars with history and historical minutiae. By means of historical criticism, they had succeeded in wresting the Bible away from the fundamentalists and confessional orthodoxy, but at great cost. The redemptive message of the Bible had been lost in the quagmire of historicism. Neoorthodoxy also criticized the fundamentalists for an inflexible, even deadening literalism that stifled free and critical inquiry and replaced faith in search of understanding with mindless credulity. When it burst forth on the American scene in the post–World War II period, neoorthodoxy offered mainline Protestants, Catholics, and Reformed Jews the possibility of affirming both the value and the importance of biblical criticism, while articulating a compelling theology.

Paradigm for Biblical Study (Philadelphia: Fortress, 1973); and idem, *Transforming Bible Study* (2d ed.; Nashville: Abingdon, 1989).

THE BIBLICAL THEOLOGY MOVEMENT

As Brevard Childs has demonstrated, a variety of understandings of theology and the Bible in America existed in the generation following World War II, although most held in common several significant features.[4] These included the following:

1. The goal was to recover the theological character of the Bible, not by the repudiation of biblical criticism, but by the renewed effort to identify the unified message of the texts. Redemptive history was especially deemed the center of the biblical message.

2. The search began to attempt to discover the unity of the entire Bible, not just the Old or the New Testament. This unity was dynamic, allowing for developments and diversity. Unity could be understood in terms of message, theme (e.g., covenant), continuity in divine revelation (e.g., promise and fulfillment), and even God.

3. Revelation was centered in history, in contrast to nature or doctrines deposited within Christian creeds. While the Bible was the human witness to this divine action, its message was not simply the result of human thought. The Bible attested to God's acts leading to the redemption of Israel and the church.

4. A distinctive biblical mentality was affirmed that, in contrast to rational, static, and abstract Greek thought, was said to be verbal, personal, and dynamic. To think biblically often meant to focus on the "words" of the Bible that were thought to embody the concreteness of Semitic thought, not on dogmas shaped by speculative philosophy or denominational self-interest.

5. The Bible was placed in opposition to its environment. In reaction against the history of religions school, biblical theologians often stressed the uniqueness of Israel's understanding. For example, Israel was thought to be unique among the nations of the ancient Near East in its conception of God acting in history, since the other cultures were thought to locate their deities primarily within the realm of nature and

4. Childs, *Biblical Theology in Crisis*, 32–50. For a somewhat different assessment, see James Barr, "The Theological Case against Biblical Theology," *Canon, Theology, and Old Testament Interpretation* (FS Brevard S. Childs; ed. Gene M. Tucker et al.; [Philadelphia: Fortress, 1988]) 3–19. Barr notes that the biblical theologians thought an alliance with history and historical research would make their case a strong one. However, they failed to realize there were theological arguments that opposed their approach.

myth. The theological implication was that this distinctiveness was considered to be especially revelatory and normative for faith. And it was thought that this uniqueness attested to the authenticity and superiority of Israel's truer understanding of God.

HISTORY AS EVENT: GEORGE ERNEST WRIGHT

Emerging during the early post–World War II period, the biblical theology movement, largely an American phenomenon, represented one of the most fertile and provocative achievements in twentieth-century religious thought. Holding the dominant position in American biblical studies for twenty years, this movement forged a majority consensus among biblical scholars in this country, evoking from many an indomitable confidence in both its procedures and its results. Indeed, the major features of biblical theology entered into American Catholicism and mainline American Protestantism in a popular form, becoming the basis for much of the lay and clerical understanding of the message of the Bible in the 1950s and 1960s.

The best-known Old Testament representative of the biblical theology movement in America was George Ernest Wright whose influential book *God Who Acts* possesses the revealing subtitle *Biblical Theology as Recital.*[5] Wright joined George E. Mendenhall, Frank Moore Cross, Jr., David Noel Freedman, and John Bright as the major representatives of the Albright school, scholars who trained under W. F. Albright and together forged the dominant tradition of Old Testament studies in North America following World War II.[6] A leading field archaeologist and biblical scholar,

5. See especially G. Ernest Wright, *God Who Acts: Biblical Theology as Recital* (SBT 8; London: SCM, 1952). Other important works of Wright include *The Old Testament against Its Environment* (SBT 2; London: SCM, 1950); "The Book of Deuteronomy: Introduction and Exegesis," *IB* (Nashville: Abingdon, 1953); with an ecumenical committee in Chicago, *The Biblical Doctrine of Man in Society* (Ecumenical Biblical Studies 2; London: SCM, 1954); with Floyd V. Filson, *The Westminster Historical Atlas to the Bible* (Philadelphia: Westminster, 1956); *Biblical Archaeology* (Philadelphia: Westminster, 1957); *Shechem: The Biography of a Biblical City* (New York: McGraw-Hill, 1965); *The Old Testament and Theology* (New York: Harper & Row, 1969); and with Robert Boling, *Joshua* (AB; Garden City, N.Y.: Doubleday, 1982), which appeared some years after Wright's death.

6. For a recent discussion of the Albright school, see George E. Mendenhall, "Biblical Interpretation and the Albright School," *Archaeology and Biblical Interpretation* (ed. Leo G. Perdue et al.; Atlanta: John Knox, 1987) 3–13.

Wright made significant use of his seminal work in field archaeology and Israelite history in establishing guidelines for doing Old Testament theology.[7] In those days, positivism guided the formation of scientific field archaeology as well as the writing of Israelite and ancient Near Eastern history.[8] As a field archaeologist and biblical historian, Wright was active both in the procurement of a corpus of data deriving from the Bible, archaeological fieldwork, and other written sources, and in their assessment for historiography. Throughout much of his life he remained unabashedly enthusiastic about the scholarly ability to reconstruct Israelite history. And he asserted that if one wished to know the God of Israel, one had to study the data and processes of history.

Wright was among the leading archaeologists of his day, candidly admitting that the driving force behind the world of biblical archaeology was "the understanding and exposition of the Scriptures."[9] He emphasized the close relationship between biblical archaeology, biblical history, and biblical theology. The Bible not only contained the history of a people in time and space, so he asserted, but also the unique confession of Israel in the God of history.

> Faith was communicated . . . through the forms of history, and unless history is taken seriously one cannot comprehend biblical faith which triumphantly affirms the meaning of history.[10]

Wright's most significant fieldwork was carried out at the biblical city of Shechem (Tell Balatah), a site important not only in antiquity but also in the annals of biblical archaeology, for it was here that scientific archaeology, biblical criticism, and biblical theology achieved their first compelling synthesis. Yet for Wright, Shechem was more than simply one of many important sites in biblical history. Shechem represented *the* site, at least for the biblical theology movement, for it was here that Wright believed the old tribal federation, with its covenant renewal ceremony, celebrated at the national sanctuary for the first time the formative acts of redemptive history (cf. Deut 26:5-9 and Joshua 8).

---

7. For a thorough study of Wright and his work, see Philip J. King, "The Influence of G. Ernest Wright on the Archaeology of Palestine," Perdue, *Archaeology and Biblical Interpretation*, 15–29; and Philip J. King, *American Archaeology in the Mideast: A History of the American Schools of Oriental Research* (Philadelphia: American Schools of Oriental Research, 1983).

8. D. Glenn Rose, "The Bible and Archaeology: The State of the Art," Perdue, *Archaeology and Biblical Interpretation*, 53–64.

9. Wright, *Biblical Archaeology*, 17.

10. Ibid.

For the Albright school, archaeology was the necessary key to unlock the mysteries of the biblical world and to place the Bible within its proper historical and cultural context. Through archaeology, Wright believed the historical character of biblical literature could be properly understood and assessed.[11] Yet it was also through the help of archaeology that one could better understand biblical theology, because the people of the Bible believed that God had acted in certain redemptive events on their behalf. Thus biblical archaeology and biblical theology go hand in hand. Taking history to be the primary avenue for divine activity and revelation, Wright then used reconstructed events as the basis for his own theological work. For Wright, confidence in the historian's reconstruction of past events gave credibility to both the ancient and the modern confession of the redeeming acts of God.

GOD WHO ACTS

In the small though very influential volume, *God Who Acts*, Wright set forth the major parameters of an Old Testament theology that were to guide his own thinking for his entire life. Here, he passionately argued that what is essential is to determine the actual course of primal events that gave birth to the people of Israel, events that may be successfully reconstructed by historical criticism. Israel's faith was grounded in and a response to historical events.

For Wright, it is the event that resides at the heart of Israel's ancient faith. The event even takes precedence over Israel's own various understandings. Israel believed that God was primarily the Lord of history whom they encountered especially in certain primal events. Without historical events—that is, events that actually occurred within and to a community dwelling in concrete time and space—there is no credible basis upon which authentic faith may be founded. Indeed, Wright thought that archaeology substantiated many of the events of the biblical story as having taken place.

Wright argued that the Bible was essentially a history book. Most important was his conclusion that field excavations on the whole substantiated the historical veracity of the Bible. Perhaps the most important case, according to Wright, was the biblical account (Joshua) of the conquest of the land of Canaan.[12] Wright thought that the accumulation of evidence from archaeological excavations made a

---

11. Wright, *Shechem*, xvi–xvii.
12. Wright, *Biblical Archaeology*, 18.

strong case for the historicity of Israel's conquest of the land of Canaan. Yet for Wright, biblical archaeology's essential purpose was not actually to prove the Bible but rather to discover and interpret the material remains of the biblical cultures that produced the Bible and gave shape to the Judeo-Christian faith.

To understand Wright, it must be stressed that while he believed that the historical character and veracity of the biblical record were supported by archaeology, its purpose was not to prove the Bible. Rather, excavations were the means to reconstruct the cultural setting and the historical background for understanding Scripture.[13]

Disdaining the categories of dogmatic theology (God, humanity, salvation, judgment, etc.) that he attributed to the early church's encounter with Greek philosophy, Wright contended that authentic theological categories must emerge from the Old Testament itself. These categories, he concluded, should not be superimposed upon the Bible from the outside. He further argued that a careful examination of the Old Testament points to the centrality of "the mighty acts of God." Indeed, these "mighty acts" present the faith of Israel and unify the diverse materials in the Old Testament.

Wright contrasted the fertility religions of the cultures of the ancient Near East, whose gods, he argued, were essentially personified natural forces, with the religion of Israel, whose God, in his judgment, was a personal deity revealed in the acts of history wrought for Israel's salvation. Neoorthodox theologians tended to place nature in opposition or subordination to history, giving unquestioned primacy to the latter. This was true of Wright. He argued that at the very heart of Israel's understanding of divine action is redemption: Israel and the world are in need of salvation; this is the ultimate goal of human history. These acts of divine redemption included the call of the fathers, the exodus, the Sinai covenant, the conquest of Canaan, and the Davidic covenant. He submitted that the primary genre for ancient Near Eastern religions was myth, while Israel's distinctive literary forms were the historical credo (Deut 26:1-9; Deut 6:20-24; Josh 24:2-13) and historical narratives.[14] These redemptive events that brought Israel into exis-

13. This point was clearly made by Wright in his essay "What Archaeology Can and Cannot Do," *BA* 34 (1971) 70–76.

14. "We can now see that though the Bible arose in that ancient world, it was not entirely of it; though its history and its people resemble those of the surrounding nations, yet it radiates an atmosphere, a spirit, a faith, far more profound and radically different than any other ancient literature" (Wright, *Biblical Archaeology*, 27). For Wright's contrast between ancient Near Eastern myth and Israelite history, see Wright, *The Old Testament against Its Environment*.

tence and guided its history attested to the sovereignty of God who alone was Lord of all.[15]

Although the specific interpretations given to these acts within the Bible itself vary, Wright contended that the core event, subject to historical reconstruction, remained for critical demonstration. And in spite of diverse biblical accounts, what these interpretations held in common was Israel's undaunted belief that God had acted to redeem them. Wright thought Israelites could express their faith so confidently, because they believed these events really happened.

Wright did not deny the importance of Israel's affirmation of God as creator for Old Testament theology. He emphasized, however, that this understanding is conveyed through the covenant relationship with God—that is, the God with whom Israel existed in covenant, the Lord of history, was also the creator who brought all things into existence and ruled over them as sovereign. He wrote: "Creation, then, is not simply the making of the world; it is what identifies history's Lord and releases into time that judging and redeeming power which is to be observed again and again in human history by eyes trained to see and interpret by faith."[16]

Israel's world, according to Wright, was a fallen world in need of redemption. Sin was pervasive both in nature and in history. Even Israel's history was often one of rebellion instead of obedience. For Israel, creation suffered from divine curse. Thus, the goal of God's redemptive acts in history was to save Israel and ultimately all humanity from the destruction of sin. Nature religion, practiced in a mythical form by the other cultures of the ancient Near East, was false, for it failed to take into consideration the corruption of creation and wrongly placed revelation within the course of natural processes. Humans also exist in a fallen state, wrote Wright, for they are responsible for their sinful disobedience to divine command. They are not the "good" creatures created by God, and thus are capable of redemption only by the sovereign Lord of history. Humans are dependent upon God for redemption, for their own misguided efforts result in tragedy and alienation.[17]

Wright came to prefer the metaphor of Israel's understanding of reality as a political world, a cosmic government, ruled over by a divine monarch. This organizing metaphor was supported by a variety of metaphors for God, including Lord, Judge, Warrior,

15. Wright, *The Biblical Doctrine of Man in Society*, 65.
16. Wright, *The Old Testament and Theology*, 95.
17. Wright, *The Biblical Doctrine of Man in Society*, 35–46.

Shepherd, and Father.[18] Especially prominent was the title of Divine Warrior, because Israel, according to Wright, believed that judgment and salvation were administered in the world by God, and at times that administration involved war in order to defeat evil and bring about salvation.[19] This sovereignty of God was also expressed in the form of covenant. The literary character of this covenant, as well as part of its conceptuality, originated in ancient Near Eastern suzerainty treaties, meaning then that Yahweh was the suzerain and Israel the vassal whose sinfulness could be restrained only in obedience to the divine will.[20]

HERMENEUTICS: BIBLICAL THEOLOGY AS RECITAL

Wright's hermeneutics took the form of a very different discourse, as revealed by his subtitle: *Biblical Theology as Recital.* He argued that hermeneutics is grounded in the *proclamation* of "the mighty acts of God" by contemporary, witnessing communities.[21] As Israel confessed and proclaimed these actions in their worship, so the proper appropriation of these events is to *recite* them in liturgy and preaching.[22] Seen in this manner, the essential faith of the Old Testament is kerygmatic and confessional. In the hermeneutical task conceived by Wright, the same event may be taken today, reclothed with new meaning, and still authentically proclaimed as a divine action of redemption. Of course, in contemporary application, historiography is abandoned, and faith becomes a matter of *preaching and confessing* the acts of God.

The impetus for Wright's theological work derived from his stance within the contemporary church. An active Presbyterian minister, Wright believed that, for the Old Testament, faith is the confessional response to the proclamation of God's saving acts. Like later believing Christian communities, Israel proclaimed and confessed its central creed of divine activity as a response to its encounter with God in its historical and social existence. In these

---

18. Wright, *The Old Testament and Theology*, 119–20.
19. See ibid., chap. 5: "God the Warrior," 121–50.
20. Ibid., 104–12.
21. Elsewhere Wright argues that the Bible "does not of itself furnish us with, or exhibit a primary interest in, propositional dogmatics in systematic form." Rather, the "doctrines" are "the Bible's *testimony* to what God has done" (Wright, *The Biblical Doctrine of Man in Society*, 9).
22. Ibid., 70–72. "Common worship, therefore, was a dominant factor in keeping the meaning of the sacred story alive as a vitalizing force in community life and as the basis of individual hope and effort" (p. 71).

active expressions, faith in the God who acts in history to save takes its vital shape.[23]

Wright also emphasized the unity of the Bible. While he worked mainly as a scholar of the Old Testament, he stressed the importance of the entire Protestant canon. This position also resulted from his confessional approach. However, he eschewed any developmental view of progressive revelation that stressed, in the old liberal fashion, the final culmination of salvation history in the person and teachings of Jesus. Rather, for Wright "the primary area of unity lies in its historical testimony to, or proclamation of, God's activity *(kerygma)*."[24]

Yet Wright noted that the problem of unity is also found in the question of the relationship between the Testaments. Wright approached biblical theology from the context of the Christian community that confesses Christ as Lord. Thus, biblical theology is christocentric, meaning that the unity of Scripture is ultimately to be found in Jesus Christ. For Wright as believer, Christ is the clue to the theological meaning of the Old Testament, for he is its final destination, even as the Old Testament is the clue to the meaning of Christ. For Wright, these "clues" have their focus in the Bible's presentation of God's redemptive activity, with Christ being the supreme act.[25] Wright came to recognize, however, especially in his more mature reflection, the dangers of what in some circles was essentially Christomonism, that is, a theology that so concentrated on Christology that the other members of the Trinity, in particular God, were either ignored or relegated to insignificance.[26]

The Reformed tradition, expressed particularly in Barthian terms, shaped the theological matrix for Wright's formulation of Israelite faith. Many mainline churches, including the Presbyterians, had suffered from the "battle for the book" since the latter part of the nineteenth century. Subsequently, there was great eagerness for a new confessional theology that encouraged critical study

23. Ibid., 76: "It is thus clear that in the Bible we have to do with a community of a most remarkable and unusual kind. Its worship, confession, proclamation and sacred literature were for the most part and centrally dominated by the understanding of God as Lord of history who had created a special community, revealed to it the manner of its life, provided for it the means of interpreting events by chosen spokesmen, and by unmerited acts and promises had given to it hope in the midst of the tragedies of history."

24. Ibid., 10.

25. Ibid., 5.

26. See Wright, *The Old Testament and Theology*, chap. 1: "Theology and Christomonism," 13–38.

of the Bible and yet seriously engaged the modern church's traditional confessions. Thus the search for a sure footing for faith, thought to reside in the scientific reconstruction of historical events, arose out of the painful modernist-fundamentalist controversies of the late nineteenth and early twentieth centuries. With biblical theology, both serious scholars and progressive preachers could embrace biblical criticism, not only because of its logic and its ability to counteract the influence of the fundamentalists but also because it was thought to have the inherent ability to secure the historicity of the faith. Biblical faith was not based on fairy tales and untrue myths but rather on recoverable historical acts that formed and sustained the Jewish and Christian communities.

REDEMPTIVE HISTORY IN JEREMIAH: JOHN BRIGHT

Another representative of the biblical theology movement and former student of W. F. Albright was John Bright. Bright's formidable works on Israelite history and Jeremiah commanded international respect, and he expressed understandings of history, archaeology, and biblical theology very similar to those of Wright.[27] Indeed, Bright's Anchor Bible commentary on Jeremiah not only was an exegetical tour de force but also presented in exemplary fashion the major features of the biblical theology movement applied specifically to a canonical text. It was not just any biblical text, for it was the Book of Jeremiah, the prophetic hero of Protestant liberalism,[28] who came to represent by painstaking exegetical analysis the major components of the biblical theology movement, the Albright school, and the important tenets of neoorthodoxy. Indeed, Bright's interpretation of Jeremiah, one of two major American studies originating in the twenty years following World War II,[29] shaped an entire American generation's understanding of this most important prophet.

---

27. John Bright, *A History of Israel* (3d ed.; Philadelphia: Westminster, 1982); idem, *Early Israel in Recent History Writing: A Study in Method* (SBT 19; London: SCM, 1956); and idem, *Jeremiah* (2d ed.; AB; Garden City, N.Y.: Doubleday, 1965).

28. See especially the classical liberal presentation of Jeremiah by John Skinner, *Prophecy and Religion* (1st paperback ed.; Cambridge: At the University Press, 1961).

29. The other was that of J. Philip Hyatt, "The Book of Jeremiah: Introduction and Exegesis," *IB* 5 (1956) 794–1142.

HISTORIOGRAPHY

Bright concluded that the formation of the Book of Jeremiah represented a lengthy process in which several streams of tradition, some oral and others written, converged. Even so, Bright argued the position that most of the materials in the Book of Jeremiah originated with the prophet, his scribal companion Baruch, and disciples who faithfully transmitted the prophet's thoughts and deeds for several generations before the final composition of the text. Thus, the poetic corpus of oracles found in Jeremiah 1–25 (source A) were considered to be the actual words of Jeremiah, perhaps even written down by the prophet and then dictated to and preserved by Baruch (chap. 36), while the prose narratives (source B, chaps. 26–45) most probably originated with Baruch or another contemporary and intimate of Jeremiah and continued to be edited and transmitted by a circle of faithful disciples. The prose sermons (source C) may not have been the actual words of the prophet, but Bright considered them a faithful recasting of Jeremiah's oracles into the vernacular common to the seventh to sixth centuries B.C.E. This work was carried out by faithful disciples within just a few generations of the prophet's death.[30] Some adaptation and occasionally even some misunderstanding of the prophet may have occurred in C, but in Bright's opinion these texts captured accurately the prophet's own thought.

With these positions in place, Bright could conclude that we know more about Jeremiah than about any other Old Testament prophet, although he denied we could write a biography of the prophet. Still, he believed a general outline of the prophet's career could "be attempted with some confidence."[31] This effort involved more than the scholar's desire to write a history of the life and message of Jeremiah. Rather, the historical prophet's thought received from Bright a privileged position in regard to authority. While not rejected out of hand, later accretions did not carry the same authority.

Affirming the historical veracity of a large part of the Book of Jeremiah, Bright argued that the most important task of the scholar was to place the life and thought of the prophet within the major social and political currents of his day. This task was made less formidable by two considerations: the efforts of tradition circles to

30. Bright, *Jeremiah*, lv–lxxviii.
31. Ibid., lxxxvii–cxviii.

date many of the deeds and sermons of Jeremiah by reference to major historical events, and the substantial body of extant historical sources from the period in which Jeremiah lived. While there were lacunae in the materials and nagging historical problems, Bright believed that much of the life and times of the prophet could be historically and accurately set forth.

BIBLICAL THEOLOGY

Like Wright, Bright was firmly anchored to the biblical theology movement. The privileging of history as the primary avenue for divine action and revelation, the importance of historical-critical method for understanding the Bible exegetically and theologically, the unity of the Bible in Christ, the authority of Scripture, and other elements of neoorthodoxy were significant features for Bright's understanding of biblical theology.[32] Even in Bright's exegetical treatment of Jeremiah, these major elements came to the fore. The task of the theologian was, for Bright, not very different from the work of the historian. The goal is to reconstruct the historical narrative of the life and thought of Jeremiah, as far as that was possible, and to place him within the dimensions of space and time. This was simply a chapter in the long narrative history of the providential shaping of the community of God and the larger history of humanity. The goal of history, according to Bright, is the movement toward the consummation of the kingdom of God, which he understood as a moral order in which peace and justice prevailed under the active and acknowledged reign of God.[33]

Bright's stance within the Christian community also shaped his understanding of both biblical theology and the prophet from Anathoth. Thus, for Bright, Jeremiah, far from being an ethical teacher and religious innovator in the style of old liberalism, became a neoorthodox preacher. This Jeremiah proclaimed Yahweh's sovereignty over history and creation, announced the redemptive acts of the God of exodus, called a sinful and wayward Israel back to the covenant at Sinai, demanded faithful obedience to the divine commandments of Mosaic law, and applied normative tradition to current events. Finding authority in his call, Jeremiah announced the impending judgment of God, the destruction of an unrepentant Judah, and exile among the nations. The one hope for Judah, both

32. Bright's major work in biblical theology was *The Kingdom of God: The Biblical Concept and Its Meaning for the Church* (New York: Abingdon-Cokesbury, 1953).
33. Ibid., 244–74.

before and after the exile, was national repentance, based on a return to God and a renewed allegiance to the covenant of Moses. Yet failing this, God's own mercy would one day precipitate the restoration of the exiles to their land.

According to Bright, Jeremiah applied the redemptive acts and covenant relationship of Israel's past to his present situation and found the nation wanting. Like other prophets, Jeremiah interpreted the course of events as proceeding according to the providence of God. The prophet found in the downfall of Assyria, not a reason for rejoicing over impending liberation, but an opportunity for national lamentation for corporate sin and the restoration of Mosaic religion. Only by national repentance could the great and fierce anger of the Lord be averted. When the nation did not fully repent, Jeremiah interpreted the coming of the Babylonians to include Judah within their empire as the work of God. The destruction of Jerusalem and the exile to Babylonia were also seen as acts of God, but the great faith of Jeremiah gave birth to the hope that one day in the future the Lord of history would redeem once again his people from captivity and bring them back to their homeland. Thus, for Bright, history was not portrayed as the story of human tragedy but as a stage of divine drama that would climax in future salvation.

Bright argued that, prior to the exile, Jeremiah used the great acts of God in Israel's redemptive past, not as guarantees of present and future salvation, but as the basis for judgment of a sinful people. Yet, before and especially after the exile, these acts of God also held out the promise of future salvation for a properly chastised and newly obedient people. The awful and terrible wrath of God brought judgment and finally the sentence of punishment to a wayward people. Yet the great acts of God in the past, who had liberated Israel from slavery in Egypt and brought the nation into being in Canaan, provided the basis for hope in future redemption.[34] The new future that Jeremiah shaped was grounded in the ancient faith, going back to Egyptian liberation, the wilderness journey, and the entrance into the land.[35] It was this hope that provided Judah in the wilderness of exile the patience to endure the trials of

34. John Bright, *Covenant and Promise: The Prophetic Understanding of the Future in Preexilic Israel* (Philadelphia: Westminster, 1976) 144: "Jeremiah's entire thinking was rooted in the recollection of Yahweh's grace to Israel in exodus and land-giving, and of the stern stipulations of his covenant, just as was the theology of Deuteronomy."

35. Bright, *Jeremiah*, xxiii.

captivity and the courage to return home to renew their lives as the people of God.

JOHN BRIGHT AND NEOORTHODOXY

Old liberalism did not easily die with the new birth of neoorthodoxy, especially among Jeremiah scholars who were raised under the pervasive influence of Schleiermacher and Harnack. Like the old liberals, Bright understood the classical prophets, including Jeremiah, often to be unique, heroic figures who considered themselves primarily to be the messengers of the divine sovereign of history, preaching often a message no one wished to hear.[36] Yet they were not cut from the same cloth of the old liberal prophets who were innovative teachers of the moral law, embodying within themselves the ethical virtues that they proclaimed. Neither were they the political revolutionaries or reformers of the social gospel who set about the task of the reconstitution of a just society. Rather, for Bright, Israel's prophets, including Jeremiah, were proclaimers of the radical sovereignty and demanding justice of God, themes grounded in the faith traditions of the past that would shape new acts of redemption in the future.

Faithful to the call to which they were predestined to submit, the prophets struggled with the Israel they addressed and the God whom they served. This is especially true of Jeremiah, for the confessions, which Bright believed came from the interiority of the prophet himself, presented the turmoil, self-doubt, and even anger directed toward God. These expressions of anguish derived from the suffering of the prophet and were captured especially in the prose narratives. But Jeremiah came to learn that the path to the consummation of the kingdom of God was the way of the cross. The suffering servant, so fully embodied in Jeremiah, was the greatest prophetic model.

Also similar to liberal Protestants, Bright portrayed the great prophets as critics of the cult, although he did not go so far as J. Philip Hyatt in arguing that Jeremiah was opposed to sacrificial religion and temple worship in principle. Rather, for Bright, Jeremiah recognized that the rituals of the cult could not sustain the vital relationship of God with Israel formulated in and continuously shaped by the covenant, a relationship that required faithful obedience to legal and moral stipulations.[37] Thus the prophet was the proclaimer of the righteousness of God, revealed in acts of

36. Ibid., xv–xviii.
37. Bright, *Covenant and Promise*, 162.

redemption and moral commandments, not the priest whose rituals could lead to the improper substitution of form for substance.

Bright also challenged old liberalism's optimistic views of human history. It is especially with Jeremiah, who, for Bright, represented the height of Israelite classical prophecy, that the undaunted optimism shared by Israel and Judah in their future, an optimism based on the election of David and the dwelling of God on Mt. Zion, faced serious challenge. For Jeremiah, the future is not unconditionally guaranteed; rather, it is one of radical alternatives: life or death, blessing or curse, and salvation or alienation. These alternatives required and demanded decision. The conditional future of the community of God is based on obedience to the stipulations of the covenant. In Jeremiah's preaching, there was the call then to radical obedience, to a grasping of the future held out by God, but only to a faithful nation.[38] In this way, Jeremiah stood, according to Bright, at one with the theology of Deuteronomy.

Jeremiah, argued Bright, never abandoned hope in Israel's destiny as the elect of God. This included both the north and the south. The prophet believed that beyond tragedy, even beyond the ashes of destruction, God would recall his people to covenant through the sheer determination of divine will accompanied by abundant grace. And God promised to enter into a new covenant with a people who would possess a transformed and obedient heart.[39] The immutable purposes of God oriented toward the redemption of the chosen could not be thwarted by the capricious forces of human-directed history. The destruction of Judah did not signal the defeat of God. In Jeremiah, conditional promise and unconditional grace received their synthesis. This is the tension, ever present among the faithful, between the salvation of unconditional grace and the obligation of obedient response.

In his formulation of the theology of Jeremiah, Bright gave an important place to "word," although this word was rooted in history. Convinced of their call to be the messengers of God, the prophets announced a compelling word, not significantly new in its substance, for it was grounded in the salvific traditions of the past, but new in its radical application to the present. The word embodied both the announcement of divine judgment against the sinful nation and the proclamation of future redemption from a God who refused to allow his people to be destroyed forever. The prophetic word, originating with God, went forth to shape the course of

38. Ibid., 140–98.
39. Ibid., 194–95.

human history, culminating ultimately in the advent of the kingdom of God.

Sin for Jeremiah permeated the human heart, although in Bright's assessment, it was far from individualistic in its expression. Sin was not merely a moral defect in the conscience and behavior of individuals. Rather, sin was both a corporate and a social evil, corporate in terms of human nature and social in the form of systemic evil, stemming from institutions corrupted by the wickedness of their human participants. The stern judgment of God must inevitably come and would assume the form of the "foe from the north," an enemy who, Bright argues, was at least eventually identified by Jeremiah as the Babylonians.

Sinful yet contrite Judah, like its ancestors before, received the promise of deliverance in the preaching of Jeremiah, because of the persistent grace of God. Yet it was not a grace freely given, totally without condition, for the covenant relationship, within which mercy and forgiveness became operative, at the same time called for moral obedience and radical faith.[40] Repentance and patient trust would lead to divine redemption, even if a period of punishment had to be endured. This repentance and obedience was to issue from the "heart," indicating that Jeremiah foresaw a transformation of human nature. Whatever Jeremiah's original view of the Deuteronomic reform, Bright thought that he soon became disillusioned with its failures and recognized that what was required was the complete transformation of human nature allowing more faithful obedience. Because human nature was depraved, it required divine re-creation. This re-creation leading to transformation was to take the form of a "new covenant" with a law written, not upon tablets of stone, but upon the human heart. The possibility of forgiveness and the return to covenant faith was offered by Jeremiah even to apostate Israel, the Northern Kingdom, that had been destroyed by the Assyrians a century before.

What caused Jeremiah the greatest opposition and suffering, according to Bright, was the clash with the official royal religion in Jerusalem. At the heart of royal religion was Yahweh's eternal covenant with the Davidic dynasty and his selection of Mt. Zion as his perpetual dwelling place (2 Samuel 7; Psalms 46; 48; 76; 89). This religion had provided the theological basis for the preaching of Isaiah, who, although extremely critical of the oppressive injustice of the monarchy and the social corruption of both the city of Jerusalem and the nation of Judah, still envisioned a future king whose

40. Ibid., 144.

reign would initiate a period when divine justice and the blessings of Shalom would prevail (Isaiah 7; 9; 11; 32). By the time of Jeremiah and the Deuteronomic reform, the royal tradition, also based on divine actions and the promises of God, had hardened into nationalistic dogma, for the conceptual formulation of eternal election and divine blessing had been misconstrued into a doctrine of unconditional guarantees for a continued existence.

According to Bright, Jeremiah stood unalterably opposed to this view of unconditional redemptive history, siding instead with the Deuteronomic formulation of the conditional promises of the covenant of Moses. In the Mosaic formulation, God's actions of redemption in history were conditionally based on the elect's faithful response to Torah. The monarchy had, for Jeremiah, a destiny that was to approximate the order of the kingdom of God on earth. Yet evil kings could and did pervert the ideals of the kingdom with social oppression and idolatry. Jeremiah's opposition to wicked kings was not to the monarchy per se but to the corruption of those who wore the crown.[41] Bright did not see Jeremiah as rejecting the royal tradition but as bringing the two covenants into creative tension. Thus it was the unconditional grace of God and the requirements of obedient response to Torah that provided the theological matrix out of which the nation was to live faithfully.[42]

In his work on Jeremiah and biblical theology, Bright stressed both the authority and the unity of the Bible.[43] Jeremiah's appeal to the historic redemptive acts of God was evidence of his own recognition of the authority of the growing corpus of scriptural traditions. Yet the prophetic oracles of Jeremiah were enduring words possessing authority and meaning far beyond the limits of their own historical period. The Word of God given historical incarnation in the preaching of Jeremiah lays claim to the lives of all future generations of the chosen people, including the New Israel. And the unity of Scripture was ultimately centered in Christ, for Christ, according to Bright, is both the center and the fulfillment of history. Thus the redemptive drama of the biblical story of the chosen people finds its ultimate climax in the ministry and nature of Jesus Christ.[44]

---

41. Bright, *The Kingdom of God*, 116.
42. Bright, *Covenant and Promise*.
43. See John Bright, *The Authority of the Old Testament* (Nashville: Abingdon, 1967).
44. Bright, *The Kingdom of God*, 10.

AN ASSESSMENT OF REDEMPTIVE HISTORY

WRIGHT'S BIBLICAL THEOLOGY

Wright's strong historical work, drawing from the methodology and discoveries of field archaeology, united with neoorthodoxy at the time that America overcame the Great Depression and emerged the victor from World War II. The biblical theology movement preached a message gladly heard by a postwar audience who had endured severe hardship finally to experience their own redemption. Tyranny had succumbed to the concerted efforts of freedom. For many in the confessing communities, the defeat of fascism must have resulted from divine action in history. Many religious conservatives also found the theological features of Wright's work compelling, because it was assumed that the historical actuality residing behind the concrete events celebrated in Israel's confession of faith apparently had been established.

There are and continue to be many important contributions to present theological inquiry by the work of scholars associated with the biblical theology movement, including Wright and Bright. There are also significant stances taken by these scholars. These include the effort to locate the theology of the biblical texts within the historical and cultural settings of their day; the recognition that the Old Testament is not only a history book or a source for history but also a compendium of the faith of ancient Israel; the effort to find a unity in both Testaments, in this case the "redemptive acts of God," while not ignoring the diversity of theological views present in Scripture; the frank admission that theological work emerges from the questions raised by those who stand within the context of contemporary communities of faith; the effort to do constructive work by construing the faith of Scripture through contemporary theology, in this case neoorthodoxy; and the recognition of the importance of correlating biblical faith with human experience.

However, as Brevard Childs has demonstrated in his book *Biblical Theology in Crisis*, some of the positions taken by Wright and other participants in the biblical theology movement have not continued to hold up under critical scrutiny.[45] Several shortcomings of Wright's and Bright's work reflect the limitations of historical criticism as a paradigm for doing Old Testament theology. The fol-

---

45. Also see James Barr, "Revelation through History in the Old Testament and in Modern Theology," *Int* 17 (1963) 193–205; and Langdon Gilkey, "Cosmology, Ontology, and the Travail of Biblical Language," *JR* 41 (1961) 194–205.

lowing are among the major questions raised by their rather imposing constructions.

First, is the search for and affirmation of the nucleus of salvation history, that is, the event ("what actually happened"), really anything more than the positivistic effort to write a history of Israel? What happens when redemptive events cannot be successfully located in history? For example, even if the patriarchs are thought to be figures within history, the myriad of periods suggested for their lives reflects the treacherous obstacles that face any historical reconstruction.[46] Even in regard to events less difficult to reconstruct, one may rightly ask with James Barr how it is possible to isolate events from their interpretation by the biblical writer, the modern historian, and the contemporary theologian.[47] To say that God delivered Israel from Egypt in the exodus is to depend completely on Israel's own interpretation. Since it is impossible to reconstruct historically the exodus "event," there remain only the varied and multiple attestations of texts that have become Scripture. Further, does not the exclusion of interpretation, and therefore "word" from the content of Old Testament faith, negate the theological value of prophecy, wisdom, and Torah?[48] For example, the faith of sages was grounded in creation and providence, not salvation history, at least before Ben Sira in the early second century B.C.E. And the Old Testament itself contends that much of the revelation of God occurred in words (including narratives and poems) and reflection on words, not simply in events experienced by the nation.

Although uniqueness may not be a necessary component for demonstrating the authenticity of Israel's faith as Wright implied, it nevertheless has been carefully documented that the non-Israelite cultures of the ancient Near East also looked to history as the arena for the actions of the gods.[49] Conversely, Israel also considered nature to be one avenue of divine action and revelation, and even used ancient Near Eastern myths in constructing their own faith

---

46. John Van Seters, *Abraham in History and Tradition* (New Haven: Yale University Press, 1975); and Thomas L. Thompson, *The Historicity of the Patriarchal Narratives* (BZAW 133; Berlin: W. de Gruyter, 1974).
47. See Barr, "Revelation through History," 193–205.
48. See Walther Zimmerli's critique in "I Am Yahweh," *I Am Yahweh* (ed. Walter Brueggemann; Atlanta: John Knox, 1982) 1–28; and idem, "Prophetic Proclamation and Reinterpretation," *Tradition and Theology* (ed. Douglas A. Knight; Philadelphia: Fortress, 1974) 69–100. For Zimmerli's approach and application, see his *Old Testament Theology in Outline* (Atlanta: John Knox, 1978).
49. See Bertil Albrektson, *History and the Gods* (Coniectanea biblica, Old Testament 1; Lund: Gleerup, 1967).

traditions that construed the nature and activity of God. Hence the location of revelation in the theologically unique and the presumption of the superiority of the historical over the mythical proved to be suspect on both counts.

What toppled the biblical theology movement from its pedestal, perhaps more than anything, has been the realization that the beginnings of Israel are largely opaque, at least historically speaking. As many historians have recently attested, the early Iron I period (thirteenth and twelfth centuries B.C.E.) in which Israel was thought to come into being as a nation suffers from the lack of sufficient sources to allow for little more than historical speculation.[50] Even in discussing the primal faith "event" of the exodus, multiple modern theories, involving significant amounts of guesswork, have been formulated in the effort to determine what happened, who participated, and under which king liberated Israel may have left Egypt. Likewise, efforts to describe historically Israel's entrance into the land, formulated in two different biblical traditions (peaceful infiltration and militant conquest), have resulted in multiple hypotheses hotly contested by modern historians in terms of time, sequence of events, the identity and number of participants, and the manner by which they left Egypt. Albright and Wright, at least through the 1950s, thought archaeology supported the conquest located in the Book of Joshua. Albrecht Alt's and Martin Noth's theory of a gradual infiltration of various groups, coupled with their joining with indigenous communities that extended back for many centuries prior to the Iron Age, was roundly criticized by the Albright school. However, recent excavations and analyses have seriously undermined Albright's thesis and suggest that the theory of gradual settlement has substance.[51] One also wonders how the "event" at Mt. Sinai, where the Bible presents Israel entering into covenant with God and receiving the Torah, could be reconstructed as a historical event when covenant and Torah, "words," are at the essence of that tradition. What has been most troublesome for the positions of Wright and others in the biblical theology movement is that the very time that was thought to be so formative for the faith of Israel is now considered the most difficult period for historians to reconstruct. All admit that their hypotheses contain much that is

---

50. See the discussion by George W. Ramsey, *The Quest for the Historical Israel* (Atlanta: John Knox, 1981).

51. J. Maxwell Miller, "The Israelite Occupation of Canaan," *Israelite and Judaean History* (ed. John H. Hayes and J. Maxwell Miller; OTL; Philadelphia: Westminster, 1977) 213–84.

speculation. Thus Wright's argument that these primal events of Israelite faith were firmly and demonstrably grounded in history carries little conviction in the present period.

WRIGHT'S HERMENEUTIC

It is interesting to note that Wright's hermeneutics, his theology as recital, is a theology of Word, given classic expression by Karl Barth, in which the Old Testament kerygma is proclaimed and confessed. One should not denigrate the importance of Wright's theological construction, based on neoorthodoxy. But the past generation has witnessed a considerable decline in the influence of both the Albright school and neoorthodoxy. Newer formulations of theology have appeared that require significant readjustment of what is at stake theologically in the Old Testament's views of God.

It should be noted, however, that toward the end of his life Wright began to make some important adjustments, and indeed his *The Old Testament and Theology* addressed a variety of matters that have generated significant theological discussion in Old Testament studies and contemporary hermeneutics for a generation. These include his important observation that the Old Testament speaks primarily of God's revelation in history but that the form of expression of that faith is narrative and not a systematic presentation;[52] the repeated contention that understanding humanity in general and in the Old Testament needs to take seriously the social nature of human existence;[53] the recognition of the importance of creation in the Old Testament construed through Israel's covenant with the God who was both Lord of history and creator;[54] the stressing of the importance of language, especially symbol, in the expression of Old Testament faith;[55] and a grappling with the problems and yet an emphasis on the importance of canon for Christian faith.[56]

BRIGHT'S THEOLOGY OF JEREMIAH

Coming out of the same confessional and intellectual tradition as Wright, Bright's approach to Jeremiah shares some of the same strengths and weaknesses. The portrait of a Jeremiah firmly an-

52. Wright, *The Old Testament and Theology*, 39–69.
53. E.g., see ibid., 68.
54. Ibid., 70–96.
55. Ibid., 151–65.
56. Ibid., 166–85.

chored within historical currents who proclaimed the sovereignty of God over creation and history and who underscored the moral requirements of the Mosaic covenant offered a compelling formulation of prophetic theology. For Bright, revelation and redemption were both part of the grand sweep of history under the providential control of God who brought judgment and salvation to an elect nation and shaped the course of future redemption for all people. Yet this admirable synthesis of historical exegesis and theological presentation has come under serious question of late.

THE QUEST FOR THE HISTORICAL JEREMIAH

Most troublesome for Bright's approach to Jeremiah studies has been the questioning of the assumption of the historical veracity of much of the book. Especially problematic is the issue of authorship. Baruch's role in the formulation of the Jeremiah tradition has been placed under critical scrutiny by many scholars. Also often debated has been the authorship of the Confessions (Jeremiah 11–20) and the Book of Consolation (Jeremiah 30–31).[57] More recently, even the authorship of other major traditions in Jeremiah has been brought into question. Robert Carroll has gone so far as to argue that Baruch's part in the redaction and composition of the book really is nothing but the creation of Deuteronomic scribes seeking to legitimate their own role and theology among the exilic and postexilic Jewish communities.[58] Indeed, the theory of a major Deuteronomic redaction of Jeremiah, especially in the composition of the prose speeches and narratives, has gained acceptance by many scholars in the academy.[59] And while the poetic oracles of source A continue to be seen as originating with Jeremiah, even this has been questioned.[60]

In addition to questions of authorship and redaction, historical difficulties also abound. The more significant questions include the identity of the "foe from the north," the date of the prophet's call,

---

57. Perdue, "Jeremiah in Modern Research," 25–28.

58. Robert P. Carroll, *From Covenant to Chaos* (New York: Crossroad, 1981) 15–16. See throughout his *Jeremiah*.

59. Winfried Thiel, *Die deuteronomistische Redaktion von Jeremia 1–25* (WMANT 41; Neukirchen-Vluyn: Neukirchener Verlag, 1973); and idem, *Die deuteronomistische Redaktion von Jeremia 26–45* (WMANT 52; Neukirchen-Vluyn: Neukirchener Verlag, 1981).

60. Siegfried Herrmann, "Forschung am Jeremiabuch: Probleme und Tendenzen ihrer neueren Entwicklung," *TLZ* 102 (1977) 481–90. Also see Herrmann's commentary, *Jeremia* (BKAT 12; Neukirchen-Vluyn: Neukirchener Verlag, 1986); and Carroll, *Jeremiah*.

the early years of the prophet's activity (prior to 609 B.C.E.), the possible priestly lineage of Jeremiah, and the fate of the prophet following his forced abduction to Egypt by revolutionaries. Especially difficult is the dating of the poetic oracles, because they contain very few historical allusions that could aid the efforts of the historian.

Then there are the difficulties associated with determining the so-called "historical" Jeremiah's own theological perspectives, even when one assumes that a somewhat accurate historical assessment of the tradition has been achieved. Thus, continuing to be debated is the question of Jeremiah's view of the Deuteronomic reform. Does he support the efforts of Josiah to return the nation to the Mosaic covenant, or does he oppose these attempts as the political ambition of the king and his political advisers? Or does he at first support the reform, only later to turn against its shallowness and obvious failures? Bright takes the last position, but only by being able to claim as historically reliable the prose tradition, an assumption not easily demonstrated. Then there is the question of Jeremiah's view of temple and dynasty. Does he see in these institutions at least one means for maintaining a proper relationship with God, or does he reject them as interloping traditions seeking to usurp the authentic Mosaic religion grounded in the exodus from Egypt and the covenant at Sinai? Bright brings both into a synthesis, but mainly by affirming the prose tradition as Jeremiah's in thought, if not in words. Other historical questions remain. Is the call tradition in Jeremiah 1 the words of the prophet, a traditional liturgy of ordination uttered by the prophet, or the composition of Deuteronomic scribes seeking to present Jeremiah in the guise of the new Moses?

These literary and historical questions take on rather imposing significance when one considers the theology of Jeremiah, especially if one wishes to set forth the theology of the historical person and not the "persona," the book, or the sources detected in the book. A careful assessment of the theological features of each of the sources reveals major differences. In the prose sermons and narratives, Jeremiah is a preacher of law, even the new Moses, who requires obedience to covenant stipulations. Indeed, he sounds very much like a Deuteronomic preacher, but is this the historical prophet or the Jeremiah reshaped by Deuteronomic redaction? Jeremiah stands in opposition to corrupt temple worship, but only in a prose sermon (Jeremiah 7; 26) also possibly written by Deuteronomic scribes who were the unsuccessful rivals to the Zadokites for control of the temple and knew post eventu of the destruction of the temple in 587 B.C.E. In the poetry (source A), Jeremiah stands in strong opposition to kings and monarchy and finds no place for the institution in any new Israel, while in the prose sermons he criticizes rulers but looks to the reestablishment of the royal institution in the future. In the confessions, he is the petulant complainer who demands the destruction of his personal enemies, following the lament tradition. In the poetry he announces destruction by the "foe from the north," yet in intense agony he intercedes for the salvation of nation and opponents. In sources A, B, and C, the prophet is the leader of the peace party who counsels submission to the foreign powers, especially Babylon, while in the speeches against the nations in Jeremiah 46–51 he sounds very much like the prophets of nationalism who used the magical power of prophetic oracles to bring destruction to foreign enemies.

These differences could be multiplied, but perhaps they are sufficient to demonstrate that there are several portraits of Jeremiah in the book along with a variety of theologies that emerge from the different traditions. Efforts to authenticate the so-called historical Jeremiah's theology, precisely differentiated from later redactional activity, are increasingly perilous.

BRIGHT'S HERMENEUTIC

It is just as challenging to attempt to recover the life and thought of a historical Jeremiah placed within the specificity of space and time as it is to attempt to recover the historical dimensions of acts of God in the Late Bronze and early Iron ages. Thus, what happens to a theology, both biblical and contemporary, that is predicated on the accurate recovery of history? And what of the multiple attestations to the God of Israel, often in significant tension even within one biblical book? What role should be given to pluralism, that is, the different tellings of the story of the chosen, or more specifically the life and thought of Jeremiah? Are the so-called later layers of tradition, assuming they may be separated out, stripped of any theological value? Or does one celebrate the pluralism and discard attempts to do any constructive work? These are important questions that face any theology that seeks some authentication in the recovery of historical events.

CHAPTER 3

History as Tradition:
The German School

TRADITION HISTORY AND OLD TESTAMENT THEOLOGY

Appearing as an important exegetical method as early as the 1930s, tradition history received its formative shape in the work of the German scholars Albrecht Alt, Martin Noth, and Gerhard von Rad.[1] A different form of the method was fashioned in Scandinavia by Harris Birkeland, Ivan Engnell, Sigmund Mowinckel, and Eduard Nielsen, to name several of its most influential practitioners.[2] Developing as a corrective to the limitations of literary and form criticism, tradition history began to reshape significantly biblical theology, especially in the seminal work of Gerhard von Rad.

It was von Rad who placed in sharp relief the major problems Old Testament scholarship encountered as a result of the limitations of literary and form criticisms.[3] Literary criticism generally followed a

---

1. Albrecht Alt, *Essays on Old Testament History and Religion* (Oxford: Basil Blackwell, 1966); Martin Noth, *A History of Pentateuchal Traditions* (Englewood Cliffs, N.J.: Prentice-Hall, 1972); idem, *Überlieferungsgeschichtliche Studien* (3d ed.; Tübingen: Max Niemeyer, 1967); and Gerhard von Rad, *Old Testament Theology* (2 vols.; New York: Harper & Row, 1962, 1965); idem, *The Problem of the Hexateuch and Other Essays* (Edinburgh and London: Oliver & Boyd, 1966).

2. Harris Birkeland, *Zum hebräischen Traditionswesen* (Oslo: Jacob Dybwad, 1958); Ivan Engnell, *Gamla Testamentet: En traditionshistorisk inledning* 1 (Stockholm: Svenska Kyrkans Diakonistyrelses Bokförlag, 1945); idem, *Critical Essays on the Old Testament* (London: SPCK, 1970); Sigmund Mowinckel, *Prophecy and Tradition* (Oslo: Jacob Dybwad, 1946); and Eduard Nielsen, *Oral Tradition* (SBT 11; London: SCM, 1954). For a detailed analysis of both the German and the Scandinavian developments of the method, see Douglas A. Knight, *The Traditions of Israel* (SBLDS 9; Missoula, Mont.: Scholars Press, 1973). For a brief overview of the method, see Walter Rast, *Tradition History and the Old Testament* (Guides to Biblical Scholarship; Philadelphia: Fortress, 1972).

3. See Gerhard von Rad, "The Form-Critical Problem of the Hexateuch," *The Form Critical Problem of the Hexateuch and Other Essays* (Edinburgh: Oliver &

"book" model for analyzing the composition of literary sources. Thus scholars thought that individuals (e.g., the Yahwist) composed their sources during a specific period of time, in one location, and for a particular audience. While these authors were thought to have used older materials and indeed may have produced compositions that were later changed by others, the model for understanding the composition of sources and books was predominantly static and one-dimensional. Form criticism focused on common literary types: their structure, oral development, and social setting. But this method was unable to work with larger complexes. Generally regarding literary types as rigid and inflexible, form critics also did not easily allow literary creativity to transform and alter genres. Furthermore, the method illustrated well the proverbial case of the inability to see the forest for the trees. Carefully and imaginatively applied, however, tradition history was a more dynamic method that both traced the development of large literary complexes and isolated their themes and social features. The method is multidimensional, allowing scholars to see the stages in the growth of a tradition over many years and in some cases even several centuries.

As a method for biblical study, tradition history undertakes four major objectives.[4] First, it seeks to determine the social group or groups responsible for the formulation and transmission of a tradition. Thus, communities of priests, sages, scribes, and prophets, to name the most common categories, are thought to be responsible for shaping traditions that reflected their own peculiar beliefs, vocabulary, and social functions. Second, tradition history is concerned with localization, that is, the role that geographical and cultural contexts play in the development and transmission of a tradition. The method also allows for the recognition that traditions were carried by their social groups during their migrations, even while leaving behind a deposit in the earlier locales. A third concern of this method, related to the first, is the discovery of the specific social, political, and religious dynamics present in the tradition. These were subject to change over the course of a tradition's growth. Fourth, the method delineates the major themes of the tradition. Theological themes, when placed within the method of tradition history, received their shape within the dynamics of Israel's evolving society and culture. This meant that the abstract categories

---

Boyd, 1958; repr., London: SCM, 1984) 1–78.
4. For a clear summary, see Rast, *Tradition History*.

stamped by the rational idealism of Walther Eichrodt's theology were replaced by a sociology of realism in which the ideas of ancient Israel were associated empirically with their concrete social matrices.

HISTORY AS TRADITION: GERHARD VON RAD

While sharing some important features with the biblical theology movement, Gerhard von Rad fashioned his own distinctive theology of history in two volumes, first published in German in 1957 (volume 1) and 1960 (volume 2). Indeed, von Rad's compelling work eventually supplanted that of Eichrodt whose exposition of covenant theology had held first rank in Old Testament theology since 1933.[5]

As a biblical scholar, von Rad was deeply concerned with recovering the history of Israel. Indeed, he enthusiastically proclaimed that "the Old Testament is a history book."[6] However, in addition to Wright's understanding that history should be based on recoverable concrete events in space and time, von Rad also contended that history was a recounting of saving history *(Heilsgeschichte)* that witnessed to God's continuing redemptive actions for Israel and the world. Further, von Rad was concerned to trace the social and historical development of Israel's theological traditions, for it was in these that Israel's faith was embodied. Thus the opening section of von Rad's initial volume outlined the development of Israelite religion and its major religious and social institutions from their origins in pre-Mosaic times to the beginnings of scribal religion in the postexilic period.[7] It was within this diachronic context that von Rad traced Israel's developing faith.[8]

The most significant difference from Wright and the biblical theology movement in America lay in the primary objective of historical research that led into biblical theology. For Wright, the primary object was to obtain the nucleus of actual events, residing behind the confessional interpretations expressing Israel's ancient faith. But, for von Rad, the primary objective was to discover the

---

5. Walther Eichrodt, *Theology of the Old Testament* (2 vols.; Philadelphia: Westminster, 1962).

6. Von Rad, *Old Testament Theology* 2:357.

7. Ibid., 1:3–102.

8. For a detailed assessment of von Rad as an Old Testament theologian, see James L. Crenshaw, *Gerhard von Rad* (Makers of the Modern Theological Mind; Waco, Tex.: Word Books, 1978).

content of this confession, trace its traditiohistorical development, and articulate its diverse understandings. By the use of tradition history, von Rad outlined the social and literary development of ongoing trajectories through the centuries of biblical Israel's historical existence. To put the contrast in succinct terms, the primary opposition between Wright and von Rad resides in what is considered to be the defining feature of biblical theology: "event" (Wright) or "word" (von Rad). For von Rad, "history becomes word, and word becomes history."[9] This did not mean that Wright ignored theological interpretations of events or that von Rad was not interested in determining the actuality or character of the historical event that may have resided behind the interpretation. However, for Wright, events had to have happened in order for them to have theological legitimacy in proclamation and response. For von Rad, it is the primacy of the word, confessed by the community and lodged within its traditions, that gives faith its authentication. While events may have resided behind confessions, the recovery of "what happened" is not necessary for faith to be true.

Von Rad was opposed to theologizing that approached its work by the articulation of bloodless, abstract concepts such as covenant, faith, and righteousness. This approach, based on the use of word studies, was part of the strategy used by the biblical theology movement that assumed that meaning was located in and derived from individual words.[10] These ideas tended to be articulated by means of generalization and abstraction. However, von Rad understood the historical task of the biblical theologian to be that of uncovering the witness of social communities to divine action within the context of tradition history. Ideas were an intrinsic part of the growth and expansion of tradition complexes, not so much in a progressive, evolutionary fashion, but rather like a river moving sometimes backward but more often forward while forming new channels and tributaries. Subsequently, each generation of Israel was responsible for determining what it meant to be the people of God in their own time by encountering tradition and reshaping it in view of their particular context and experience.

THE LITTLE CREED

The linchpin of von Rad's theology was the isolation of what he considered to be confessions of faith that were embedded within

---

9. Von Rad, *Old Testament Theology* 2:357.

10. See James Barr's devastating critique of this assumption in his important book, *The Semantics of Biblical Language* (London: Oxford University Press, 1961).

larger literary texts. He argued that Israel's earliest faith was expressed in what he determined was an ancient, historical creed found in Deut 26:5b-9, going back, so he proposed, to a liturgy of thanksgiving uttered during a festival of first fruits at a local sanctuary (cf. Deut 6:20-24; Josh 24:2b-13). Von Rad argued that this creed, either a confession by or a hortatory address to the congregation within a liturgical setting, is a succinct expression of the redemptive acts of God and contains the earliest faith of Israel.[11] These redemptive acts include the promise to the fathers, the exodus from Egypt, the wandering in the wilderness, and the gift of the promised land. Von Rad attached great significance to the absence of any mention of the revelation at Sinai in this so-called early creed. He concluded from this "absence" that covenant and Torah were later developments and thus were not an early part of the primal faith centering on the redemptive acts of God. Indeed, for von Rad, it was not until the post-exile that the reference to Sinai is included within the creedal faith (Neh 9:6f.). This means that the Sinai tradition, which embodies laws detailing the character of divine justice, had a separate and later origin and was not originally related to the earliest tradition of the redemptive acts of God.

The Hexateuch (Genesis through Joshua) contains, for von Rad, two large tradition complexes that developed over several centuries. The exodus-settlement tradition, very early in its history, incorporated the promises to the ancestors and celebrated God's guidance and redemptive activity, while the Sinai tradition portrayed theophanic vision, the coming of God to his people, and the entrance into a covenant relationship. It is not difficult to see that von Rad is differentiating between what he considers to be "law" (Sinai) and "gospel" (exodus-settlement). Originally, the cultic setting for the exodus-settlement tradition was the offering of first fruits during the Feast of Weeks. Thus the creed was the earliest part of the religious narrative of this important pilgrimage festival at a time when ownership of the land was a live issue. This would have been shortly after the entrance into the land but before the emergence of the monarchy of David some two centuries later. Von Rad concluded that the sanctuary where this religious narrative originated was Gilgal, near Jericho. Here the territorial boundaries of the tribes were ritually recognized.

In terms of origin, the Sinai tradition, in von Rad's view, is perhaps the latest stage in the development of the Hexateuch. It

---

11. This creed found expression in cult lyrics (Psalms 78; 105; 106; 135; 136), again demonstrating its liturgical setting.

developed as the religious narrative of the sanctuary of Shechem, the chief northern Israelite temple from the time of the tribal federation during the formative period of the judges. The two dominant features, the coming of God and the entering into covenant, presuppose some grand festival, most probably the Feast of Booths, celebrated during Israel's autumnal New Year. Even the structure of the Book of Deuteronomy, which presents the reformulation of historic faith and covenant, reflects the major features of a cultic ceremony: historical presentation of the events at Sinai, the reading of the law, the sealing of the covenant, and blessings and curses. Deuteronomy derives from the formal pattern of this liturgy. And its characteristic mentioning of "today" emphasizes that the saving events, which provided the basis for covenant and law, were the objects of response by the assembled community. In saying yes to God's redemption, formalized within the renewal of the covenant, salvation is reactualized liturgically in the community's present experience. In the ceremony of covenant renewal, the Lordship of God over Israel is reaffirmed.

Von Rad then proceeded to trace the development of these two major hexateuchal traditions, indicating how they were eventually included in the major literary sources of J, E, D, and P. The treatment of J by von Rad is illustrative of this development. For von Rad, central for J was the exodus-settlement tradition, although this writer did include an early form of the Sinai complex. But it was a considerable period of time before the combination of these two traditions was generally accepted. J was responsible for the first blending of the "two fundamental propositions of the whole message of the Bible: Law and Gospel."[12] In addition, the Yahwist was responsible for the inclusion of the creation tradition, also late in being accepted by the community of faith as a redemptive activity of God. With this inclusion of creation, however, the Yahwist indicated that the purpose of Israel's redemption was to reconcile all humanity to God. This secularization of redemptive history and covenant by the Yahwist led to the development of a spiritualized faith in which the cultus was tolerated but not seen as fundamentally important. Indeed, the theological problem of the Yahwist was that the sacral sphere no longer guaranteed the truth of the creeds. Now it is the theological emphasis on the providential direction of history that is developed. This understanding enabled new traditions to appear, grounded in Israel's continuing history.

12. Von Rad, "The Form-Critical Problem of the Hexateuch," 54.

New traditions came to include the promise of an eternal dynasty to David (2 Samuel 7; Psalm 89) and the selection of Zion (Jerusalem) as the dwelling place of God (Psalms 46; 48; 76). God is not limited either to the past or to the sacred sphere but even now is active in history to effectuate redemption through new agents and events. This included creation, although this affirmation of divine action never achieved a commanding and normative status as an independent tradition, except in wisdom literature. Rather, for von Rad, creation was but the prolegomenon to salvation history. Seen as ancillary to redemption, creation theology was held in suspicion because of its possible association with fertility religion and natural revelation. While creation was certainly known by Israelites who witnessed its central place in the religions of the ancient Near East, it was not appropriated by their faith until very late. According to von Rad, decisive for this appropriation was the prophet of the exile, Second Isaiah, who spoke of creative redemption. However, this prophet, he contended, still gave primacy to revelation and redemption in history.

It is important to remember that, for von Rad, the two major traditions in the Hexateuch, exodus-settlement and Sinai, originated and developed over the years within liturgical celebrations. These two traditions represented, not the attempt to write history in the modern sense, but the efforts of successive generations to articulate and celebrate their faith within worship. Nevertheless, the ancient faith could be taken by the shapers of theological tradition, such as the Yahwist and the prophets, and given a spiritual character that validated the authenticity of belief outside worship. The sacred and the secular continued to be the two spheres, at times in direct tension, that expressed the vital faith of the chosen people.

THE TRADITIONING PPROCESS

The major thematic traditions isolated by von Rad were quite similar to those of Wright: the promise to the fathers, the exodus, the Red Sea victory, the wilderness wandering, the land of Canaan, and the later additions of Sinai covenant and law, the David-Zion complex, and creation. Unlike Wright, however, the emphasis was not placed on the nucleus of demonstrable events but on their interpretations that continued to develop and change over the years. Wright saw his task to be the reconstruction of Israelite history, out of which one could then begin to do Old Testament theology. This scholarly reconstruction of history differed at times rather dramatically from Israel's own accounting. The tension between Israel's own accounting of its story and the history of Israel reconstructed by scholars was, for von Rad, a great problem, one that he never fully resolved. Even so, he took much more seriously Israel's own rendering of its history than did Wright. Indeed, what Israel says about God's action is primary for Old Testament theology.[13] Thus the proper mode of engaging and actualizing the faith of Israel, for von Rad, is "retelling." And what Israel says is not dependent for its legitimacy on the actual occurrence of events or the ability of the historian to "prove" that these events took place. While von Rad does not appear to doubt that some sort of historical experience lay behind the redemptive acts, the real significance of the traditions resided within the development of the content of the faith expressed in words. In von Rad's formulation of the task of biblical theology, one is by necessity forced to take seriously what Israel *says* about its own salvation history. For von Rad, Israel's faith is not grounded in history but in a *theology* of history.[14] This is the fundamental difference from Wright. Indeed, for von Rad, Israel's theology, and therefore our own, is the critical engagement and response of each generation to the proclamation of the ancestors. Each generation of necessity had to determine what it meant for them to be Israel in their own time and place. The role of the believer was not passive but active in creating and reformulating tradition. In the context of worship, Israelites represented and reactualized, that is, made living and new, the faith for their own contemporary existence. In and through ritual, the community made the past present and thereby participated in the sacred stream of redemptive history. The same process, suggested von Rad, is at work today in believing communities, especially in liturgical settings.

Perhaps more clearly than Wright, von Rad recognized the tension between competing presentations of the faith. For von Rad, historical-critical method demonstrates the development of Israelite religion in all of its multiplicity. Therefore it is not only impossible to argue for a unifying center that is indigenous to the text but it is also wrongheaded to engage in a systematic rendering of faith in abstract categories. Israel's faith is presented in flowing streams of various traditions and cannot be authentically rendered by a system. Further, the pluralism of Israel's faith, in part due to the very

13. Von Rad, *Old Testament Theology* 1:105.
14. Ibid., 1:106.

nature of the canon as a collection of texts, also derives from the moving and changing streams of tradition that pass through many generations of witnessing communities.

OLD TESTAMENT HERMENEUTICS

In addressing the issue of hermeneutics, von Rad argued that Old Testament traditions continued into the New Testament, where they received new formulations. Thus the relationship between the Testaments was not one of radical discontinuity.[15] However, what of von Rad's understanding of the meaning of the Old Testament for modern Christianity?

For von Rad, tradition history contains three hermeneutical features: typology, promise-fulfillment, and reactualization. Redemptive acts as historical events were unrepeatable, once-for-all occurrences. However, in a new understanding of typology, von Rad argued that the events of Old Testament salvation history became the prototypes for the New Testament's corresponding antitypes.[16] This means that salvific events in the Old Testament pointed beyond themselves to acts in the future, especially and most important the Christ-event. In von Rad's words, "The primeval event is a type of the final event."

Von Rad took the promise-fulfillment scheme and argued that each event points beyond itself to ever greater and more significant fulfillment, until the Christ-event provided the ultimate culmination of history.[17] This allows the Christian to read the Old Testament as a "book of ever increasing anticipation."[18] Inherent within the formulation of each redemptive tradition was the feature of divine promise pointing toward new and even greater fulfillment in the future. Each development in the tradition allowed for God to enter into it once again, leading to both different interpretations and similar, though new events. Especially for the prophets (and this is the point of origin for von Rad's understanding of promise-

15. Unlike Rudolf Bultmann who contrasts Old Testament law with New Testament grace and points to the failure of Old Testament promises as a serious hermeneutical dilemma ("The Significance of the Old Testament for the Christian Faith," *The Old Testament and Christian Faith* [ed. Bernhard W. Anderson; New York: Harper & Row, 1963] 8–35).

16. See von Rad, *Old Testament Theology* 2:364–87.

17. Ibid., 2:319–35, 357–87.

18. Ibid., 2:319.

fulfillment), there was to be a new exodus, a new covenant, a new Jerusalem, and a new David. Indeed, even creation, which von Rad saw as a redemptive "act," was to become new.

Von Rad saw this hermeneutic as intrinsic to the Old Testament itself, for it understood that there were ever new fulfillments and that the community always lived between the now and the not yet, in anticipation of additional and at times greater fulfillments that resided still in the future. God was not held captive by the past but was ever active, willing and able to effectuate new acts of salvation in the present and the future.

For von Rad, this faith in a God of history, the present, and the not yet is expressed most clearly in the psalms (especially the laments), the prophets, and Deuteronomy. Here there are always breaks within the continuity of historical development, where God intrudes to inaugurate periods of new beginnings. There is the fulfillment of the Old in the New, yet this too opens itself to new possibilities. While von Rad attributed a "once-for-all" character to God's ultimate and final act in Jesus Christ, the tradition opened itself ever again to new possibilities, revitalized understandings, fresh hope, and an anticipated final climax in the eschaton. Von Rad contended that his version of typology was rooted in history, whereas allegory was invalid because of its ahistorical nature.

NEOORTHODOXY AND CONFESSIONAL CHRISTIANITY

Like Wright and Bright, von Rad approached his theological work from within the confessing church. Von Rad's Lutheran heritage, construed by neoorthodoxy, is represented in several of his theological affirmations: revelation in history, the sovereignty and providence of God, the Lordship of Christ, human nature, justification by faith, law and gospel, Word and confession, and the normative character of Scripture.

For von Rad, history reigned supreme as the primary mode of revelation. While the pagan nations searched for religious meaning and guidance in the sacral orders of nature, Israel looked to salvific events in history as the medium for understanding the activity and nature of God. It was especially in history that God had been active to deliver Israel from destruction and to bring it into existence as the chosen nation. Through the reactualization of past redemptive acts of God in confession and liturgy, the present community reexperienced the salvation of old. Thus one finds a sacramental view of the events of salvation history and the means by which they were liturgically reactualized or enacted in the life of the worshiping community. And the anticipation arose from these liturgical experiences that new acts of God in the immediate and distant future yet waited to greet the faithful community.

Von Rad also affirmed that divine sovereignty extended over all creation. Creation was not viewed as a Greek cosmos but as a unity that originates in the divine will and continues only by God's sustaining effort that moves creation and history toward their divinely appointed goal.[19] For von Rad, creation was viewed not so much as a doctrine as it was a salvific act, indeed the first as well as the prolegomenon for many others. Israel did not see creation as nature in some scientific sense or as a sacral sphere infused by divine forces, or gods, vying for control. Israel's creation faith did not allow for either the divinization of sex or the use of idols that were made from natural materials. Nor did this faith find expression in the timeless or recurring seasonal myths that were dramatically performed in fertility religions in order to renew the vitality of the earth. Rather, Israel viewed creation, contended von Rad, as the first of God's salvific acts that preceded all others.

As the Lord of history, God was, for von Rad, the one whose acts of redemption brought Israel into existence as the covenant people. The redemptive acts of God, recited in the ancient creed, were the formative events that shaped Israel's life as the community of God and continued to sustain Israel throughout its history.

As a Christian Old Testament scholar, von Rad's religious confession came to shape his views of Scripture and Israelite faith. In maintaining continuity between the Testaments, and between Israel and the church, he held that Christ claimed the traditions of Israel for himself. The early church saw in him the ultimate fulfillment of Israel's redemptive faith. He held that in Christ there is continuity with the old, and yet also the dawn of a new beginning. The kingdom of God had come in the newness of the Christ event.

Further, the New Testament writers read the Old Testament and its redemptive acts as the precursors of the Christ-event. Giving this tendency a prophetic cast, von Rad placed this development within the scheme of promise and fulfillment.[20] Each new act of redemption pointed beyond itself to greater and more lasting fulfillment, until the climax of God's eschatological act of redemption in Jesus Christ. Thus the unity of Scripture was found in redemptive history,

19. Ibid., 2:338–39.
20. Ibid., 2:328–29.

culminating in the Christ-event. While elements of the interpretation of the Old Testament by the New are not valid for today, the thrust of tradition, the increasing expectation, and the fulfillment in Christ are of lasting value for Christians.

In articulating his view of human nature, von Rad believed that God had given humans the freedom to choose their way of life before or apart from God. Yet the basic tendency of humans was to digress from God's commandments. The general thrust of the Old Testament is to speak of a fallen humanity ever in opposition to God and always needing forgiveness and divine guidance.[21] Even the chosen are incapable of obeying God in a consistent fashion. Humans needed what Jeremiah and Ezekiel called a transformation of the heart, an act of divine creation that shapes human nature to have the very capacity for responsive obedience. Sinful humanity also required mediation with the Holy. The mediators could be and often were priestly officials who guarded the sacred sphere, but the more significant ones were prophetic intercessors who suffered vicariously for a sinful nation. These were Moses in Deuteronomy, Jeremiah, and the Servant in Second Isaiah. Only in Jesus Christ, asserted von Rad, was the law perfectly fulfilled and the sins of a fallen humanity borne by a sinless victim. For von Rad, Christ was the ultimate mediator, for in his life and death humanity was reconciled to God.

Justification by faith was also central to von Rad's Old Testament theology. Faith was the one and only possible authentic response to God by Israel.[22] There was not just a glance backward to the redemptive acts of old but also a forward look by which one may move into the salvific action of God's future. The Old Testament, especially Deuteronomy and Deuteronomic theology, renders judgment on the sinfulness of people. Yet radical faith demanded the abandonment of self and the acceptance of the grace of God. The hidden God continued to address Israel with the new Word. In this way Israel was able to live by faith. What is new in the gospel is that the proclamation of the redemptive acts of God becomes incarnate in the Word that confronts humanity with an either/or decision. With "yes" to the divine encounter, humanity stands justified before God. Israel's "yes" to the redemptive events of the past and its open affirmation of new acts yet to come allowed Israel to par-

21. Ibid., 2:348.
22. Ibid., 2:378.

ticipate in the final justification rendered by faith in Jesus Christ as Lord.

In struggling with Luther's dichotomy between law and gospel, von Rad emphasized that the Old Testament was not only a statement of judgment but also a repository of grace.[23] Significant for von Rad was the fact that Israel was elected prior to the giving of the commandments. God's judgmental and demanding will was incorporated into law which, nonetheless, was related to the preceding acts of grace. Law was recited liturgically as evidenced in its formation in a series. Even so, the law was never firmly fixed; rather, it remained flexible and open to the mystery of God. The saving event that brought Israel into existence was intrinsically related to the moral responsibility demanded by the imperatives of divine law. Law, including the so-called sacramental orders, was to regulate an existing, redeemed community.

Even so, Israel understood that it was saved, not by legalistic obedience, but by God's acts of merciful redemption, given primal expression in the exodus event. Israel never legitimately understood its relationship to God to be defined exclusively or even primarily in legal terms. Rites, sacrifices, and moral deeds could never lay claim, in and of themselves, to divine favor. Israel was saved by grace, not by human works of imperfect moral obedience and ritual performance.

For von Rad, the prophets were the first to preach the wrath of God and to require their community to submit to law. This preaching of the law was new in Israel. The prophets based their indictments in oracles of judgment on specific legal statutes. However, Israel's primary sin was that of failing to respond to God's gracious action of salvation, not that Israel violated this or that commandment. At the ground of Israel's sin was the rejection of freely offered salvation and God's continued will to save. Human obedience to law was not, on the whole, a prerequisite for salvation. It was only with Ezekiel that Israel is condemned for failing to fulfill the law.

This understanding of law and gospel finds expression in von Rad's treatment of the two major traditions of the Hexateuch: law (Sinai) and gospel (exodus-settlement). For von Rad, the exodus-settlement tradition, which speaks of the gifts of redemption, preservation, and land, was earlier, primary, and normative, while the

23. Ibid., 2:388–409.

later tradition of law was less significant. As faith required guidance by law for Paul and Luther, so for von Rad faith in the redemptive acts of God, involving both a backward and a forward look, necessarily led to the desire for moral obedience made possible by the Torah.

Finally, von Rad discusses the importance of the confessional response to the divine Word that embodied the redemptive acts of God. For the Old Testament, von Rad stressed that the Word of God creates the world and directs human history.[24] Priestly and prophetic oracles partook of this creative power that, on the one hand, transformed, directed, and redeemed human life and, on the other, counteracted sin and evil. Symbolic acts, both ritual and prophetic, shared the same sacred power. Through dramatic performance and spoken confession in liturgy, both the mystery and the redemptive power of God were experienced.

TRADITION HISTORY AND THE BOOK OF JEREMIAH

Von Rad's traditiohistorical approach to Old Testament theology shapes his presentation of the prophets. He begins by placing these spokespersons for God solidly within the developing life and faith of Israel. The prophets, like other social groups, are both carriers and transformers of tradition.

Reacting against classical liberalism, von Rad opposed earlier portrayals of the prophets as original thinkers and highly individualistic loners whose intimate relationship with God gave shape to a radically new theology.[25] For von Rad, the prophets were more properly understood within the larger religious and historical context of the ancient Near East and earlier generations of Israel. However, the prophets' use of myth and ritual from the ancient Near East and their appropriation of traditional ideas and images from both pagan and Israelite sources in no way reduced the power and significance of their message. Von Rad also went much further than Bright and Wright in arguing against the false dichotomy drawn between the spirituality of the prophets and the cultic religion of the priests. In fact, von Rad entertained the idea that the early prophets were official spokespersons of the cult, perhaps even functionaries of the sanctuaries. This view was even more pronounced in the

---

24. Ibid., 2:80–98, 352–56.
25. See ibid., vol. 2, for von Rad's assessment of the broad contours of classical prophecy.

Scandinavian school.[26] Von Rad noted that the early prophets were intercessors on behalf of Israel, speaking for the corporate body, often, it seemed, within the context of official worship ceremonies. On occasion they even uttered curses against the nation's enemies. Thus, as late as the ninth century B.C.E., the prophets were a part of the cultus.

For von Rad, however, the classical prophets marked a new development in Israelite prophecy. While there was not a radical break with the past, the prophets of the eighth century reformulated the prophetic tradition. On the one hand, even the classical prophets were closely bound to the traditions of Israel's historic faith. The exodus, guidance through the Sinai, the gift of the land, law and covenant, creation, the promise to David, and Zion as the city of God were theological traditions on which the classical prophets based their preaching. In these they find their legitimation, Israel's continuing identity, and the theological images and symbols available for reinterpretation. The ancient traditions of faith were encountered and made new.

Yet, always open to the freedom of God, the message of the classical prophets also represented something radically new. The old was passing away, and new acts of God were imminent. A new exodus, a new covenant, a new creation, to name several examples, were to be wrought by the Lord of history. For von Rad, these new acts, in one sense, were continuous with those of the past, and yet, in another, they embodied fresh and even greater experiences of divine redemption. There was both continuity and discontinuity with the past.

In breaking with the past, the classical prophets attacked the cult and announced divine judgment, not only against the enemies of Israel, but even against the chosen people themselves. The classical prophets found their authority, not in an office in the cult, but in the experience of their individual call. In this divine-human encounter, they were commissioned to challenge the past orders of religious piety and in unprecedented fashion to announce the radical judgment of God. Unlike their Canaanite and some of their early Israelite counterparts, the classical prophets were not driven into ecstasy by the spirit, for by the eighth century this phenomenon had essentially ceased.[27] Rather, for von Rad, it was their encounter

26. See, e.g., Alfred Haldar, *Associations of Cult Prophets among the Ancient Semites* (Uppsala: Almqvist & Wiksells, 1945).

27. Ezekiel represents a problem for von Rad, since ecstatic experiences induced by the spirit or "hand" of God appear to be evidenced in this prophet.

with the Word of God, first experienced in the call and personally directed to them, that gave them their authority and shaped their understanding of the divine will. Von Rad emphasized, however, that the freedom of the prophet was never lost in this encounter. Indeed, there were experiences in which the call seemed so overwhelming that the prophets were unable to resist. Yet, for von Rad, prophets were free to accept or to reject the divine commission and did not completely surrender their freedom to God.[28]

Their call signaled a radical break with their individual past and thrust them into a role that endured throughout the remainder of their lives. The old was passing away; now the new is about to dawn. This individual break with the past was paralleled by God's own dealings with Israel. Divine judgment of Israel's past was accompanied by the promise of new acts of redemption that would break into history. Prophetic life and message became entwined, and the prophets found themselves compelled by a will much stronger than their own. In the primal experience of the call and later encounters with the Holy, prophets were detached from their own feelings and thoughts and filled with the emotions of God. And in the experience of the emotions of God, the prophet came to understand both God's governance of history and view of the human situation.

Important is von Rad's contention that it is the Word which is the bearer of revelation and possesses authority, not an event behind the interpretation. Prophets were bearers of the divine word that they announced and proclaimed. Using the messenger formula to introduce their speeches ("thus saith the Lord"), the prophets understood themselves as messengers who spoke the oracles delivered to them by God. These speeches, which were couched in a variety of forms, were arranged into small complexes either by the prophets themselves or by their disciples who transmitted the prophetic traditions. These collections were designed to demonstrate that the prophetic word was power-laden language that directed the course of history by bringing destruction and dispensing salvation. These powerful words could never become void or empty of creative force; rather, they continued to find fulfillment in new and significant ways. The disciples believed that fresh meaning could always be extracted from prophetic collections, even when their original historical context and meaning long since had been forgotten.[29]

These adaptations of prophetic words were not spurious distortions; rather, they represented the renewal and re-creation of tra-

---

28. Von Rad, *Old Testament Theology* 2:70–79.
29. Ibid., 2:45.

dition that continued to have power and meaning. Thus, unlike the Albright school, von Rad did not give primacy to the earliest layer of prophetic tradition, presumably closest to if not actually deriving from the prophet himself. Rather, the many layers of tradition possessed an authentic character. This traditioning process was "a perfectly normal and theologically legitimate procedure."[30] Since the prophet's words continued to accompany Israel on its historical journey, later generations who encountered these oracles were not only summoned to faith by the generative power of prophetic discourse but also felt free to reinterpret them within new and different settings. This trajectory of tradition was indeed the authentic hermeneutic that was articulated by Israel's own theologizing. Radical openness to the future allowed continuous reinterpretation, a process that did not do violence to the past but gave it new life.

THE THEOLOGY OF JEREMIAH

Von Rad's explication of the theology of Jeremiah begins with his customary description of the historical context in which the prophet lived.[31] The collapse of the Assyrian empire, the contest between Egypt and Babylonia for control of Syro-Palestine, and the ultimate establishment of Babylonian hegemony are rehearsed along with the heroic although ultimately futile struggles of Judah to achieve political independence. Indeed, Jeremiah's message and life achieved significance in interaction with these most critical events. Perhaps the most significant historical factor in shaping the prophet's message, suggested von Rad, was the "foe from the north," an enemy from Mesopotamia, eventually identified as Babylonia, who would carry out divine judgment against Judah (see Jeremiah 4–10). This theme of a northern enemy appears in the preaching of Jeremiah from its inception in 627 B.C.E. to its conclusion sometime after the fall of Jerusalem in 587 B.C.E.

Von Rad points to the significance of Jeremiah's identity as a northern Israelite prophet from the village of Anathoth in the tribe of Benjamin. Like Hosea, upon whom Jeremiah was dependent, the prophet grounded his preaching in the theological traditions derived from the older, Israelite complex of exodus, covenant at Sinai, and conquest and not from the southern traditions of Judah centered in the promise to David and Zion as the city of God. These northern traditions were cultivated by Jeremiah's priestly family, Levites whose famous ancestor, Abiathar, had been exiled to Ana-

---

30. Ibid., 2:47.
31. Ibid., 2:188–219.

thoth by Solomon. Abiathar had been one of David's two chief priests, but he was exiled as a result of the power struggle between Solomon and Adonijah, two of David's sons who vied for the throne. Abiathar suffered from the misfortune of supporting Adonijah. When Solomon succeeded to the kingship, he selected Zadok, the founder of the Zadokite priesthood, as his chief priest, and exiled Abiathar. While the Zadokites nurtured the David-Zion tradition, the Levites in the north, including the family and descendants of Abiathar, maintained the older traditions of the exodus, the Sinai covenant, and the conquest of Canaan. After the Assyrian conquest in the late eighth century B.C.E., many northern Levites went south to preach in Judah.

Von Rad argued that the sacred traditions of Israel are the basis for the three major elements of Jeremiah's preaching: proclamation of divine judgment, individual laments, and announcement of future salvation. Common to all is von Rad's emphasis on the power of the divine word that goes forth to direct human history and to create the possibility of faithful response. In Jeremiah's early preaching, he speaks of the threat of a "foe from the north" who would carry out Yahweh's will in bringing not salvation to the chosen people but destruction. Israel and Judah both had been faithless to the election and covenant traditions and subsequently were placed under the threat of divine punishment. Prior to Josiah's death in 609 B.C.E., Jeremiah held out the possibility of repentance and the averting of destruction. However, after the battle of Megiddo and the death of the king, Jeremiah points to God's final rejection of his people.[32]

Von Rad emphasized the importance of the redemptive acts of Yahweh in the laments of Jeremiah that speak of suffering, accusation, and the silence of God. The Psalter, of course, contains the response of the community to the acts of divine redemption in hymns (Psalms 78; 105; 106; 135; 136), thanksgivings (Psalms 18; 21; 65; 66; 75; 92; 118), and laments (Psalms 7; 22; 44; 52; 58; 60; 74; 80; 83; 85; 89; 90). Laments typically mention the gracious acts of God in saving the people in the past, complain about the silence and inactivity of God in the present, and sometimes conclude with expressions of confidence in coming redemption. Unique in prophetic literature, however, is the presence of laments in the Book of Jeremiah (11:18—12:6; 15:10-21; 17:14-18; 18:18-23; 20:7-13; 20:14-18). These "confessions" speak of the prophet's struggle with

---

32. See, e.g., the temple sermon in Jeremiah 7.

both his call and the justice of God. Persecution by his enemies and the failure, at least for a time, of the judgment from the north to materialize resulted in a darkness of the soul that threatened the prophet's faith. Jeremiah questioned the justice and faithfulness of God in much the same way that Israel responded to the threat of judgment. Where was the God whose acts of redemption in the past had rescued the faithful from an existence under threat?

According to von Rad, Jeremiah's prophetic life, in a sense, became a via dolorosa (see Jeremiah 37–45). Through his own suffering (confessions and passion story), Jeremiah came to experience the terrifying darkness of "godforsakenness," even as Judah was to experience that terror in its own dark night of the soul. For von Rad, this personal struggle of the prophet reflected the near-collapse of God's relationship with the chosen. Yet in the intensity of their struggles, Jeremiah and eventually Judah discovered an essential feature of faithful life: the concealment of God is the only means that enables people to have the possibility of true human-divine dialogue.

After the judgment of God rendered by the "foe from the north," Jeremiah used the same ancient traditions as the basis for hope in new and gracious acts of God in the future. These new acts, grounded in the redemption of old, included the reuniting of Israel and Judah, the return from exile, and the establishment of a new covenant that would command the obedience of a faithful people whose hearts were transformed (see especially Jeremiah 30–31). While the David-Zion tradition had no significance in the prophet's proclamation of judgment, his eschatological preaching did make a place for a future Messiah (see Jer 23:5-6 and 30:21). However, the new emphasis of the prophet is placed upon one who, in representing divine rule on earth, risks his life and thereby provides access to God in a personal way. Distinctive to Jeremiah is the view that the royal mediator opens up the possibility of salvation to those who give their lives and hearts to God.

A THEOLOGICAL ASSESSMENT OF
VON RAD'S HISTORY AS TRADITION

Von Rad's articulation of Old Testament theology has been and continues to be a commanding presentation. Its distinguishing features include a descriptive, historical articulation of Israelite religious traditions; an important place for the hermeneutical process at work in the Bible by which each generation engaged its traditional faith and reformulated it for their own present; a serious effort to forge a unity between the Testaments not only by means of the traditioning process but also by pointing to Christ as the culmination of history; the use of promise and fulfillment as a hermeneutical structure intrinsic to the traditioning process; and the interpretation of Scripture within the setting of the modern church. Von Rad did not write a systematic Old Testament theology shaped by a single center. But he did point to several tradition complexes that provided thematic coherence for the presentation of the faith of Israel. Von Rad's constructive work tended to be done in writings that represented a stage beyond the descriptive work of his two-volume theology. Yet he did not leave entirely the constructive task to others.

While continuing to serve as a formidable rendering of Old Testament faith, von Rad's theology still has several limitations.[33] He has tended to use characteristic features of Deuteronomic theology to shape the various Old Testament traditions. The so-called ancient credo may be only a Deuteronomic summary, not a primitive core of faith developing into long-standing trajectories, while the organizing principle of "proclamation and response" is also Deuteronomic.[34] Of course, there is nothing inherently wrong with using certain elements of Deuteronomic theology, but why privilege these over others in the Bible?

One may also criticize von Rad for tracing the development of each tradition of faith without attributing any significant theological value to the principles of discontinuity and plurality. To point out the discontinuous and plural nature of Old Testament faith without some incorporation of these observations into theological method is not very satisfying.

Von Rad's theology also faces the same challenge that confronted Wright and the biblical theology movement in America: how to integrate successfully certain parts of the canon, especially wisdom and law, into a comprehensive Old Testament theology. Not only did wisdom literature find its theological grounding in creation, it expressed very little interest in sacred history or even national his-

---

33. See especially James Barr, *Old and New in Interpretation* (London: SCM, 1966); idem, "Trends and Prospects in Biblical Theology," *JTS* 25 (1974) 265–82; and Reventlow, *Problems of Old Testament Theology*, 110–24.

34. J. Philip Hyatt, "Were There an Ancient Historical Credo in Israel and an Independent Sinai Tradition?" *Translating and Understanding the Old Testament* (ed. Harry Thomas Frank and William L. Reed; Nashville: Abingdon, 1970) 152–70.

tory before Ben Sira in the second century B.C.E. The theology of law is based on the primal event of revelation at Sinai. Yet neither of these themes was a part of the early creed, at least according to von Rad. For him, the full development of the theological traditions of creation and the revelation at Sinai as themes of a confessing faith occurred only in the exilic and postexilic periods.

The theological struggle to find an important place for creation is illustrated, according to von Rad, by the Yahwist. The J narrative regards creation as a preface to salvation history that begins with Abraham in order to extend the blessing of Israel to all nations. Yet for creation to be regarded as a saving event, von Rad had to make creation into a work in time, much the same as the exodus. Given the primacy of redemption in his Old Testament theology, von Rad searched for this view of creation as a soteriological act and found it very late, in Deutero-Isaiah's redemptive theology. Von Rad attempted, not very convincingly, to include wisdom under the rubric of the "response to salvation history," even though these themes are absent in the corpus until the second century B.C.E.[35]

Von Rad's presentation of the theological significance of Torah is also open to serious debate. He regarded the Sinai tradition as secondarily placed into the tradition of the wilderness wandering. And of course, the ancient creed, as he determined it, did not mention this event.[36] He argued that it is only in the postexilic period that the law assumed primacy in Jewish religion and received its full theological development. For von Rad, of course, this was not entirely a welcome development. He saw this as something of a digression from a theology of redemption grounded in both the gracious acts of Yahweh and Israel's justification by faith (see Abraham's response to God's call) and as a movement toward a theology of works-righteousness. According to von Rad, the law, not election rooted in gracious acts of saving history, now defined who belonged to the people of God.[37] The law became absolute, timeless, and unconditional, regardless of the situation. True, the law was

---

35. Von Rad addressed this deficiency in his *Wisdom in Israel* (Nashville: Abingdon, 1972) when he indicated that wisdom reflected theologically on the nature and activity of God revealed in everyday experiences of the world. For von Rad, the sages, except Qoheleth, affirmed that creation was good and came to express their trust in the graciousness of the creator. Even Job finally places his destiny and that of creation back into the hands of God. For a detailed treatment, see Leo G. Perdue, *Wisdom and Creation: The Theology of Wisdom Literature* (Nashville: Abingdon, 1994).
36. Von Rad, *Old Testament Theology* 1:187.
37. Ibid., 1:90.

strongly linked to salvation, but redemption now was merited by obedience to divine commandments. Prior to the post-exile, he argues, the purpose of the law was to serve the people by guiding them through their history as the chosen of God. After the exile, the purpose of the people was to serve the law. Von Rad saw the door to casuistry open, and saving history as a movement through time and space came to an abrupt halt.[38] Israel was no longer linked to the nations but now was separate and apart. The theological richness of Torah is not explored and set forth by von Rad, and this is perhaps the greatest weakness of his presentation.

Von Rad's work in the area of hermeneutics also is open to question. Certainly, the principle of promise and fulfillment and the practice of "retelling" are important in understanding the nature of traditioning and the re-presentation and reactualization of Old Testament faith. Each generation encounters the "word" and re-experiences its saving power through faith and confession. However, typology is not very useful as a hermeneutical principle. Typology derives from precritical thinking unencumbered by the shock of the Enlightenment and presupposes one continuous story of faith, not the multiplicity of traditions, interruptions, and fragmentation that von Rad so adroitly reveals in his descriptive work.[39] Events become extracted from their space and time to point to "like" events in the future. The scholar most responsible for describing Old Testament theology as redemptive history moves away from the language and conceptualities of history to another mode of discourse and understanding when he approaches hermeneutics.[40]

---

38. Ibid., 1:91.

39. For an overview of the critical responses to von Rad and the difficulties posed by history in general, see Reventlow, *Problems of Old Testament Theology*, 59–124.

40. In Germany, especially among the scholars who continue the von Rad–Alt–Noth *Schule*, the program for doing theology remains essentially that of von Rad. What is needed is greater clarity and more refined results. See especially Rolf Rendtorff, "Alttestamentliche Theologie und israelitisch-jüdische Religionsgeschichte," *Gesammelte Studien zum Alten Testament* (Theologische Bücherei 57; Munich: Kaiser, 1975) 137–51. Rendtorff (the major Old Testament participant in the Pannenberg *Schule*) is one of von Rad's students who has developed his teacher's views by attempting to bring together the history of actual events uncovered by historical criticism and the history of Israel's own self-attested faith. For Rendtorff, it is impossible to believe simply that God acted in certain, uninterpreted ways that are discernible to the historian. Indeed, these acts are interpreted and constantly reinterpreted. No event occurs without the interpretation which is its meaning. But more important, Rendtorff contends that the traditions of the thematic acts are themselves history, i.e., they are constructed

Von Rad certainly worked as a Christian interpreter of the Old Testament, standing within his own confessing community. Would his presentation of Old Testament theology have been improved by the inclusion of a more constructive, integrative, and systematic approach? This is a major question, but it would have enabled contemporary theologians and those who stand within confessing Christian communities of faith to access better von Rad's theology, or, better stated, theologies.

To push further the issue of doing a constructive Old Testament theology, what of questions emerging from the contemporary community of faith that von Rad's treatment does not answer, at least directly? Sexism, racism, environment, war, the Holocaust, and social justice, to name a few pressing issues, are not addressed by von Rad's theology, presumably because he thought these belong to contemporary theology and ethics.

One may question an approach that does not posit a center that allows for a systematic presentation. As a historian, von Rad has made a strong case for denying that any one theme or tradition resides at the center of Israelite faith. For a descriptive stage of Old Testament theology, this is most probably true. Is it not possible, however, for a theologian, even a historical theologian, to move to another stage or level in theological discourse and set forth a center that unites various elements into a more systematic treatment?

Von Rad's treatment of Jeremiah is admirable. He places the prophet within his historical and cultural setting, the long stream of prophets in Israel, and the theological traditions of Israelite faith. At the same time, he addresses in cogent terms the specific features of the life and thought of the prophet, bringing to light, for example, the unique presence and importance of the confessions.

Yet several problems confront von Rad's theological presentation of Jeremiah. What is one to do, for example, with Jeremiah's appropriation of the theology of creation, particularly the chaos tradition, in describing the "foe from the north"? Or, what of the

---

within time and space by historical communities and open to historical understanding. These traditions include actual events, but they cannot be separated into two parts: facts and interpretation. Israel's history occurs both within the "outward" events that are the subject of the historian and the "internal" events that exist in the multilayers of tradition. There is the unity of word and event through which the knowledge of God comes. For Rendtorff, revelation comes in "the event which is announced in the Word in its context in the history of the tradition." For a purely descriptive approach, following the historical development of Israelite theology, see Werner H. Schmidt, *The Faith of the Old Testament: A History* (Philadelphia: Westminster, 1983).

wisdom texts that made their way into the prophetic traditions (e.g., Jer 17:5-11)? Von Rad could have examined these specific examples of two traditions in Jeremiah, but he does not do so.

Then there is the substantial problem posed by the continuities and discontinuities resulting from the Deuteronomic editing of the Book of Jeremiah. In this redaction, Jeremiah becomes the "new Moses" who is both the preacher and the interpreter of the (Deuteronomic) law. Would this representation of Jeremiah as the "new Moses" be a digression and perhaps even misrepresentation, given von Rad's treatment of Torah?

Von Rad's formulation of Old Testament theology, illustrated by his assessment of the Book of Jeremiah, remains a formidable presentation even today. However, the weaknesses mentioned above have demonstrated how an Old Testament theology, grounded in history, even a history of traditions traced out within a reconstructed narrative history of Israel, faces serious challenges and carries with it inherent limitations.

CHAPTER 4

History as Liberation: Social Science and Radical Theology

The paradigm of history remains a significant model for biblical study and Old Testament theology, in part because it has adapted well to new methodological developments. Since the 1970s, however, a renewed emphasis on the social sciences has led, not only to the reshaping of the study of the Bible, but also to the reformulation of the tasks of both biblical theology and contemporary hermeneutics. Perhaps the most provocative example of the combination of the historical paradigm with social-scientific study that leads into biblical theology and eventually contemporary hermeneutics is the work of Norman Gottwald. The two primary and related features of Gottwald's formidable work are his social-scientific analysis of ancient Israel and his theological work that is largely informed by liberation theology.

SOCIAL-SCIENTIFIC STUDY OF THE OLD TESTAMENT

While the concerns and application of the social sciences have shaped modern biblical scholarship for the past century, the significant use of social-scientific methods to reconstruct Israelite history and religion has developed at a rapid pace since the 1970s.[1]

1. See Walter Brueggemann, "Trajectories in Old Testament Literature and the Sociology of Ancient Israel," *JBL* 98 (1979) 161–85; Norman K. Gottwald, "Sociological Method in the Study of Ancient Israel," *The Bible and Liberation* (ed. Norman K. Gottwald; rev. ed.; Maryknoll, N.Y.: Orbis, 1983) 26–37; Bruce J. Malina, "The Social Sciences and Biblical Interpretation," Gottwald, *The Bible and Liberation*, 11–25; J. W. Rogerson, "The Use of Sociology in Old Testament Studies," *SVT* 36 (1985) 245–56; Gerd Theissen, "The Sociological Interpretation of Religious Traditions: Its Methodological Problems as Exemplified in Early Christianity," Gottwald, *The Bible and Liberation*; and Robert K. Wilson, *Sociological Approaches to the Old Testament* (Guides to Biblical Scholarship; Philadelphia: Fortress, 1984).

Historical criticism has been traditionally an eclectic combination of methods from the humanities (literature, philosophy, art, and even to a certain extent archaeology and history). The use of methods from sociology and anthropology gained prominence in the generation prior to World War II, but interest waned for a time after the war. The recent reemergence of the use of methods from sociology and anthropology has been due in part to their successful accommodation to historical-critical interests. The focus of these methods is not primarily on national history or the development of religious institutions or ideas as separate from other features of communal life; rather, the focus is on describing the changing social organization of ancient Israel throughout its lengthy history. The thrust tends to be macrocosmic in the sense of understanding the internal workings of the entire society rather than focusing on only one particular feature. The models of analysis available for comparative study and applied to past societies, such as those represented in the Bible, derive from the contemporary world: Western European and American societies (sociology) and "primitive" contemporary cultures (anthropology). Because of this, some caution is always in order, since the transference from modern societies and current "primitive" cultures to ancient ones must negotiate its way past such pitfalls as the anachronistic imposition of contemporary models of human interactions on the past, reductionism, and an ignoring of the specificity of particular social configurations. Nevertheless comparative work based on the principle of analogy may offer keen insights into certain sociological and anthropological possibilities for assessing the social realities of the Old Testament world.

An important element in the description of societies through the lenses of these models is social knowledge, including ideologies that legitimated and supported the various patterns for and functions of human relationships. This means that biblical writings are considered social products written by and reflecting the interests of groups who interacted with both institutions and significations of communal life, including the family, economy, government, legal system, military, education, and religion. And these social products reflect a group's or a community's particular view of things or, in other words, their social construction of reality.[2]

The move from social world to biblical theology, informed by the

---

2. Norman K. Gottwald, "Social Matrix and Canonical Shape," *TToday* 42 (1985) 307.

social sciences, requires the demonstration of how the "assertions of that theology correspond to socioeconomic, political, and cultural interests and desiderata in ancient Israel."[3] Any understanding of God must be grounded in the concrete social life of the community. At the same time, the social identity and life of the communities of the interpreter of Scripture and the one translating the theology of the text for the present must also be assessed.

Generally speaking, social-scientific study in Old Testament scholarship complements rather than replaces historical-critical work. Old Testament scholars who use social-scientific explanatory models attempt to "grasp the typical patterns of human relations in their structure and function, both at a given moment or stage (synchronics) and in their trajectories of change over specified time spans (diachronics)."[4] Synchronic analysis focuses on a particular historical moment that provides a cross-section of social life, while diachronic study looks at the development of social organizations over a period of time.

Specifically, Israelite societies over the centuries are arguably comparable to typical patterns of social organization in general, and through sociological and anthropological study they may be compared to specific types of social arrangements in the present. Israelites are seen to think and act within certain social patterns that made up particular expressions of changing social organizations. These expressions include institutions, roles, statuses, values, meanings, and symbols that are a part of complex networks of economics, law, military, religion, and politics comprising the larger social system. These expressions are viewed within the social sciences through the lens of typical models for social interaction. At the same time, historical, literary, and archaeological work should complement sociological analysis. These help the scholar using social-scientific method to identify the "data" that may be used for reconstructing Israelite society as it developed and changed over the years.

The social sciences identify several models that typically describe the ways human communities are organized. These models are general theories that describe major forms of human interaction and the meaning systems that these models develop in order to legitimate and maintain the important features of social organization. Major models for social organization include the structural-

3. Ibid., 318.
4. Gottwald, "Sociological Method in the Study of Ancient Israel," 27.

functional (or order) paradigm, the conflict model, and symbolic interaction.[5]

The structural-functional model proposes that human communities develop and continue to create and maintain order and harmony.[6] In this largely static model of order, humans interact within commonly accepted patterns or structures that are grounded in mutually shared purposes or functions.[7] There is thought to be a general consensus involving the important values that make up a meaning system that shapes and informs behavior. Acceptable change is slow and occurs within basic institutions that influence each other. Thus a society that is well balanced and "healthy" tends to be stable and well integrated. Behavior that is not based on commonly accepted values and that does not grow out of slow, adaptive change is considered deviant and potentially destructive. Various forms of social control (e.g., law, military, and custom) are used to produce conformist behavior. The inherent weakness in the model is that constraints imposed on human freedom are themselves potentially destructive.[8] The model may too easily lend itself to the view that people freely enter into a societal consensus. The constraints of social control, imposed by those who are in positions of power, may lead to the elimination of "deviance," resulting in a fascist social organization.

The conflict model contends that struggle is inherent in the development, continuation, or decline of human societies.[9] Change is considered to be endemic to social interaction. The issue is whether change is slow and deliberate or disruptive and subversive. According to this model, societies are composed of various and often competing social groups that have different values and specific interests that are not commonly shared by all. Competing groups may use compromise and cooperation to realize their goals.

5. For an introduction to social models, see W. D. Perdue, *Sociological Theory* (Palo Alto, Calif.: Mayfield, 1986). Malina's essay provides a clear overview of social models ("The Social Sciences and Biblical Interpretation," 11–25).

6. Important representatives of the paradigm of order include Emile Durkheim, *The Division of Labor in Society* (New York: Macmillan, 1933); Robert K. Merton, *Social Theory and Social Structure* (New York: Free Press, 1968); and Talcott Parsons, *The Structure of Social Action* (Glencoe, Ill.: Free Press, 1937).

7. Malina, "The Social Sciences and Biblical Interpretation," 16.

8. Ibid., 17.

9. Important examples of conflict theory include Karl Marx, *Capital: A Critique of Political Economy* (3 vols.; New York: International Publishers, 1967); Herbert Marcuse, *Reason and Revolution* (New York: Humanities Press, 1954); and Jürgen Habermas, *Toward a Rational Society* (Boston: Beacon, 1970).

However, if the interests and values of certain groups are not supported or allowed to come to expression because of the imposition
of constraints, they may use various means of conflict (from mild
coercion to total struggle) to obtain their interests and to realize
their values. Dissent and conflict are seen as "normal" features of a
society as long as competing groups may find their values and interests protected. However, if these are not protected within the
equilibrium that had been achieved by cooperation, then struggle
that seeks to change or, in extreme cases, subvert the social order
may occur. According to conflict theorists, conflict is inevitable, for
it is endemic to all forms of human interaction.[10]

A third theoretical model for human organization is symbolic
interaction.[11] This model argues that societies comprise systems of
symbols that inform human perceptions and motivate behavior.
Ideally speaking, people, institutions, perceptions, and actions are
thought to embody these meaning-conveying symbols. These symbols derive their range of meanings by the definitions given them by
participants in the society. The social organization of individuals
and groups is formed and informed by the symbolic meanings that
are given to values, objects, and ways of acting. Shared definitions
provide the basis for social equilibrium, although change is produced by the ongoing response to new situations.[12]

The use of the social sciences to write a social history of Israel has
led to the reconfiguration of ways of doing Old Testament theology.
Old Testament theology, seen descriptively, becomes ideology, that
is, it functions to legitimate and maintain the interests and values of
different social groups or the larger social organization as a whole.

LIBERATION THEOLOGY

Social-scientific methods have also contributed significantly to
conversations involving Old Testament hermeneutics when combined with the concerns of contemporary or confessing theologies.[13]
This is not to suggest that social-scientific methodologies are necessarily linked to any particular contemporary theology. Indeed, an
Old Testament scholar using social-scientific methods may not
demonstrate an interest in modern theology of any kind, although
one may well look askance at those who argue they are operating out

10. Malina, "The Social Sciences and Biblical Interpretation," 17.
11. See George Herbert Mead, *Mind, Self and Society* (Chicago: University of
Chicago Press, 1934).
12. Malina, "The Social Sciences and Biblical Interpretation," 18.
13. Wilson, *Sociological Approaches to the Old Testament*, 7.

of a methodological approach that is not guided by values to which they either give at least some allegiance or in which they have some interest. This is true of most scholars in any field who carry out their work. Methodologies and their applications are not value free.

Other scholars, however, have connected their social-scientific analysis to rather clear theological and hermeneutical interests. The active expression of these hermeneutical concerns is comparable to that of Wright and von Rad whose indebtedness to neoorthodoxy is present in the formulation of their respective Old Testament theologies. Perhaps the most engaging cases of the combining of social-scientific methodology with contemporary theology are those which use both conflict theory and liberation theology to describe the social organizations and ideologies of human communities and social groups in ancient Israel.

Liberation theology has many, often diverse expressions, including African-American, Third World, feminist, and womanist, to name some of the more general categories.[14] Within these larger areas are significant varieties of formulation. However, much liberation theology and many liberation movements that may not have a theological component generally operate out of a conflict social model (Marxist, neo-Marxist, or socialist). And liberation theology has identifying themes that are common to most of its diverse expressions: solidarity with the oppressed, the liberation of the downtrodden, the humanization of both the oppressed and oppressive social structures that deny full humanity to certain groups, the empowerment of oppressed groups to live lives of integrity, the value placed on the experience of oppressed peoples, and the rejection of authoritarianism and hierarchy. Since feminist theology will

---

14. We shall deal with feminist theology below, in chapter 7. For a basic introduction to both African-American theology and Latin American liberation theology with bibliography, see Ferm, *Contemporary American Theologies*. Among the classics of Latin American liberation theology are Gustavo Gutiérrez, *A Theology of Liberation* (Maryknoll, N.Y.: Orbis, 1971); idem, *We Drink from Our Own Wells: The Spiritual Journey of a People* (Maryknoll, N.Y.: Orbis, 1984); José Miguez Bonino, *Doing Theology in a Revolutionary Situation* (Philadelphia: Fortress, 1975); and Juan Luis Segundo, *Liberation of Theology* (Maryknoll, N.Y.: Orbis, 1976). For introductions to Latin American liberation theology, see Leonardo and Clodovis Boff, *Introducing Liberation Theology* (Maryknoll, N.Y.: Orbis, 1987); Robert McAfee Brown, *Gustavo Gutiérrez: An Introduction to Liberation Theology* (Maryknoll, N.Y.: Orbis, 1990); and Arthur F. McGovern, *Liberation Theology and Its Critics: Toward an Assessment* (Maryknoll, N.Y.: Orbis, 1989).

be addressed in chapter 7, a brief listing of major themes in Latin American liberation theology follows.[15]

Originating in countries in which the poor have long been victims of oppressive regimes that have extended policies formulated during the period of European colonialism, Latin American liberation theology has important defining features that undergird its diversity of expression.[16] The starting point is the realization that for Latin American liberation theologians, context is critical. Subsequently, they have argued for a theology that would reflect the situation and culture of Latin America and not the history, issues, and culture that is the context for European theology. Central to liberation theology, of course, is the emphasis placed on the practical application of the gospel's emphasis on liberation and continuing reflection on its practical application. There has also been significant use or adaptation of sociological conflict theory, particularly Marxism or neo-Marxism, in providing the social-critical basis for liberation theology.

While the focus of liberation has been on the humanization of the poor by freeing them from the shackles and degradation of poverty, there are also the related theological objectives of freedom from sin, selfishness, and oppression. Practice and critical reflection on practice are the bipolar features of liberation theology, and together they comprise what liberation theologians refer to as praxis. For some liberation theologians, orthopraxis, not orthodoxy, is the primary consideration of theological reflection.[17]

Liberation theologians base their objective of freeing the oppressed on the exodus from Egypt and the teachings and actions of Jesus in the Gospels. Liberation for the downtrodden is the actualization of the commandments of God to love and care for the neighbor. Love is actualized in solidarity with the oppressed, in experiencing their lot, and in capturing their vision of both life with God (spirituality) and the reign of God (social justice). In Latin America, the victims of social injustice are most commonly the poor, although liberation theology includes all people and groups who are the victims of oppression. To enter into solidarity means to oppose the oppressors, those modern pharaohs whose repression leads to the victimization of the downtrodden. Yet to enter into solidarity also

15. For the impact of liberation theology on the churches in North America, see William K. Tabb, ed., *Churches in Struggle* (New York: Monthly Review, 1986).
16. See Leonardo and Clodovis Boff, *Introducing Liberation Theology*, 49–63.
17. Miguez Bonino, *Doing Theology in a Revolutionary Situation*, 81.

means recognizing that all people, including the poor, are fully human, a recognition that is often denied by oppressive social systems.[18] Thus the task is to proclaim a liberating gospel in a world that is often nonhuman in its treatment of the oppressed. Conscientization is the means by which the oppressed achieve their full human dignity. This usually involves active struggle in various forms. Struggle is directed against oppression in both the spiritual and human (sociopolitical) realms. For some liberation theologians, even radical means may be used in the struggle for liberation, including revolution against tyrannical regimes.

The experience of the oppressed is seen as a defining, epistemological characteristic for liberation theology. Their piety, compassion, love, celebration of life, serenity, and moderation are the defining features of faithful living. Theology that is not informed by their experience and consequent vision of God and the kingdom is limited in its scope and character.[19]

For liberation theology, God is one who expresses partiality toward the poor:

> God is especially close to those who are oppressed; God hears their cry and resolves to set them free (Exod. 3:7-8). God is father of all, but most particularly father and defender of those who are oppressed and treated unjustly. Out of love for them, God takes sides, takes their side against the repressive measures of all the pharaohs.[20]

God is the redeemer *(gō'ēl)* of the Old Testament, the one who saves the poor from their affliction. This same redeemer freed the slaves in Egypt and commissioned them as the people of God to liberate other captives from their prisons. The revelation of God occurs in the historical setting of the liberation of the oppressed. The paradigmatic act for divine liberation in the Old Testament is the exodus.

In Christian liberation theology, Jesus Christ is the one who identified with the poor, suffered their misery, preached the good news to them, opposed and was oppressed by repressive rulers, and through word and deed initiated the dawning of the kingdom, that realm of nearness to God in which justice would reign supreme. The ministry of Christ represents the paradigm and forefront of active liberation. The crucifixion represents both Jesus' rejection by human authorities and the sacrificial acceptance by God. In the resur-

18. Gutiérrez, *A Theology of Liberation.*
19. Ferm, *Contemporary American Theologies*, 62.
20. Leonardo and Clodovis Boff, *Introducing Liberation Theology*, 50–51.

rection, life triumphs over death and freedom over oppression. The resurrection anticipates the culmination of the universal reign of God.

In Christian liberation theology, the Holy Spirit continues to dwell with God's people and becomes the means by which persons are able to live in peace and justice, one with the other. The Holy Spirit, as the divine presence that identifies and struggles with the oppressed, works for the transformation of human society in order to eliminate oppression and discrimination.

The kingdom of God is the goal of salvation history. Working out of a theology of realized and future eschatology, the kingdom is viewed as both present in a partial manifestation and not yet in its final and complete realization. The kingdom embraces all of history as well as its culmination. It is the manifesto of liberation theology that faith must be put into action in order to free the oppressed and enter into community with God until the final culmination of the kingdom becomes a complete reality. And the kingdom includes both creation and eternity. With the new heaven and the new earth, creation and history and eternity and time are joined together in their totality as one. In the liberation of history, there is the redemption of creation. In the liberation of creation, there is the redemption of history.

Finally, the people of God are to be both the sign and the instrument of liberation. In response to the grace of God's salvation extended to them, the church as the community of the redeemed who embody in themselves servanthood are to be active in their preaching of a liberating gospel to all, but particularly to the poor. In the communion experienced by poor base communities, the church shares with others both love and justice. Through action and divine encounter (prayer, worship, Bible reading), the church and its members experience true spirituality. It is this spirituality that is the wellspring of liberation. Rejecting the tyranny of authoritarianism and hierarchy, these base communities of the poor point the way authentically to the culmination of the kingdom of God. In its worship and celebration, and in its piety and struggles for social justice, the church embodies the liberation and liberating experience offered to all.

Liberation that brings about the humanization of the oppressed may occur only by changing the systemic structure of oppressive societies, including economics and politics. Evil is not simply personal, it is intrinsic to human societies in general. Only in the church's transformation of oppressive structures through active and even revolutionary change is it possible for the oppressed to be liberated and to achieve their full humanity.[21]

NORMAN GOTTWALD AND LIBERATED ISRAEL

The most engaging and prodigious example of the combination of conflict theory with liberation theology in Old Testament studies is the work of Norman Gottwald.[22] For Gottwald, the symbols and ethical teachings of religion may play an important, if not necessary, role in human liberation. Nevertheless Gottwald's concern for contemporary hermeneutics, especially in the struggle for freedom, is a major force in shaping his scholarly work. In the introduction to *The Bible and Liberation,* two primary aims of this collection of essays as well as his own work are identified:

1. To bring to light the actual social struggles of our biblical ancestors and to locate the human and religious resources they drew upon in the midst of those struggles.
2. To tap the biblical social struggles and religious understandings as important resources for directing us in the social struggles we are presently engaged in.[23]

The hermeneutical concerns of liberation theology that shape the analysis of some practitioners of social-scientific methodologies are clearly set forth in the introduction to *The Bible and Liberation.* Here, various destructive chasms are identified that the essays in this volume attempt to overcome: "the chasm between religion and the rest of life," "the chasm between the past as 'dead history' and the present as 'real life,'" "the chasm between thought and practice," and "the chasm between biblical academics and popular Bible study."[24]

21. For an introduction to African-American liberation theology, see Ferm, *Contemporary American Theologies,* 41–58. Among the best examples of African-American liberation theology are James Cone, *Black Theology and Black Power* (New York: Seabury, 1969); idem, *A Black Theology of Liberation* (New York: J. B. Lippincott, 1970); idem, *God of the Oppressed* (New York: Seabury, 1975); J. Deotis Roberts, *Liberation and Reconciliation: A Black Theology* (Philadelphia: Westminster, 1971); Major Jones, *Christian Ethics for Black Theology: The Politics of Liberation* (Nashville: Abingdon, 1974); and Cornel West, *Prophesy Deliverance! An Afro-American Revolutionary Christianity* (Philadelphia: Westminster, 1982).
22. See especially Norman K. Gottwald, *The Tribes of Yahweh* (Maryknoll, N.Y.: Orbis, 1979); and idem, *The Hebrew Bible—A Socio-Literary Introduction* (Philadelphia: Fortress, 1985).
23. Norman K. Gottwald, "The Bible and Liberation: Deeper Roots and Wider Horizons, *The Bible and Liberation,* 2.
24. Gottwald, "The Bible and Liberation," 2.

The social-scientific approach of Gottwald builds upon histori-cal-critical method, only the primary philosophical framework is conflict theory (largely Marxism or neo-Marxism), not positivism. Gottwald has shifted the interpretative enterprise away from his-tory as events or as tradition to social analysis that proceeds from the impetus of a basic affirmation: the movement of history is toward liberation.

Laying the grounds for his social-scientific assessment of ancient Israel, Gottwald argues against the notion that Israel's social system represents a static order of equilibrium that does not change over the years. Rather, his major contention is that change is inherent to Israelite society as well as to all social systems, change that is not always slow, adaptive, and orderly but rather at times may be dis-ruptive and even chaotic.[25]

Working out of a conflict model, Gottwald contends that for ancient Israel meaning systems, actualized in various patterns for human interactions, authorized valid distributions of human and natural resources as well as the use of power. These distributions and uses of power were expressed overtly and symbolically through religious rite and various means of socialization (e.g., education) as well as through cooperation, persuasion, and force.

According to Gottwald, the engine that drives all societies is the distribution of resources and power. This is illustrated in the area of economics where a particular emphasis is placed on both the mode and the control of production. But economics also involves politics and culture, for those who control production and reap its benefits are in positions of political power.

Gottwald argues that the major determinant for human history is the material condition of life, not religious ideas, although religious ideas are a part of the ideologies that express the values and self-interests of various groups concerned with their share of resources and access to power. Israelite society, like all human societies, ar-gues Gottwald, consists of competing groups who seek in various ways to have their interests and values supported by the broader society. Of course, this does not always happen through cooperation and compromise. Accordingly, human history in general, as well as Israelite history in particular, reflects the tensions and conflicts between competing groups, tensions that are most severe in the oppression of various communities and groups by elitist rulers.

Gottwald traces Israel's history through three major movements: the intertribal confederacy (Israel's revolutionary beginnings), the

25. Gottwald, "Sociological Method in the Study of Ancient Israel," 27.

monarchy (Israel's counterrevolutionary establishment), and home rule under great empires (Israel's colonial recovery). His analysis is not simply a description of the historical trajectories of ancient Israel devoid of his own evaluative, social comment. Rather, Gottwald clearly assesses the virtues and vices of the social institutions and ideologies operative in ancient Israel and in a straightforward way argues that the social organization and values of the intertribal confederacy found in Israel's revolutionary beginnings are ethically superior to those represented by the royal state. The monarchy and the Israelite royal state are viewed by Gottwald as inherently corrupt and evil. Indeed, the folly of this counterrevolution contributed to the eventual subjection of Israel to the empires as a colony.

Revolutionary Israel

The starting point for understanding Gottwald is his intertribal confederacy (revolutionary Israel). At the beginning of his discussion, Gottwald investigates the great traditions and traditionists: the Yahwist, Elohist, Deuteronomic History, P, the redaction of JEP, and the common source (G) of J and E. While these sources were produced after the demise of revolutionary Israel, Gottwald argues that they contain oral traditions that provide some understanding of the prerevolutionary peoples, values, and social organizations that eventually combined to form the intertribal confederacy in the early Iron Age (1200 to 1000 B.C.E.). These oral traditions ("low literature") arose primarily among lower-class peoples who desired self-determination in place of the intervention and control of the ruling groups.[26] The basic literary types, according to Gottwald, were instructional and celebratory, for they incorporated both the ethical values and the popular beliefs of a folk culture. The settings for the shaping of these early oral traditions were the public assemblies and covenant renewal ceremonies of a pre-state people. The history-like themes (see von Rad and Wright) that were recounted and celebrated were placed in a historical sequence by a later traditionist (e.g., J), but the sequence was not necessarily the actual historical order. These themes are the primal history (creation to Abraham), the patriarchs (Abraham, Isaac, Jacob), the descent into Egypt (Joseph), slavery and the exodus (Moses), the wilderness sojourn (Moses), law and covenant at Sinai (Moses), the conquest of Canaan (Joshua), and the consolidation of

---

26. Gottwald, *The Hebrew Bible*, 14.

the conquest (Judges).[27] For Gottwald, the original core was the exodus and conquest (cf. von Rad). This core was expanded by the addition of the stories of the ancestors, the sojourn in the wilderness, and the covenant and law at Sinai.

Gottwald finds in this largely oral literature of intertribal Israel traces of accounts of earlier ancestors who may be placed into two categories: the ancestors (fathers and mothers) of Israel and the great deliverer Moses. The stories of the ancestors, argues Gottwald, became a part of Israelite tradition during the intertribal period. Jacob was the ancestral hero of northern tribes located in the areas of Ephraim and Manasseh, while Abraham and Isaac were southern heroes of Judah and the northern Negeb.[28] These ancestral stories were combined into a unified tradition only during the period of the confederacy of tribes.

Gottwald argues that the tribes preserved these stories, not primarily because they expressed religious practices and beliefs, but because they reflected the tribes' concerns with economic production, reproduction, and self-defense.[29] Accordingly, the ancestral stories reflect the desire for a community with a future that is possible only by having offspring, a fertile land, and a defense against internal and external threats. The groups who told and handed down these stories required sons to continue their existence, pastureland and farms especially located in the highlands and often outside the control of Canaanites, and an adequate defense to ensure their survival in the face of the larger, more powerful city-states. These ancestral stories indicate that those who handed them down were only marginally integrated into Canaanite society. For Gottwald, these groups decided to be marginals, choosing to exist in small communities with their own social organization and values. Although these groups were led by males, Gottwald argues that it is clear from the traditions that there were strong women who played significant roles.

The prerevolutionary traditions also contain materials about Moses and derive from a group of state slaves who left Egypt and migrated to Canaan. These slaves, suggests Gottwald, were most probably former Canaanites and their descendants who had either migrated to Africa or were forcefully taken as slaves by the warrior kings of Egypt, especially during the period of the New Kingdom

27. Ibid., 144.
28. Ibid., 173–74.
29. Ibid., 175.

(the Late Bronze Age). This Moses, who bore an Egyptian name, led an uprising of slaves who escaped into the desert, although he died prior to the entrance into Canaan.[30] These early traditions attribute to Moses, a Levite, the worship of a new deity, Yahweh, and the introduction of a new cultus that included either a tent or an ark, some form of sacrifice, and quite possibly a covenant relationship between a community of former slaves and the God of liberation. This group consisted of breeders and herders, gardeners, and fishers who had been turned into state slaves by the kings of Egypt. Perhaps numbering only a few hundred, this Moses group had a primal experience that was later paradigmatic for the many other pre-Israelite groups in Canaan: liberation from the oppression of kings. The Moses group struggled to unite to form a community of equals with leaders who would replace the oppressive control of Egyptian rulers. They struggled against imposing odds to escape the threats of disease and famine. Finally, they also sought to define new roles for women, active in the struggle for liberation, within an emerging social organization.[31]

Gottwald then turns to consider the origins of Israel in Canaan. In essence three theories, existing in many variations, have been used as explanatory models: conquest, gradual infiltration, and revolution.[32] Before the 1970s, the conquest theory provided the most popular explanation of Israel's formation as a people in Canaan. Attempting to correlate Joshua 1–12 with archaeological excavations of Late Bronze and Iron I sites or occupation levels, this theory posits a blitzkrieg invasion of Canaan by twelve united tribes under the leader Joshua who, having left Egypt, entered Canaan from the east and subsequently conquered many of the city-states. The destruction of numerous Canaanite cities during the end of the Late Bronze and the beginning of the Iron I periods, which archaeology was thought to support, lent credence to the literary portrait in Joshua 1–12. Primitive settlements, built either on the destruction layers of earlier Late Bronze cities or on long-abandoned areas, were thought to provide early sedentary evidence for Israelite occupation.

Major difficulties with this theory have arisen that undermine much of its credibility, as Gottwald clearly demonstrates. First, an alternative literary portrait, especially in Judges 1 and Joshua 13–

---

30. Ibid., 223.
31. Ibid., 225.
32. Ibid., 261–76; and Rose, "The Bible and Archaeology," 53–64.

19 (the so-called negative conquest tradition), often conflicts with the conquest theory. In addition, excavations of various cities reported to have been conquered or defeated by Joshua and the Israelites in Joshua 1–12 do not always support the conquest model. Ai had not been occupied for centuries; Jericho, if inhabited at all at the end of the Late Bronze period, could have been no more than a fort or small unwalled settlement; and Gibeon gives no evidence of Late Bronze material culture, except for some scant examples of Late Bronze tomb pottery. Further, there is no explicit supporting evidence that even those sites which experienced destruction at this time were destroyed by invading Israelites. The destruction could have been caused by Egyptians, rival Canaanites, seminomadic tribes, or even revolutionaries. Indeed, some of the cities may have burned by accident and not by war. These difficulties have led to a modified version of the conquest theory that posits Joshua as the leader of a few tribes who took at least some of the cities. Consolidation of Israelite gains occurred throughout the period of the judges, until, it is argued, David brought the entire region under Israelite control for the first time.

The second theory is that of gradual infiltration over a period of centuries. This theory, championed especially by Albrecht Alt and his student Martin Noth, depicts a long period of largely peaceful settlement in unoccupied areas of Canaan, especially the highlands, by various, usually unrelated groups until David brought the region under Israelite hegemony. Hence the negative conquest tradition in Judges and Joshua 13–19 is given more credence than Joshua 1–12. The latter is simply a later Deuteronomistic retrojection of David's or perhaps even Josiah's efforts many years later. The social, political, and religious organization during the Iron I period was the twelve tribe league (amphictyony).

The third theory, embraced by Gottwald, is revolution which blends well with his use of a conflict model for describing Israelite society. Building on the work of George Mendenhall,[33] this theory proposes that early Israel consisted primarily, not of pastoral nomads invading Canaan from the outside, but of former lower-class and marginal Canaanites who rose up against the ruling classes of the Canaanite city-states and in some cases were successful in deposing these tyrants. The parasitic ruling class consisted of royal families, merchants, bureaucrats, and large landowners. Gottwald

---

33. George E. Mendenhall, *The Tenth Generation: The Origins of the Biblical Tradition* (Baltimore: Johns Hopkins University Press, 1973).

contends that this ruling class, not the masses of Canaanites, was the enemy attacked and either exterminated or expelled. Thus he concludes that, historically speaking, there was no mass genocide of the Canaanite population of the city-states as depicted in Joshua 1–12. These Canaanite peasants, located largely in the farming villages situated near the large walled cities, were joined by pastoral nomads and 'apiru in their struggle. According to Gottwald, the catalyst for this partially successful revolution, which had been brewing for several centuries, was the Moses group, former slaves who escaped from Egypt and entered the land of Canaan proclaiming the gospel of liberation championed by a divine warrior. This message incited the Canaanite peasants to active revolt, to rise up and take control of what they had produced and thus was rightfully theirs. He contends, then, that early Israelite history was a revolutionary social movement taking control of production and placing it in the hands of the people.

Gottwald's description of Canaanite social organization followed the economic model of the Asiatic mode of production in which peasant farmers and herders were exploited by the ruling classes in Canaanite city-states.[34] These rulers were largely aristocratic warriors, merchants, bureaucrats, and landowners who monopolized trade and imposed on the oppressed peasants and herders heavy taxation, military service, and forced labor. Together, these masses of deprived marginals supported through their economic labor the luxury of the privileged classes.[35] Religion was used to legitimate and sustain this oppressive system.

Gottwald argues:

> In time, probably with the arrival of the exodus Israelites, the religion of Yahweh became the socioreligious ideology and organizational framework that won over these rebellious peoples and helped to forge them into an effective revolutionary movement that expelled the tributary mode of production from the highlands and substituted a system of free peasant agriculture within a loose tribal design.[36]

This was a lengthy process that required the arming and training of peasants, the learning of subsistence agriculture in the hill country,

---

34. Gottwald, *The Hebrew Bible*, 272–73; and idem, "Early Israel and the Canaanite Socioeconomic System," *Palestine in Transition: The Emergence of Ancient Israel* (ed. David Noel Freedman and David Frank Graf; Social World of Biblical Antiquity 2; Sheffield: Almond, 1983) 25–37.

35. Gottwald, *The Hebrew Bible*, 272–73.

36. Ibid., 273.

and indoctrination in a religious ideology in which egalitarian existence and militant revolt against oppressive overlords were central features. This process continued from the end of the Late Bronze period until the time of David, who brought the revolutionary efforts to an end and set up a counterrevolutionary royal state.[37]

Gottwald combines this theory of revolution with his depiction of the social structures of early Israel in Iron I. These included a tribal confederacy, individual tribes, protective associations of extended families, and extended families or households.[38] These structures represent a "retribalization" of Israelite social relations that reacts against the statism of Canaanite society.

While somewhat critical of Martin Noth's amphictyony of premonarchical Israel,[39] Gottwald nevertheless posits the existence of an intertribal, albeit loosely knit organization in Iron I. He argues that this confederacy consisted of tribes who worshiped Yahweh, practiced economic egalitarianism, bore arms to oppose military threats, and recognized various patterns of social interaction that included extended families, the militia, ritual, the Levitical priesthood, and the Kenites. Bound together by covenant, the adult males of the tribes met periodically (either annually or every seven years) in an assembly to renew their covenant, celebrate and affirm the major components of their religious and social ideology, shape and transmit by instruction laws and customs, adjudicate tribal disputes, and engage in common defense by means of tribal levies, appointing leaders, and mustering troops for war. By egalitarianism or social equality Gottwald means "the organizational principle of equal access to basic resources for all adult members of the society."[40]

In positing an intertribal confederacy, Gottwald rejects both the social depiction of Israel's ancestors as largely pastoral nomads invading Canaan from the desert[41] and the model of the amphictyony borrowed from Greek, Etruscan, and Old Latin city-state

37. Ibid., 275.

38. For a detailed description, see Gottwald, *The Tribes of Yahweh*, 237–386.

39. Martin Noth, *Das System der zwölf Stämme Israels* (Stuttgart: Kohlhammer, 1930). Also see idem, *The History of Israel* (rev. ed.; New York: Harper, 1960) 53–138.

40. Gottwald, *The Tribes of Yahweh*, 697, 798–99 n. 635; and idem, "Two Models for the Origins of Ancient Israel: Social Revolution or Frontier Development," *The Quest for the Kingdom of God: Studies in Honor of George E. Mendenhall*, ed. Herbert B. Huffman (Winona Lake, Ind.: Eisenbrauns, 1983) 17 n. 35.

41. Gottwald, *The Hebrew Bible*, 277–80.

leagues.[42] In their place, Gottwald offers a retribalization model that describes early Israel as primarily deriving from a large majority of tribal peasants, together with an assortment of pastoral nomads,[43] 'apiru, merchants, craftsmen, and priests. Economically they engaged in free agriculture; the breeding of sheep, cattle, and goats; the production of handicrafts; and limited trade. Agriculture was enhanced by terracing, irrigation, and metal tools. The various groups of tribes banded together for self-defense and internal economic support.

The next social organization, according to Gottwald, was the tribe, an autonomous association of extended families who lived mostly in villages. These groups of families intermarried, shared a common worship, and practiced mutual aid (both economic and military). Each tribe convened not only during pilgrimage festivals to celebrate and shape their common religious and social traditions but also during times of military threat. Levitical priests in local sanctuaries also transmitted and taught tribal traditions. Tribal elders made the decision to go to war and settled internal disputes.

Protective associations of extended families lived in the same or contiguous villages or sections of larger settlements, practiced intermarriage, celebrated common cultic traditions, settled local disputes through the courts, organized a militia for the tribal wars, and offered mutual economic aid to association families. The heads of these families were the decision-making body and may have served also as lay priests. However, Gottwald does not think these associations were exogamous, property-owning clans to which families were subordinated.

The primary social group in Iron I, argues Gottwald, was the extended family or household that was "a primary residential and productive socioeconomic unit of two or more generations."[44] Kinship was determined patrilineally and residence was patrilocal (i.e., wives lived with the families of their husbands). Extended families

---

42. Ibid., 280–84. For a discussion of the amphictyony, see Henry E. Chambers, "Ancient Amphictyonies, Sic et Non," *Scripture in Context* 2 (ed. William W. Hallo, James C. Moyer, and Leo G. Perdue; Winona Lake, Ind.: Eisenbrauns, 1983) 39–59.

43. Gottwald argues that pastoral nomadism and agriculture are related symbiotically. Agriculture, however, is the dominant mode of production. The type of pastoral nomadism that Gottwald presents involves seasonal change of pastureland, not migration. He rejects the argument that early Israel resulted from either the invasion of desert nomads or their slow infiltration and eventual settlement in Canaan.

44. Gottwald, *The Tribes of Yahweh*, 341.

produced and raised children within the institution of marriage, were largely economically self-sufficient, supplied participants for the militia to pursue tribal wars of self-defense, transmitted common values and beliefs through education and other forms of socialization, and engaged in the collective worship of larger units as well as in more private familial celebrations (e.g., the Passover).

Early Israelite society, for Gottwald, was an experiment in egalitarian social organization, meaning that adult members of extended families had "equal access to resources" for economic production, while the family provided the social unit for sexual reproduction necessary for continued existence.[45] Power was also distributed, for it was not located in any one group or in a particular person. There was no centralized authority, although there was some influence of the various social organizations on one another.

Gottwald notes that leadership was primarily male, although he contends that women benefited from the new system. Unlike amphictyonies which were largely religious in nature, the intertribal organization or confederacy emphasized mutual aid in the face of economic difficulties and military threats. Tribal elders were responsible for legal decisions, priests instructed the people in religious ideology and practices, and military leaders ("charismatic judges") emerged to lead the militia of the tribes into battle against the threats from without. Efforts represented by Abimelech to move toward a centralization of power in the form of kingship (see Judges 9) were strongly opposed.

Counterrevolutionary Israel

The collapse of revolutionary Israel was due, in Gottwald's judgment, not simply to the external Philistine threat, but also to the increase in power and affluence of certain Israelite familial chieftains and priesthoods in Ephraim, Manasseh, Benjamin, and Judah. These chieftains and priesthoods contended for power, until finally David moved the social model of leadership from "chieftainship" to "hierarchic kingship" and succeeded in making Israel an ancient Near Eastern state.[46] In the absence of imperial power throughout the ancient Near East, David and then Solomon instituted a sociopolitical organization that would continue even after the breakup of the United Kingdom following the death of Solomon.

---

45. Gottwald, *The Hebrew Bible*, 285.
46. Ibid., 323.

Gottwald points to four structural changes in social organization that accompanied the institution of the monarchy:

1. Political centralization in the royal house in Jerusalem gave to the king powers of taxation and conscription. A standing military and royal bureaucracy became the instruments of royal rule.
2. Social stratification led to the concentration of wealth in the hands of a "parasitic nonproductive class" consisting of the royal family, merchants, and landed nobility.
3. Land ownership slowly transferred from families to the upper class, with former owners becoming day laborers and tenant farmers. This led to the undermining of the tribal character of Israel.
4. Monarchial rule led Israel into foreign adventures involving trade, diplomacy, and war. Growing failures in these efforts brought increased economic exploitation of the people, a process aided by political propaganda.[47]

For Gottwald, the traditions that point to, and at times undergird, this social transformation from confederacy to monarchy include the Yahwist, Psalms, Wisdom, and the David-Zion complex. J is viewed as either a warning against the excesses of royal power or as a legitimation of the new directions. Be that as it may, Gottwald contends that it is clear that both Psalms, especially the royal ones, and Wisdom were sponsored by the court, indicating that piety and the intellectual enterprise were under royal control.

Important for Gottwald is his contention that the ideological basis for the empire assumes the form of the promise to David and the selection of Zion (Jerusalem) as the political and religious center of the nation. The covenant with David in 2 Samuel 7 (cf. Psalm 89), assuming the ancient Near Eastern form of a royal grant, was viewed as Yahweh's unquestioned promise of future dynastic rule and thus was at odds with the conditional covenant of Moses that based the relationship of the people with Yahweh on their faithful obedience to moral and legal responsibilities. This new, royal covenant now placed the relationship between Yahweh and the people squarely on the shoulders of the royal dynasty. Closely related is the theology of Jerusalem (Zion) as the cosmic mountain, the habitation of Yahweh, and thus the center of the cosmos that secures reality against the threats of chaos in historical and mythic incarnations (see Psalms 46; 48; 76). The cultus, concentrated in the Solomonic temple, was under royal control and through its rites and ideology secured dynastic rule in the hands of the house of David.[48]

47. Ibid., 323–25.
48. Ibid., 335–36.

COLONIAL RULE

Gottwald argues that the conflict between two social organizations and their ideological undergirdings, surviving elements of the intertribal confederacy supported by the Mosaic covenant and the counterrevolutionary royal state legitimated by the David-Zion complex, continued throughout the later history of Israel. With the death of Solomon, the empire dissolved and civil war led to the creation of two royal states, Israel and Judah. For geopolitical reasons, Israel was drawn more into Near Eastern politics, leading ultimately to its demise at the hands of the Assyrians in the late eighth century B.C.E. Judah, by contrast, enjoyed a longer history, in part because it was more isolated from world affairs and in part because of the stability afforded by the dynastic principle and the uninterrupted rule of the house of David (except for the one short-lived coup organized by Queen Athaliah) until the exile of Zedekiah following the fall of Jerusalem to the Babylonians.

One may trace critiques of the royal states especially in the Elohist, the prophets, and the reform movement of Deuteronomy (see also the Deuteronomic History). In their strong criticisms of royal abuse, each of these draws on the intertribal tradition undergirded by the Mosaic covenant.[49] The significant point for Gottwald is that these critics remembered an intertribal confederacy that offered equality to all its members and avoided political adventurism in the form of foreign entanglements.[50] Indeed, some radicals went so far as to argue that over the long haul it would be better to be subject to foreign empires than to continue an oppressive system of local monarchic rule that victimized its own people.[51] To follow Gottwald, Jeremiah was caught up in the transition from Judah as a counterrevolutionary, royal state to a colony subject to foreign imperialism. Now, Jews from 596 to 63 B.C.E. were spread throughout the ancient world, with some remaining in Palestine and others living in the Diaspora. In either case, Jerusalem was the religious and cultural center of Judaism, but the foreign empire held military and political power and dominated the distribution of natural and human resources. For Gottwald, Jews in Palestine were one of many "semiautonomous homelands," while the dispersed settlements were "minority religiocultural communities."[52]

---

49. Ibid., 346–404.
50. Ibid., 373. Gottwald notes: "Social equality and sociopolitical hierarchy did not readily mix, and it was the former that steadily lost ground to the latter."
51. Ibid., 374.
52. Ibid., 421–22.

THE HERMENEUTIC OF LIBERATION

The theological extension of Gottwald's social history is liberation theology that praises the Lord of the exodus but condemns the God of the monarchy. Underlying this central affirmation is Gottwald's basic hermeneutical contention that religion and its symbols reflect, criticize, legitimate, and advocate social systems. Especially critical for understanding Gottwald is his contention that there are moments when religion opens a society up to new possibilities by moving beyond the traditional and the customary, something that Gottwald calls the "impossible possibility."[53] These new breakthroughs may occur, contends Gottwald, only when a social group commits to total struggle. This is Gottwald's hermeneutical key, for it moves his work away from being merely descriptive, sociological functionalism to a theological posture that allows religious ideas and symbols to play a most significant role in shaping social movements and their culture. In this way, the Yahwism of early Israel can become an ideological (or theological) vision for struggling peoples seeking the possibilities of their own liberation and identity.

The major features of Gottwald's theological position are explicitly set forth and articulated, although a full presentation has not yet materialized. What he has discussed, however, is the nature of theologizing in view of a shift toward social-scientific interpretation of the Bible.[54] Gottwald argues that this methodological shift requires a major reorientation of usual assumptions about the theological task. First, the theological enterprise should view the materials in the Bible as ideological products, that is, views and values that derive from people living within a particular social matrix. Simply put, theology is ideology.[55] Second, the theological enterprise should regard the biblical traditions as one means for the social formation of Israel, that is, as containing directives for the creation and legitimation of social organizations that define human relationships and activities.[56] Third, the theological enterprise can

53. Gottwald, *The Tribes of Yahweh*, 701.

54. Norman K. Gottwald, "Biblical Theology or Biblical Sociology? On Affirming and Defining the 'Uniqueness' of Israel," *Radical Religion* 2 (1975) 42–57; idem, "The Theological Task after *The Tribes of Yahweh*," *The Bible and Liberation*, 190–200; and idem, *The Tribes of Yahweh*, 667–709.

55. Gottwald, *The Tribes of Yahweh*, 668.

56. Gottwald, "The Theological Task," 191; and idem, *The Tribes of Yahweh*, 668.

no longer merely extract the religious essentials (i.e., lasting ideas and universal values) from the social matrix that gave them shape and embodiment, thereby relegating the social setting to so much "background."[57]

Gottwald, of course, is most taken with the social organization of what he calls the intertribal confederacy of early Israel between the end of the Late Bronze Age (1200 B.C.E.) and the rise of the monarchy and the accompanying royal state in the late eleventh century B.C.E. At the center of this "village-based retribalizing movement," argues Gottwald, was the religion of Yahweh that did share various features with other ancient Near Eastern religions: the high god is a personal power responsible for what is and what happens; this high god is active in creation, history, morality, and the social order; the understanding of the high god is expressed through natural and human analogies; the high god receives the attributes of powerful, just, and merciful and is responsible for conducting human affairs; the high god enters into a reciprocal bond with a people; and the interpretations of the high god are made by particular representatives of a people.[58]

More important for Gottwald, however, are what he sees as the distinctively peculiar or exceptional views that distinguish Israelite religion from the religions of the ancient Near East. These distinguishing marks provide the focus for Gottwald's own critical, reflective theologizing.[59] First, Yahweh requires exclusive recognition and commitment by the people of Israel who must reject loyalties to other deities and all other allegiances. While not strict monotheism (Gottwald prefers the term "mono-Yahwism"), Yahweh is still seen as the unrivaled center of the life of the people, shaping and directing all matters pertinent to their existence.

Second, only Yahweh is active in the world, not the many gods in mythic traditions who vie for power to control the cosmos. Yahweh is the "sole ultimate actor in all phenomena of decisive importance to a community."[60] Third, and perhaps most important for Gottwald's own quest for an authentic hermeneutic, Yahweh "is conceived by egalitarian sociopolitical analogies."[61] By contrast, nature

57. Gottwald, "The Theological Task," 193.
58. Ibid., 192–93; and idem, *The Tribes of Yahweh*, 676–78.
59. Ibid., 193–94; and idem, *The Tribes of Yahweh*, 679–91.
60. Gottwald, *The Tribes of Yahweh*, 681.
61. Ibid., 682. "It seems that it is primarily from the historicosocial struggle of a sovereign intertribal community that the major analogies for conceiving Yahweh are drawn" (p. 685).

images are rare and, when used, are subordinate to sociohistorical categories. While the masculine images for Yahweh dominate the traditions, Gottwald argues that this may be no more than "cultural drift," where the name Yahweh perhaps developed from an appositional title for the Canaanite high god El. Historically, "he" is the appropriate reference for Yahweh, but the rejection of the concept of a divine consort with whom Yahweh sires sons and daughters indicates that gender was not important in Israelite theology. Rather, Israel seeks ways to express "the indivisibility and completeness of the deity."[62] Furthermore, Yahweh is a deity of the people, not of a city or of nature or of a particular sacred place. A "warrior-leader" who brings Israel into existence, enters in covenant with the nation, and defends it against all threats, Yahweh remains the sovereign in relationships with people. However, Yahweh does require equality among those who come together in the new social experiment.

Fourth, Israel's understanding of power, justice, and mercy produces a more critical reflection on how these features are to come to expression in human relationships. Indeed, these elements are unified and rationalized as divine manifestations directed by one purposive will. These elements receive their concrete expression in sociohistorical actions and functions, the paradigm for which is the liberation of Israel from bondage and the establishment of an egalitarian, intertribal community in Canaan.

Fifth, Yahweh enters into a covenant with an egalitarian people existing in an intertribal society. This is the social matrix for understanding the people of God and indeed Yahweh as well. Yahweh was not in covenant with a city, a sacred place, an occupational group, or even a people through biological descent. Women share in this equality as members of the household and have prominent places in the larger social system. Gottwald admits, however, that early Israel's leaders were still primarily males, and correspondingly human analogies for God are essentially male. Nevertheless Gott-

---

62. Ibid., 685. Gottwald is quick to note that "Yahweh's asexuality was apparently not invoked to challenge or to shatter male dominance in the Israelite society as a whole—in the decisive way, for example, that class dominance was challenged and shattered by Yahweh's liberating action. The overthrow of class dominion in early Israel had the indirect effect of improving the status of women relative to their status in Canaanite society, but there was no frontal assault in Israel on several forms of feminine subordination."

wald argues that "it seems as appropriate to refer to Yahweh as 'she' as to call Yahweh 'he.'" Finally, the interpreters of Yahweh are "egalitarian functionaries," not privileged priests or royal aristocrats. Leadership was invested in charismatic authority, not in the hierarchy of a state or a bureaucracy.

In his discussion of the "socioeconomic demythologization of Israelite Yahwism," Gottwald argues that earlier biblical theology shares the weakness of religious idealism that ignores the social character of theological formulations. In seeking to speak of Israel's distinctive theology, Gottwald argues that it is better to depict "Yahweh as the symbolic bonding dimension of a synthetic, egalitarian, intertribal counter-society, originating within and breaking off from hierarchical, stratified Canaanite society."[63] Yet Gottwald also argues that Yahweh "stood for the primordial power in historical development" that provided the impetus to transcend existing social limits and to press forward to new realizations.[64]

With these elements firmly in mind, Gottwald gives a social-scientific definition to common theological terms from the Bible:

> "Yahweh" is the historically concretized, primordial power to establish and sustain social equality in the face of counter-oppression from without and against provincial and nonegalitarian tendencies from within the society. "The Chosen People" is the distinctive self-consciousness of a society of equals created in the intertribal order and demarcated from a primarily centralized and stratified surrounding world. "Covenant" is the bonding of decentralized social groups in a larger society of equals committed to cooperation without authoritarian leadership and a way of symbolizing the locus of sovereignty in such a society of equals. "Eschatology," or hope for the future, is the sustained commitment of fellow tribesmen to a society of equals with the confidence and determination that this way of life can prevail against great environmental odds.[65]

Gottwald also gives social-scientific interpretations to important understandings of God in the Bible. The "jealousy" of Yahweh is "the singularity and excessive passion of the Israelite social revolutionary movement."[66] Or Yahweh's absence from Sheol and asexuality are expressions of the reaction against the attempt of rulers to

63. Ibid., 692.
64. Ibid., 693.
65. Ibid., 692.
66. Gottwald, "The Theological Task," 194.

manipulate people with their fear of death and their sexual pas-sion.[67] Indeed, even the events of salvation history that were central to the theological articulations of Wright and von Rad receive social definitions. These paradigms are "modes of engaging history as the sphere of social struggle."[68] Thus the conquest of Canaan became paradigmatic for all efforts at socioeconomic existence freed of tyrannical, hierarchical systems. Even when these paradigms and the social system that gave them expression were suppressed by the development of a royal state with a new ideology, they continued to provide the basis for social struggle and survived the cataclysmic end of the monarchic system.

The theme of Israel's election by God is

> an absolutizing of an experiential social reality into dogmatic general claims as the special property of a group. It is an instance of the objectification and reification of an actual reality into such a form and context that it becomes an embalmed relic and grotesque parody of the original truth.[69]

Necessitated and perhaps even justified by the radical demands of social struggle against Canaanite imperialism, the theology of elec-tion eventually became the undergirding support for the evils of Israelite particularism, when Israel developed another social system (i.e., the monarchy).

The God language of early Israel, according to Gottwald, re-flected

> the heterogeneous, classless, decentralized association of tribes con-ceived as a brotherhood—and at least in larger measure than in Ca-naanite society, as a sisterhood—of social, economic, and political equals, and as a society striving for cultural meanings and purposes in the absence of clear precedents.[70]

This religious symbolism expressed the efforts of early Israel to end two millennia of hierarchical, socially stratified, imperialistic existence in the ancient Near East, supported and legitimated by very different religious symbols.

For Gottwald, the power of the religious symbolism of early Yah-wism was derived from "its integration within and penetration of a

---

67. Ibid., 194; and idem, *The Tribes of Yahweh*, 694–95.
68. Gottwald, *The Tribes of Yahweh*, 698–99.
69. Ibid., 702.
70. Ibid., 700.

total struggle situation."[71] The Yahwism of early Israel represented a singular commitment to liberation, self-rule, self-defense, productivity of resources, reproduction, and social equality. He argues that the only way for those symbols to be reemployed authentically today is "in a situation of social struggle where people are attempting a breakthrough toward a freer and fuller life based on equality and communal self-possession."[72] For theology to interact with social context, both in the past and in the present, what is required is an altering of consciousness and a radical commitment to restructuring the values and priorities of the larger world.[73] The hermeneutical task is to assess what our own challenges are and then to find and adapt those religious images, old and new, that will aid us in "mastering our circumstances." This ultimately would require such a radical reformulation that we would indeed "found a new religion."[74]

Religious symbols, to continue to be valid, must aid in the achieving of social goals through struggle. When religious symbols serve the purposes of docility and passivity, when they inhibit social progress toward liberation, and when they legitimate the vested interests of ruling classes and elitist groups, then they must be negated and discarded. New, authentic religious symbols should develop only at those critical conjunctures of "lawful social process and human freedom," that is, when the evolutionary development of human societies embrace the values and formulations of liberation.[75]

For Gottwald, the biblical portrait of revolutionary Israel and its God of the poor should be used to disrupt oppressive power relationships.[76] This God who enables and empowers the poor opposes capitalist systems that allow elitist groups to exploit workers, control production, and monopolize wealth. To allow this God to shape Christian understanding of economics would radically transform capitalist economies and their political systems. In their place, argues Gottwald, should emerge both socialist systems in which the

71. Ibid., 701.
72. Ibid., 701.
73. Gottwald, "The Theological Task," 199.
74. Gottwald, *The Tribes of Yahweh*, 704.
75. Ibid., 708.
76. Norman K. Gottwald, "From Biblical Economies to Modern Economies: A Bridge over Troubled Waters," Tabb, *Churches in Struggle*, 138–48.

people are owners of what they produce and political systems that would support the new economic realities.[77]

Finally, Gottwald speaks of Israel's covenant theology as embracing both culture and nature as well as history.[78] Images of father point to God's role as "deliverer and protector" as well as one involved in family and reproductive elements. The paradigm of blessing within the covenant reflects elements of "femininity." The God of revolutionary Israel was involved not only in the social processes of the people but also in the processes of nature on which the people depended for existence. Gottwald rejects the dichotomies between history and nature (creation) and masculine and feminine. What was at stake for Gottwald in revolutionary Israel's time was a "participatory" culture (Israel) versus a hierarchic culture (Canaanite city-states).

JEREMIAH AND THE THEOLOGY OF LIBERATION

Gottwald's theological understanding of Jeremiah is grounded in his social description of Israel's movement from an intertribal confederacy (revolutionary Israel), to a royal state (counterrevolutionary establishment), and finally to a colony within various world empires. In this movement, Jeremiah's criticisms of the monarchy and the Judean state are based in part on the ancient traditions of the intertribal confederacy. Gottwald contends that elements of the founding vision of revolutionary Israel, that society of equals, continued in the voices of the prophets during the period of the monarchy and in various social organizations that developed during the period of colonialism.

The sociopolitical reform of Josiah, which adopted, at least in part, the agenda of the Deuteronomic reformation, ended with his death at Megiddo in 609 B.C.E. The effort to rebuild a Davidic empire collapsed, and Judah found itself first under Egyptian and

---

77. Gottwald argues that "socially committed Christians should hold up the mirror of biblical Israel before the churches so that the freshly glimpsed social image out of the past can prompt new self-appraisal of 'social mission'—of what it means to be a self in this society and what it means to be a church! We Christians should deny any *easy* claim to affinity with those early Israelites, unless we too are willing to hazard our present life toward that fuller human existence that lures us onward in time" ("The Impact of Ancient Israel on Our Social World," *Currents in Theology and Mission* 6 [1979] 93).

78. Norman K. Gottwald, "The Biblical Mandate for Eco-Justice Action," *For Creation's Sake* (ed. Dieter T. Hessel; Philadelphia: Geneva, 1985) 32–44.

then under Babylonian rule. The attempts by successive kings of Judah to gain political independence from the empires to the north were opposed by Jeremiah who saw the "foe from the north" (eventually identified as the Babylonians) as the agent of God. Thus Jeremiah argued that the only hope for survival into the future was to assume the role of a willing vassal to Nebuchadrezzar II.

However, for Gottwald, Jeremiah's preaching was not simply a matter of political expediency or a prophetic theology removed from the sociopolitical developments in the life of the nation. Gottwald sees Jeremiah's radical stance as consistent with the early criticisms of the royal state, criticisms grounded in the values of social justice defined by a theology of liberation and at work within the constitutional operation of the Mosaic covenant of the intertribal confederacy. Unless there was true repentance on behalf of the leadership and an abandonment of the oppressive rule of the counterrevolutionary establishment for the values of the Mosaic covenant, the destruction of the nation was inevitable.[79]

Gottwald argues that the Book of Jeremiah reveals two opposing political alignments of leaders, prophets, and priests during the period of 609 to 586 B.C.E., that is, from the death of Josiah to the fall of Jerusalem.[80] The "autonomy" party, according to Gottwald, supported political independence for Judah, opposed Babylonian rule, thought that national survival depended on self-rule and the continuation of the present system of leadership, and legitimated their agenda by an appeal to Yahweh's will revealed in the royal traditions. By contrast, Gottwald contends that the "coexistence" party, which included Jeremiah among its leaders, supported submission to Babylonian control, thought that survival for the people was possible without the present form of leadership, argued that the present governing system and its leaders inside Judah would only continue policies of social oppression, and saw the problem not in terms of conflict between two states (Babylonia and Judah) but as interclass struggle between the rulers and the people.[81] It was not simply a class struggle, however, argues Gottwald, since there were powerful members of the ruling class (e.g., the family of Shaphan) who supported the views of Jeremiah. Ultimately, the "coexistence" party lost and rebellion broke out twice, resulting finally in the destruction of Jerusalem and the beginning of the exilic period.

79. Gottwald, *The Hebrew Bible*, 395–96.
80. Ibid., 402–04.
81. Ibid., 403–04.

What was considered most extreme by Jeremiah's contemporaries, according to Gottwald, was the prophet's view that true reformation on the basis the covenant could occur only within the context of Neobabylonian rule. Gottwald argues that Jeremiah at first thought that this reform could occur within the social organization of the royal state, as long as Judah willingly submitted to the Neobabylonian empire. However, after the revolutions of Jehoiakim and Zedekiah, the prophet reached the startling conclusion that internal reform within existing social institutions was no longer possible. Finally, after the failure of Zedekiah's rebellion, Jeremiah indicated that the next stage of national life would develop without the institutions of temple and monarchy. The opportunities for reform would have to be carried out under the political control of the Neobabylonian empire. Indeed, Jeremiah committed his life to reform under the auspices of Babylonian rule by choosing to remain in the country and support the efforts of Gedaliah, the governor appointed by Nebuchadrezzar, at the city of Mizpah.

The vision of a reformed community is found in the Little Book of Comfort in Jeremiah 30–31. Gottwald sees these materials as largely the product of later editors who shaped the Jeremiah tradition.[82] Important for Gottwald is a portrayal of a future people who may well anticipate the end of their cultus and yet who continue the values incorporated in the laws of the old intertribal covenant.

It would follow that the theological grounding of Jeremiah was in the old intertribal traditions of the God of liberation who led oppressed slaves from Egypt, guided them through the wilderness, entered into covenant with them at Sinai, and gave them the land of Canaan. By contrast, his opponents found their theological base in the David-Zion complex with the guarantees of the continuation of the Davidic dynasty and the inviolability of Jerusalem. Both traditions were inseparably part of two different, often conflicting social organizations: the intertribal confederacy (at least remnants thereof) and the royal state. Efforts to correlate these conflicting societies and their traditions, for example in the enterprise carried out by Deuteronomy and the Deuteronomic History, were not successful. As Gottwald would argue, egalitarianism and hierarchy are incompatible ideologies.

82. Ibid., 401.

LIBERATION THEOLOGY AND REVOLUTIONARY ISRAEL: AN ASSESSMENT

The fundamental premise in Gottwald's work is his rejection of idealism's portrayal of religion as an abstract system of beliefs and practices that may be separated from the matrix of social life. By contrast, Gottwald contends that religion is inextricably linked to the social patterns and functions of human communities.[83] As a result, his contribution to the way we think of doing Old Testament theology is quite extraordinary. He has taught us that the abstract thinking of idealism, carried into the realm of biblical theology, is a "bloodless" entity divorced from actual existence. Theologizing that is separated from social matrices and actual practice is also irrelevant to human life.[84] And better than tradition critics, Gottwald has taught us that theology is caught up in the fabric of human life and therefore expresses political, social, and economic values and concerns. Indeed, critical theological reflection must engage the social life from which it originates.[85]

Gottwald also has helped us to see more clearly the possible ideological nature of religious beliefs and symbols. While one may disagree with the position that theology is nothing more than ideology, assessing the theological traditions of the Old Testament by raising the questions of how and in what way they may express the self-interest of groups and may seek to maintain and legitimate existing or proposed social organizations is an important effort. Gottwald accepts tradition history's position (see Noth and von Rad) that the main Pentateuchal themes are developed within the cult as confessional responses, but he also develops the view that part of these tradition complexes undergirds a subversive, egalitarian social organization. This means that Wright's and von Rad's "mighty acts of God" are cultic confessions of a subversive social movement, at least in their original expression.[86]

83. See especially the review by Walter Brueggemann, *"The Tribes of Yahweh*: An Essay Review," *JAAR* 48 (1980) 441–51.

84. In Gottwald's words, his focus on the material culture and social character of Israel leads to *"a rejection of forms of theology that separate religion from theology and that abstract religious beliefs from the socially situated locus of the religious believers"* (*The Tribes of Yahweh*, 701).

85. Wilson argues: "It is no longer possible to engage in theological reflection without taking into account the role of the Old Testament's social matrix" (*Sociological Approaches to the Old Testament*, 83).

86. See Brueggemann, *"The Tribes of Yahweh,"* 444.

Gottwald follows the conundrum of Wright and von Rad in his contention that theological truth must exist in history, at least history as the processes and organization of actual social life, if not also the temporal sequence of events, including especially those identified with divine salvation. And Gottwald finds at least the partial validation of his particular expression of liberation theology in an egalitarian peasant society existing in Iron I Israel. Indeed, by reference to the origins of Israel and the use of Scripture, Gottwald's social reconstruction becomes a powerful source for legitimating liberation theology in the present.[87] The theological contribution of Gottwald is especially important in the articulation of a theology that opposes authoritarianism and life-denying oppression. He brings to light quite clearly the theology of the Old Testament God as redeemer *(gō'ēl)* and sustainer, especially of the poor and oppressed. A theology of liberation subverts oppressive systems, both in the ancient world and in the present.

Regardless of how brilliant this synthesis of liberation theology and social-science theory is, Gottwald's work has elicited serious criticism and at times rather heated debate. A critical response to Gottwald may be placed in four categories. The first three have to do with his own sociological analysis, especially of Israel's beginnings in Iron I, and the fourth points to questions about his theological method and the conclusions that he draws.[88]

THE SOCIAL-HISTORICAL RECONSTRUCTION OF ISRAEL'S ORIGINS

Much of the debate stimulated by Gottwald's work has centered on his sociohistorical reconstruction of early Israel.[89] Gottwald's

87. See Gottwald, *The Bible and Liberation.*
88. No attempt will be made to offer a critical evaluation of either the political, social, and economic analysis and views that undergird the various presentations of liberation theology or of the theoretical basis for Gottwald's social-scientific work. However, some critical responses to the theoretical base of his arguments have been offered. E.g., J. W. Rogerson ("Was Early Israel a Segmentary Society?" *JSOT* 36 [1986] 17–26) criticizes Gottwald's use of anthropological data from Africa to support the idea that Israel was a segmentary lineage society (i.e., there was no centralized power; rather, power was distributed through groups with equal status). Rogerson argues that early Israel represents more probably a segmentary state: "It may well have been an association of chiefdoms, the genealogies of whose ruling families are to be found in the OT" (p. 23). For a recent summary of critical responses to the theoretical basis and social analysis of contemporary liberation theology, see McGovern, *Liberation Theology and Its Critics.*
89. In addition to Brueggemann, *"The Tribes of Yahweh,"* see Frederic R. Brandon, "Norman Gottwald on the Tribes of Yahweh," *JSOT* 21 (1981) 101–10;

reconstruction of intertribal Israel combines four major features: the revolt model, an Israelite confederacy, an interdependency of urban and rural societies, and an interdependency between nomadism and rural town life. While each of these may be questioned, the linchpin of the entire reconstruction is the revolt model.

Much of the difficulty that Gottwald faces in his social reconstruction derives from the fact that the Iron I period defies easy and precise description and reconstruction.[90] Primary literary sources are very limited, and what we have in the Bible are reinterpreted literary sources reflecting many later hands. The growing accumulations of archaeological data detailing Israel's origins and early history are open to various, plausible historical reconstructions, none meriting special favor.[91] For example, excavations reveal that Ai was not inhabited at the end of the Late Bronze period, and hence the biblical description of the taking of the "city" in Joshua 7–8 is not historical. Even so, Gottwald contends that the Iron I inhabitants who settled this abandoned site, lived in poorly constructed houses, made crude pottery, and were incapable of reconstructing the ruined fortifications of the EB III city were early Israelites who believed in a God of liberation and possibly joined in a revolt against oppressive Canaanites. The most recent excavator of Ai argued that the early Iron I settlers were Canaanites, only later driven away by Hebrews in the late twelfth century B.C.E.[92]

Indeed, a number of Canaanite cities were destroyed in the transitional period from Late Bronze to Iron I, but what evidence exists that these were destroyed by invading Israelites who sparked an internal peasants' revolt? It is just as plausible to posit Egyptians, rival Canaanite cities, non-Israelite desert raiders, and accidental fires as being responsible for the destruction. One also wonders why it is that the Israelite presence archaeologically attested in Iron I is largely in the western hill country, precisely in those areas on the periphery of the territory controlled by the Canaanite city-states.

Alan J. Hauser, "Israel's Conquest of Palestine: A Peasants' Rebellion?" *JSOT* 7 (1978) 2–19; Werner E. Lemke, "Interpreting Biblical History through the Eyes of Sociology and Politics: The Work of George Mendenhall and Norman Gottwald," *Conservative Judaism* 39 (1986) 67–80; A. D. H. Mayes, "Review," *JTS* 32 (1981) 472–83; and Thomas L. Thompson, "Historical Notes on 'Israel's Conquest of Palestine: A Peasants' Rebellion,'" *JSOT* 7 (1978) 20–27.

90. J. Maxwell Miller and John H. Hayes, *A History of Ancient Israel and Judah* (Philadelphia: Westminster, 1986) 54–119.

91. Miller and Hayes, *A History*, 68–72.

92. Joseph Callaway, "Excavating Ai (Et-Tell): 1964–1972," *BA* 39 (1976) 18–30.

Indeed, the evidence for new settlements at the end of the Late Bronze period and extending into Iron II points to areas that were agriculturally quite marginal and thus not generally populated by the Canaanites.[93]

Further, there is scant evidence to support a peasant revolt from either the primary or biblical literature. While the Amarna correspondence speaks of social unrest in the Late Bronze Age in Canaan, the term *'apiru* is used in a variety of ways. And there is little evidence they represented an alternative social system to that of the Canaanite city-states. It seems for some scholars quite a stretch to deduce from a few narratives like Rahab's harboring of spies in her house in Jericho that there was significant revolutionary activity within the Canaanite city-states.

Gottwald's positing of an intertribal confederacy is also largely constructed on a great deal of interesting but debatable supposition. The pan-Israelite confederacy reflected in the overarching theological and literary structure given to the materials in Joshua and Judges by the Deuteronomic History can just as plausibly be interpreted as a retrojection into the past by a Deuteronomic school in the eighth, seventh, and even sixth centuries B.C.E. seeking an alternative to the monarchy and its evident failures.

ROMANTICISM AND INTERTRIBAL ISRAEL

It is interesting that a scholar who uses social-science methods that operate out of generalities still intimates that the theologically authentic is unique. In spite of Gottwald's search for common features to which social-scientific analysis points, it nevertheless is that which sets Israel off from the nations that receives value. What Israel holds in common with its ancient Near Eastern neighbors carries little theological weight. Thus Wright and von Rad argued that the "mighty acts of God" (e.g., the exodus) were the cornerstone of Israelite faith. This God who acted in history was contrasted with the fertility deities in Canaanite myth. In a sense, Gottwald has continued this emphasis on "the mighty acts of God,"

93. Thompson, "Notes on 'Israel's Conquest,'" 25. See the work by Moshe Kochavi indicating that "the first phase of Israelite Settlement occurred in the hill country where there were no Canaanite cities, or where the settling herdsmen were at least tolerated. It is Alt's *Landnahme* that seems to be in accord with this phase" ("Israelite Settlement in Light of Surveys," *Biblical Archaeology Today. Proceedings of the International Congress on Biblical Archaeology, Jerusalem, April 1984* [Jerusalem: Israel Exploration Society, 1985] 47–60). He goes on to suggest that expansion into the lowlands was a later stage of occupation which "gained momentum with the Monarchy." Also see Joseph A. Callaway's "Response" in *Biblical Archaeology Today*, 75.

but now what is theologically essential and unique to the cultural setting is a Yahwism in which a divine warrior liberates the oppressed and acts within a social organization that promotes equality of members.

Gottwald also seems to share with Wellhausen and Albright the positing of a "golden age" that was eventually subverted by later developments. Wellhausen and Albright both pointed to pristine beginnings that they thought contained the essence of authentic religion. To recapture these origins, at least their spirit, is the object of the hermeneutical quest. This quest also may lie at the heart of Gottwald's affirmation: the social genius of early Israel should inspire later communities to move toward new forms of liberation, with or without religious symbols.

SOCIAL RECONSTRUCTION OF REVOLUTIONARY ISRAEL

Gottwald has been criticized for anachronistically reading his own social and theological perspectives into the ancient past.[94] It would indeed be exciting to find the modern values of egalitarianism, inclusivity, revolution against oppressive governments, and an important place for women in the Iron I tribal communities of the hill country. Yet there are major questions about his social reconstruction.

Some scholars have indicated that the argument lacks much concrete evidence. Others have indicated that sociologically speaking it is also plausible to argue that early Israel developed a differentiated, hierarchical, male-dominated, oppressive system because of the authority invested in male family heads who even had the power of life and death over wives, children, and slaves.[95] In regard to Israelite law, the vesting of such power in the hands of male family heads is attested in even the earliest legal codes of Israel. And there is much in the narrative texts that contradicts the social world of revolutionary Israel posited by Gottwald. Certainly, many of the stories in Judges suggest that egalitarian ideals and an important place for women were not always present. These stories include Jephthah's sacrifice of his daughter because of his stupid, hasty vow (Judges 11); Samson's lustful appetite for "strange" women and his one-man crusade of vengeance against the hated Philistines (Judges 13–16); and the wanton rape and murder of the Levite's concubine

94. Mayes, "Review," 476.
95. Miller and Hayes, *A History*, 91–94. See E. R. Wolf, *Peasant Wars of the Twentieth Century* (New York: Harper & Row, 1969). Indeed, Larry Stager has argued that inequality in Israel existed before the rise of the Israelite monarchy ("The Archaeology of the Family in Ancient Israel," *BASOR* 260 [1985] 1–35).

by Benjaminites and their subsequent decimation by other tribes seeking revenge for the hideous crime (Judges 19–20).

Gottwald responds to his critics, in part, by arguing that the social revolution was incomplete. He has indicated that the "battle for social equality was not simply between Israel and its neighbors; it was a battle internal to Israelite society."[96] He calls the development of revolutionary Israel an "opening toward equality" in which structures were established in order to promote equality, "understood as approximately equal access through extended families to the basic resources or means of production."[97] While social equality was not complete, there was an intentional effort to remove obstacles to equal access. "In short, Israel was egalitarian in its conscious deployment of society power."[98]

THEOLOGICAL LIMITATIONS OF REVOLUTIONARY ISRAEL

In addition to questions about Gottwald's social reconstruction, there are significant theological issues emanating from his view that there is no way of engaging in "God-talk" apart from the social matrices of human life.[99] Indeed, Gottwald's approach is critical Marxism that understands religion, including Yahwism, in materialist terms. Simply put, for Gottwald material interests involving the ownership and control of production and the holding of power are primary in the formation of social organizations. This means that religion is an ideology that legitimates the interests of particular social groups. Gottwald's approach opposes the contention of idealism that ideas, including religious ones, are primary in the formation of social communities.

Even so, Gottwald, while primarily adhering to a Marxist position, still allows for Yahwism not only the function of legitimating a social movement but also of facilitating it as well. This is the fundamental tension in Gottwald's work, although he certainly leans more heavily in the Marxist direction. In any case, it is never clear that Gottwald allows for the possibility of transcendence as separate or apart from social organizations and processes. Indeed, he seems not to. The major theological liability in accepting this approach is the loss of transcendence. If one grants that all as-

96. Gottwald, "Two Models for the Origins of Ancient Israel," 18.
97. Ibid., 18.
98. Ibid., 19.
99. See the discussion by Brueggemann, *"The Tribes of Yahweh,"* 441–50. Brueggemann notes: "Then the substantive question is whether such a theological move can be anything other than mere ideology, an ideology which costs more than it gains."

sertions of Old Testament theology are expressions of Israelite social life, it is impossible to argue, as Scripture does, that God transcends the symbols, images, and representations of human culture.[100] Of course, Scripture may be sociologically naive and simply wrong. But carried to its logical extreme, Gottwald's argument makes God a social symbol with no existence outside the matrix of communal life. With this materialist understanding of social organization and the production of culture, theology is reduced to a set of religious symbols expressing the ideology of a social group that may help to facilitate, legitimate, and maintain the formation of social communities. It seems that, for Gottwald, God cannot exist outside the interstices of material culture and social relations. In fact, religion and theology are reduced to social ethics, but not theological ethics: human behavior is authentic and valid only when it leads to the enhancing of liberation for all. But the value of liberation and the effort to free oppressed groups do not necessarily belong to a religious paradigm. The experience of the Holy (i.e., worship), the search for harmony with nature, and spirituality, unless they are intimately part of the fabric of social life, have little place in Gottwald's biblical theology or hermeneutic.

To provide a specific example, the loss of transcendence in Gottwald's biblical theology and hermeneutic means that creation theology is limited to its connections to the social life of human communities. One could speak of ecology, but only as it relates to the interests of a particular social organization or group within that organization. One could not speak theologically of creation, as James Gustafson does, prior to the appearance of Homo sapiens.[101] Nor may one speak theologically of God after the disappearance of Homo sapiens either through extinction or the cataclysmic end of the solar system in which the earth is found.

For Gottwald, all theological traditions in the Old Testament must be ideologies that promote the worldviews and special interests of particular groups and communities. Yet, if transcendence (even in the broad sense of a norm or source for authority that stands outside the individual or human self) is eliminated, how does one evaluate as "good" or "bad" any ideology? How does one

---

100. See Bernhard W. Anderson, "Biblical Theology and Sociological Interpretation," *TToday* 42 (1985) 292–306. Anderson notes that sociological interpretation, carried to its extremes, makes Yahweh only "a symbol for the values and identity of the social group, perhaps on the order of Uncle Sam in the political history of the United States" (p. 300).

101. See James Gustafson, *Ethics from a Theocentric Perspective* (2 vols.; Chicago: University of Chicago Press, 1981, 1984).

argue against a sapiential doctrine of retribution that blames the poor as being responsible for their own misery? Or how does one argue that liberation is a virtue that is preferred over some form of slavery? Or, taken into the present, how does one argue that neo-Nazis or skinheads are wrong? The view that theology is ideology also means that if Scripture cannot be divested of its ideological character, "how can the Bible be the medium of the Word of God who transcends all ideologies and who cannot be domesticated in human word-worlds?"[102]

This is not to deny that theological traditions in the Old Testament may at times present the particular views and interests of the social groups that produced them. But if God is more than a human symbol and if the human words of Scripture in any fashion or in some measure contain the Word of God, then a valid hermeneutic for critically engaging Scripture needs to be developed that transcends ideology. Bernhard W. Anderson points to some examples of how Scripture itself has on occasion transcended ideology: when Israel's life was brought under the criticism of the moral requirements of the covenant; when human words evoke a sense of wonder in the presence of the Holy, a wonder that is grounded in a God who is experienced as wholly other; and when traditions continued beyond their original social setting engage later communities with a divine word.[103] These provide a good starting point, but certainly Gottwald's approach has sharpened the question: how is theology different from ideology?

In addition to transcendence, there is also a great deal of other Old Testament theology that is ultimately lost, if Gottwald's positions are accepted. Much theology after the fragmentation of revolutionary Israel, especially "God-talk" located in biblical traditions produced by very different societies from the Iron I community he posits (monarchic, colonial, protorabbinic, and proto-apocalyptic), would be discarded, except for those expressions which carry forth the values associated with liberation that he finds in revolutionary Israel.[104] A good deal of royal theology, prophetic theology (at least that of the centrist prophets), wisdom theology,

102. Anderson, "Biblical Theology and Sociological Interpretation," 300.
103. Ibid., 301–3.
104. Gottwald notes that his focus in *The Tribes of Yahweh* has been on the Iron I intertribal community which did undergo many changes over the successive centuries but that what he has to say about the first two centuries of Israelite social existence will impact dramatically the way that later societies and their literary expressions will be treated (p. 668).

Torah theology, protorabbinic theology, and protoapocalyptic theology would have to be dismissed.[105]

One may also argue, in this regard, that liberation is not the final purpose and objective of even the paradigmatic event of the exodus from Egypt, or, for that matter the new exodus from Babylonian captivity. In both instances, liberation is for the purpose of Israel's becoming the people of God, a covenant community called to service in humble obedience to divine instruction. Theologically conceived, it is not the experience of freedom that is exalted in the Bible but rather the love of God and neighbor practiced by a servant people. Liberation is the instrument or means by which obedience and service in the name of love are enhanced, but not the ultimate and final objective of human striving. Or, as Langdon Gilkey indicates, freedom itself is not a theological virtue. It is what one chooses to do with freedom that is the critical issue in identifying virtue.[106]

Of course, none of this may be especially troubling to Gottwald. He concludes that in the social evolution of the human species religion indeed may one day die out. But he does allow for the possibility that future societies may choose to affirm "transcending images and celebrations," but religion as a "mystifying accompaniment of class rule" will be discarded.[107]

Gottwald does not argue that modern society should attempt to reconstruct the social reality of revolutionary Israel. Indeed, the real value, hermeneutically speaking, of such social-historical study is analogical: it should spur us on to detect what forms of life and ideas

---

105. In his response to the theological approaches represented by Gottwald and Brevard Childs, Brueggemann argues for a bipolar approach to Old Testament theology, one that "legitimates structure and legitimates pain." He notes that, for Gottwald, Old Testament understandings of God emerge from social life, while, for Childs, God tends to reside beyond historical contingencies. For Brueggemann, the affirmation of both polarities ("God is above the fray" and "God is in the fray") is critical in the presentation of Old Testament theology ("A Shape for Old Testament Theology, I: Structure Legitimation," *CBQ* 47 [1985] 28–46). The traditional categories, of course, are transcendence and immanence. Thus certain Old Testament traditions (especially creation and wisdom) reflect a coherent and rational theology: the world is ordered and governed by God. Yet the extreme may be the improper legitimation of totalitarianism in imperial government. Thus the critical balance to this pole is "the cry of pain" that opposes structure and calls for liberation. The latter is where Gottwald's theology makes an important contribution.

106. Langdon Gilkey, "Power, Order, Justice, and Redemption: Theological Comments on Job," *The Voice from the Whirlwind: Interpreting the Book of Job* (ed. Leo G. Perdue and W. Clark Gilpin; Nashville: Abingdon, 1992) 159–71.

107. Gottwald, *The Tribes of Yahweh*, 706.

are oppressive and inhibit the expression and development of human life in our own time and then establish both an ideology and a praxis that will enable us to remove these obstacles and establish a fully liberated life.[108]

GOTTWALD'S THEOLOGY OF JEREMIAH

How well Gottwald's assessment of the theology of Jeremiah works depends in part on his reconstruction of the history of Israel: from revolutionary society, to subversive monarchy, to subjugated colony. Jeremiah's theology is grounded in the premonarchial traditions of exodus and covenant and not in the David-Zion traditions of Judah. While several important features of Gottwald's revolutionary Israel are open to question, certainly Jeremiah's powerful criticism of monarchy and kingdom may well have originated and continued within the remnants of a village-agrarian society at odds with royal ambitions. Also convincing is Gottwald's presentation of Jeremiah as the spokesman for the "peace" party that advocated accepting Babylonian rule and carrying out religious and social reform within the political configuration of empire and vassal. Gottwald allows us to see Jeremiah as moving theology beyond a nationalistic agenda whose success is explicitly confirmed by historical triumphalism to a righteous community that struggles to articulate and live out its faith and piety within the rule of an oppressive empire.

Jeremiah does not appear to be a revolutionary attempting to subvert by aggressive actions a monstrous Babylonian empire, at least until some distant future (see Jeremiah 50–51). Yet the prophet did look forward to a new covenant and a repentant people who lived in peace with God and neighbor without the institutions of national cult and royal monarchy.

CONCLUSION

Gottwald's work is bold and imaginative. Even if one disputes major elements of his social-scientific reconstruction, its magnitude and importance cannot be ignored by either social historians or theologians. Also, its combination with liberation theology provides a most formidable theological presentation, even when critically examined. While the history of oppression may be recon-

---

108. Ibid., 705.

structed in part, including that of the biblical world, it should be noted that the validity and integrity of liberation theology are not necessarily dependent on the existence of an Iron I egalitarian society. There are pieces of the fabric of an egalitarian society that have presented themselves in the past, and glimpses may be seen in biblical materials. Indeed, these may be projected into the future through the imagination and then lived into being by prophetic existence in the present.

PART TWO

Old Testament Theology:
Cosmology and Anthropology

CHAPTER 5

History and Creation:
Myth and Wisdom

Since World War II, history, variously conceived, has dominated both the content and the method of Old Testament theology. However, during the past generation critical voices have been heard that point to the limitations of history. To concentrate primarily on the content of history means that much of the Old Testament is either ignored or slighted. This is particularly true of texts and traditions in which creation plays a prominent role. For example, the wisdom literature, prior to Ben Sira in the early second century B.C.E., has nothing to do with history as a theological category but much to do with creation and providence. The same is true of many psalms. Law also has very little importance in theological presentations that emphasize history, except as a reference point for either the revelation at Sinai or the ideal of liberation. This is not to suggest that history is not an important category for theologizing in the Old Testament, but it is to say that this category cannot, in and of itself, subsume most of the Old Testament within its confines.

In considering questions of methodology, the use of historical criticism to present Old Testament theology, even with refinements and different philosophical orientations, continues to face serious problems. First, while the method may present the history of Israelite society and religion (including religious beliefs, symbols, and rituals), historical criticism has no obvious procedure for overcoming the gap (Lessing's "ugly ditch") between the historical past and the present situation. At best, a historical critic may argue by analogy that the historical context and the theology of a particular text is like a situation today, or that the traditions are reformulated in a continuous stream into the present period. However, few Old Testament theologians move beyond the canon. Hermeneutical inquiry into the Bible is often left to contemporary theologians to ponder.

Second, the method offers no means of critical evaluation of a theological tradition that is reconstructed. The historical critic is limited to the description of certain views about God. Critical evaluation of the description is not a part of the repertoire of approaches within this methodology. Third, the method fragments the biblical texts into a variety of different understandings of God, community, and creation, and is not concerned, much less able, to bring them into relationship. The method is quite successful at pointing to the multiple theologies of Israel but has no procedure for writing an overarching theology. For the Old Testament theologian to engage in a systematic synthesis, she or he has to move beyond historical criticism to another kind of methodology. Fourth, positivism limits theology in religious data accessible to "scientific" methods, while neo-Marxism limits God-talk to the realm of social ideas. There is the fundamental underlying assumption that reality is humanly or socially constructed.

Fifth, the reign of the Enlightenment, including its ways of knowing and its approaches to and understandings of power, is being contested by approaches in which different epistemologies and power arrangements are formulated. We may well be in that uncomfortable and unsettling "betwixt and between" time of transition when either the old is passing away and the new is not yet, or at the very least the hegemony of an intellectual age is to be severely restricted. In either case, the comfortable certitude of "scientific knowledge," grounded in Enlightenment objectivity that interestingly enough largely eliminated either transcendence or its referential knowledge, no longer continues to convince and convict in ways that it did only a generation ago.

All of this means that history no longer dominates the scene of Old Testament theology, as it did in the first generation following World War II. Of course, the objective is now that of pointing to different methods and themes that have appeared in the past twenty years for undertaking Old Testament theology. In the late 1970s, this collapse of the domination of history as the way of conceiving the interpretative enterprise has occasioned thematic methodological shifts to other paradigms. One of these shifts is the move to creation, which is not only a thematic change but also often involves the employment of new methods.[1]

---

1. See Reventlow, *Problems of Old Testament Theology*, 134–86; and Hayes and Prussner, *Old Testament Theology*, 273–76. For a recent presentation of creation theology in the Old Testament, see the work by R. J. Clifford, "The Hebrew

CREATION AND MYTH

CREATION IN CONTEMPORARY THEOLOGY

The increasing number of studies of creation in Old Testament scholarship has been stimulated in part by the same issues that have led to the reemergence of the importance of creation in contemporary theological discussion. Of course, anthropology has been a constant in theological discourse in the twentieth century,[2] but what has especially developed over the last generation has been a renewed interest in cosmology.[3] This interest in cosmology has resulted in part from the existential crises of our age mentioned in the first chapter: the possibilities for nuclear holocaust and the pollution of the planet.[4] The extinction of life at human hands is a very real threat. Another stimulus has been the recognition that it is impossible intellectually to speak of history, redemption, and anthropology without setting forth the relationship of these fundamental themes to cosmology. In some important sense, the understanding of human nature, history, and redemption are defined by the meaning of cosmology, even as the meaning of cosmology is defined, at least in part, by reference to these other theological themes.[5]

Finally, the interest in creation, and particularly cosmology, has been aided by the collapse of earlier models of scientific method (mechanistic, positivistic, and materialist) occasioned by new insights and subsequently an altered scientific methodology to advance these understandings (e.g., DNA, quarks, quantum mechanics, black holes). A spirit of humility among many scientists about the "certainty" of the knowledge produced and a growing appreciation for interesting and insightful analyses of values and mystery have shaped a climate in which intellectual discourse between

---

Scriptures and the Theology of Creation," *Theological Studies* 46 (1985) 507–23; and idem, "Creation in the Hebrew Bible," *Physics, Philosophy, and Theology: A Common Quest for Understanding* (ed. Robert Russell et al.; Notre Dame, Ind.: University of Notre Dame Press, 1988) 151–70.

2. See, e.g., Wolfhart Pannenberg, *Anthropology in Theological Perspective* (Philadelphia: Westminster, 1985).

3. See especially Robin Lovin and Frank Reynolds, eds., *Cosmogony and Ethical Order* (Chicago: University of Chicago Press, 1985); Julian Hartt, "Creation and Providence," *Christian Theology* (ed. Peter Hodgson; Philadelphia: Fortress, 1982); and David Tracy and Nicholas Lash, eds., *Cosmology and Theology* (Concilium 166; New York: Seabury, 1983).

4. See Winter, *Liberating Creation*.

5. See Gustafson, *Ethics from a Theocentric Perspective*.

scientists and theologians is occurring. Indeed, many scientists are equally concerned by the crisis of possible extinction at the hands of human bomb makers and polluters. An earlier period of hostility between science and religion has been replaced by a greater openness that has encouraged dialogue and mutual learning.[6]

MYTH AND RITUAL IN EUROPE

In addition to contemporary theology, history of religions and anthropology also have stimulated important work in Old Testament creation theology. Indeed, in thinking about creation, biblical scholars often have turned to these two related disciplines especially to understand the nature and structure of myth.[7] Before and then during the period of the significant synthesis of salvation history in America and Europe, two circles of Old Testament scholars, the so-called British Myth-Ritual school of S. H. Hooke and the Scandinavian school, used theoretical insights from cultural anthropology and the data of ancient Near Eastern cultures to develop the notion of a common mythic and ritual pattern present throughout the ancient Near East, including Israel.[8]

Basing his theory on a diffusionist model, Hooke did not simply argue that myths from Babylonia spread throughout the Fertile Crescent and eventually made their way into the literature of the Bible. Rather, he argued there was a common ancient Near Eastern religious pattern of myths and associated rituals that made their way into Hebrew religion. Myth and ritual were inextricably linked together. According to Hooke and his circle, the Babylonian New Year's Festival dramatically presented the death and resurrection of the god Marduk, recited the myth of creation, portrayed the ritual combat in which Marduk defeated the dragon, consummated the sacred marriage between Marduk and his consort, and concluded with the triumphal procession climaxing in his enthronement. Through the power of ritual performance and mythic word, the world was re-created and destinies fixed.

The imaginative reconstruction of this myth and ritual pattern

6. Tracy and Lash, "Editorial Reflections," *Cosmology and Theology*, 87–92.

7. For a survey, see J. W. Rogerson, *Myth in Old Testament Interpretation* (BZAW 134; Berlin: W. de Gruyter, 1974).

8. See S. H. Hooke, ed., *Myth and Ritual* (London: Oxford University Press, 1933); idem, *The Labyrinth* (London: SPCK, 1935); and idem, *Myth, Ritual, and Kingship* (Oxford: Clarendon, 1958); Sigmund Mowinckel, *Psalmenstudien* 1 (reprint, Amsterdam: P. Schippers, 1961); and Ivan Engnell, *Studies in Divine Kingship in the Ancient Near East* (Oxford: Basil Blackwell, 1967).

significantly impacted the understanding of Israelite religion, influenced studies of biblical theology's conceptions of time and space, and even supported such major tenets of classical liberalism as universalism. While serious questions have been raised about both the theoretical base and the conclusions of this approach (the rejection of the diffusionist theory of culture, the separation of myth from ritual, and the criticism of attempting to force a wide variety of data from culturally distinct areas into a common pattern), the Scandinavian school has continued to advance this distinctive synthesis.[9]

MYTH IN AMERICAN OLD TESTAMENT CIRCLES

During the reign of the biblical theology movement, very little theological interest in myth and ritual developed in this country. Yahweh was the Lord of history, not a nature deity in cosmogonic and world maintenance myths. Myth was placed in opposition to history, including even salvation history, and while it was recognized that Israel may have held some things in common with its ancient Near Eastern neighbors, only the distinctive, not the common, was given important theological value.

The theoretical base for this position came from the popular book, *The Intellectual Adventure of Ancient Man (Before Philosophy)*, written by H. and H. A. Frankfort and Thorkild Jacobsen.[10] These ancient Near Eastern scholars, following the theories of Ernst Cassirer and Lucien Lévy-Bruhl, argued that primitive human thought, represented in the high cultures of the ancient Near East, was mythopoeic, that is, addressed the world and its objects as a "Thou," not an "It."[11] Furthermore, a mythopoeic way of looking at reality primarily perceives things in wholes, not in their analytical parts. The basic type of literature that expressed this primitive, in contradistinction to modern, thought was poetry, and more specifically, poetic myth.

However, in the search for the distinctive character of Israelite religion, Henri Frankfort wrote in his chapter on the Hebrews that the break with mythopoeic thought began to occur with Israel. For Frankfort, the relation of the Hebrews to God took place through

---

9. Benedikt Otzen, Hans Gottlieb, and Knud Jeppesen, *Myths in the Old Testament* (London: SCM, 1980).

10. H. and H. A. Frankfort, *The Intellectual Adventure of Ancient Man (Before Philosophy)* (Chicago: University of Chicago Press, 1946).

11. Ernst Cassirer, *Language and Myth* (New York: Harper & Brothers, 1946); and Lucien Lévy-Bruhl, *Primitive Mentality* (New York: Macmillan, 1923).

the avenue of history, as opposed to the ancient Near Eastern gods who were mediated through nature. Yahweh was a transcendent deity who at times became immanent in history, not nature.[12]

Frank Moore Cross, Jr., has been the leading mythologist of the Albright school that has generally subscribed to the theses of *The Intellectual Adventure of Ancient Man*.[13] Cross has argued that the Israelites mythologized historical events, such as the victory at the Red Sea (Exodus 15). This argument in part may issue from his assumption that there must be a historical kernel for Israel's religion to be distinctive and even true.[14] Mythic language was borrowed from Canaan and elsewhere to enable Israel to speak of divine transcendence. Cross took to task von Rad and other members of the German school for their late dating of creation theology. According to his argument, the name Yahweh was an abbreviated form of the longer cultic formulation, "He is the one who creates the (heavenly) armies." Cross argued that very early on Yahweh was both a creator deity and a divine warrior who fought on Israel's behalf.

Among American scholars who have contributed significantly to the understanding of creation as a theme in Israelite religion and Old Testament theology is Bernhard W. Anderson. His studies of creation construct a synthesis that brings together the theological work of scholars like von Rad and the study of Israelite myth and religion by historians of religion, including Frank Moore Cross. Among Anderson's writings is an important collection of classic articles that deal with Old Testament creation, introduced by his own insightful, programmatic essay.[15] Here he provides a very clear summary of the development of creation theology in separate tradition complexes.

12. The work of T. H. Gaster is that of a folklorist who compiles parallels to Old Testament texts, rites, and customs. Influenced by the conceptions of mythopoeic thought *(Before Philosophy)* and myth as expressive of existential experience (Bultmann), Gaster contrasts the personal God of Israel with the personification of natural forces in Near Eastern religion *(Myth, Legend, Custom in the Old Testament* [2 vols.; New York: Harper & Row, 1969]).

13. See Frank Moore Cross, Jr., *Canaanite Myth and Hebrew Epic* (Cambridge: Harvard University Press, 1973).

14. The processes of the mythologization of history and the historization of myth are addressed by a former student of Cross, J. J. M. Roberts ("Myth Versus History," *CBQ* 38 [1976] 1–13).

15. Bernhard W. Anderson, ed., *Creation in the Old Testament* (Issues in Religion and Theology 6; Philadelphia: Fortress, 1984). See his earlier *Creation versus Chaos: The Reinterpretation of Mythical Symbolism in the Bible* (New York: Association Press, 1967).

Anderson argues that there are two very different traditions of creation in the Old Testament: the older exodus-covenant formulation in which Yahweh is warrior and creator of a people, and the later David-Zion tradition. The former is represented by the Song of the Sea in Exodus 15 which contains the mythic pattern of the defeat of chaos, enthronement on the sacred mountain (temple), and proclamation of kingship over the cosmos (cf. the battle with chaos represented by the Baal cycle). Anderson contends that this mythic hymn traces the origins of Israel to a historical event, not to primeval times. By contrast, the second tradition, the election of David and Zion, is grounded in the order of creation. In contradistinction to the horizontal (historical) axis of meaning, this mythic tradition is vertical (cosmic) in explaining the origins and continuation of monarchy and temple through which the saving benefits of God are mediated. This worldview that speaks of the primeval origins of society in creation is, in Anderson's view, an adaptation of Canaanite mythology.

Anderson continues his categorization of the traditions of creation in the Old Testament by examining Psalm 104, placed under the rubric "Creation and Creaturely Dependence." Attributing the origins of the psalm to Egypt (King Akhenaten), he concludes that it entered Israelite religion through the medium of the wisdom tradition. According to Anderson, Psalm 104 is a true cosmogonic myth in which the battle with chaos leads to a harmonious order where every creature is assigned a proper place and time. Closely related to this psalm is Gen 1:1—2:4a, a cosmological myth that was formed in the Priestly circle. Finally, Anderson returns to his previous work on Second Isaiah under the category of "Creation and New Creation," where history, soteriology, and creation are combined into eschatological vision.

NEW DEVELOPMENTS IN THE STUDY OF MYTH

In important ways, Old Testament scholarship has continued to draw on the new and formative work on myth in anthropology.[16] Claude Lévi-Strauss, Mary Douglas, Victor Turner, Clifford Geertz, and Edmund Leach, to name a few leading theorists, have provided structural, mythic, social, and ritual models for assessing and understanding cultures and the way creation myths provide the con-

---

16. See especially H.-P. Müller, *Mythos, Tradition, Revolution: Phänomenologische Untersuchungen zum Alten Testament* (Neukirchen-Vluyn: Neukirchener Verlag, 1973).

textualization for custom, religious practice, and law.[17] Mircea Eliade and Paul Ricoeur have provided a theoretical base for understanding the mythical nature of language in the Old Testament.[18] Their pervasive influence is seen in the work of quite a number of biblical scholars. We mention only three examples: Claus Westermann, Brevard Childs, and Frank Gorman.

Westermann appropriates Eliade's contention that myth is primarily concerned with preserving and maintaining the orders of the present and with providing security against forces that threaten current existence, not with explaining, as a response to human curiosity, what happened in the past.[19] Childs has learned from Malinowski and Eliade that "myth is a form by which the existing structure of reality is understood and maintained."[20] Their influence is present also in his contention that the actions of deities in primeval times were both deterministic and paradigmatic for the present order of reality (nature and society).

17. Claude Lévi-Strauss, *Structural Anthropology* (New York: Basic Books, 1963, 1976); idem, *The Savage Mind* (Chicago: University of Chicago Press, 1966); idem, *Totemism* (Boston: Beacon, 1963); Mary Douglas, *Purity and Danger* (Harmondsworth: Penguin, 1970); idem, *Natural Symbols* (New York: Pantheon Books, 1970); Victor Turner, *The Ritual Process* (Chicago: Aldine, 1969); Clifford Geertz, *The Interpretation of Cultures* (New York: Basic Books, 1973); and Edmund Leach and D. Alan Aycock, *Structuralist Interpretations of Biblical Myth* (Cambridge: Cambridge University Press, 1983).

18. Mircea Eliade, *Cosmos and History: The Myth of the Eternal Return* (New York: Harper, 1959); idem, *Myth and Reality* (New York: Harper & Row, 1963); idem, *The Sacred and the Profane* (New York: Harcourt, Brace, & World, 1959); and Paul Ricoeur, *The Symbolism of Evil* (New York: Harper & Row, 1967).

19. Johannes Hempel wrote an insightful essay in 1953 ("Glaube, Mythos und Geschichte im Alten Testament," *ZAW* 65 [1953] 109–67) in which he took on Bultmann's argument that myth was primarily the attempt of primitive humans to achieve self-understanding. Hempel contended that this anthropological, existential character of myth is only one of many ways that myth functioned in the ancient world of the Old Testament. To demythologize myth is to destroy a primal category for expressing a very real and immediate experience of God, not unlike that experience in the modern pietistic understanding of prayer and the experience of forgiveness. However, Hempel did contend, as did Cross, that Israel mythologized history. Hempel placed biblical myths into the categories of theogony, cosmogony, soteriology, and revelation. Also insightful, although marred by his own strong hesitancy to attribute true myth to Israel, is the work by J. L. McKenzie (*Myths and Realities* [Milwaukee: Bruce Publishing Co., 1963]). McKenzie correctly rejected the idea that myth is necessarily associated with ritual or was produced only by primitive minds. He argues that while ancient Near Eastern cultures told myths, they did not break through to a true perception of God and succeeded only in speaking about the phenomenal world. By contrast, Israel, which did have its own myths, received the true revelation from God.

20. Brevard S. Childs, *Myth and Reality in the Old Testament* (SBT 27; London: SCM, 1960).

Drawing on the works especially of Clifford Geertz and Victor Turner, Frank Gorman analyzes the relationship between myth, social status, and ritual in the Priestly code and concluded the following. For P, Yahweh is the God of creation who spoke into being all of creation, although the pollution of the earth led to the divine decision to return the orders of life to chaos.[21] After the new creation of the world and the creation of Israel as a "nation of priests" set apart, Yahweh eventually brought into existence the priestly cult that was designed to maintain the ongoing order of creation and life and to restore it when it had been violated. Basic to the structural order of creation, as well as society and cult, is its establishment through divisions and boundaries: time (festival and common), space (sacred and profane), categorization of objects and actions (clean and unclean), and status (priests and laity). Gorman argues that the ritual enactment of the spoken word maintains and restores the created order. In this way humans participate in the event of creation. Especially insightful is Gorman's argument, drawing on Turner's understanding of installation, that the ritual of consecration for the priesthood in Leviticus 8 is a rite of passage for Aaron and his sons, from "death" to their ordinary status in society to "life" in their priestly roles.

MYTH AND CREATION: THREE CURRENT EXAMPLES

Significant presentations of creation theology in the Old Testament have appeared in recent years that draw on contemporary theology and cultural anthropology. All three address the important relationship between history and creation. These include the work of three scholars who approach history and creation in distinctive ways: Jon Levenson, Claus Westermann, and Rolf Knierim.

CREATION AND THEODICY

One of the best, more recent treatments of creation comes from a student of Frank Moore Cross who carries forth his teacher's interest in Canaanite myth and the Divine Warrior. Jon Levenson's book, *Creation and the Persistence of Evil*, grows out of his concern to address the difficult questions posed by the Jewish Holocaust.[22]

21. Frank Gorman, *The Ideology of Ritual: Space, Time and Status in the Priestly Theology* (JSOTSup 91; Sheffield: JSOT, 1990). Also see Robert L. Cohn, *The Shape of Sacred Space* (AAR Studies in Religion 23; Chico, Calif.: Scholars Press, 1981).
22. Jon Levenson, *Creation and the Persistence of Evil: The Jewish Drama of*

He asks whether, in view of the Holocaust, it is possible to reconcile a doctrine of divine sovereignty with the equally important affirmation of the life-sustaining justice of God. To answer this fundamental question of post-Holocaust thought, Levenson presses forward with three objectives. First, he seeks to demonstrate that *creatio ex nihilo* is an inadequate characterization of creation in the Hebrew Bible. This has led in turn to ascribing "a false finality or definitiveness" to creation that both ignores the vulnerability and fragility of the cosmos and fails to appreciate the drama of God's omnipotence over creation. Second, Levenson detects a general lack of appreciation of the relationship of the Priestly creation story with the liturgy of cult. This leads to a common failure to understand the significant role of ritual in the forming and sustaining of the cosmos. Third, Levenson wishes to work out the relationship between cosmos and history, not only in understanding God as both creator and Lord of history, but also in appreciating the dialectic of human submission to divine suzerainty and God's dependence on humanity.

In Part One of his volume, Levenson points to the basic tension between the mastery of God and the vulnerability of order. While Genesis 1 suggests that God has always reigned supreme, other accounts speak of the time when God comes to assume leadership over the divine council. Instead of discounting one or the other portrayals, Levenson develops a model of dialectical theology in which the two poles interact in creative tension.

Levenson argues that it is especially within Israel's historical experience that chaos has seemed to gain the upper hand. Thus the assertion of Yahweh's sovereignty is often opposed by the contesting of that lordship. Levenson believes that liturgy, by activating divine power, mediates the two contradictory affirmations of God as Lord of creation and history, on the one hand, and as the one who is contested and even appears at times to be defeated, on the other. Further, Israel at times projected the combat myth into the future. In the eschaton (cf. Isaiah 24–27), God will once for all defeat the chaos monster, death will be vanquished, and the cosmos will be ultimately secure. Yet this final mastery over chaos is grounded in hope that issues forth in a confession of faith. Israel stands before, not after, the cosmic victory.

In the second section of his book, Levenson develops the dialectic expressed in the alternation between chaos and cosmos, especially

---

Divine Omnipotence (San Francisco: Harper & Row, 1988).

in the Priestly account of creation. While Israel may have had a seven-day festival that was the New Year's celebration of the re-actualization of cosmogony and enthronement, P eventually dissociated creation from New Year's and connected it instead to the Sabbath. With Sabbath rest, there was the cessation from the time of opposition to divine rule. Sabbath worship was the way that the cultic community came to participate in the ordering of creation on a weekly basis.

Sacred space is also important, Levenson maintains, because the temple is a microcosm of the perfect and harmonious world as it ought to be. In the ritual building and rededication of the temple, once again humans participate in the divine ordering of the world. In sacred space and time, Israel proleptically participates in the defeat of chaos and the transformation of chaos into order.

Finally, in Part Three, Levenson takes up the dialectic of cosmos and history expressed in the two idioms of creation and covenant. In the mythic battle with the dragon, Israel came to express its monotheistic faith. By monotheism Levenson means that for Israel there is the exclusive enthronement of God over the divine council and the uncompromising commitment to obey his commands. The other idiom of monotheism, covenant, also requires unswerving loyalty to God. Covenant love is threatened primarily by the seduction of other gods who promise more for less. Even as God's kingship over the cosmos was dependent on Israel's constant reaffirmation in worship, so God's rule over history required the repetition of the covenant in ritual celebration and loyal, but freely given, obedience. The actualization of divine power requires the worship and testimony of God's people. God's sovereignty depends on Israel's faithful response.

Yet, according to Levenson, Israel must be free to recognize and then submit to divine rule. This tension between autonomy and heteronomy, human freedom and submission to God, is explained by reference to Near Eastern suzerainty treaties. The vassal freely enters into covenant with the suzerain and recognizes his lordship. Yet behind every treaty is the implied threat that violence will be inflicted on the weaker party. Thus there is no real alternative to God's suzerainty. Even so, to avoid war the suzerain must woo the vassal. This element of courtship mediates between autonomy and heteronomy. Likewise, God both woos and commands Israel's faithful response. "Those who stand under covenantal obligation by nature and necessity are continually called upon to adopt that relationship by free decision. Chosen for service, they must choose to serve. This is the paradox of the dialectic of autonomy and heteronomy."[23] It is the autonomy of humanity that makes it possible for people to argue with God and win, but it is also the heteronomy of humankind that brings them into submission. Thus, within this "larger, dialectical theology, both arguing with God and obeying him can be central spiritual acts."[24]

Levenson's work is both provocative and often compelling as he uses Near Eastern mythology and Israelite covenant theology to set forth a dialectic in which divine omnipotence and limitation are held together in an uneasy tension. At the same time, there are several areas where he may be pressed for further explication. First, one wonders whether Levenson has tended to superimpose the mythic pattern of the battle with the dragon on too much of the Old Testament. One may argue that there are texts with root metaphors of word, aesthesis, and fertility that may not so easily fit his paradigm of combat or eschatological resolution of combat proleptically realized in the cultus. Second, the form-critical thesis of a suzerainty treaty used by Levenson to explicate Israel's understanding of covenant and the theological tension between autonomy and heteronomy has come under serious criticism, both as a literary construct and as an appropriate analogy for understanding Israelite covenants. To use this model for understanding Israel's covenant raises questions about the interpretation given to covenant.

Nevertheless this is an important book that moves theological inquiry in an important direction. It provides a systematic presentation of the various materials in the Hebrew Bible without negating the plurality of voices that speak, and there is critical reflection on the hermeneutical value of these voices.

THE DIALECT OF HISTORY AND CREATION: CLAUS WESTERMANN

The most significant work in creation theology among German Old Testament scholars has been done by Claus Westermann.[25] As Walter Brueggemann has correctly observed,[26] Westermann brings together two major theological poles in the Old Testament that are

---

23. Ibid., 148.
24. Ibid., 153.
25. Claus Westermann, *Creation* (Philadelphia: Fortress, 1974); idem, *Genesis 1— 11* (Minneapolis: Augsburg, 1984); idem, *Blessing in the Bible and the Life of the Church* (Philadelphia: Westminster, 1978); and idem, *Theologie des Alten Testaments in Grundzügen* (ATD Ergänzungsheft 6; Göttingen: Vandenhoeck & Ruprecht, 1978).
26. Walter Brueggemann, "A Convergence in Recent Old Testament Theologies," *JSOT* 18 (1980) 2–18.

fundamental to its depiction of God: soteriology (history) and blessing (creation). In discussing the first pole, Westermann largely retraces the path worn bare by von Rad in positing the thesis of an ancient historical credo, the themes of which are developed in the exodus-Sinai complex and then the covenant of Deuteronomy. Here Yahweh is the redeemer who liberates and continues to save his chosen people. Salvation is the goal of history.

The second pole, for Westermann, focuses on creation texts, psalms, and the wisdom literature in addressing the theme of blessing, that divine power which enhances and sustains life. Blessing is divine power that preserves the ongoing order of life and creation. Breaking with von Rad who saw creation merely as the first of God's historical acts, thus a continuum from beginnings into history, Westermann argued that creation is beyond history. However, he also contended that, unlike the salvific acts of God that were recited, creation was the presupposition of faith but not the object of its confession. Creation is the ground of history that takes on its specific redemptive character in the life of Israel. Here we move with Westermann into the arena of creation theology concerned with securing the present by linking the order of reality to primal origins, that is, to the doctrine of *creatio continua*. Thus history and creation form a sweeping dialectic that embraces the whole of Old Testament theology.[27]

The Subordination of History to Creation: Rolf Knierim

While he has not yet written a comprehensive theology of creation, Rolf Knierim has several programmatic essays that are highly significant.[28] Knierim's "prolegomenon" represents one of the best

---

27. Also moving into a dialectic of Old Testament themes is the work of Samuel Terrien, whose book *The Elusive Presence: Toward a New Biblical Theology* (New York: Harper & Row, 1978) contains in its title what, for him, is the center (God) of Old Testament theology. While God continues to defy precise location and understanding, Terrien argues that interpretation, even theology itself, must recognize the aesthetic dimension of Israelite faith just as much as the ethical and historical side represented in most Old Testament theologies. In the Psalter and Wisdom corpus, reality is comprehended as an aesthesis, a world of beauty into which one enters and finds life, order, and even playfulness. God is made present by each of these avenues. Thus it is impossible for the theologian to attempt to subsume all of Old Testament thought under the categories of ethics, history, and instruction in law. Other categories should include beauty, wisdom, grace, and love. What is most promising about Terrien's work is his combination of history, language, and creation.

28. Rolf Knierim, "Cosmos and History in Israel's Theology," *Werden und Wirken des Alten Testaments* (Göttingen: Vandenhoeck & Ruprecht, 1980) 59–123; and idem, "The Task of Old Testament Theology," *HBT* 6 (1984) 25–57.

efforts since Walther Eichrodt to argue for a systematic presentation of Old Testament theology. While Knierim makes use of historical-critical methods, he tends to see Old Testament theology as a discipline within theology in general and not as a subject that develops out of a subdiscipline of historical criticism (e.g., von Rad's use of tradition history). In addition, Knierim's work is constructive in that he advocates moving the articulation of Israel's theological reflection into the present and engages in critical evaluation of that articulation. In contrast to many, Knierim subordinates history to creation.

Recognizing the plurality of Old Testament theologies in the text, Knierim seeks a monotheistic structure that relates and systematizes these features into a consistent whole.[29] This monotheistic structure is defined as "the universal dominion of Yahweh in justice and righteousness." The Old Testament, says Knierim, does not speak about God alone but about God in relationship to a reality that consists of cosmos and nature, history and society, and the individual. The task of the Old Testament theologian is to relate these three spheres to the sovereignty of God. "Justice" and "righteousness," which include the fundamental concept of order, are the key in describing and understanding this relationship.

Knierim contends that the most universal domain of God's sovereignty is creation, not history: God's sovereignty is not contingent on history but precedes, transcends, and will follow history. While humans are dependent on the cosmos for life, they were not originally a part of its order. Indeed, the continuation of the cosmos does not require human beings, although it is often threatened by their presence. History, thus, is subordinate to cosmos. In addition, Knierim argues that human history and Israel's own election receive their meaning only when they witness to and act out God's universal dominion.[30] Israel had to learn that neither human history nor their election as the chosen people was the arena of and testimony to God's ultimate glory but rather that history, including especially salvation history, was the realm in which the struggle for the meaning of creation was carried out. Israel's deliverance from oppression points out and witnesses to God's more extensive liber-

29. Knierim is critical of von Rad's tradition history approach for pointing out the plurality inherent in the theology of the Old Testament but doing nothing to address the problem. He is also critical of the canon scholars, since the canon simply concretizes the problem of plurality and does little to address it.

30. "History fails or is justified to the extent that it is in step with the just and righteous order of the world" (Knierim, "Cosmos and History," 94).

ation of the world from chaos. Israel's history and world order both have one and the same purpose: liberation from chaos and oppression. The ultimate goal of history is to achieve harmony with God's good creation.

According to Knierim, two types of social existence actualize the liberation of nature from chaos. One is *měnûhâ*, the "rest" in which Israel is given the promised land as a gift and learns to exist in an agrarian life-style within the cosmic cycle. Second, Israel is to implement justice and righteousness in society. This justice, which is identified with world order, is actualized by specific actions of the righteous community.

In speaking of cosmology, Knierim stresses two features: space and time. Ordered space, often captured in the phrase "heaven and earth," distinguishes between two fundamental realms within creation, the place where God dwells and the inhabited world of human beings. This points to a systematic understanding of creation as bipartite and even reflects what is fundamental about reality itself. This basic dualism, world of God and world of humans, cannot be overcome, unless creation return to chaos.[31] But even more central, argues Knierim, is the affirmation that the cosmos is not self-originating and self-perpetuating but is created and sustained by God. This means, then, that God alone is the "ground and guarantor of the unity and the wholeness of the world." Thus it is monotheism, the unity of the creator, that keeps the world from the oblivion of chaos. At the same time, this structure of space, which Knierim calls the "ultimate theodicy," is ordered and supported by the justice of God.

Knierim also examines the dualism of time: cosmic (cyclical) and historical (linear). God's righteous power sustains the cycle of time that rules creation and interrupts history in salvific acts of deliverance. The connection of both types of time also is rooted in the unity of God. However, historical (human) time, ultimately dependent on God, is subordinated to cosmic time. While history has a later beginning and may come to an abrupt and final halt, cosmic time precedes the appearance of human beings and will continue after their disappearance. Even eschatology is expressed in the language and thought of a new creation in which cosmic space and time, threatened by human evil, are revitalized. History, including linear time, is to be subservient to the salvific intentionality of God

---

31. Thus the attempted violation of this separation in the Tower of Babel episode in Gen 11:1-9 leads to the alienation of the nations from each other and from God.

who also establishes and continues the just and beneficent order of the cosmos. "History fails or is justified to the extent that it is in step with the just and righteous order of the world."[32] Knierim's articulation of the task of Old Testament theology is both clear and provocative. He moves from the merely descriptive level to systematic and critical-reflective levels, making open judgments about the centrality of the sovereignty of God grounded in and expressed through righteousness and justice. His highly rational, systematic presentation does not obscure the diversity of the theological traditions present in the canon, but at the same time moves beyond the paralysis of pluralism. Traditions or texts that do not meet the standards and insights of the "monotheistic structure" are subjugated to those which do.

If Knierim is to be faulted, it is in being perhaps a little too rational and systematic. The human experience of the chaotic character of reality in history and creation (nature) may not receive enough consideration in his formulation. Nor does he allow chaos to pose a serious threat to divine sovereignty. In contrast to Israel's theological reflections, creation is not fragile or subject to annihilation. It is the experience of the chaotic, not merely in human form, that is so very fundamental, so much a part of the mythic world in which Israel existed and of our own, especially since the disintegration of liberal idealism occasioned by world war and holocaust.

Finally, the language of the text itself, in all of its multiple forms and levels, narrative as well as poem, does not receive enough consideration in this approach. Language, especially metaphor, creates those narrative worlds of imagination into which humans enter and exist, realities at once both blind and visionary, worlds in which Apollo struggles with but is embraced by Dionysus. It is the world of vision and dance, of aesthesis, which is absent from Knierim's discursive, rational construction.[33]

---

32. A very similar approach to Old Testament theology is developed by Hans Heinrich Schmid in his collection of essays, *Altorientalische Welt in der alttestamentlichen Theologie* (Zurich: Theologischer Verlag, 1974). In these essays, Schmid contends that creation is the "broad horizon of biblical theology" and is rooted in the ancient Near Eastern understanding of world order. For a full, systematic treatment of "order," see Hans Heinrich Schmid, *Gerechtigkeit als Weltordnung* (BHT 40; Tübingen: J. C. B. Mohr [Paul Siebeck], 1968). Brueggemann likewise has pointed to the common ancient Near Eastern theology of creation and providence in which Israel participates, yet from which it struggles to be free. The peculiarity of this latter element, contends Brueggemann, is in Israel's historical experiences ("A Shape for Old Testament Theology, I: Structure Legitimation," 28–46).

33. Contrast Terrien, *The Elusive Presence*, who makes room for beauty, joy, and imagination.

WISDOM AND CREATION

It is not fortuitous that considerable scholarly interest in wisdom literature began at the same time the biblical theology movement was beginning to stumble under the weight of serious criticism. As is well known, salvation history plays no role, indeed is not even mentioned, in wisdom texts before Ben Sira in the second century B.C.E. However, in the rebirth of interest in wisdom in the late 1960s and early 1970s, there was considerable enthusiasm to attribute much of biblical literature to the sages, thereby negating wisdom's ignoring if not denial of salvation history as the arena for revelation and divine action. Von Rad, for example, placed wisdom under the rubric of "Israel before Jahweh: Israel's Answer," indicating that, like the psalms, Israel's sapiential corpus was a response to the salvific acts of God in history. In one of his early essays, James Crenshaw questioned the legitimacy of finding wisdom and wisdom influence throughout the Old Testament corpus.[34] His was more than a tedious tracing of sapiential language or its lack in books outside the traditional wisdom corpus. Instead, he set forth rather stringent criteria (linguistic and conceptual) for defining wisdom and wisdom influence in order to return the sages to their time-honored home of the wisdom collection of Job, Proverbs, Qoheleth, Ben Sira, and the Wisdom of Solomon. Proponents of salvation history now found it more difficult to co-opt wisdom as a part of their theological enterprise. Consequently, theologians of the Old Testament had to address a wisdom tradition that did not embrace salvation history until the early second century B.C.E.

Many scholars today would readily affirm Walther Zimmerli's contention that wisdom "thinks resolutely within a theology of creation,"[35] although there is yet to appear a major comprehensive study that sets forth the creation theology of wisdom literature.[36] Subsequently, attention should be drawn to several preliminary studies that suggest new directions and offer formative theological insights into wisdom and creation.

There are four major approaches to the presentation of creation in wisdom theology: anthropology, world order, theodicy, and the dialectic of anthropology and cosmology. Creation is studied by

---

34. James L. Crenshaw, "Method for Determining Wisdom Influence upon 'Historical Literature,'" *JBL* 88 (1969) 129–42.
35. Walther Zimmerli, "The Place and Limit of the Wisdom in the Framework of the Old Testament Theology," *SIAW*, 316.
36. See Perdue, *Wisdom and Creation*.

means of the terms of understandings of myth in the history of religions and cultural anthropology and as a theme that may be delineated within a corpus of litcrature according to various literary methods. Up to the present time, nothing approaching a comprehensive treatment of one or more of these approaches has appeared.[37]

ANTHROPOLOGY

Among those who have understood wisdom to be the human quest to master life,[38] Walther Zimmerli has been the most articulate. In his early writings, Zimmerli argued that "wisdom is radically anthropocentric."[39] He illustrated this contention by focusing on Qoheleth's central question: "What is good for humanity in living?" Later on, a more mature Zimmerli still considered anthropology to be at the center of sapiential reflection.[40] However, an anthropological center was found within the sages' reflection on creation with a view to determining the role and place of human beings in the world-historical situation made possible by God. For Zimmerli, the goal of the wise person who lives before God is "to master life," that is, to rule over the creation as God's representative and to engender the values and discipline of a sapiential existence that leads to divine blessing. Wisdom's path is not solely dependent on human reason and individual experience; rather, it is forged by the engagement of reason and experience with the revelation of God in the cosmos and sapiential tradition.

WORLD ORDER

Cosmology is a second organizing principle for the presentation of creation theology in wisdom literature.[41] Several scholars (es-

37. See Perdue, *Wisdom in Revolt: Creation Theology in the Book of Job* (JSOTSup 112; Sheffield: JSOT, 1991).
38. These include Walter Brueggemann, *In Man We Trust* (Atlanta: John Knox, 1972); John Priest, "Where Is Wisdom to Be Placed?" *SIAW*, 281–88; idem, "Humanism, Skepticism, and Pessimism," *JAAR* (1968) 311–26; O. S. Rankin, *Israel's Wisdom Literature* (Edinburgh: T. & T. Clark, 1936); and Walther Zimmerli, "The Place and Limit of Wisdom," 314–26.
39. Walther Zimmerli, "Zur Struktur der alttestamentlichen Weisheit," *ZAW* 51 (1933) 177–204.
40. Zimmerli, "The Place and Limit of Wisdom."
41. Hartmut Gese, *Lehre und Wirklichkeit in der alten Weisheit* (Tübingen: J. C. B. Mohr [Paul Siebeck], 1958); Hans-Jürgen Hermisson, "Observations on the Creation Theology in Wisdom," *Israelite Wisdom* (ed. John G. Gammie et al.; Missoula: Scholars Press, 1978) 43–57; Horst Dietrich Preuss, "Das Gottesbild der älteren Weisheit Israels," *SVT* 23 (1972) 117–42; idem, "Erwägungen zum theologischen Ort alttestamentlicher Weisheitsliteratur," *EvT* 30 (1970) 393–417;

pecially Hartmut Gese, Hans Heinrich Schmid, and Hans-Jürgen Hermisson) have produced important studies that focus on world order. Gese begins his study with Egyptian *ma'at*, the daughter of Re, the sun god, and the embodiment of "order, truth, and justice." At the beginning of time, the creator established *ma'at* as the cosmic and social order for regulating all existence. And in the Osiris-Horus myth and ritual that represented the transfer of power to the new king, Horus succeeds his dead father, Osiris, to the throne and becomes the incarnation of *ma'at*. Through just rule, the order of creation and of society is undergirded and sustained.[42] The principle of retribution by which the good were rewarded and the evil punished became central to sapiential ethics. There were limits to *ma'at*, however. The mystery of the gods and the limits of human knowledge made it impossible for *ma'at* to be perceived in its totality. Imperfections in creation—for example, those who were born with deficiencies or handicaps—underscored the troublesome flaws even in the work of the creator. Periods of crisis brought forth serious questionings of a simplistic theory of retribution grounded in cosmic and social order.

While Israel's sages, argues Gese, appropriated much of this thinking in their wisdom literature, they gave a more important place to divine freedom. Yahweh was not shackled by immutable laws but was free to act as he so chose. This radical freedom of God broke through the Egyptian emphasis on causality in which actions met with predetermined results. Rather, the freedom and grace of God received a more pronounced place in sapiential thinking in Israel.

Hans Heinrich Schmid's prolific writings on world order have developed Gese's groundbreaking thesis. Schmid's more elaborate treatment of order in Israelite and ancient Near Eastern thought appeared in 1968: *Gerechtigkeit als Weltordnung*. Although not limited to wisdom texts, Schmid's book systematically analyzed the major spheres of order in Egyptian, Sumero-Akkadian, and Israelite cultures: law, wisdom, nature/fertility, war/victory, cult/sacrifice, and kingship. He observed that it was especially the royal tradition that encompassed all other spheres. In Egypt, where a more pronounced doctrine of order was developed, the creator was believed to have brought *ma'at* into existence to replace chaos. Thus, for

---

Schmid, *Gerechtigkeit als Weltordnung*; and idem, "Creation, Righteousness, and Salvation;" Anderson, *Creation in the Old Testament*, 102–17.
42. Gese, *Lehre und Wirklichkeit in der alten Weisheit*, 5–32.

example, Re was the "Lord of *ma'at,*" and *ma'at* was his divine daughter. As the son and devotee of Re, the king had responsibility for maintaining and actualizing both the order of creation and human society. Wisdom was the attribute of the king that gave him the capacity for orderly, beneficent rule. And the sages, particularly Egyptian officials (e.g., Ptahhotep), worked in the service of the king, thereby bringing social structures into harmony with creation. The sages were understood as issuing "instructions of *ma'at*" that, when taken into the heart, enabled one to live in concert with the world and the human community. Wise acts constituted and realized both world and social order. In Schmid's judgment, a similar, although less pronounced, understanding of world order developed in Mesopotamian cultures. In the Sumerian myth of Inanna and Enki, for example, one hundred laws *(me)* were thought to govern all reality and provided the collective structure that maintained the continuation of reality. Here too the king as sage was responsible for the ongoingness of order.

In turning to Israel, Schmid contended that while ancient Near Eastern conceptions of order were appropriated through a Canaanite medium, the unity of reality embracing the major areas of order in Egypt and Mesopotamia was fragmented. While law, wisdom, and kingship were the spheres in which *ṣdq* ("justice," "righteousness," "order") functions, it is especially rare in the traditions of cult, war, and to a certain extent nature.

The Hebrew term for order, according to Schmid, is expressed in the root *ṣdq,* although one should differentiate between *ṣdq* ("justice"), which originally designated cosmic order made concrete in wisdom and law and actualized in the social realm by the king, and *ṣdqh* ("righteousness"), which embraced behavior and thought that created and sustained a just and beneficent order in cosmos and society.[43] The one who engaged in order-creating behavior is the *ṣaddîq* ("righteous one") who lives in harmony with God and society and experiences well-being in life. Schmid also stressed that the understanding of order in Israel was historically nuanced, at least until the exile. This implies that prior to the end of the state of Judah, the freedom of God and human limitations meant that order was not a static, mechanistic principle operating in and through a system of retribution but was historically conditioned. After the exile, however, certain circles developed a mechanical theory of retribution and an ahistorical conception of order in which human

43. Schmid, *Gerechtigkeit als Weltordnung,* 67.

actions led inevitably to certain consequences. It is this distorted conception of order that led to the radical protest of Job.[44] In several publications, H. D. Preuss has also characterized wisdom theology as "thoughts about order" (Ordnungsdenken) established through observation, experience, and tradition.[45] However, Preuss emphasized that older wisdom was quite secular and became theological only at a much later stage of its history. For Preuss, retribution was a continuous component of this way of thinking, and the causal relation between deed and consequence was so inflexible that it tended to negate the possibility of divine freedom, even when the tradition became more theologically nuanced. A crisis developed in wisdom thought because of two factors: collective experience led to the realization that a moral order was not universally and unquestionably in operation in the world, and increasing emphasis was placed on the freedom of God. After the dramatic failure of the attempt to bring older wisdom within the sphere of Israelite faith (see Job and Qoheleth), the remnant of continuing tradition was radically transformed. Then wisdom became the "fear of God," a successful, although somewhat misguided attempt, according to Preuss, to place the tradition within the parameters of Yahwistic faith. Indeed, the seriously altered character of later wisdom demonstrated how much Israel had to transform the originally pagan, order-thinking wisdom to alleviate the erupting exilic and postexilic crisis that could have led to the total disintegration of its tradition.[46]

44. For a detailed discussion of the historical nature of wisdom, see Hans Heinrich Schmid, Wesen und Geschichte der Weisheit (BZAW 101; Berlin: W. de Gruyter, 1966). Schmid demonstrates that, contrary to some presentations, the wisdom tradition does respond to historical contingencies. Thus, while wisdom is not centered in salvation history, it is not ahistorical in its approach and response to reality. Rather, the tradition has a historical consciousness that strongly affects its interpretation of human experience and God.

45. Preuss, "Erwägungen zum theologischen Ort alttestamentlicher Weisheitsliteratur."

46. Preuss denies to wisdom any legitimate place in either normative Old Testament theology or Christian faith. This is based on his conclusion that wisdom thought is essentially pagan and contributed nothing distinctive or important. Indeed, the "fear of God" which is absent in older wisdom becomes a constitutive feature of the later tradition because of the impress of Yahwistic faith. Pointing to salvation history as the normative theological tradition for both Old Testament theology and Christian faith, creation, retribution, and sapiential empiricism are deprecated as natural theology. Therefore wisdom has no theological value ("Alttestamentliche Weisheit in christlicher Theologie?" Questions disputées d'Ancien Testament [BETL 33; ed. C. Brekelmans; Louvain: University Press, 1974] 165–82).

A final example of approaching wisdom theology through cosmology appears in the work of Hans-Jürgen Hermisson. In his important study of the wisdom saying, Hermisson detected what he considered to be constitutive for sapiential thought: the saying is a form connecting deed and result, thereby recognizing, transmitting, and creating an order of life.[47] In a later article, he extended his argument about the basic form of Israelite wisdom to a comprehensive statement about sapiential theology.[48] In Hermisson's view, wisdom sought regularity in the multiplicity of phenomena, a regularity observable in both nature and human society. This regularity led to a unified construction of reality that established a correspondence between what was observed and its perception. The developing sapiential epistemology led to the articulation of a creation theology in which order in the world was consistent with the process of human perception and the knowledge it acquired. The same regularity, purpose, and beauty of wisdom as human perception were part of the essential nature of creation itself. This insight provided human life its raison d'être, for it implied that existence had purpose: to live so as to actualize and experience the beneficent order of creation. Sapiential teachings provided guidance for the proper way of existing in the world.

THEODICY

Several scholars have approached wisdom theology by the avenue of theodicy, proposing that the questioning of the justice of God is the key to understanding the sapiential literature.[49] Perhaps the best example of this approach is James Crenshaw.

Arguing against the prevailing tendency in the 1960s to extend wisdom's domain by encompassing much of the Hebrew Bible, Crenshaw argued for specific linguistic and thematic criteria that reflected the thought and influence of the wise.[50] The effect of this argument for theological discussions was to force wisdom back within the confines of recognized wisdom literature and thus to the

---

47. Hans-Jürgen Hermisson, *Studien zur israelitischen Spruchweisheit* (WMANT 28; Neukirchen-Vluyn: Neukirchener Verlag, 1968).

48. Hermisson, "Observations on the Creation Theology in Wisdom," 43–57.

49. James L. Crenshaw, "Popular Questioning of the Justice of God," *ZAW* 82 (1970) 380–95; idem, "Prolegomenon," *SIAW*, 1–45; idem, "In Search of Divine Presence," *RevExp* 74 (1977) 353–69; and Burton L. Mack, "Wisdom Myth and Mytho-Logy," *Int* 24 (1970) 46–60.

50. Crenshaw, "Method for Determining Wisdom Influence," 129–42.

centrality of creation, not sacred history. With Wisdom dwelling securely in her linguistic house, James Crenshaw pronounced theodicy the center of sapiential God-talk.[51] In contradistinction to salvation history's redeeming God who entered history to rescue the perishing, the sages collapsed the myth of history with thunderous accusations against the justice of God. With sacred history coming under attack because of individual and national experiences of chaos and the demonic, most notably the Babylonian holocaust, Job, Agur, and Qoheleth moved from direct attack on the justice of God, to satire, and eventually to resignation.[52] Yet the sages, including Qoheleth, did not abandon the enterprise of theology during its "crises." Rather, they shaped a theology that reoriented God-talk away from a dominant and singular reliance on history to the importance of creation.[53]

Turning to creation, so Crenshaw argues, the sages articulated a theology designed to defend the justice of God. In the midst of a crisis of faith and meaning, they appealed to creation in order to affirm the possibility of discovering the nature and activity of God and coming to meaning in wholeness. Ben Sira was responsible for the clearest argument that "the original creative act and *creatio continua* bear witness to the justice of God."[54] According to Ben Sira, God created all things in oppositional pairs.[55] Each pair consists of something valued and something worthless, something positive and something negative, something good and something evil. This dualism of good and evil is, for Ben Sira, at the basis of creation and operates under the impress of divine service to reward

---

51. Crenshaw, "Questioning of the Justice of God," 380–95; idem, "The Shift from Theodicy to Anthropodicy," *Theodicy in the Old Testament* (ed. James L. Crenshaw; Issues in Religion and Theology 4; Philadelphia: Fortress, 1983) 1–16; and idem, *A Whirlpool of Torment* (Philadelphia: Fortress, 1984).

52. James L. Crenshaw, "The Human Dilemma and Literature of Dissent," *Tradition and Theology in the Old Testament* (ed. Douglas A. Knight; Philadelphia: Fortress, 1974) 235–58.

53. Crenshaw argues that wisdom's open and honest efforts to construct a strategy to defend the justice of God led to the development of creation theology. He makes the following points: "(1) The threat of chaos in the cosmic, political, social realms evokes a response in terms of creation theology; (2) in wisdom thought, creation functions primarily as defense of divine justice; and (3) the centrality of the question of God's integrity in Israelite literature places creation theology at the center of the theological enterprise" ("Prolegomenon," 27).

54. Crenshaw, "Prolegomenon," 34.

55. James L. Crenshaw, "The Problem of Theodicy in Sirach," *JBL* 94 (1975) 47–64.

the good and punish the wicked. For Crenshaw, it is the failure of history by itself to support the doctrine of divine justice that calls forth the authenticity of wisdom's theological witness.[56]

THE DIALECTIC OF ANTHROPOLOGY AND COSMOLOGY

Gerhard von Rad's approach to the theology of creation in wisdom has continued to offer a balanced and incisive overview. For von Rad, the early sages focused their attention on the immediacy of human experience and the desire to master life.[57] This earliest expression of wisdom was gnomic in its literary form and experiential in its epistemology. In their observations, the early sages perceived a connection, consistency, and regularity, although this regularity was never shaped into an all-embracing order comparable to the Greek cosmos. The incomprehensible and the mysterious tended to defy human insight, making absolute clarity and epistemological certitude an impossibility. According to von Rad, the patterns of regularity and the contingencies that even the sage could not anticipate were both a part of the reality of human life.

Von Rad argued that it was only in a later, more mature stage of development that the sages reflected theologically on the nature of reality. This theological reflection, contends von Rad, ultimately resulted in the positing of a creator who not only originated and maintained all life but also was revealed by the "voice" of creation (Proverbs 9; Job 28; Sirach 24) to those who "feared God" and answered Wisdom's call.[58] Thus one has in the wisdom tradition a development from human experience to cosmology and from anthropology to theology. This move to creation theology paralleled the development in other traditions that gave this theme normative status no earlier than the sixth century B.C.E.

Von Rad later changed his evolutionary description of wisdom's development and contended that for the sages religious perceptions and rational understanding were not differentiated as separate activities in the effort to understand what was actually the same reality.[59] Indeed, for von Rad, to experience the world was also, to a certain extent, to experience God, not in a pantheistic sense, for the

---

56. For a critique of theodicy as having precedence over creation, see Perdue, *Wisdom in Revolt*.

57. Gerhard von Rad, "Die ältere Weisheit Israels," *KD* 2 (1956) 54–72 (=*Old Testament Theology* 1:418–41).

58. Von Rad, *Old Testament Theology*, 1:441–53.

59. Von Rad, *Wisdom in Israel*, 61.

mysterious God still transcended the world and human perception. However, the encounter with God still came within the moment of human experience and perception of the world.

Throughout his life, von Rad denied that the sages operated with a retributive system of justice. There was not a direct and necessary result from human actions that led to reward or punishment. Rather, for von Rad, "good" was neither a virtue nor a value; rather, it was a "power" or "blessing" that enhanced life.[60] Accordingly, divine freedom and the limitations of human knowledge were intangibles that made it impossible to assure success in human action. But this recognition also led to a positive openness to new experiences and understandings. In the final analysis, the sages trusted in divine grace and affirmed the value and goodness of life. Even when Job cannot, at least for a time, trust in the creator, God in the theophany demonstrates divine support and care for the sufferer. This leads Job confidently to place the destiny of the world in the hands of God, or so says von Rad.

Rainer Albertz and Peter Doll, two students of Claus Westermann, applied their teacher's analysis of the two major creation traditions in the Old Testament ("the creation of humans" and "the creation of the world") to Israel's wisdom literature.[61] Albertz examined Job, while Doll dealt with the remaining wisdom corpus. The first tradition speaks of God's creation of individuals and finds its form-critical location in the lament and its response in the oracle of salvation. The individuals remind God of the care taken to shape them and then beseech the creator to deliver them from their difficulty. In the thanksgiving, the broken relation between creator and creature is restored, and God is given grateful thanks. The motive is to create trust in the turning of God to deliver humans from catastrophe. Creation is not limited to a once-occurring action in the remote primordial past but is ever recurring in the conception and birth of new individuals through an event that is intimate and primal to human creatures. Further, the creation of the individual obligates God to a lifetime of support and care for the human creature. Creation and providence go hand in hand.[62]

60. Ibid., 80.

61. Peter Doll, *Menschenschöpfung und Weltschöpfung in der alttestamentlichen Weisheit* (Stuttgarter Bibelstudien 117; Stuttgart: Katholisches Bibelwerk, 1985); and Rainer Albertz, *Weltschöpfung und Menschenschöpfung* (Calwer Theologische Monographien, Reihe A: Bibelwissenschaft 3; Stuttgart: Calwer, 1974).

62. Albertz argues that the original form of the tradition was the creation of a

The second tradition, "the creation of the world," focuses on God as the creator of heaven and earth who continues to exert sovereignty over creation. The form-critical location for the tradition is the hymn that praises God's creative power and majestic place as the one who providentially governs the world in justice and love.

According to Doll, the older tradition, that of the creation of humanity, is found in the earlier strata of wisdom (Proverbs 10–29) and incorporates two themes: the creation of rich and poor, which emphasizes the responsibility of the well-to-do for the deprived, and the creation of organs of perception, which are the means to enable one to become wise. The social setting for these sayings is the agrarian village in which the exploitation of small farmers is opposed (cf. Amos). The tradition continues from the early period into the post-exile.

By contrast, the tradition of the creation of the world is embedded in the late stages of wisdom, including the poems in Proverbs 1–9 and Job 28, in which wisdom becomes a theological construct. Here the social setting moves from the royal school providing training for officials (the middle stage of the tradition) to the temple school. Wisdom and cult are closely related, and all wisdom moves within the sphere of religion ("the fear of God"). This move toward the world creation tradition involves not so much the praise of God as creator as it does the authentication of the wisdom tradition by placing its origins in "the beginning" and legitimating it as the way to the knowledge of creation and its orders. This development continues in Sirach (chaps. 1; 24) and in Baruch (3:9f.) with the increasing identification of wisdom with Torah. The confluence of both streams (cosmology and anthropology) occurs in Sirach, Baruch, and the Wisdom of Solomon, although the shift is from God's acts as creator of the world to a doctrine of predestination and theory of nature. Now nature is brought into the service of retribution to reward the righteous and punish the wicked.

In his examination of creation theology in Job, Albertz continues this separation of the two traditions.[63] In the dialogues, Job makes use of the tradition of the creation of the world in describing the frightening power of God as the majestic creator and ruler of the cosmos (Job 9:5-10). However, the function is not to praise, as is the case in the hymn, but to accuse God for lack of compassion and care

---

primeval man or humankind from which derived the specific formulation of the creation of the individual (*Weltschöpfung und Menschenschöpfung*, 81–87).

63. Albertz, *Weltschöpfung und Menschenschöpfung*, 132–50.

for creatures, including humans and especially Job. Job makes use of this tradition to emphasize the radical gulf separating a powerful, unresponsive God and weak, insignificant humanity. Job also refers to the creation of humanity (Job 10) in connection with the cosmic tradition in order to demonstrate the tension between the two. The normal intention of the anthropological tradition is to effectuate God's turning to the human creature who, in desperate circumstances, is in need of redemption. By contrast, Job uses the tradition to indict God for failing to turn toward him.

Job's friends use the creation of the world tradition in ways very different from Job's use. In Job 5:9 16, Eliphaz speaks of God's deliverance of the poor and deprived who turn to him. Eventually they are exalted, while the wicked are humbled. According to Albertz, Eliphaz uses the tradition in its typical fashion, at least in the beginning of the debate, to affirm the relationship of trust. Job should turn to God, who will graciously save. By the end of the dialogues, however, the situation is very different. Attributing Job 26:5-14 to Bildad, and placing the disputed section between 25:1-3 and 25:4-6, Albertz contrasts the incomprehensible power of God with weak and insignificant humanity. Therefore, how can a weak mortal like Job dare to call God into question? Unique is Bildad's combining the tradition of the creation of the world with the motif of the battle with chaos, normally found in laments, not hymnic praise. This use of the tradition is done to humiliate and put insignificant Job in his place. The use of the creation of humanity tradition is also distinct. Instead of using it to emphasize the compassion of God, Eliphaz underscores the radical distance between God and humanity (Job 4:17, 19; cf. 25:4—Bildad). Thus the relationship between humans and God, stressed in the penitential formulation of this tradition, is absent in the speeches of Job's friends.

The "Speeches of God" by contrast use only the tradition of the creation of the world. Arguing that the form is hymnic self-praise, Albertz contends that the tradition is used also for the purposes of debate, not simply for praise or instruction. Instead of the usual announcement of salvation by a priest to the one who has presented a lament, God comes in theophany to challenge Job to a war of words. The awe-inspiring presentation of the creation and rule of heaven and earth emphasizes the sovereignty of God. Even so, God's care for his creation, including wild and fearsome creatures, illustrates quite well divine compassion. Yet this is done not to establish trust between creator and creature but to demonstrate the unbridgeable gulf between the awesome God and insignificant humanity. God, not Job, nurtures creation. The theme of the chasm between God and humanity parallels that of the friends, but with one difference. God is not simply the frightening despotic power who exerts unchallenged rule but also the compassionate deity who cares for creation.

The later Elihu speeches (Job 32–37) make almost unparalleled use of the creation of humanity tradition. Its functions, however, are peculiar. On occasion Elihu uses the tradition to stress that he too is a human creature of God, just like Job and the friends, thereby legitimating his prerogative to speak and be heard. Elsewhere Elihu uses the personal relation between the creator and himself to emphasize that he must say what is acceptable to God. The tradition of the creation of the world is also significantly present in Elihu's speeches. But he uses the tradition both to humiliate Job as an insignificant mortal and to point to God's use of nature, especially meteorological elements, to punish and reward. What one has in Elihu's speeches is a more abstract depiction of creation, more descriptive of the phenomena of nature than was the case earlier.

Finally, Roland Murphy's presidential address before the Society of Biblical Literature approaches the understanding of wisdom's creation theology under the principle of anthropology and cosmology. For Murphy, creation is not a "strange" theological tradition that is secondary to salvation history and therefore must be ingenuously brought within authentic Israelite religion. Indeed, Israel made no separation between creation and redemption, but had a legitimate place for both within the articulation of its faith. In describing the "wisdom experience," Murphy stressed that there is no radical difference between faith and reason for the sages, for they believed that their experience of the world in its many facets was also, to some extent, an experience of God. Wisdom is comprised not only of admonitions and human insight but also of both "an attitude" and "a dialogue with the created world."[64] This dialogue is made possible because creation speaks a language open to human understanding, an understanding that recognized that the revelation of God comes through the language of creation. According to

---

64. Roland E. Murphy, "Wisdom and Creation," 6. Murphy is critical of the concept "world-order" as appropriate for understanding wisdom's approach to creation. Certainly there is regularity in creation and experience, but the image of the wooing and even marriage of Woman Wisdom mitigates against any rather sterile, systematic conception like order (p. 9).

Murphy, Woman Wisdom is none other than the voice of God calling creatures to experience the gift of life in all of its fullness. For Israel, there was no distinction between rational and revealed revelation. In its experience of the world, Israel came to know God, although only imperfectly.

CREATION THEOLOGY IN JEREMIAH

Presentations of the theology of Jeremiah have focused largely on salvation history and divine judgment, the Mosaic covenant as the basis for punishment and hope, and the pathos of God and prophet. However, theologies of this prophetic book pay little attention, if any, to the importance of creation. While the following cursory outline is only suggestive, three significant features of creation theology in Jeremiah will be highlighted. Although they are closely related, it is heuristically useful to describe them separately. These features include the dialectic of creation and history, the creation and destiny of the individual, and wisdom and creation.

Creation theology is prominent in the poetic oracles of Jeremiah (source A) that represent the layer of tradition that is judged by many to be the closest to the historical prophet. The Deuteronomic redaction (both narratives and prose speeches) generally ignores creation, except for its serving as a thematic prolegomenon to Yahweh's acts of salvation. Later poetic additions—for example, those embedded within the "Oracles against the Nations" in Jeremiah 46–51—make limited use of creation theology, particularly the chaos tradition, developing within burgeoning prophetic eschatology during the postexilic period.[65]

The Dialectic of Creation and History

Among the poetic oracles in Jeremiah 1–25 (source A) is a collection of judgment speeches that depicts the coming of the "foe from the north": 4:5-31; 5:1-9; 5:10-17; 5:20-31; 6:1-8; 6:9-15; 6:16-30; 8:4-13; 8:14—9:11; 9:17-22; 10:17-25. The enemy comes from the north and a distant land, speaks a foreign tongue, is an "ancient" and "enduring" nation, has great warriors, is merciless, attacks unexpectedly and with boldness, rides on swift horses and chariots, is

---

65. For an introduction to the various creation traditions and their dominant metaphors, see Perdue, *Wisdom in Revolt*. The root metaphors are battle (the myth of conflict between the god of creation and order and the god of chaos or death), fertility, word, and artistry.

armed with bows and spears, and uses battle formations. While this enemy is undoubtedly a historical foe in Jeremiah's own poetic speeches (source A), the identity is not made explicit except in the later prose redaction (see Jeremiah 25 and 36). Unless one chooses to regard the foe as Scythians belonging to an Assyrian alliance, there is no real alternative to Jeremiah's viewing the foe as the Babylonians. The dialectic of creation and history is present in two related ways: the use of the mythical language of the battle with chaos in the description of the destruction this invasion brings, not simply to Judah, but to the entire cosmos; and the borrowing of elements of the theophanic hymn in which Yahweh, as sovereign Lord, does battle with chaos to reestablish rule over the earth.[66]

The tradition of the "foe from the north" is replete with images of chaos in describing the destruction wrought by the enemy. Their destruction leaves the land and its cities devastated, without human habitation (Jer 4:7, 23-26, 29; 6:8; 9:11; 10:22, 25). Perhaps the most shocking and yet captivating depicting of the enemy's devastation as the return of creation to primordial chaos is found in Jer 4:23-26. Drawing especially on Genesis 1-2, the cosmos, following the enemy's invasion, is described as tōhû wā-bōhû, "without form and void" (Gen 1:2), while the heavens are without light (Gen 1:3-5; see Jer 13:16). After the destruction, there "was no 'ādām (human)" (see Gen 2:5), and the birds of the air had fled (see Gen 1:20-21).[67] The land, which had been fruitful (see Gen 1:11-12), became a desert (see Gen 2:5). This poem also draws on the chaos tradition's description of the "quaking" (rā'aš) of the cosmos, in this case the hills and mountains (cf. Judg 5:4; Ps 18:8).[68] Even so, this return to chaos is not due to the power of the invading enemy; rather, it results from the fierce anger of Yahweh (Jer 4:26).

The theophanic tradition is grounded in the mythical depiction of the battle of Yahweh with the chaos monster for rulership of the earth. Following the primeval victory, Yahweh creates and orders the world, and keeps chaos at bay. In one of the oracles concerning the "foe from the north," Yahweh speaks of his power in sustaining creation by mentioning his containment of Yam ("Sea"), the chaos monster who rules the waters, by the formation of sand barriers or

---

66. For a discussion of the myth of the battle with chaos, see Perdue, *Wisdom in Revolt*, 47–56.

67. In a subsequent text (Jer 9:9), the cattle and the beasts are gone (cf. Gen 1:24-25). Only the jackals remain to inhabit the ruins of former cities (Jer 9:10; 10:22).

68. See Brevard Childs, "The Enemy from the North and the Chaos Tradition," *JBL* 78 (1959) 187–98.

beaches (Jer 5:22; see Job 38:8-11; Ps 104:6-9; Isa 51:9-10). In subsequent battles, usually occurring on a cyclical basis each New Year's, Yahweh's defeat of chaos brings new vitality to creation. In poetic imagination, which stimulates Jeremiah's own envisioning of reality, historical enemies embody this mythical challenge to Yahweh's rule. Only, in a dramatic twist, it is Yahweh who unleashes this enemy, or incarnate chaos, to bring judgment to the apostate nation of Judah and the cosmos. Instead of defeating the threatening enemy, Yahweh now sustains and aids them, and their victory results, at least in poetic imagination, in the return of the cosmos to chaos, especially depicted as an uninhabited waste devoid of life and in particular human habitation.

Jeremiah's contention that the judgment of devastation against the disobedient nation results in the cataclysmic upheaval of nature is obvious hyperbole. Even so, it underscores both the prophet's faith in Yahweh's sovereignty over cosmos and history and his argument that Judah's denigration of covenant existence lays waste to God's good creation. For Jeremiah, Judah's covenant with Yahweh entails more than a relationship built on historical destiny in which the chosen, because of their faithfulness and justice, would be not only the most favored among the nations but also the instrument by which other peoples would be blessed by glorying in the creator of heaven and earth (see Jer 4:1-3). This covenant also binds the nation with the creator and sustainer of all life. Jeremiah's is truly a universal vision. Judah's loyalty to covenant and faithfulness to Yahweh would lead to the well-being of all creation and of all life. The people's recalcitrance, by contrast, leads to the savagery of war and empire building that results in cruel destruction and not the blessing of life grounded in the glory of Yahweh. Their transgressions against justice and covenant loyalty result in the return of God's good creation to the oblivion of chaos.

In addition to judgment, creation theology plays an important role in the prophet's theology of hope and future salvation. In looking to the past, Jeremiah remarked that Israel's birth in the event of the exodus was indeed an act of creation. The liberated people moved through the wilderness, described in the language of chaos, before entering into the good land of promise (Jer 2:6-7). In speaking of future salvation, grounded in a theology of hope, Jeremiah speaks of a return home in which not only the nation would be recreated but creation itself would be renewed (see Jeremiah 30–33, the Book of Consolation). The exiles will return home, Israel and Judah will be reunited, a new covenant between the chosen and

God will be established, the law will be inscribed upon the human heart, and the land will once again be inhabited and fruitful. Creation theology figures prominently in this collection of salvation oracles and is expressed not only by reference to the mythic battle with chaos and the theophanic tradition but also by the pronouncement of prophetic word and confessional response. In speaking eschatologically, more is intended than a tentative wish for the future. Rather, the power of prophetic language, grounded in the Word of Yahweh, speaks reality into existence. In the confessional response, both by prophet and then by people, the community not only affirms but participates in the drama of eschatological hope.[69]

The theophanic tradition depicting the Divine Warrior going forth to battle the wicked is once again present, signifying the mythical triumph of God over chaos and evil as the new order of salvation is instituted (Jer 30:23-24). The covenant is not simply limited to Yahweh and reunited Israel and Judah but is extended to all living things, both human and animal (Jer 31:27-28). Yahweh promises that the perpetuity of redeemed Israel's existence and ongoing covenantal relationship are grounded in the very order and stability of creation that derive from his divine power (Jer 31:35-36). Israel's descendants would cease to be, only if the expanse of heaven and earth could be measured and its unfathomable mystery open to understanding (Jer 31:37).

In the confessional response, expressed in the prayer of the prophet, following his purchase of his cousin's land, Jeremiah begins his recounting of Israel's sacred history and fall from grace with a hymnic address of the Lord God "who made the heavens and the earth by your great power and by your outstretched arm" (Jer 32:17). Jeremiah 33 continues in this same vein when Jeremiah, shut up in the court of the guard, refers to Yahweh as the one who created the earth (33:2). This same creator will one day forgive his people and will bless them with such goodness that the nations will come to fear him. The desolated and uninhabited wasteland will again flourish, and the "captivity of the earth" (33:11, not simply the land of Israel) will be restored. With Israel's defeat by the Babylonians, the creator has accompanied the exiles into captivity. But in a future deliverance, Israel's redemption is to be but a part of the greater liberation of the cosmos. Jeremiah's own confessional re-

---

69. For a discussion of "word" as a root metaphor in creation theology, see Perdue, *Wisdom in Revolt*, 42–46.

sponse, as a function of prophetic mediation and representation, becomes the voice of a hopeful people who praise Yahweh for his redemptive acts, admit their sins, and anticipate the joy of new resurrection.

The use of mythical language to describe the destruction and salvation of Israel and Judah is more than just poetic redescription of historical event, demythologization of myth, or mythologization of a historical tradition. Indeed, the use of mythical imagery involves these things. But it is far more. Theologically conceived, Yahweh is both the creator of heaven and earth and the sovereign Lord of history who guides human affairs, even bringing destruction, at least for a time, to the chosen people. The dichotomy between creation and history, while heuristically useful in describing Jeremiah's understanding of God, leads to serious misunderstanding, if the two dimensions of divine lordship and activity are placed in opposition, or if history is given priority. It is because Yahweh is creator that he expresses his divine sovereignty over history. Yahweh's covenant with and through Israel binds him, not only to all other peoples, but also to the entirety of all creation.

Finally, in the "Oracles against the Nations" (Jer 25:13-38; chaps. 46–51), one finds once more creation language. The introduction in 25:13-38 depicts the Divine Warrior rising up to do battle with the wicked and oppressive nations of the earth, demonstrating his sovereignty and reclaiming his kingship. One should especially note that in the oracles against Babylon (chaps. 50–51) creation becomes a cosmic choir that with one voice sings at the rise of destroyers from the north who will devastate Babylon (51:48). Now the chaos tradition is used to describe the eschatological defeat of Babylon, with heaven and earth serving as a heavenly choir rejoicing at the fall of the earthly tyrant.

Another mythical tradition of creation centers on fertility as the divine potency that leads to the producing of new life and the revitalization of old existence.[70] However, in his calling forth this mythical language, the prophet once again combines it with Israel's salvation history, following the lead of an earlier northern prophet, Hosea. Like Hosea, Jeremiah speaks of Israel's primal relationship in Egypt and the wilderness, prior to the entrance into Canaan, in images of courtship and marriage (Jer 2:1-3). Even as the marriage of a fertility god and his royal consort (e.g., Baal and Anat) led to the revitalization of the powers of fructification and productivity for

70. Perdue, *Wisdom in Revolt*, 32–38.

soil and people, so Israel and its sacred land, with the consummation of its marriage with Yahweh, were the "first fruits," that is, the first and best of the harvest, dedicated to sacred possession (Jer 2:3). Also following Hosea (see Hosea 2), Israel's yoking herself in unholy union with false gods and faithless national suitors led to divorce (Jer 3:1—4:4). Israel behaved like a faithless wife, and her religious and political apostasy led to the pollution of the land (cf. 23:10), the withholding of rain (3:2-3), and the decree of divorce (3:12-13). This violation of the sacred marriage covenant defiled the land (2:7-8) and led to its sterility.

The same imagery is used in the important poem located in Jer 31:15-22 that contrasts the nation's despairing present with its hopeful future. In the opening of the poem, the voice of a dead Rachel is heard weeping over her children who are no more. This ancestral mother of Joseph (the father of Ephraim and Manasseh) and Benjamin cannot be comforted, for her children (the Israelites) have perished in the Assyrian holocaust. Yet the conclusion of the poem indicates that in the future restoration, "Yahweh creates something new": faithless daughter Israel will "enfold" *(tĕsôbēb)* a man.[71] Here the prophet promises that Israel will have posterity to continue into the future. The new creation is Yahweh's proleptic gift of a hopeful future.

The covenant lawsuit (Jeremiah 2 and 3) borrows language from divorce proceedings and becomes the official means for moving to terminate the relationship between Yahweh and Israel. In these divorce proceedings, creation is called upon as a witness. However, Yahweh goes beyond the letter of the law of divorce to offer to take back a repentant Israel as covenant partner (chap. 3).

THE CREATION AND DESTINY OF HUMANITY

As Claus Westermann and Peter Doll have noted, two creation traditions are present in the Hebrew Bible and the mythology of other ancient Near Eastern cultures: the creation of humanity and the creation of the cosmos. While the difference between the creation of humanity and of the cosmos has been too sharply drawn,

---

71. For a discussion of the meaning of this controversial verse, see Bernhard W. Anderson, "The Lord Has Created Something New": A Stylistic Study of Jer 31:15–22," *CBQ* 40 (1978) 463–78. The interpretation of giving birth makes proper sense in a poem in which the initial strophe speaks of a deceased mother weeping over her dead children. Thus, the poem moves from death (exile) to life or birth (return from exile and new posterity).

this dichotomy remains a useful heuristic device for getting at the creation traditions of the Hebrew Bible, including Jeremiah.[72]

The most prominent use of the tradition of the creation of humanity occurs in the call of Jeremiah (1:4-10). At the heart of this tradition are two metaphors that describe humanity's nature and role in the cosmos: king and slave. Several biblical texts speak of human existence in royal terms, particularly the Priestly narrative in Gen 1:1—2:4a and Psalm 8. Here humans represent divine sovereignty in ruling over the cosmos. Other biblical texts describe humanity as slaves who are created to carry out the wishes and decrees of Yahweh and the divine council (see the Yahwist's account of creation in Gen 2:4b-25 and the Book of Job). These texts draw on the Mesopotamian understanding of humanity's role and place in the cosmos, an understanding in which even kings are slaves of the gods.

Central to the call of Jeremiah is the language of Yahweh shaping him in the womb and, even before birth, predestining him to serve as a "prophet to the nations." This compares to a variety of creation texts in which Yahweh is seen as the father, mother, and midwife who shapes the fetus in the womb, aids in the birthing process, and then shapes the destiny of the newborn (see Job 10 and Psalm 139). In spite of the protest of Jeremiah, Yahweh's will prevails. Royal language is found in Jer 1:10 when Yahweh announces to Jeremiah that he is being "set this day over nations and over kingdoms" (cf. the coronation psalms, Psalms 2 and 110). By means of the power and authority of the prophetic word, Jeremiah will indeed rule over nations and kingdoms, determining their destiny. In a fashion consistent with other examples of entwining creation and history, Jeremiah's life and destiny are enfolded in the creation and history of the nation. This striking case of Yahweh's creating and predestining Jeremiah while in the womb is countered by the final "confession" (Jer 20:14-18) in which the prophet, in Joban despair, if not defiance, curses his birth, wishing that he had died in the womb. This is the most provocative example of Jeremiah's rejection, at least temporarily, of his divine destiny.

Jeremiah also draws on the tradition of the creation of humanity in portraying the birth and destiny of the chosen people. The judgment against Israel in Jeremiah 2 is, in part, described as unfaithful

---

72. For a discussion of the tradition of the creation of humanity and its two root metaphors of king and slave, see Perdue, *Wisdom in Revolt*, 61–72.

children who regard fertility gods, not Yahweh, as their parent. This apostasy occurs in spite of Israel's status as the favored son (Jer 3:14, 19; 31:9, 20; cf. Joseph in Genesis 37–50). As noted above, birth imagery is used to describe Yahweh's "new creation," that is, the giving to the nation a posterity who will continue into the future.

WISDOM AND CREATION

Before Ben Sira in the early second century B.C.E., Israel's wisdom literature looks to creation, not to salvation history, as its theological center.[73] Indeed, salvation history is absent in Job, Proverbs, the Wisdom Psalms, and Qoheleth. The impact that wisdom had on the prophet Jeremiah and the later Jeremianic tradition bearers has not yet been explicated in any detailed fashion.[74] However, there are texts that point to wisdom's influence either on Jeremiah's own presentation of creation theology or on his later redactors.

The sages' affirmation of the existence of a just and life-giving cosmic order, established by God at creation and sustained by divine wisdom, is at the basis of Jeremiah's judgment oracle concerning the "foe from the north" and his conflict with the "wise" (in this context political counselors and interpreters of the law) in Jer 8:4-13. The sages thought that individual and corporate wise behavior, that was in line with cosmic order, led to well-being. Cosmic order had to do with both continuity and regularity as well as justice and righteousness. And although the cultivation of wisdom and insight allowed the sages some understanding of order, mystery as well as contingency were given their due in the quest for understanding.

In contrasting Judah's obstinate refusal to repent, Jeremiah makes use of two rhetorical questions (a common wisdom form) in 8:4 to indicate how irrational their behavior is when compared to normal, intelligent ways of acting. Further on, in the same oracle (8:7), Jeremiah contrasts birds' instinctive knowledge of migration

---

73. See Perdue, *Wisdom and Creation*; and idem, "Cosmology and the Social Order in the Wisdom Tradition," *The Sage in Israel and the Ancient Near East* (ed. John G. Gammie and Leo G. Perdue; Winona Lake, Ind.: Eisenbrauns, 1990) 457–78.

74. For the best treatments, see Raymond van Leeuwen, "The Sage in the Prophetic Literature," Gammie and Perdue, *The Sage in Israel and the Ancient Near East*, 303–6; and his essay on the understanding of wisdom in prophetic literature in *In Search of Wisdom: Essays in Memory of John G. Gammie* (ed. Leo G. Perdue, Brandon B. Scott, and William J. Wiseman; Louisville, Ky.: Westminster/John Knox, 1993).

in following seasonal changes with the people's ignorance of divine instruction (believed to be contained in the teaching of the wise and in law codes produced by lawyers and judges trained in the wisdom tradition). Even worse, those entrusted with wisdom and law, the sages, have falsified Yahweh's instruction and discipline for life. It was the responsibility of the sages to teach the people knowledge of God and to counsel the king wisely and judiciously. This "counsel" was to result in well-being and "peace" *(šālôm),* but it has led instead to ignorance, obstinacy, and a rejection of the prophetic word (see 18:18).[75] It is this lack of knowledge, grounded in willful disobedience and disregard for the life-giving and just teaching of Yahweh, that leads to the coming judgment.

Jeremiah's idol satire in 10:1-16 also borrows from wisdom's theology of creation. As von Rad has noted, idol satires are a part of the wisdom tradition especially in the Wisdom of Solomon where idolatry is condemned, not as a violation of commandments against idol making, but as an example of irrational and foolish behavior.[76] Idolatry is satirized in several ways by Jeremiah. Idols have human origins, are stupid pieces of wood that cannot offer life-giving instruction, are impotent, cannot move or speak, and cannot do good or evil. Most significant is the contrast with Yahweh who is the creator of heaven and earth and who originated and sustains the cosmos by his wisdom (10:12-16; see 51:15-29). This section affirms not only that God is creator and sustainer, in contrast to impotent and stupid idols, but also that he has chosen Jacob as his inheritance (10:16). Once more, Jeremiah combines creation theology with Israel's election.

Wisdom's theology of creation is not only used by the prophet in the formulation of his oracles of judgment. As noted above, when Jeremiah envisions a new future for Israel and Judah, he grounds that approaching reality in the order, mystery, and unlimited expanse of creation. The regularity, continuation, and expanse of creation serve as God's guarantee that Israel will have a future (31:35-37).

In addition to a theology of creation that deals with cosmic order, the sages also speak of Yahweh's creation of humanity in general and the individual in particular. Of special interest to the anthropology of the sages was the notion that Yahweh knows the heart

---

75. For a discussion of the prophet's conflict with the wise, see William McKane, *Prophets and Wise Men* (2d ed.; London: SCM, 1983).
76. Von Rad, *Wisdom in Israel,* 177–86.

(i.e., mind) of human beings. This theology of creation, à la the sages, is found in a wisdom collection of diverse materials in Jer 17: 5-11. Verses 5-8 contain a wisdom poem of two strophes, strikingly similar to Psalm 1, that contrasts the destruction that comes to the wicked man with the blessing that enhances the well-being of the god-fearer. More to the point of creation, however, are the rhetorical question and the saying concerning the human heart in 17:9. Pessimistic in the statement that the human heart is corrupt and deceitful (cf. Qoheleth), Yahweh is represented as the one who "searches the heart and knows the mind" and thus as the one who distributes just desserts to each person (17:9-10).

CONCLUDING EVALUATION

The attention given to creation has led to the rethinking of both critical methodology and the presentation of Old Testament theology. In order to access the richness of creation theology in the Old Testament, a variety of methods within cultural anthropology have been used, resulting in very important insights. In addition, what the Bible shares with its culture becomes more obvious, as the mythical traditions of the ancient Near East are recognized as important resources for the Old Testament's expression of creation theology.

Theological discourse also takes a new shape, or perhaps returns to an earlier form, since the construct of history and a sole reliance on historical criticism usually point out the pluralities of theological understandings within the Old Testament and arrange them within a sequential or linear development. Once again, a theme (in this case creation, not covenant) that yields itself more easily to systematic treatment reshapes the way the theology of the Old Testament is presented. And a systematic presentation lends itself more easily to conversation with contemporary theology.

Of course, the potential danger resulting from the attention given to creation is to break its fundamental connection to history and therefore another important feature of providence. A balanced presentation notes that creation and history are both significant theological constructs in the Old Testament, even though one book or tradition may ignore or limit its interest in one or the other. This is why Brevard Childs's emphasis on the canon provides an important corrective to one-sided efforts to select a "canon within a canon" and to articulate a theology that is not inclusive of the theological dimensions of the entire Old Testament. We now turn to consider Childs's contribution to the ongoing debate.

PART THREE

Old Testament Theology: Scripture and Metaphor

CHAPTER 6

From History to Scripture:
Canon and Community

The dominance of the historical paradigm, as both method and theme, for approaching Old Testament theology in the generation immediately following World War II began to be questioned in the 1960s with the appearance of a variety of new issues and approaches. Interest in creation, along with the various methods used in its presentation, did not lead to an alternative to history and historical criticism, but it did produce a more balanced view: history and creation (along with the various methods for accessing them) were the two important poles of Old Testament theology.

Recent years have witnessed a second new direction in Old Testament theology: the move from history to text. This direction, in its various forms, has produced at times what are considered to be alternatives to history and historical criticism. This direction in biblical study is concerned, not with the history of events residing behind the text or with developing traditions that eventuated in the present canon; rather, it is concerned with the character, structure, composition, content, and theological status of the text itself. In approaching the text, scholars have followed two quite different paths. One path is taken by Brevard Childs who regards the Old Testament as Scripture; another path has been traveled by those scholars who interpret the Bible as literature by using a great variety of literary methods. What the two approaches share is a common affirmation that meaning is primarily located not in the mind of the author or in how the original audience may have understood what was written or said but in the boundaries of the text itself. And some literary approaches, especially New Criticism, emphasize with Childs's canonical approach that the original historical setting of the text, even if it may be recovered, does not contribute in important ways to the meaning of the text. Instead, the text means by construing its own reality.[1]

At this point, caution is in order. One should avoid making rather bold claims for a paradigm shift that places history and literature or history and Scripture into oppositional, either/or categories or that consigns historical criticism to the graveyard of methodological relics.[2] It may be somewhat imperious to argue that newer methods have superseded or rendered passé earlier ones. Indeed, analysis of language and literary examination, as well as the theological status of the text as Scripture, are important to the overall interpretative enterprise in that they raise and then seek to answer at times rather different questions than those posed by historical critics. In addition, regardless of claims to the contrary more recent approaches invariably make use of older methods in pursuing answers to their questions, even as older methods draw from the insights of newer ones.

Nevertheless analytical dichotomies are necessary for critical inquiry, before serious reflection may lead to understanding. Thus it is useful to focus on the distinctive features of new methods, not only in order to understand their ways of proceeding and their particular nuances, but also to distinguish them from earlier approaches. To contend that this movement from history to text portends a major paradigm shift in the way Old Testament study in general and Old Testament theology in particular are to be done is one thing. To say that this movement replaces history and historical criticism is another, much more questionable assertion. Certainly, the tyranny of positivistic history is now at an end, and its domination of the theological enterprise among Old Testament scholarship has been questioned sufficiently enough to allow, not only for other philosophies of history (e.g., feminism or neo-Marxism) to make their contributions, but also for quite different methodologies to develop and be applied. Significant change is now under way, opening up some very exciting possibilities for Old Testament the-

---

1. Brevard Childs (*Introduction to the Old Testament as Scripture* [Philadelphia: Fortress, 1979] 74) makes some important distinctions between newer literary methods and his own approach. But, in spite of his protests against the comparison, there are significant similarities.

2. Walter Wink's arguments concerning the hermeneutical demise of historical criticism are greatly exaggerated and distorted *(The Bible in Human Transformation).* See the more balanced assessment by Rolf Rendtorff, "Between Historical Criticism and Holistic Interpretation: New Trends in Old Testament Exegesis," *SVT* 40 (1988) 298–303.

ology. One example of these is represented by the work of Brevard Childs.

THE CANONICAL APPROACH: BREVARD CHILDS

THE THEOLOGICAL BANKRUPTCY OF HISTORICAL CRITICISM

In his *Introduction to the Old Testament as Scripture*, Brevard Childs[3] pronounced the historical-critical method to be theologically bankrupt.[4] The reason, for Childs, is simple: it does not lead, in his estimation, to Old Testament theology, much less to biblical theology and then to hermeneutics in the form of constructive and normative theology for the confessing church. For Childs, an appropriate approach to the Old Testament recognizes that its books are intrinsically theological and, for believing communities, in some fashion authoritative.

3. A helpful assessment of Childs's work is made by Mark G. Brett, *Biblical Theology in Crisis?* (Cambridge: Cambridge University Press, 1991). Theologically, Childs is a Barthian and a Presbyterian. Hence, he largely continues the theological emphases of neoorthodoxy. Childs's postcritical approach to biblical interpretation and particularly Old Testament theology, and his assault on the limits of historical criticism, have developed under two influences: Barth's criticism of exegesis as a historical-critical approach and the postmodern criticism of modernism's grounding in the rationalism of the Enlightenment.

4. Childs, *Introduction to the Old Testament as Scripture* (also see his "Interpretation in Faith," *Int* 18 [1964] 432–49). Childs offers a communal lament on behalf of many scholars who have often expressed their dismay at the difficulty in moving from historical criticism to Old Testament theology, much more to contemporary theology, thereby affirming the reality of Lessing's "ugly ditch" separating historical inquiry from theological articulation. Other important works by Childs include "The Exegetical Significance of Canon," *SVT* 29 (1977) 66–88; "The Sensus Literalis of Scripture: An Ancient and Modern Problem," *Beiträge zur alttestamentlichen Theologie* (FS Walther Zimmerli; ed. H. Donner et al.; Göttingen: Vandenhoeck & Ruprecht, 1977) 80–93; "Some Reflections on the Search for a Biblical Theology," *HBT* 4 (1982) 1–12; *The New Testament as Canon: An Introduction* (Philadelphia: Fortress, 1985); *Old Testament Theology in a Canonical Context* (Philadelphia: Fortress, 1985); "Die Bedeutung des jüdischen Kanons in der alttestamentlichen Theologie," *Mitte der Schrift? Ein jüdisch-christliches Gespräch* (ed. M. Klopfenstein et al.; Bern: Peter Lang, 1987) 265–81; "Die theologische Bedeutung der Endform eines biblischen Textes," *TQ* 167 (1987) 242–51; "Biblische Theologie und der christliche Kanon," *Jahrbuch für biblische Theologie* 3 (1988) 13–27; and *Biblical Theology of the Old and New Testaments: Theological Reflection on the Christian Bible* (Minneapolis: Fortress, 1993). For a series of critical responses to Childs, see the essays by Bonnie Kittel, James Barr, Joseph Blenkinsopp, Henri Cazelles, George Landes, Roland Murphy, and Rudolf Smend, followed by Childs's reactions to his critics in *JSOT* 16 (1980) 2–60. Also see *HBT* 2 (1980) 117–211 for essays by James Sanders, James Mays, Douglas Knight, Bruce Birch, and David Polk, followed by Childs's response; and the essays in the collection edited by George Coats and Burke Long *(Canon and Authority: Essays in Old Testament Religion and Theology* [Philadelphia: Fortress, 1977]).

For Childs, historical criticism has mistakenly approached these texts as being primarily ancient documents containing information about Israelite religion and social history. They indeed may be historical documents, but, more important, for the church they are theological texts. If the texts are locked in the past and therefore decanonized as authoritative Scripture, then it is not possible to move to theological analysis and appropriation by later communities of faith. Thus the interpretative efforts of historical criticism are not appropriate for theological exegesis.[5]

Historical criticism, in Childs's view, also has failed theologically because of three key omissions: first, it has ignored the canonical form of the text that bears the authority and normative value of Scripture given it by the community of faith;[6] second, historical criticism has failed to understand the "canonical process" that eventually construed the final shape of Old Testament books; and third, historical criticism has tended to ignore the creative dynamic operating between sacred books and the communities that not only produced them but also came to honor them as normative and authoritative. In general, Childs argues that this threefold failure has resulted from an overriding concern by scholars either to reconstruct the history behind the text or to trace the growth of traditions within the biblical corpus, instead of comprehending the theological questions that produced the canon.

While Childs does have some rather harsh words to say about historical criticism, he does not regard the approach as a useless or outdated configuration of methods. It is clear that he often uses its tools in pointing to the canonical process at work in the religious community and in analyzing the canonical form of the final text. However, he indicates that the method often does not lead to an appreciation for and understanding of the theology of the text. Indeed, he incriminates some practitioners of the method for even using historical and sociological arguments to oppose the theological and scriptural character of the biblical text. In the place of historical criticism, he offers what he considers to be a postcritical, canonical approach to Scripture, biblical theology, and hermeneutics.[7]

5. Childs, "Interpretation in Faith," 440: "Theological exegesis is a disciplined method of research fully commensurate with its material."
6. It should be noted here that while Childs acknowledges that he makes some distinction between "Scripture" and "canon," a clear differentiation is not obvious.
7. See Childs, *Introduction to the Old Testament as Scripture*, 69–83, for the description of his methodology.

INTRODUCTION TO THE OLD TESTAMENT AS SCRIPTURE
AND THE CANONICAL APPROACH

In essence, Childs makes two fundamental assertions that reside at the basis of his approach. First, the canon, not history, is the proper and primary context for interpretation. This means, among other things, that the interpretation of a single text occurs within the entire canon. Second, Childs argues that the Old Testament is a normative, authoritative collection of texts that is intrinsically theological. This means that the texts were intentionally shaped by communities of faith to address a Word of God to future generations. Any appropriate method for interpretation, for Childs, must begin by acknowledging these two fundamental assertions.

Childs contends that any proper understanding of canon must take into account both its historical and theological dimensions. The development of a canon consciousness, that is, an awareness of the authority of certain sacred writings for faith and practice, developed, in Childs's estimation, quite early in Israel's historical existence (Deut 31:24f.; 2 Kings 22; the law of Ezra; Isa 8:16; Jeremiah 36). The canonical status of Torah and the prophets is well attested by Ben Sira (second century B.C.E.), while the writings achieved final canonical status by the beginning of the common era as indicated by the stabilization of the consonantal Hebrew text. Childs admits that the historical-critical method can help us retrace fragments of the historical development of canon, but this is not his major concern. Rather, he wants to demonstrate that a canonical process was at work, although only recoverable in part, throughout the growth of the Bible. In other words, people standing within communities of faith were actively at work to shape sacred texts that would address not only themselves but also later generations.[8] This canonical process involved the slow development of texts and traditions, beginning in the early preexilic period and concluding in the synagogue during the Hellenistic period.[9]

---

8. Mays, "What Is Written," 155: "Because canon as Childs defines it involves a unity of the historical and the theological, he is convinced it can be employed as a context and stance which overcomes the established tension between canon and criticism and will establish an approach to the Old Testament as scripture which makes a full and consistent use of the historical study."

9. Childs notes that at times the canonical form of the text enables it to transcend its historical setting, while at other times, the canonical context works historical material into its very core and makes full use of a public witness to common historical reality. He adds, "The canonical process is, in no way, divorced from the historical process in my view, but the two processes retain their own integrity and are not to be fused" ("A Response," *HBT* 2 (1980) 204).

Even more important to Childs is the theological dimension of canon. He stresses that the formation of the canon is a process of theological reflection within Israel, a reflection that derived from the impact that certain writings had upon the community of faith, especially in the context of religious use. The concern of the shapers of the canon was to create a formulation of the divine word that would lay authoritative claim upon successive generations who had not participated in the events and circumstances of the original revelation. Childs does not doubt that there were "events" that resided behind traditions of faith, although he is skeptical that these often can be successfully reconstructed. Indeed, he is openly critical of scholarship for producing much that is hypothetical and little that is certain in historical matters. Besides, it is the Word contained within the canonical text for Childs that is revelatory, not the particularities of the historical and social circumstances that may have influenced those authors, tradents, and editors who produced the tradition over many years.

How, then, does Childs suggest we interpret the text? The major features of the canonical approach to the Old Testament include the following. First, the essential task is descriptive, that is, the interpreter attempts to understand the particular shape and function of individual books in the Hebrew canon. It is a formalist concern with final shape. Second, the interpreter concentrates on the final form of the text instead of attempting to reconstruct the historical stages of a book's development. Childs concedes that it is probable that the earlier stages of a book were considered authoritative at one time by certain groups, and yet, once canonization occurred, it is only the final form that continues to exercise authority for ongoing communities of faith. Earlier traditions and sources, even if they may be successfully isolated, are not authoritative once the canonical process was completed and the consonants of the Hebrew text stabilized in the first century C.E. Third, the canonical approach takes seriously the community of faith and practice that not only shaped the sacred literature but was itself shaped by it. The community to which Childs refers is not the historical society of ancient Israel that developed and changed over the years but more a collective group of people who together made decisions regarding selection and canonical shape over the centuries.[10] The appropriate successors of this general collective community are communities of

10. Brett calls this a "hermeneutics of consent" (*Biblical Theology in Crisis?* 98).

believers who regard the Old Testament as authoritative for life and faith even after the canon had been completed.[11]

THE CANON AND OLD TESTAMENT THEOLOGY: PRELIMINARY CONSIDERATIONS

In *Old Testament Theology in a Canonical Context*, Childs applies the canonical approach of his earlier *Introduction* specifically to the task of doing Old Testament theology.[12] It is here that one may determine whether Childs's claims about the theological value of the method in his *Introduction* do indeed bear fruit.

He begins with what are now the familiar arguments heard before in his earlier introduction. Once again he asserts that earlier approaches, in this case theological ones, have only led to conflicting depictions and fragmented results. These include even the great classics of Eichrodt and von Rad. The root cause of these problems is the disagreement about how theological reflection relates to historical criticism. Hence, he argues that "a canonical approach to the Scriptures of the Old Testament opens up a fruitful avenue along which to explore the theological dimension of the biblical text."[13] Childs then surveys the development of Old Testament theology as a discipline and notes the continuing problems for which we need fresh solutions: the tension between *religionsgeschichtliche* and theological tasks, coherence/unity, the history of interpretation, and the relation of Old Testament theology to Judaism and Christianity. In presenting his own Old Testament theology, Childs thinks not only that these problems of methodology will be addressed and answered but also that the Hebrew canon may be allowed a more important place to address the theological concerns of the church.[14] Hence the major components of this explicitly theological approach include the following.

Similar to the argumentation in his *Introduction*, he asserts that the primary object of theological reflection is the Hebrew canon, not

11. Clues of canonical shaping include the overall structure of the book; prescripts, conclusions, superscriptions; an editorial assignment of a historical setting to a book; the relations between the author's vantage point and the audience; the function of the implied audience; the function of the pseudonymous author or indirect authorship; and the placing of documents side by side that leads to the omission, addition, or separation of materials (see Childs, *The New Testament as Canon*, 48–53).

12. Childs, *Old Testament Theology in a Canonical Context*. See pp. 1–19 for his overview of problems and the major features of the canonical approach to Old Testament theology.

13. Ibid., 1.

14. Ibid., 6.

the history of the various communities of ancient Israel and early Judaism that existed behind and produced this text. Childs allows that the use of the Old Testament as one source for reconstructing the history and religion of Israel is appropriate within a historical paradigm. However, it is not an appropriate theological paradigm.

In his theological work, Childs makes it even more clear that the canonical process focuses not only on the final shape of books but also on the tripartite structure of the canon. Thus the canonical model examines the theological interaction of these three collections of texts (say, creation and history, or narrative and law). This creative and flexible way of relating various parts of the canon in the actualization of interpretation not only allows for but truly invites new varieties of combinations.[15] Childs uses the term "intertextuality" to refer to using Scripture to interpret Scripture, since he argues that there was an intended dialogical character at work in the shaping of the canon. Texts were meant to be read by reference to each other, both in illumining and in sharpening debate. In Childs's view, even silence plays a key role. For example, the relegating of the conquest tradition to the past meant that it was locked there forever and was not to be regarded as authoritative for later communities. Through this interior dialogue of the canon, "some texts were subordinated, others raised to new importance, others relativized in the light of the larger collection."[16]

Also similar to the argumentation in his *Introduction*, Childs emphasizes the role of the communities of faith in theological discourse. He asserts that the theological witness of the text cannot be heard apart from the voices of the communities of faith who have interacted with the canon both in its rather lengthy development and then after its final formulation in theological appropriation. This hermeneutical interaction with the developing texts began in early preexilic times and extended into the Greco-Roman period when the Hebrew Bible was canonized by the rabbis. This witness has continued in the hermeneutical engagement by ongoing communities of faith.

With the origin and development of Christianity, however, the Old Testament also became a part of this religious community's Bible and therefore an important source for Christian theology and practice as well as for the Jewish community. The efforts of the Gnostics to reject the Old Testament as Scripture were declared

15. Ibid., 13.
16. Childs, "A Response," *HBT* 2 (1980) 204.

heretical by normative Christianity. This means for Childs that the Old Testament, as a legitimate and revelatory part of Christian Scripture, must be placed in a dialectical relationship with both the New Testament and the ongoing Christian community.[17] Since Judaism traces an unbroken continuity from the Hebrew Bible (Tanak) into the rabbinic tradition, the relationship is continuous, not dialectical. This argument, of course, reflects Childs's own Protestant understanding of Scripture.

Childs also seeks to address other issues that make the use of the Old Testament as Scripture by Christians distinctive from that of the Jewish community. He notes that the discipline of Old Testament theology is a Christian, not a Jewish, enterprise.[18] Childs does not attempt to write a theology of the Hebrew Bible, a biblical theology, or a contemporary theology. Rather, he sets forth descriptively a theology of the Old Testament from the perspective of a Christian who stands within a tradition that regards this collection as one part of the received canon. This does not mean that Childs attempts to christianize the Old Testament, for the Old Testament is an independent witness to Jesus Christ in a pre-Christian form. But it does mean that he approaches the text as a confessing Christian standing within a Christian community of faith.[19]

Childs acknowledges that Jews have used the Old Testament (or Hebrew Bible) in a way that does not necessitate the doing of biblical theology. That is, there is in Judaism both continuity between Scripture and tradition and an acceptance of the legitimacy of oral commentary on the Old Testament. Thus a very different enterprise is undertaken when Judaism addresses the questions of authority and norms. Childs also notes that the search for a "center" to Old Testament theology is a distinctively Christian enterprise, not a Jewish one.

While recognizing that it is impossible to ask Christians to read the Old Testament as though the Christ-event had not occurred, Childs argues that Christian hermeneutics cannot simply force the Old Testament into a promise (OT)-fulfillment (NT) schema, since there are other, even New Testament options to this. Rather, for the

17. Childs argues that Christians need "to hear Israel's witness in order to understand who the Father of Jesus Christ is" (*Old Testament Theology in a Canonical Context*, p. 9).

18. Ibid., 8.

19. In an earlier work, Childs affirms: "The genuine theological task can be carried on successfully only when it begins from within an explicit framework of faith" ("Interpretation in Faith," 438).

church, Childs asserts that biblical theology is both an innerscrip-
tural dialectic between the Old and the New Testament and
between the Christian community and a canon that has two testaments. While the Old Testament can only reflect one witness to
Christian theology, it is still a part of Christian Scripture. Thus he
avows that "the task of Old Testament theology is . . . not to christianize the Old Testament by identifying it with the New Testament
witness, but to hear its own theological testimony to the God of
Israel whom the church confesses also to worship."[20] Childs adds:
"It is still necessary to hear Israel's witness in order to understand
who the Father of Jesus Christ is."[21] Finally, in this regard, Childs
contends that even though the Old Testament of the continuing
Christian community often was the Septuagint, it is important for
present-day Christians to use the Hebrew canon in order to promote
dialogue between Jews and Christians.

In relating biblical theology to systematics, Childs notes that the
canonical approach combines the descriptive and the hermeneutical tasks. Modern theological interpretation may not be content
with only describing the faith expressed in the Hebrew Bible. There
is also a hermeneutical dimension, for the interpreters must continue to struggle with the issues of faith and practice to which
Scripture points. This ultimately means then that Scripture is normative for the life of the church. Thus the interpreter, who takes on
the theological task, stands within the community (Israel and the
church) of faith and attempts to discern the will of God by engagement of Scripture and tradition.

Childs concludes the description of his approach by allowing that
there is no single key to getting at Old Testament theology, although
the canon is the object of reflection as well as the context in which
understanding may occur.[22] At times even historical as well as systematic interpretations may be preferred. In the final analysis, the
real concern for Childs is not really how the interpretation is
achieved but rather its compelling quality.

OLD TESTAMENT THEOLOGY IN A CANONICAL CONTEXT

Laying aside introductory matters addressed in the opening chapter, Childs then presents his own theology. He does so in the form of
nineteen additional chapters, each of which deals with a largely self-

20. Childs, *Old Testament Theology in a Canonical Context*, 9.
21. Ibid., 9.
22. Ibid., 15–16.

contained theme or subject: five deal directly with some aspect of revelation (e.g., "The Old Testament as Revelation"), three pertain to law ("The Law of God," "The Theological Significance of the Decalogue," and "The Role of the Ritual and Purity Laws"), four present a theology of sacred roles and offices (Moses, judges, kings, prophets, and priests), one is devoted to the cultus, another to the major social institutions of Israelite life, two handle anthropology ("Male and Female as a Theological Problem" and "The Theological Dimension of Being Human"), one is directed toward ethics, and two handle eschatology ("Life under Threat" and "Life under Promise"). Childs neither formulates a center around which these themes and subjects may revolve nor attempts to integrate them into a system, although it would not be difficult to shape them into a larger set of topics ("Revelation"; "Law"; "Sacred Offices"; "Covenant: The Chosen, Cult, and Society"; "Anthropology"; "Worship and Ethics"; and "Eschatology"). These are largely self-contained essays that rarely interact with each other in the larger totality of the book. Indeed, Childs's own Old Testament theology is largely devoid of "intertextuality," although he makes significant use of this principle in enabling biblical texts to interact. It is also rather surprising that, while Childs has much to say about the Old Testament's understanding of God throughout his volume, there is not a chapter that explicitly concentrates on the nature and character of the deity. The closest to this is the third chapter, "How God Is Known," although the concern here is with revelation.

In his own explicit presentation of Old Testament theology, Childs primarily uses the canon as a context. On occasion he uses what he calls the principle of intertextuality to indicate how one part of Scripture comments on, interacts with, or illustrates another. This includes Childs's use of the tripartite structure of the canon to make a theological argument or to demonstrate how a theme was presented in various ways and readdressed by later canon shapers. At times Childs will even trace a theme through Scripture; for example, he does this in a limited way with the commandment, "You shall not kill." Elsewhere, he points to the importance of the canonical shape of an Old Testament book for articulating a theological theme. However, he has little to say about the canonizers and the community that interacted with Scripture. The community is discussed somewhat abstractly in two chapters: "The Recipients of God's Revelation" and "Structures of the Common Life." In addition, there is not much in the volume that addresses the issues raised in his introduction about the relationship between the two canons in Christianity. In any case, the following discussion will illustrate how his distinctive canonical approach is brought to bear on the presentation of Old Testament theology.

Chapter 2 addresses the subject of "The Old Testament as Revelation" by contrasting a canonical use and understanding of the subject with those of analytical philosophy (especially the work of James Barr) and sociological analysis represented by Norman Gottwald.[23] For Childs, the canonical approach allows one to understand the Old Testament as revelation in both a vertical and a horizontal sense. Revelation is horizontal in that the canonizers attempted to formulate the tradition in such a way as to address authoritatively future generations of believers. The vertical dimension of revelation involves Israel's "reception, collection and ordering of the experiences of the divine."[24] For Childs, this allows Scripture to be authoritative revelation grounded in the reality of a transcendent God. The theology of the Old Testament cannot, for Childs, simply be ideology, that is, the symbolic expression of the social realities of historical Israel.[25] This is a direct challenge to Gottwald and those who follow his approach. For Childs, Gottwald's approach "destroys the need for closely hearing the text on its verbal level."[26]

In chapter 3, "How God Is Known," Childs begins his search for the knowledge of God as revealed in Scripture as a believer within a confessing community. This quest to know God in the Hebrew canon is not anachronistic; rather, it is a recognition of the church's acceptance of the Old Testament as an authoritative witness to the nature and reality of God.[27] And Childs stands within the community of faith as he seeks to come to an understanding of God.

Childs then notes the various ways in which God is revealed according to the Old Testament. A canonical approach stresses that God is revealed in creation and rejects both the contrasting of creation with history and the subordination of one to the other.[28]

---

23. Childs has had a running, lively debate with these two scholars for the better part of a generation.

24. Childs, *Old Testament Theology in a Canonical Context*, 23.

25. Ibid., 26. As noted in chap. 4 above, Gottwald's social-scientific approach "starts from the premise that biblical writings are social products" ("Social Matrix and Canonical Shape," 307). For Gottwald, Childs does not give a proper place to the social reality of texts.

26. Childs, *Old Testament Theology in a Canonical Context*, 25.

27. Ibid., 30.

28. Ibid., 33.

The same is true for God's revelation through wisdom, an avenue of understanding and a corpus of literature that have often been neglected or relegated to a minor status by Old Testament theologians. For Childs, this literature presents important testimony to God's revelation in creation through wisdom. While revelation in history is another important dimension of divine self-disclosure, Childs notes that it is not different in kind from creation. Numerous examples point to texts that speak of both creation and history as avenues of divine activity and self-disclosure.[29] Finally, Childs points to the revelation of God through names that testify to divine nature.

In his chapter on "The Law of God," Childs addresses, at least indirectly, the problem of the Sinai revelation to which von Rad had pointed. Von Rad had indicated that the absence of Sinai in the early historical credo (see Deut 26:5-9) relegated it to an unimportant and late (postexilic) status. This resulted in the theological diminishing of this tradition of Israelite faith. By contrast, Childs, in his use of the canonical approach, indicates that Sinai is the fullest expression of the will of God in the Old Testament, and indeed stands at the very heart and soul of the Pentateuch.[30] By means of a canonical approach that does not devalue Sinai as a tradition of late importance, Childs offers a series of significant theological insights. Some of the more salient observations include the following. First, Sinai is connected to the exodus from Egypt, thus removing legitimate opposition between law and freedom. Second, the events of Sinai (covenant and law) provide the culmination of the formation of Israel as the people of God. Third, all laws and legal collections are grounded in Sinai, even those that obviously originated later. This one paradigmatic "moment" in the life of Israel becomes the "norm by means of which all subsequent history of the nation is measured."[31] Fourth, Deuteronomy functions canonically to emphasize that Moses' new interpretation of the Torah invites engagement and reactualization for future generations who had not themselves participated in the Sinai event.

Important suggestions are made by Childs in his treatment of ritual and purity laws in chapter 8.[32] For him, a canonical approach argues against contrasting ethical and ritual laws. Even so, the can-

---

29. Ibid., 38.
30. Ibid., 53–56.
31. Ibid., 54–55.
32. Ibid., 86–90.

onizers do not remove the features of ritual laws that point to their sociohistorical context. Thus, they are, in Childs's designation, "time-conditioned." To remove these in order to find an underlying ethical principle or motivation is, in Childs's estimation, a questionable hermeneutical move. In addition, other portions of the canon deal with purity laws in ways that elicit theological reflection. For example, he points to prophetic criticism of the cultus, especially when Israel separates justice from ritual obedience. Ultimately, for the prophets, Israel's sinfulness and inability to merit God's favor through reliance on ritual and their own efforts at justice lead to dependence on divine mercy.

Childs's exposition of Israel as "the recipients of God's revelation" (chap. 9) deals with covenant theology in the canon.[33] Not only is covenant the central theme in the Pentateuch, Deuteronomy reactualizes it for future generations. In his arguments that the prophets cannot be understood without allowing them the fundamental view that Israel is the special people of God, Childs opposes a long-standing argument that the concept of covenant was not historically present until the development of the Deuteronomic traditions in the seventh and sixth centuries B.C.E.

Childs's examination of the sacred roles and offices of Israel is found in chapters 10–13.[34] In dealing with these, he eschews sociological description in favor of a canonical approach that allows for theological reflection. Several examples of Childs's interpretation should suffice to demonstrate how he approaches canonically these roles and offices. To begin, he argues that there are many diverse traditions that are in tension over their depiction of Moses. Significant is the realization that Moses not only has a unique role, he also encompasses all other roles: priest, prophet, lawgiver, deliverer, psalmist, and sage.[35] However, the most important point for Childs is that Moses is the mediator of the covenant who "transfers his unique role to a written record" (i.e., the "law of Moses").[36] This point fits in quite nicely with the entire thrust of his canonical reading.

Also illustrative is Childs's treatment of the problem of false prophecy.[37] Referring to the canonical shaping of Jeremiah 23–29,

33. Ibid., 94–95.
34. Ibid., 108–54.
35. Ibid., 108–12.
36. Ibid., 110–11.
37. Ibid., 133–44.

Childs contends that the canon dealt conclusively with this problem by arguing that the true prophet speaks the word of God, while the false prophet lies. The community can make this distinction by recognizing that "the truth of prophecy is determined by God's confirmation in action."[38] By reference to historical action, later communities of faith had the means by which to distinguish between true and false prophets.

One other example of the canonical shaping of an office in Israel is the priesthood. Shunning historical reconstructions, Childs argues that a canonical approach recognizes that the postexilic form of the priesthood becomes normative, although its diachronic development at times is woven into the text. This normative form focuses on the roles of the priesthood as distinguishing between clean and unclean (profane and sacred) and as knowing the divine will. Finally, the canonical presentation contrasts the ideal, normative priesthood with corrupted forms and practice.[39]

The best example of Childs's use of the canonical shape of a book to discuss one of his theological themes is his analysis of the Book of Leviticus in chapter 14, "Benefits of the Covenant: The Cultus."[40] On the one hand, Childs notes what is missing in this book. He argues that Leviticus selects only a small number of elements pertaining to the cultus, and even these do not refer to their specific religious settings or the "mechanical" features of ritual. He observes that this text neither presents a theory of sacrifice and atonement nor demonstrates any interest in the psychology of the worshipers. On the other hand, Childs considers it worthy of note that Leviticus and its expression of the cultus are placed within the revelation and covenant of Sinai, that primordial moment for Israelite faith. He also emphasizes that Leviticus is organized primarily by means of the repetition of certain key phrases (e.g., "a pleasing odor to Yahweh"). All of these are brought together in Childs's basic theological argument that Leviticus is not a manual for the Israelite cultus but rather a theological book that seeks to illustrate how the cult is "to engender obedience to the covenant." Indeed, he thinks that its canonical shape indicates that the theology of the book is already removed from the actual history of Israelite worship.[41]

Childs's comments on "The Shape of the Obedient Life" (chap.

38. Ibid., 139.
39. Ibid., 152–53.
40. Ibid., 156–61.
41. Ibid., 160.

18) focus on worship and ethics. For example, he argues that the canonical function of the Psalter has been redirected by the insertion of Psalm 1 at the beginning. Through the lens of this introductory Torah psalm, the prayers of Israel are not simply directed to God as a response to divine activity and grace but are now understood as "God's fresh word to his people."[42] In illustrating his remarks on ethics, he contends that the patriarchal narratives do not present the human characters as models of moral behavior for emulation but as both illustrations of "God's faithfulness to his promise" and examples of those whose sinfulness God forgives.[43]

Childs's last two chapters deal with eschatology and apocalyptic: "Life under Threat" and "Life under Promise."[44] Noteworthy are Childs's remarks concerning the canonical shaping of books and larger collections to underscore the importance of eschatological hope. This shaping includes the prophetic pattern of judgment followed by oracles of promise, the joining of psalms of lament with those promising salvation, the reinterpretation of the king in the royal psalms as the future messiah, the arrangement of Genesis by reference to the theme of promise, and the editing of the historical books that indicates that the promises to David are to be realized by a future community.[45]

BIBLICAL THEOLOGY OF THE CHRISTIAN CANON

Childs uses the paradigm of the canon approach in presenting a comprehensive theology of the Old and the New Testament.[46] He also addresses many of the questions raised by his earlier formulations of the nature and tasks of Old Testament and biblical theology. Following a prolegomenon that outlines the history of the discipline, contemporary paradigms, and classic formulations of Christian presentations,[47] Childs delineates the major features of his new approach to biblical theology under four major headings: "The Problem of the Christian Bible" (pp. 55–69), "A Canonical Approach to Biblical Theology" (pp. 70–79), "From Witness to Subject Matter" (pp. 80–90), and "Canonical Categories for Structuring a Biblical Theology" (pp. 91–94). Here he builds on his

42. Ibid., 207–8.
43. Ibid., 216, 220.
44. Ibid., 222–47.
45. Ibid., 238–40.
46. Childs, *Biblical Theology of the Old and New Testaments*.
47. Ibid., 3–51.

earlier work but addresses specifically the issues and problems inherent in doing a theology of the entire canon.

In his section on "The Problem of the Christian Bible," Childs clearly articulates the interpretative problems posed by the bipartite nature of the Christian canon that contains two testaments, Old and New. He notes that the central issue is Christian claims about the Old Testament that also functions as Scripture within Judaism. Noting the difficulty of attempting to trace the historical development of the canon, Childs concludes that the Old Testament probably did not reach its final form and achieve normative status as a canon until the first century C.E. He also notes that the Christian church historically has functioned with a "narrow" (Jerome) and "wider" (Augustine) canon until the Reformation, when Protestants returned to the Jewish Bible for defining the contents and limits of the Old Testament.

Following this brief survey, Childs articulates the theological issues at stake in the multiplicity of Old Testament canons. First, he argues that the Christian Bible in its various canonical formulations, including the Old Testament, functioned in normative ways as Scripture. The presence or absence of the so-called Apocrypha does not change or detract from this fundamental understanding of the Old Testament as Scripture for both the varieties of Christian confessions and Judaism. Second, the reformers wished to return to the "most pristine and purest form" of the Old Testament, although, in Childs's estimation, it is not true that their decision to eliminate the Apocrypha from Scripture was due only to the working of the Holy Spirit or that significant theological differences resulted. He notes that the value of the larger Roman Catholic canon is that the importance placed on tradition clearly recognizes the church's continuing use of Scripture as one of several authorities, although there is the risk of subordinating the authority of Scripture to human tradition. Third, and most important, Childs argues that "the basic theological issue at stake can be best formulated in terms of the church's ongoing search for the Christian Bible."[48] While this search will not reach a final discovery, the very process of seeking is "constitutive for Christian faith." The tension between Scripture and tradition, both of which contain the Word of God, produces theological vitality, not polarization.

Childs then moves in his prolegomena to a delineation of the distinctive features of his canonical approach, already outlined in

48. Ibid., 67.

previous publications. However, he also seeks to address some of the criticisms raised by earlier scholarly reactions to his work, in particular the ambiguity of the term "canonical." Childs clarifies his understanding and use of the term (and related ones) in the following ways. He explains that the term is a "cipher" for the variety of factors at work in the development and shape of the biblical witness. Under the general rubric of "cipher," Childs distinguishes four separate, though related, uses of the term "canonical." First, the term refers to the ongoing faith community's attribution of authority to developing traditions and writings that made their way into the Bible. Second, "canonical" refers to the process that led to the development and final shape of the canon, that is, to the process of "canonization." This means there was a continuing "canon consciousness" that was at work in the literature and the faith community. Third, the term, in underscoring the importance of theological forces that led to the formation of the Bible, keeps us from limiting explanations of canon development to only historical, redactional, and sociological factors. Fourth, the term influences the ways that modern interpreters regard the biblical text. This means that the understanding of contemporary readers is created, at least in part, by the degree of their identification with the faith community of those who shaped the canon. He summarizes his understanding of canon in the statement: "The term canon points to the received, collected, and interpreted material of the church and thus establishes the theological context in which the tradition continues to function authoritatively for today."[49]

Childs also addresses the criticism that his approach is primarily formal and literary and thus lacking in theological content. He explains that literary text and theological character and function are fundamentally entwined, that is, they cannot be separated into unrelated categories. Childs also responds to the criticism of some social-scientific and liberation theologians that his approach removes the canon from contextualization, that is, from the crucible of human faith communities engaging Scripture and political-social realities. He argues that the canon was shaped by communities of faith who responded to divine interruptions into history. To appeal to another external entity as authoritative in the formative process of the development and shape of the canon, be it ideology or social group, is to replace the theological character of a community witnessing to divine action by producing a normative canon with a

49. Ibid., 71.

very different understanding of the role of the community and the nature of the Bible. The danger for Childs is that a one-sided emphasis on the community as social organization and religion as the symbolic projection of human beings may lead to the loss of transcendence.

Childs then sets forth in a comprehensive way the distinctive features of the canonical approach to the two Testaments of the Christian Bible. He begins by arguing that the relationship between the Old and the New Testament is not simply historical but also theological. Using the language of redaction critics and tradition historians, he notes that the process of the shaping of the entire Christian canon was the result of tradents and redactors within faith communities developing layers of texts and reformulating earlier traditions. However, he nuances this activity as theological, that is, redactors and tradents received the texts and traditions as authoritative and wished to shape them in ways that would allow them to continue to have authority for later generations of believing communities. Even so, this transmission process is not true of the entire Christian Bible, for there are streams of Old Testament tradition that did not flow into the New Testament.

In the appropriation of the Old Testament, the church made many theological moves: typology, law and gospel, the church as the New Israel, and prophecy and fulfillment. Writers of the New Testament searched the Old Testament and claimed that it witnessed to Jesus Christ. The tripartite canon of law, prophets, and writings was changed to Pentateuch, historical books, wisdom and hymnody, and prophecy. With prophecy at the end, the church was able to shape more clearly an eschatological expectation of the coming of the messiah and the birth of the Christian community. Placing prophecy at the end of the Old Testament canon enabled the church to see its relationship to its Jewish past, not so much in historical terms but in regard to the revelatory value of the divine Word spoken by Israel's prophets. The Old Testament pointed beyond itself to the New. This does not mean, argues Childs, that the church attempted to christianize the Old Testament, for the shape of its books remained largely unchanged. Indeed, the church even considered the Old Testament canon closed. However, for Childs, the New Testament is not simply citing the Old Testament and reflecting on its meaning in the light of the new revelation of the Christ-event. The new redemptive activity of God in Jesus Christ goes beyond a recasting of the earlier canon.

The New Testament also is not simply a midrashic exposition of the Old Testament. And there are significant discontinuities between the Testaments. Even so, one cannot present a simplistic formulation of the Old and the New Testament into the categories of law and gospel, as does Bultmann. Each of the two Testaments contains a measure of both. Childs further argues that the Old Testament cannot be regarded as a witness to failure that leads to its rejection. However, he acknowledges that his earlier focus on the citations of the Old Testament by the New for getting at biblical theology stands in need of significant revision.[50]

Childs articulates the following canonical "guidelines" for shaping a biblical theology.[51] First, the integrity of the individual Testaments (Old and New) needs to be honored. While the Old Testament bears witness to the New, the voice of the former is not silenced by the language of the latter. The promise set forth by the Old Testament should not be removed by the fulfillment of the New. Second, biblical theology cannot simply be understood as the New Testament's interpretation of the Old, "as if the Old Testament's witness were limited to how it was once heard and appropriated by the early Church."[52] Rather, the Old Testament continues to speak as Scripture, not simply to the Jewish community, but also to the church. As revelation, the Old Testament, even for the church, continues to possess a "vertical" and "existential" character. The Old Testament must continue to be heard in its own terms as Scripture and not discarded by the incorrect view that it is now displaced by the New. Third, the Christian, including the Christian theologian, cannot limit modern biblical theology to New Testament theology. Childs argues: "Both testaments make a discrete witness to Jesus Christ which must be heard, both separately and in concert."[53] And fourth, the Christian must listen to and reflect on the discrete witness of the two Testaments, including their continuities and discontinuities. The connections and tensions between the two Testaments cannot be treated by a singular hermeneutic, whether it be promise and fulfillment, typology, tradition history, or another scheme.

In his section "From Witness to Subject Matter,"[54] Childs then addresses two issues: the theological task of biblical theology and

50. Ibid., 76. See Childs, *Biblical Theology in Crisis*, 114f., for the earlier proposal regarding citations of the Old in the New.
51. Childs, *Biblical Theology of the Old and New Testaments*, 77–79.
52. Ibid., 77.
53. Ibid., 78.
54. Ibid., 80–90.

the connection between biblical theology and contemporary theology. While respecting the discrete witnesses of both Testaments, Childs nonetheless argues that the major objective of biblical theology is "to understand the various voices within the whole Christian Bible, New and Old Testament alike, as a witness to the one Lord Jesus Christ."[55] The discrete witnesses of both Testaments are shaped into one common confession. This understanding rejects both a linear view of a development from the Old to the New Testament and the understanding that the New corrects the Old. Rather, both bear witness to the one Lord. Biblical theology is dialogical, not simply in the sense of conversation between the historical communities of faith and the reality of God's redemptive acts, but also between contemporary communities of faith in conversation, guided by the Holy Spirit, with the reality shaped by earlier witnesses. By including contemporary communities in the hermeneutical process of understanding and responding to the witness of Scripture, biblical theology, for Childs, is normative, not merely descriptive. For Childs, systematic theologians today need to be more biblical, even as biblical theologians need to be more systematic or constructive in their formulations.

Finally, Childs sets forth the "canonical categories for structuring a biblical theology."[56] First, he argues that the Old Testament's witness to divine activity is to be set forth within the history of ancient Israel. The Old Testament's understanding of God is articulated, not in the form of a systematic treatise abstracted from history, but within the ongoing life of Israel. Even so, Childs disputes the contention of Wright and von Rad that the Old Testament is a history book. It is a history book in that it sets forth the story of Israel from its origins to its reconstitution in the post-exile and describes at least in part the social and religious institutions that shaped its corporate life. However, biblical theology is not to be equated with the tasks and objects of the history of religions. In following the canonical approach to biblical theology, Childs argues that the redemptive events and institutions of Israel's corporate life continued to be shaped and reinterpreted by the tradents who transmitted the materials that came to comprise the Bible. In contradistinction to von Rad, Childs argues that the voice of Israel's testimonies to redemptive activity is heard, not in the traditions

55. Ibid., 80.
56. Ibid., 91–94.

shaped by the tradents of Israel, but in the "canonically shaped literature of the Old Testament."[57]

Second, Childs argues that the canonical approach does not regard the New Testament's witness primarily as a redactional layer of Old Testament traditions. Nor does this approach consider the Christian community as simply a historical extension of earlier Israel. While there are continuities between the two, that is, between the Old and the New Testament and between Israel and the church, there are also discontinuities. Nevertheless the New Testament still witnesses to God's redemptive act in Jesus Christ in terms of the Old. The New Testament transforms the Old, but only in the effort to speak theologically of the meaning of the Christ-event.

Following his prolegomena, Childs moves into "The Discrete Witness of the Old Testament," setting forth its theological understanding in its own terms.[58] To do this, Childs seeks to achieve the following methodological goals. These are (1) placing the Old Testament witness within the original setting of Israel's history; (2) following the development of this witness within the story of Israel; and (3) noting both the unity and the disunity within Old Testament faith.

In his discussion of these three goals, Childs makes several important points. As a historical community that witnesses to divine reality, Israel's voice is given theological priority over other voices that speak through the literatures of the ancient Near East. Further, Israel's voice expressed in its Scripture is revelatory and not simply a source for historical reconstruction. Similarly, as approached by Childs, Israel's history is a canonical history that was shaped and formed as an authoritative history, for it experiences and bears witness to God's redemptive activity.

To escape the impasse reached by conservative scholars who use critical method only as long as their theological convictions are not disturbed and liberal scholars who hide behind the presumed objectivity of historical criticism that they think allows them to escape theological judgments, Childs offers the following points. First, there should be a constructive relationship between viewing Israel's history confessionally and neutrally. Both dimensions are true, but they are required for a complete understanding of Israel's history. Second, Israel's history, as witnessed by the believing communities, involves both divine and human participants. Third, Israel's historical experiences cannot simply be chronicled within the develop-

57. Ibid., 92.
58. Ibid., 97–106.

ment of the nations of the ancient Near East any more than the salvific events of Israel's life can be set forth as distinctive from the entirety of the historical process. The limitations of both extremes are lessened by the presence of the other. Fourth, Israel's history is selectively presented by the witnessing communities. Some materials are selected and transmitted, although reshaped, while others are eliminated or repressed. What these points mean for Childs is the recognition that there exists a dynamic tension between Israelite history as reconstructed by contemporary scholars and the confession of the historical community of Israel to divine redemption at work in its ongoing life. The solution he offers is that of viewing the collective life of Israel as a canonical history, that is, as a history that entwines human life with divine activity by reference to the normative shape of Scripture.

THE THEOLOGY OF JEREMIAH IN A CANONICAL CONTEXT

Childs's brief treatment of Jeremiah in his *Introduction* allows one to determine at least the major parameters of his assessment of the theology of this prophetic book.[59] Again, it should be stressed that this is not a full-blown theological treatment, even in the limited sense of Old Testament theology as over against biblical or contemporary theology. Childs's *Introduction* sets forth a canonical approach that yields itself to theological work, but it is not intended to be even a descriptive Old Testament theology. Childs does refer to Jeremiah in numerous places in his Old Testament theology, especially in his contrast of true and false prophecy, although his overall approach is primarily thematic. Thus the following remarks will begin with the section on Jeremiah in his *Introduction*.

Childs follows his standard procedure: an examination of the major historical-critical problems leads him to conclude that traditional scholarship has reached an impasse in solving these difficulties. Like many Jeremiah scholars before him, he recognizes that the most important problem in this prophetic book is the relationship between the poetry and the prose. After exploring the various solutions offered, he concludes that scholars are divided in their assessments of this relationship and have not reached a consensus.

---

59. Childs, *Introduction to the Old Testament as Scripture*, 339–54. Also see the work of Childs's student, Christopher Seitz, *Theology in Conflict: Reactions to the Exile in the Book of Jeremiah* (BZAW 176; Berlin: W. de Gruyter, 1989); and idem, "The Prophet Moses and the Canonical Shape of Jeremiah," *ZAW* 101 (1989) 3–27.

Childs notes that, while most scholars trace the poetry (source A) back to Jeremiah, there is strong disagreement over the question of the prophet's relationship to the prose, including the speeches (source C) and the biographical narratives (source B). Some scholars stress historical continuity between the poetry and the prose, noting that Jeremiah may have uttered prose speeches (source C) and that Baruch, the scribe of Jeremiah, perhaps was responsible for the biographical narratives (source B). Others see little relationship between the two traditions, and several have even attributed the prose to an extensive Deuteronomic redaction of Jeremiah.

With this scholarly impasse duly documented, Childs then turns to consider how the canonical method leads to a viable solution of the poetry-prose dilemma and finally to some important theological insights. In proposing a solution to the problem of the poetry and prose, Childs argues that these diverse materials represent two different forms of the prophet's proclamation, emerging from two different settings: the twenty-three-year period for the individual poetic sayings (source A) and the later reshaping of these materials by Jeremiah himself into a call to repentance (source C). Childs contends that the stimulus for the reshaping was the impact that Israel's sacred Scripture, in this case Deuteronomy, made on the prophet. Jeremiah came to understand himself as standing in a long line of prophets who preached repentance on the basis of the law. This led Childs to reinterpret Jeremiah's prophetic activity in the mode of Deuteronomy's preacher of judgment. This is the first, and perhaps most interesting, feature of Childs's assessment of the canonical shaping of the Book of Jeremiah.

The second element of the canonical shaping of the Book of Jeremiah, for Childs, is later Deuteronomic editing. The Deuteronomic pattern of interpretation is noticeable, he argues, in the frame of the book: the additions to the prophet's call in 1:15f. and chapter 52, a prose narrative taken from 2 Kings 24 that details the fall of Jerusalem. For Childs, this "deuteronomic framework serves to interpret the significance of Jeremiah's ministry for the life of the nations within the larger economy of God's plan."[60] The interpretation of Jeremiah as a preacher of the law and repentance is found in the Deuteronomic editing of the early poetic speeches in chapters 1–25 (cf. 7:1f.; 11:1f.; 21:1f.; 25:1f.).

Childs argues that a third feature of the canonical shaping of Jeremiah is evidenced by the materials that speak of both the life

---

60. Childs, *Introduction to the Old Testament as Scripture*, 348.

and the interiority of the prophet. These materials consist of two different types: the "confessions of Jeremiah" found scattered throughout chapters 11–20 and the prose narratives (B) in chapters 26–45. In the latter, prose summaries of speeches are often found among the narrative stories of events in the prophet's life. Childs argues that the emphasis of these stories is theological: their shaping is designed to demonstrate from Jeremiah's own history "the rejection of the Word of God," a theme conspicuous throughout the entire prophetic corpus. The biographical narratives demonstrate also that Jeremiah's proclamation consisted of both word and deed. His life interfaced with his preaching. This is also true of the confessions, for his inner turmoil led to reflection on and struggles with the prophetic office and the theology of judgment. Finally, the biographical material demonstrates that Jeremiah's office and message were understood in relationship to the Deuteronomic portrayal of the preacher of judgment.

Two other features of the canonical shaping of Jeremiah are noted by Childs in his assessments of "the oracles of promise" (chaps. 30–33) and "the oracles to the nations" (chaps. 46–51). "The oracles of promise," picking up and developing other occurrences of future redemption, emphasize in no uncertain terms that hope was always a part of the message of Jeremiah, regardless of the judgment that Judah faced. Thus salvation is ultimately the anticipated outcome of the divine plan for the nation. In the shaping of the Book of Jeremiah, this anticipated salvation is given an eschatological character, for it is directed, not simply to Judah, but to Israel as well. Even so, argues Childs, the expected covenantal response was not passivity by the people of God but the actualization of hope within the "life of the community who lived in expectation toward righteousness."[61]

"The oracles to the nations" in the Masoretic text are found at the conclusion of the book (chaps. 46–51), while the Septuagint, quite possibly following an earlier stage of redaction, places them after 25:13a. Childs suggests that the rearrangement in the Masoretic text may have resulted from two factors: the influence of other prophetic books that have similar oracles at the end and the concern to maintain a close connection between the oracles of Jeremiah 1–25 and the biography in chapters 26–45. Thus there were two canonical forces at work in the placement of these oracles, an external influence exerted by several other prophetic books and an internal

61. Ibid., 352.

dynamic seeking to relate larger units of material in a theologically coherent way. Nevertheless Childs contends that the theology is the same for both the Masoretic and the Greek text: Yahweh, the God of Israel, directs the course of all human history. Thus judgment and salvation for Israel and Judah are placed within God's universal rule of human history.[62]

Childs concludes with three "theological and hermeneutical implications" of the application of the canonical approach to Jeremiah.[63] First, this interpretation avoids the unfortunate devaluing of materials considered "inauthentic," that is, not directly from the prophet himself. While Childs does not seek to claim that the prose tradition is always historically accurate, he does contend that his canonical approach "acknowledges the normative theological shaping of the material by the canon." In this sense, the later shaping of the tradition has theological and normative value.[64]

A second theological implication drawn by Childs is that the canonical shaping of the Book of Jeremiah points to the close relationship between the law and the prophets. Scholars have attempted to ascertain the historical Jeremiah's relationship to or view of the reform of Josiah (see 2 Kings 22–23) in order to establish some connection to the Book of Deuteronomy that, at least in an earlier stage of formation, most probably was the basis for Josiah's efforts. The difficulty with this effort by scholars is Jeremiah's silence about the reform. However, the canonical approach notes that Jeremiah was placed within the tradition of a preacher of the law, thus enabling a later community to see how the law was to function prophetically in guiding their lives. This approach avoids placing the law and the prophets in opposition to each other and keeps from subordinating the former to the latter.[65]

Finally, the third implication to which Childs points is the larger issue of prophetic collections as Scripture. This prophetic book points to the importance of the canonical process in establishing a new context, that is, a scriptural context, to interpret the growing tradition. As a sense of canon led to the development of normative Scripture, these prophetic texts were used to shape later traditions that would eventually become canonical. Given this canonical shaping, the final form of the text of Jeremiah bears the witness of

62. Ibid., 352.
63. Ibid., 353–54.
64. Ibid., 353.
65. Ibid., 353.

the confessing community and conveys that community's under-standing of the prophetic word for future generations.

Of course, Childs also approaches Jeremiah, not as an individual book, but as a part of the canon. Thus, in Childs's thematic treatment of Old Testament theology, Jeremiah is cited in some thirteen of the twenty chapters. The canon, including of course the Book of Jeremiah, becomes the context for treatment of theological themes addressed by interpreters of Scripture from the perspective of their own theological contexts.

In addition, chapter 12 ("True and False Prophets") makes substantial use of Jeremiah, particularly chaps. 23–29.[66] The theological issue is ultimately one of truth, that is, how to distinguish between a true and a false prophet. There are texts that seek to set up criteria for making this important distinction (Deuteronomy 18 and Jeremiah 23 and 28). The former seeks to protect the community against false prophets who, by speaking a word of judgment in the name of Yahweh that does not come to pass, "terrorize the community with threats of coming disaster."[67] By contrast in Jeremiah 28, Jeremiah opposes a false prophet (Hananiah) who seeks to "lull the people to sleep with false hopes of peace and security."[68] These examples indicate how difficult it was for the community to discern divine truth from human falsehood.

Arguing against the existential interpretations of Zimmerli and von Rad that emphasize that "the criterion of truth resides alone in a fresh word from God *hic et nunc,"* and against James Sanders who proposes that the problem of truth was a hermeneutical one of timing (judgment or salvation, depending on the time and circumstances), Childs examines Jeremiah 23–29 by means of the canonical approach and concludes that the proper criterion for establishing true prophecy is "God's confirmation in action."[69] This means that in the shaping of the Book of Jeremiah, criteria were offered for making the distinction that in essence turned on historical confirmation of what the prophet said, and in the course of events Jeremiah's words were proven true: God brought judgment against Jerusalem and the nation.[70] There are other characteristics of true prophecy and the true prophet discerned by Childs in Jere-

---

66. Childs, *Old Testament Theology in a Canonical Context*, 133–44.
67. Ibid., 133.
68. Ibid., 134.
69. Ibid., 136–39.
70. Ibid., 140–41.

miah 23–29: the message's clarity of content and the moral life of the spokesperson. But only the course of history can truly make the determination as to what is true.

Finally, Childs approaches the witness of Jeremiah within the larger parameters of his fully developed biblical theology. One should begin by recalling Childs's emphasis on taking seriously the distinctive witness of the Old Testament. There is a vertical and even an existential dimension of the Old Testament witness, including the distinctive voices that express that witness, for the believing community in the present.

Childs addresses Jeremiah indirectly within the larger context of "The Prophetic Tradition."[71] Eight topics comprise this section: "The Biblical Presentation," "The Origins of Prophecy," "The Historical Scope of the Prophetic Tradition," "The Formation of the Prophetic Corpus," "The Cessation of Prophecy," "The Relation of the Law and the Prophets," "Development and Change within the Prophetic Tradition," and "Prophetic Themes of Promise."

In characterizing the "biblical presentation," "origins," and "formation" of the prophetic tradition, Childs admits that the materials are diverse, have undergone major redactional revisions, and contain only very limited evidence for tracing their historical development. As is true in his *Introduction*, Childs argues that the material contained in the prophetic corpus does not allow for a reconstruction of the history of the "movement" and its various types. Instead, Childs argues, the interest of the Old Testament is theological and focuses primarily on the call of the prophets, not on the means or modes of inspiration. Social-scientific reconstructions not only are speculative in that they move beyond the limits of the evidence but are also heavily rationalistic and tend toward "demythologization."[72] Childs notes the diversity in the prophetic tradition in several examples, including the different trajectories that make their way into the thinking of early Christianity (especially Jeremiah and Deutero-Isaiah and their language of "new covenant, vicarious suffering, new creation, suffering servant") and rabbinic Judaism ("temple, cult, priesthood, law").[73]

---

71. Childs, *Biblical Theology of the Old and New Testaments*, 167–80.
72. Ibid., 168–69. Childs appears to be suggesting that a phenomenology of prophecy is developed that removes God language from view and replaces it with sociological and anthropological categories for explaining the nature and character of prophecy. For example, prophecy is a social institution directly related to the Israelite monarchy or ecstasy is a psychological state that explains the prophetic phenomenon of inspiration and revelation.
73. Ibid., 176.

Childs points to the canonical or theological shaping of the prophetic tradition by the Deuteronomists ("The Historical Scope of the Prophetic Tradition") who are the first to develop "a genuine theology of the prophets."[74] This theological rendering of prophecy includes Moses as the paradigm for all legitimate "word" prophets, the emphasis on the validity and claims of the covenant, the articulation of criteria for distinguishing between true and false prophets, Israel's history of disobedience, the prophet as the preacher of repentance (a message that largely goes unheeded), and especially the sequencing of a series of promises and fulfillments that end with the tragedy of the exile. This Deuteronomic editing of the prophetic corpus, according to Childs, "left its decisive stamp on Jeremiah."[75]

Childs's remarks concerning "The Relation of the Law and the Prophets" cover familiar territory. Rehearsing the scholarly debate that has recognized the tension between the law and the prophets, Childs takes the position that "the prophets can only be understood by assuming the authority of Israel's ancient covenantal law which they used as a warrant for their message of divine judgment."[76] However, according to Childs, this does not mean that the prophets are only commentators on the law or that their independence and freedom are denied by the constrictions of legal prescription. For Childs,

> There is a radical newness to the prophets' message, a deeper plunge in the reality of God, a freedom of prophetic function (von Rad, *Theology*, II, 70ff.) which cannot be contained within the category of mere commentary.[77]

Childs sides with Walther Zimmerli, not with Gerhard von Rad, in arguing that the Torah embodies both "law and gospel" existing in dialectical tension and that the prophets understood their role to be the proclaimers of judgment to a disobedient people.

Childs directly speaks to the rendering of "promise" in Jeremiah when he notes that Jeremiah makes use of the renderings of future hope in the faith traditions of earlier Israel. He argues that chapters 30–31 articulate a message of promise to the northern tribes who

---

74. Ibid., 170.
75. For an overview of the Deuteronomic redaction of Jeremiah, see Perdue, "Jeremiah in Modern Research: Approaches and Issues," Perdue and Kovacs, *A Prophet to the Nations*, 1–32.
76. Childs, *Biblical Theology of the Old and New Testaments*, 174.
77. Ibid., 175.

had experienced the Assyrian destruction of their state but do so by pointing to a return to Jerusalem to worship Yahweh. However, "the main point," as Childs sees it, is the recognition that "Jeremiah's promise of hope . . . has been articulated in the language and traditions of Deuteronomy, most likely in the early post-exilic period."[78] This does not mean that Childs is reverting to a historical-critical paradigm that would suggest that Jeremiah's prophetic message may have been distorted but rather that this group of tradents "accorded special authority" to this prophet.

AN EVALUATION OF CANON THEOLOGY

While Childs's canonical approach has elicited significant discussion about a variety of issues and questions,[79] this evaluation will center on two areas: the canonical approach's rendering of Old Testament theology and, more specifically, his understanding of the theology of Jeremiah.

THE OLD TESTAMENT AS SCRIPTURE: THE CANONICAL PROCESS

The contributions to Old Testament theology by Childs are both provocative and significant. Above all, he reminds us that, in the view of Judaism and Christianity, the Old Testament is Scripture and embodies not only the religious ideas of historical communities but also, and more importantly, witnesses to the Word of God in ways that must be taken seriously by ongoing communities of faith. Thus Childs clearly distinguishes his approach from efforts to present the history of Israelite religion. The Bible was not intended primarily to be a collection of ancient records, readily accessed by contemporary historians intent on doing historical reconstruction but rather a sacred canon that is normative and authoritative for the faith and practice of living religious communities. Thus Childs draws a very clear line between Old Testament theology that is approached by confessing scholars from within believing communities and the history of Israelite religion that is presented by scholars

---

78. Ibid., 178.
79. See the responses in *JSOT* 16 (1980) by James Barr, Joseph Blenkinsopp, Henri Cazelles, George Landes, Roland Murphy, Rudolf Smend, and others. Also see the critical response to the theological implications of the method by John Hayes (Hayes and Prussner, *Old Testament Theology*, 268–73). Barr has especially taken Childs to task in *Holy Scripture: Canon, Authority, and Criticism* (Philadelphia: Westminster, 1983).

of the academy who may or may not have an interest in the hermeneutical implications of their study for modern faith. This means
that what is studied, that is, the Bible, is viewed differently by an
Old Testament theologian (canon) than by a historian (cultural
artifact). The chief object of study for the Old Testament theologian
is the canon, in particular the distinctive witness of this part of the
canon which needs to be heard as normative Scripture in its own
terms, while the historian cannot limit his or her attention to these
books without a consideration of the data of history provided by
archaeology and the literatures of the ancient Near East. Indeed,
any and all material available for study (the Bible, other written
records including ancient Near Eastern sources, and the material
culture of archaeology) is scrutinized and used in historical reconstruction.

Childs's contribution to Old Testament theology also resides in
his rejection of the position of romanticism that the earliest voice
within a text is the truly authentic and even normative one in
contrast to later voices that do not merit the same hearing by interpreters and their communities of faith. There has been a general
tendency among Old Testament scholars to play down the theological contributions of tradents, redactors, and authors of later
sources who contributed to the shaping of an Old Testament tradition before it received its final form. The Old Testament theologian, approaching the material with hermeneutical interest, and
the academician seeking to reconstruct the history and meaning of
the text, both have generally privileged either for theological or
historical reasons the earliest recoverable stage of biblical texts.
Childs has strongly argued that it is the canon and final form of Old
Testament books that require a full hearing and serious response by
believing communities. While earlier voices may be heard by means
of the application of historical-critical method, the later voices cannot be ignored or less valued by confessing communities and still
allow for the Old Testament to function as Scripture. Not all interpreters will follow Childs to his conclusion in arguing that only the
final, canonical form of the text is authoritative and normative for
contemporary confessing communities. But he requires the church
and academy to attend to the canonical form and not simply to the
earliest recoverable stage.

Childs's approach also allows the Old Testament canon to address the Christian community and to be heard. The Old Testament
is not simply a collection of books with antiquated ideas of passing
historical interest that are replaced by the New Testament, but it

also contains within it a Word of God that addresses normatively and authoritatively future generations, including our own. Childs's objective in his *Introduction* is to point to the canonical shape of each individual book in the Old Testament and then to indicate the hermeneutical implications for both Old Testament theology and contemporary hermeneutics, but his task is not to write a constructive, systematic Old Testament theology that indicates exactly what the meaning of a text is for contemporary believers in their context. Even in his Old Testament theology and biblical theology, he seeks mainly to describe how the canonical approach extrapolates and sets forth major theological themes in the Old Testament, but he does not attempt to bring these into serious conversation with contemporary theology. Nevertheless these formulations of the canonical shape of individual books and Old Testament themes are expected to contribute in important ways to later stages of theological reflection in biblical theology and contemporary hermeneutics.

This emphasis on hearing the Old Testament means, for Childs, that it is not superseded or discarded by the appearance of the New Testament. He notes that early Christianity valued the Old Testament as Scripture and continued to do so even after the finalizing of the New Testament canon. The Marcionite heresy, which often is latent within the ongoing history of Christianity, continues to threaten the value of the Old Testament as Scripture. Thus Childs's work reminds the church that the Old Testament must continue to be addressed and heard as Scripture.

Childs also is refreshingly open about his own stance as a Christian interpreter of Scripture. He approaches his work, not from the position of historical curiosity, but from that of a believer who stands within a confessing community whose faith continues to seek understanding. His own work as scholar is shaped by his Christian confession. This parallels the frankness of many feminist and liberation interpreters who openly admit that they work out of a particular paradigm of belief or philosophical orientation. Indeed, Childs believes that Old Testament theology is Christian theology. Thus he is not attempting to write a theology of the Hebrew Bible appropriate for Jews, although he makes an effort to remain in dialogue with them. This is one reason he accepts as the authoritative collection of texts the traditional Jewish Hebrew canon and not the Greek canon of the Septuagint or the later Vulgate, even though the latter were the Bible for the large majority of Christians until the Reformation.

Childs's approach also offers fresh insight into the meanings of texts, because the context is not primarily history but rather the canon. Meaning changes when context changes, whether one is speaking of a social-historical setting, a literary corpus, or a theological tradition.[80] Through intertextuality Childs demonstrates that each passage of Scripture should be read and illuminated by reference to the entire canon. This does not lead Childs to diminish the diversity of voices in the text but places the various books and sections into dialogue.

Finally, Childs reminds us not only of the theological nature of the Old Testament but also of the importance of believing communities who shaped and were shaped by the texts that were selected for canonical inclusion. These communities inevitably made choices as to what to transmit, and for Childs these choices represent the decisions and insights of many generations of faith. The movement is away from a one-sided emphasis on the original author to include the recognition of the importance of the community of faith in the canonical process.

With this said, however, there are still important questions and concerns that should be raised. One of the most difficult problems facing the interpreter of Childs has been Childs's lack of clarity in speaking of rather key terms.[81] This is true even of the crucial term "canon." At times it refers to the final form of an individual book like Jeremiah, in contrast to earlier stages in the composition of a book. At other times, it is either an abstract theological concept apparently deriving from systematic or confessional theology that conveys certain understandings of the authority and revelation inherent in Scripture or a normative value attributed by a community at some unknown time to a text or collection of texts. Sometimes it is a collection of texts, specifically the Hebrew Bible of early Judaism, that contains boundaries that exclude other writings. At other times, canon is a context in which theological interpretation is to occur. Even when Childs attends to this criticism in his biblical theology by summarizing his various understandings of the term, the variety of uses in the context of his writing does not always yield

---

80. See the essay by Erhard S. Gerstenberger, "Canon Criticism and the Meaning of Sitz im Leben," Tucker, *Canon, Theology, and Old Testament Interpretation*, 20–31. Gerstenberger discusses the incarnation of the "Word of God" in social history and indicates that this is the major problem he has with Childs.

81. See Margaret Davies, "Review of Old Testament Theology in a Canonical Context," *JTS* 37 (1986) 442–45.

clarity. It is also not clear how Childs would differentiate canon from Scripture, although he apparently has some difference in mind. This multifaceted understanding of canon, not to mention equally ambiguous terms such as canonical process, canonical intentionality, and canonical integrity, makes it difficult at times to grasp clearly what Childs intends as he speaks in various places about his interpretative enterprise.

One also wonders why "canon" in any or all of the above understandings should be given primary consideration in the interpretation of the Bible, in biblical theology, and at times it seems even in modern hermeneutics. Childs may well have his reasons and an argument to make, yet these are not explicitly brought together in a full and clear statement. Instead, he seems mainly to work from the assumption that canon, theologically conceived as authoritative revelation, has this privileged status. What of the authority and theological value of events, persons, communities both ancient and modern, and tradition? What of reason and experience? Certainly, these elements come into play in Childs's efforts to enable Scripture to speak to a present community. It would be helpful if Childs would address the importance of these areas in matters of contemporary hermeneutics and authority. In contrast to Protestantism, Judaism and Roman Catholicism do not privilege Scripture to the virtual exclusion of later tradition. Why should interpreters who come from a variety of different religious traditions do so? One wishes that Childs would be far more explicit about his own particular religious tradition and theological understandings and then indicate how canon is understood and functions within his specific community of faith. It is clear, however, that Childs is expressing a theological conviction about canon that is heavily weighted by his own Protestant understanding. Childs should simply make his own confessional stance more clear and then articulate some arguments for his privileging of canon.

Perhaps the most serious question raised by Childs's version of the canonical approach is the loss of the sustained importance of historical particularity in canonical interpretation.[82] Childs does

---

82. James Luther Mays points out that the major tension facing the Old Testament theologian resides in the relationship between faith and history, "between a literature whose origin is sought in historical causes and whose meaning is seen as a function of its ancient setting and a theology which seeks to read it as authoritative scripture for contemporary believing" ("What Is Written," 152).

not deny that it may be possible to identify early sources or stages of tradition along the way to the development of the canonical text. And when these are identified, they should be brought into conversation with the final shape of the canonical book and the canon as a whole. It is not true that he abandons historical-critical research as he carries out his canonical approach, although he often points to the hypothetical character of the results of this type of study. For Old Testament theology, however, and indeed for subsequent stages in critical reflection (biblical theology and contemporary hermeneutics), historical particularity receives little theological significance for Childs.[83] This is due to his consistent argument that the canon was shaped to transcend the particularities of the social history of texts, communities, and tradents in order to address all future generations of believers. This is why, he argues, it is so difficult to reconstruct the historical circumstances of most texts. If historical circumstances were so important, he asks, why are they often ignored or obscured by those who shaped the canon? It is only when some redactors and tradents (see the Deuteronomistic History and Jeremiah, to name two examples) were concerned to provide dates and other sociohistorical information, even if modern scholars think this information is at times wrong or distorted, that Childs consents to the view that the historical context is important for the canonical meaning of the text.[84]

This point of the lack of theological value associated with historical particularity is taken even further by Childs's argument that it is the canonical intentionality of the text, not that of the original author or redactor, that is important.[85] Here Childs is joined by

83. Childs points to the problems of history in his excursus "The Theological Problem of Old Testament History," *Biblical Theology of the Old and New Testaments*, 196–207.

84. Brett disagrees that Childs totally dispenses with the theological importance of historical particularity. He thinks that Childs is not looking for lasting religious ideas but rather is seeking to discover how the canonical form might enable historical data to continue to have significance beyond their time and place (*Biblical Theology in Crisis?* 76–115).

85. Childs's former student, Gerald Shepherd, supports his teacher in this contention ("Hearing the Voice of the Same God through Historically Dissimilar Traditions," *Int* 36 [1982] 21–33). See the critique offered by Sean E. McEvenue, "The Old Testament, Scripture or Theology?" *Int* 35 (1981) 229–42, who argues not only for the importance of authorial intention but also for the importance of historical particularity. See Joseph Blenkinsopp, *Prophecy and Canon: A Contribution to the Study of Jewish Origins* (Notre Dame, Ind.: University of Notre Dame Press, 1977) 142–43. See also the essay by Roy Melugin, "Canon and Exegetical Method," in the same volume (pp. 48–61). Melugin uses the terms "synchronic" for Childs's understanding of context and "diachronic" for the

some modern literary critics and phenomenologists who argue that meaning is found within the literary boundaries of the world of the text and not within the mind of the author. This also means for Childs that the understanding of the original audience, even if it could be recaptured, is of no real theological importance. Childs submits that canonical texts were shaped to transcend their historical contexts to speak a Word of God to future communities.

This lack of the consistent importance of historical particularity for canonical interpretation is seen in Childs's treatment of those involved in the shaping of what eventually became Scripture over many generations and even many centuries. Childs avoids wanting to say who they may have been by arguing that the lack of importance attributed to their identities is evidenced by the fact that the text succeeds in hiding them from view. Since for Childs the canonical process began in the early preexilic period, these canonizers must have been authors, tradents, and redactors who over the centuries shaped the canon. However, should one not want to understand how they interacted with their own religious communities and cultures? Is it unimportant to attempt to determine what influence their historical setting may have had on their thinking, even if theories and hypotheses necessarily have to be developed to get at this interaction?[86] But for Childs, to ask these questions of identity is to suggest that their social and historical context as well as their own intentions were of importance in shaping the canon and therefore carry important theological weight. For Childs, these are not consistently important in the Bible and thus are considered irrelevant theologically. He asserts that the primary intention of the shapers of the canon is to transmit a tradition becoming Scripture that would address not only their own but indeed future generations. It is interesting to note, however, that at times he will remark that Deuteronomic redactors, for example, were instrumental in the canonical process. Even so, he usually avoids historical speculation about the canonizers as not being very useful and indeed generally unimportant for the canonical meaning, especially since this type of historical imagination directs attention to the canonizers instead of to the canonical process and the text.[87]

---

understanding of those who point to the importance of social history as context for interpretation.

86. See George M. Landes, "The Canonical Approach to Introducing the Old Testament: Prodigy and Problems," *JSOT* 16 (1980) 36–37.

87. Paul Hanson outlined his own interactional model (text and community) in his volume *Dynamic Transcendence* (Philadelphia: Fortress, 1978). The key

There is one other ramification of Childs's rejection of historical particularity as important to the theological enterprise and that is the issue of ideology as seen through the eyes of a hermeneutics of suspicion. While Childs is not in agreement, it is reasonable to assume that social groups in ancient Israel, including those to which authors and redactors and tradents belonged, at times shaped ideologies of self-interest that eventually entered the Old Testament. The canonical approach does not have an obvious place for a critical, much less self-critical hermeneutics of suspicion in working with biblical texts. This is a significant shortcoming and could legitimate, if not corrected, a tendency toward absolutizing of even theologically distorted or inappropriate biblical views, including ones that are sexist, patriarchal, homophobic, and supportive of genocide and slavery.[88]

The debate about the locus of meaning cannot be resolved here. The primary point is that words, sentences, or even texts can convey meaning that is significantly different and even distorted when removed from the original context(s) of the author and audience. Obviously, any text can be taken out of an original setting and placed in a new one that is totally different. And meaning invariably changes. This occurs internally to the Bible in the traditioning and

---

feature is the movement from a static model of theology (God, the Bible, hermeneutics) to a dynamic one. Now see his *The Called People: The Growth of Community in the Bible* (New York: Harper & Row, 1986). James Sanders has constructed his own formula for canon criticism which has important ramifications for doing Old Testament theology, especially by emphasizing the ongoing interaction between community and text. This interaction is traced diachronically through the growth of the canon and into the present context of the church (Sanders, "Canonical Context and Canonical Criticism"; and idem, *Canon and Community: A Guide to Canonical Criticism*; also see Sanders, "Adaptable for Life: The Nature and Function of Canon," *Magnalia Dei: The Mighty Acts of God* [ed. Frank Moore Cross, Jr., et al.; Garden City, N.Y.: Doubleday, 1976] 531–60; and idem, *From Sacred Story to Sacred Text* [Philadelphia: Fortress, 1987]). Unlike Childs, Sanders sees canonical criticism, as he prefers to call the approach, developing out of historical criticism and being the next logical step after redaction criticism. The major difficulty with Sanders centers on his affirming pluralism and diversity in the canon, but without addressing the problems that pluralism raises. By acknowledging but not dealing with the difficulty, he embraces the fragmentation that represents major obstacles to the presentation of Old Testament theology in any systematic or constructive form.

88. See Gottwald, "Social Matrix and Canonical Shape," 318; and Walter Brueggemann, "Review of Old Testament Theology in a Canonical Context, by Brevard Childs," *TToday* 4 (1986) 286. Brueggemann argues: "By dismissing and excluding historical perspective, Childs—when he wants—is able to make things flat and absolute in ways that are not always convincing" (p. 286). There also is no obvious place for self-criticism that exposes ideological tendencies in the interpreter.

redactional process, and it occurs as biblical texts continue to enter new social and cultural contexts. Words, once uttered, take on a life of their own as they find opportunity to settle into new contexts. Texts create a world of meaning, a vision of reality, although not by themselves. Worldviews also require the active participation of interpreters and context. Do not the historical and cultural particularities of the later audience play a large role in determining what a text is "heard" to say? Context becomes important, but now it is the context of the interpreter or new audience or different literary tradition that assumes importance and not the original context. If this is the case, then why should one deny significance to the earlier contexts of author and redactor in the interpretative enterprise?[89]

To represent these issues surrounding historical particularity as unimportant for the understanding and even appropriation of the Old Testament as Scripture appears to remove all remnants of human culture as a significant consideration in theological discourse. There is a conversation, but it is between believers and non-believers and culture. Can theological discourse that enables faith to seek understanding simply dismiss culture?

The lack of significance given to historical particularity also means that Childs cannot be very explicit about the function of Scripture within the believing communities of ancient Israel.[90] In addition, it is arguable that even from a biblical perspective the presence of God is located also within the imperfections of human culture, not predominantly in the written words of the text or spoken words of the text.[91]

One may rightly laud Childs's efforts to counteract the theological judgment by some scholars that the earliest stage of a tradition is "authentic" and normative, while later stages are "inauthentic," less historical, if not untrue, and thus not as valuable for understanding

---

89. Sanders, "Canonical Context and Canonical Criticism," 186. Sanders argues that Childs's view of communities in effect eliminates their importance in producing and handing down the text.

90. Ibid., 186. Sanders asks: "How can one be so concerned to rehabilitate the function of Scripture in the believing communities when he effectively denies the importance and humanity of those very communities by ruling out ancient historical contexts in discussing ancient texts—not only the original ones but the subsequent historical contexts through the periods of intense canonical process?" (p. 190). Sanders is concerned not only to trace the historical development of canon but also to determine how traditions functioned authoritatively within these historical communities (*Canon and Community*, 24).

91. Bruce Birch, "Tradition, Canon and Biblical Theology," *HBT* 2 (1980) 122.

Israelite theology or for contributing to matters germane to modern faith. Childs helps us to appreciate the theological legitimacy of later redactors and bearers of tradition who attempted to reappropriate an earlier message for a new setting and different community. However, just as troublesome for some is his denying of normative, theological value to earlier stages in the tradition. Now Childs admits that these earlier stages perhaps were authoritative for their communities when they were first shaped and for a time, perhaps, even later, but only the final form of the text is Scripture for those living after the canon was closed. But one might ask Childs, why should the interpreter, either as modern scholar or confessing believer or both, identify the final form of the text with the truly authentic voice? Why also should one prefer the work of a late canonizer from the postexilic or Hellenistic period who shaped the meaning of the tradition in another direction over the words of the historical voice, say, of Jeremiah, uttered several centuries earlier? Is one not especially privileging the views of the canonizers in late Judaism who finalized the form of the text? Childs's main explanation seems to be that the canonical books in final form, not an earlier stage, were canonized. Yet even he admits that the decisive forces of canonization were at work throughout the biblical period, not simply at the end. Thus authority should not be located only at the end of the process any more than it should be solely identified with the beginning. Rather, the recovery of stages along the way to the completion of the canon could well speak authoritatively to future generations of believers.[92]

Then there is the issue of the plurality and diversity of voices that are heard even within the same book, not just within the larger canon. Indeed, this plurality of voices is the most significant problem posed by the canon. At most, Childs will speak of intertextual dialogue, tensions, and dynamic interactions within a text or the entire canon, noting that Scripture does not attempt to harmonize differences. He is also careful to trace a theme through Scripture, indicating the variety of ways it develops and changes. Yet, is this really enough, especially for a theologian concerned with allowing Scripture to address modern faith? What happens when a Jeremiah, as best as we may understand him, and his canonizer are in conflict, or when a later tradent either misunderstood the prophet

92. See Douglas A. Knight, "Canon and the History of Tradition: A Critique of Brevard S. Childs's *Introduction to the Old Testament as Scripture*," *HBT* 2 (1980) 127–49; Birch, "Tradition, Canon and Biblical Theology," 113–25; and Barr, *Holy Scripture*, 94.

or offered a contrary theological position? What happens when a significant theological meaning from an earlier stage of a text or a book is altered or even negated by a later stage or book? What happens when various positions in Scripture are taken on almost every theological issue? To be fair to Childs, he is not writing a constructive theology where such judgments presumably would be made, but some guidance here, if only in a preliminary form, would be helpful in making discriminations between positions that lead to the affirmation of one, the negation of another, or still the reformulation of a new one resulting from the blending of several. After all, it is the canon itself that raises the problem of pluralism; it is not a problem created by scholars. Pointing out the theological richness of diversity is important, but certainly pluralism carries with it significant difficulties that require theological reflection and response.

One of the major concerns with Childs's approach is his decision to privilege as theologically normative and authoritative, that is, as Scripture, one form of the canon: the Jewish canon of the late postexilic period which survives in the Masoretic text, as over against the larger Roman Catholic canon or the various Greek canons, including that represented by the Septuagint. Childs's argument is that the Old Testament has primarily been transmitted through Judaism, and this very fact allows for a common Scripture with Christianity. This in turn sets the stage for fruitful dialogue between Christians and Jews.[93] And he attempts to rescue his privileging of the Jewish form of the Old Testament by submitting that there are not really important differences between the books considered canonical by Christians and Jews and that even the inclusion of the so-called Apocrypha did not significantly alter the content of Scripture's witness. Yet it is the canon as a collection of sacred books that often divides, not only Jews and Christians over the question of the New Testament, but also various groups of Christians (Protestant, Roman Catholic, and Orthodox).[94] In contrast to the Jewish Bible, the Roman Catholic canon includes the so-called deuterocanonical books, while the Coptic canon contains even a larger number.[95] To say that the content of the faith is not

93. Barr, *Holy Scripture*, 151–52.
94. James Barr, "Childs' Introduction to the Old Testament as Scripture," *JSOT* 16 (1980) 22.
95. See Jared Jackson's review in which he raises the issue of different sequencing of books by the various collections. This, he argues, also has to do with interpretation ("Review of Old Testament Theology in a Canonical Context," *HBT* 9 [1987] 71–72).

significantly altered by the inclusion of the Apocrypha is certainly open to serious skepticism, while to argue that the quest for the canon helps to constitute faith contributes very little to this theological crux.

One often hears from Childs, especially in but not limited to his *Introduction*, that historical criticism is "theologically bankrupt" because it does not lead to Old Testament theology and then to contemporary hermeneutics. Childs's major motivation in shaping a canonical approach is that it will lead to theological presentation. However, what of important work done in the area of Old Testament theology by historical critics? In his *Introduction*, it does not seem fair play for Childs largely to ignore the theological work that has been done by historical critics and then to take historical criticism to task for being theologically bankrupt. While there are inherent difficulties in historically proving that a confessional "event" like the exodus actually happened, the moves to biblical theology and then to the faith of modern confessional communities by scholars such as Wright and von Rad, for example, are theological contributions worthy of serious consideration. It is true that in his later writings Childs acknowledges the value of previous Old Testament theologians like Gerhard von Rad and Walther Zimmerli. But to ignore these efforts in his *Introduction* leads to an unbalanced presentation that does not take into full consideration the theological insights and contributions of historical critics whom he often takes to task.[96]

Finally, Childs is not consistent in arguing that, on the one hand, streams of tradition that did not flow into later texts, including the New Testament, are implicitly negated (e.g., the conquest of Canaan) or, on the other hand, should be heard as a distinctive witness in their own terms. Would it not be better to negate the horror of conquest by reference not only to its absence or reformulation in later biblical traditions but also to the criteria of norms functioning within contemporary hermeneutics? In other words, why not simply negate this tradition as theologically illegitimate for contemporary faith? Why not simply render a value judgment and defend it in theological terms that derive from one's own tradition of faith?

CANON THEOLOGY AND THE BOOK OF JEREMIAH

Childs's analysis of Jeremiah in his *Introduction* makes an important contribution to the understanding of this book. Childs en-

96. Barr, "Childs' Introduction," 20.

gages the most complex of problems, that of the relationship between the poetry and the prose, and succeeds in relating the two theologically. That is, Jeremiah reshaped his earlier poetic sayings in response to the "preacher of judgment" in a book that had become Scripture in his own day: the Book of Deuteronomy. Childs also gives an authentic voice to the canonizers who shaped the Book of Jeremiah into its final form. He does not deny them authenticity, as many earlier historical critics have tended to do.

While Childs often points to what he considers only hypothetical and conflicting interpretations offered by historical critics that their methods may not successfully resolve, one may suggest that many of his alternative understandings are just as open to question and often not all that new. For example, as noted above, Childs in his *Introduction* argues that it is Jeremiah himself who is responsible for reinterpreting his prophetic activity and his earlier oracles in the light of the preacher of judgment set forth in Deuteronomy. This is Childs's key example of the canonical process at work in the Book of Jeremiah, for Deuteronomy, if not an earlier form of that tradition, had already begun to achieve the authoritative status of Scripture. Thus the prophet takes this tradition as Scripture and uses it to reinterpret his ministry and prophetic oracles. Yet, how does Childs know it is Jeremiah who takes this step? It is just as logical and convincing to argue, as many scholars have, that this step is taken by either Baruch or a later Deuteronomic editor. Perhaps late canonizers are responsible for reinterpreting Jeremiah in the light of Deuteronomy or a postdeuteronomic tradition. In any case, this interpretation of representing Jeremiah in the role of a Deuteronomic preacher is a long-standing one in Jeremiah studies, whether the step is taken by Jeremiah himself or by a later person or group who reshapes his life and message. Indeed, Childs, in his later biblical theology, appears to shift his position by noting that the Deuteronomic school had a major influence on shaping this prophetic text, although he draws up short of saying that these redactors altered or distorted the message of the prophet to whom they accorded a special authority.

Then there is the question of the canonical text of Jeremiah. For Childs, it is always the Masoretic text that is the "vehicle" to the canonical text. Historically speaking, Childs is probably correct in pointing to the first century C.E. as the time when the consonants of the pre-Masoretic text were stabilized, although competing textual traditions produced by other groups (Masoretic and non-Masoretic) and even written in different languages (e.g., Greek) certainly existed before the living communities that transmitted them ceased to exist. But the point is not to reiterate the fact that different religious communities, both Jewish and Christian, have different canons. Rather, it is to ask why Childs privileges the Masoretic text over the ancient versions even in cases when it is obvious that the Masoretic textual tradition is at times very problematic. Can the textual tradition be improved by later communities through textual criticism?[97] What of the fact that there are competing Masoretic families of texts and variance even within the same family. One might even go beyond this to historical errors in the canonical text. Should they be retained? Childs does respond to this query. To have a canon means that "the theological 'data' on which the church's identity is grounded does not lie in the events themselves, or in the text itself, but in the canonical text which has interpreted the events and which receives its meaning in the context of a community of faith." Does this mean that textual errors are a part of the canonical tradition and should not be removed?[98]

This area under discussion illustrates clearly the difference between Childs and historical critics in their handling of textual traditions. According to one school of thought, the Septuagint, which appears to represent an earlier short Hebrew text of Jeremiah, is the more historically original. That is, it is closer to the historical Jeremiah, for it has undergone less expansion because of later redaction.[99] The Masoretic text, by contrast, reflects a later Hebrew recension, and even a different family of Hebrew texts. For Childs, by contrast, the Masoretic text, not the Septuagint, is the canonical tradition for understanding the theology of the Book of Jeremiah. However, one is then puzzled when Childs qualifies his position by noting that the competing canons of different Catholic communities, containing some texts written or preserved in Greek, do not represent a major change in the content of the faith.

This is the tension that Old Testament scholars face who belong to communities of faith: to engage in historical study, in this case textual criticism, may lead the interpreter to regard the Septuagint of Jeremiah as historically the preferred text. To engage in theological construction, at least as represented by Childs, the same scholars should move into a different mode and work with the Masoretic tradition, for it is, in Childs's judgment, a better vehicle to the original canonical text. For Childs, the canonical approach

97. Roland E. Murphy, "The Old Testament as Scripture," *JSOT* 16 (1980) 40–41.
98. Childs, "A Response," *HBT* 2 (1980) 207.
99. See Perdue, "Jeremiah in Modern Research," 10–14.

and its Masoretic text are privileged theologically as Scripture, while historical criticism and its arguments that a version or another textual tradition are to be preferred are denied any real theological importance. What may be true historically is not necessarily true theologically, and what may be true theologically is not necessarily true historically.

There is also the question of the different placement of the oracles against the nations in the Masoretic text and the Septuagint. Certainly, two, if not more, communities of faith in a different historical and social context made different decisions. In any case, the different locations of the "Oracles against the Nations," contrary to Childs, could lead to different theological understandings of the Book of Jeremiah. To place them in the middle of the book suggests that the coming judgment against Judah in the form of Babylonian invasion, following the defeat of Egypt by Nebuchadrezzar at Carchemish in 605 B.C.E., is but a stage in God's judgment against the nations and ultimately against Babylon itself. To place them near the end more clearly indicates that judgment will be followed by salvation, precipitated by the fall of the nations and especially Babylon.[100] Childs is correct in arguing that the general theological point is the same: Yahweh is the Lord of history who brings both judgment and salvation. However, the placement of the oracles does offer possibilities for important theological refinement.

CONCLUSION

Certainly there is much value in the canonical approach, for it reminds both the interpreter and the believer of important questions to pose in faith's quest for understanding. Childs's many contributions to theological discourse are of great significance, and his positions are particularly provocative. However, the occasional polarization between the canonical approach and historical criticism is unfortunate, for both may have an important role to play even in theological discussions and contemporary hermeneutics. Instead of seeing the canonical approach as the panacea for leading to the presentation of Old Testament theology even as Scripture, it would be better to include it as one approach among many others that have value in relationship to the questions asked and the answers discovered.[101]

100. Childs, *Old Testament Theology in a Canonical Context*, 38.
101. See Brett, *Biblical Theology in Crisis?*

CHAPTER 7

From History to Metaphor:
Literary Criticism
and Feminist Hermeneutics

Since the 1960s, the methodologies and insights of literary criticism and the phenomenology of language have been applied increasingly to biblical interpretation and Old Testament theology and have produced significant results. Among the results have been important literary studies in the areas of metaphor and rhetorical criticism, the subjects of this chapter. Developments in the study of metaphor and rhetorical criticism have been combined, on occasion, with feminist hermeneutics to shape new ways of doing Old Testament theology. This is not to suggest that feminist theology is always or even necessarily linked to literary criticism. Indeed, some feminist scholars work out of a diachronic, social-scientific model for liberation theology in similar fashion to Norman Gottwald. For example, two feminist biblical scholars who use historical-critical method within the larger matrix of liberation theology are Carol Meyers and Elisabeth Schüssler Fiorenza.[1] However, the contemporary church's concern for inclusive language, especially ways of speaking about God, is reflected in feminist efforts to pay close attention to the language of the biblical text. Thus the rhetorical character of texts is examined to find feminine images for God, recover women's stories, undermine patriarchy, and expose sexism.

FEMINIST THEOLOGY

Feminist theology began to achieve prominence in the 1970s, accelerated by the struggles of women for liberation for the last

---

1. Elisabeth Schüssler Fiorenza, *In Memory of Her* (New York: Crossroad, 1983); and Carol L. Meyers, *Discovering Eve: Ancient Israelite Women in Context* (Oxford: Oxford University Press, 1988).

century.[2] There is, of course, significant diversity in feminist theology. It is neither a method nor an ideology. A great variety exists in regard to theory, analysis, and objectives. Distinctions are now being made between first generation feminist theology and second generation. The first generation concentrated mainly on the critique of patriarchy and pointed to the limitations of theology that did not take women's issues and women's experiences seriously, while the second generation is now moving beyond critical evaluation to a more systematic presentation. The reshaping of theological language is under way in contemporary feminist hermeneutics and modern study of the Bible.

There are important themes and emphases that bring together the diverse expressions of feminist theology. Responding to systemic oppression and victimization, women's liberation is a multifaceted response that seeks through a variety of strategies to effectuate social, economic, political, cultural, and religious change that not only will eventuate in the equality of women but at the same time will lead to the recognition and authentication of their full humanity. Many forms of social existence use gender to support male domination (patriarchy) and female subordination.[3] The ideological undergirding of patriarchy is sexism. Feminism actively seeks to identify the various manifestations of sexism, misogyny, and patriarchy, forces that exploit and subordinate women, and then to

2. Among the many important works in feminist theology are Anne Carr, *Transforming Grace: Christian Tradition and Women's Experience* (San Francisco: Harper & Row, 1987); Mary Daly, *Beyond God the Father: Toward a Philosophy of Women's Liberation* (Boston: Beacon, 1978); Jacquelyn Grant, *White Women's Christ and Black Women's Jesus: Feminist Christology and Womanist Response* (Atlanta: Scholars Press, 1989); Carter Heyward, *Touching Our Strength: The Erotic as Power and the Love of God* (San Francisco: Harper & Row, 1989); Rosemary Ruether, *Sexism and God-Talk: Toward a Feminist Theology* (Boston: Beacon, 1983); Letty Russell, *Human Liberation in a Feminist Perspective—A Theology* (Philadelphia: Westminster, 1974); *Feminist Interpretation of the Bible* (ed. Letty Russell; Philadelphia: Westminster, 1985); and Susan Thistlethwaite, *Sex, Race and God: Christian Feminism in Black and White* (New York: Crossroad, 1989). For recent surveys of feminist theology, see Pamela Dickey Young, *Feminist Theology/Christian Theology* (Minneapolis: Fortress, 1990). For an example of feminist biblical interpretation, see *The Women's Bible Commentary* (ed. Carol A. Newsom and S. H. Ringe; Louisville, Ky.: Westminster/John Knox, 1992). Trible's article "Five Loaves and Two Fishes" provides a succinct summary of feminism and its impact on biblical theology. Also see D. C. Bass, "Women's Studies and Biblical Studies: An Historical Perspective," *JSOT* 22 (1982) 6–12; and Katherine Doob Sakenfeld, "Feminist Perspectives on Bible and Theology," *Int* 42 (1988) 5–18.
3. Trible, "Five Loaves and Two Fishes," 280. Trible defines patriarchy as "the institutionalization of male dominance over women in home and society at large."

subvert them by means of a variety of different strategies. As a manifestation of the sinful distortion of the image of God that involves both male and female, patriarchy is prophetically opposed and subverted.[4]

Because sin permeates all areas of human life (e.g., sex, economics, class, and family), feminists operate on the understanding that sexism is but one of many related forms of pervasive oppression that include racism, fascism, capitalism, and colonialism. Thus, there is often an explicit concern to work with other oppressed groups to subvert all forms of oppression that lead to the denial of full humanity to any person or group. Indeed, there is at times even an expressed desire to liberate the oppressor.

In the examination of sexist exploitation of women, feminists have recognized that religion has been used or misused to oppress women and other groups. This has led to the rejection of religion, including Christianity, by some feminists. Yet religion is also recognized as a powerful means by which to achieve liberation. To this end, there is a critical evaluation of religion and religious texts in order to deny to authentic religion myths, stories, rituals, symbols, and language that are oppressive, but yet at the same time to discover as well as create religious language and celebrations that are liberating.

Feminist theologians, historians, and biblical scholars have sought to recover women's stories in the Bible and Christian tradition in the effort to recognize the important contributions of women in religious history that had been lost, forgotten, or suppressed by patriarchy. There are various means of getting at these stories, including a "hermeneutics of suspicion" that attempts to identify evidences of patriarchy's efforts to suppress women's voices. This recovery of women's history represents, not merely an antiquarian interest in the past or the expression of pride in women's accomplishments, but also the desire to find new models for women in roles of leadership. The implication is that women would not be forced into male or patriarchal models of leadership that are oppressive.

Of great importance is the question of language. Feminists have recognized that, because of the power of language, "whoever names the world owns the world."[5] In large measure, men have dominated the naming process. Recognizing that traditional God language is

---

4. Ibid., 281.
5. Sallie McFague, *Metaphorical Theology* (Philadelphia: Fortress Press, 1982) 8.

largely patriarchal (God is father, king, lord, suzerain), feminist theology emphasizes that God is beyond gender (male or female), even though there are metaphorical ways of talking about God in sexual terms: God as male but also God as female. Inclusive language is broader in scope, however, than the matter of God-talk. Religious language describes human beings as well as God, and even language about God says a great deal about who human beings are. Thus, to limit metaphors for God to male terms (father, king, ruler, and lord) creates and legitimates a social reality in which males rule over women who are cast in a subordinate role.[6]

Discovering in the tradition language that either is demeaning to or affirming of women helps in the effort to shape a contemporary discourse in society and religion that recognizes the full humanity of all. Other metaphors for God, some new and others suppressed or residing forgotten within the tradition, have been proposed, including, for example, God as mother, friend, and lover.[7]

Of course, many other questions and concerns that are being raised and addressed by feminists impact contemporary and even biblical theology. For example, feminists raise the question of whether there is a distinctively female experience, consciousness, or embodiment that separates women from men. This question has major epistemological implications for various disciplines and their practice, including theology: women's experience may be used by feminists as a source for doing theology or even as a norm that evaluates theological expressions, including those in the Bible.[8] For feminists, theology that does not take into account or reflect women's experience is inauthentic. This point may be taken a step further by the argument that women's experience should contribute to the norms for evaluating theology.

Related to the matter of women's experience is the question of the relationship between the sexes. Are they enemies or partners? How may they relate authentically to each other in ways that affirm the full humanity of each, or is this even possible?

In more recent feminist theology, efforts are under way to con-

---

6. "Patriarchal language for God promotes an entire way of thinking, social constructions of race, class, and gender, for instance, that benefit males, especially white, affluent males" (Sallie McFague, "Mother God," *Motherhood: Experience, Institution, Theology* [ed. Anne Carr and Elisabeth Schüssler Fiorenza; Concilium; Edinburgh: T. & T. Clark, 1985] 138–43).

7. Sallie McFague, *Models of God: Theology for an Ecological, Nuclear Age* (Philadelphia: Fortress, 1987).

8. See Young, *Feminist Theology/Christian Theology*, 49–69.

struct a hermeneutic that embraces a common methodology. Some feminist theologians are no longer content only to evaluate critically religious traditions; rather, they now seek to develop a method with norms that not only undermine theologies that are patriarchal but that also allow constructive feminist theology to be written. How successful these efforts will be remains to be seen. Be that as it may, the present task is to present examples of feminist interpretations of Scripture that impact Old Testament theology in general and the Book of Jeremiah in particular. We shall begin with an understanding of the character of metaphor and then look at metaphorical theology as shaped by Sallie McFague.

METAPHOR AND RELIGIOUS LANGUAGE

Religious language about God is metaphorical in content, function, and meaning.[9] By means of its root metaphors a culture conveys its understandings of God and most cherished beliefs.[10] However, the effort to understand how metaphor works as an important element of language is often a slippery and elusive task. Nevertheless the following features are important in the understanding of metaphor.

One should begin by recognizing that metaphor is more than an example of rhetorical flourish by which a factual, literal meaning is given poetic enhancement. Rather, a metaphor says that one thing is something else. In describing its grammatical and linguistic character, metaphor in essence interfaces two distinctly different things

9. Among the many important studies on metaphor, see Ian Barbour, *Myths, Models, and Paradigms* (New York: Harper & Row, 1974); Max Black, *Models and Metaphors* (Ithaca, N.Y.: Cornell University Press, 1962); Frederick Ferré, "Metaphors, Models, and Religion," *Soundings* 51 (1968) 327–45; George Lakoff and Mark Johnson, *Metaphors We Live By* (Chicago: University of Chicago Press, 1980); I. A. Richards, *The Philosophy of Rhetoric* (New York: Oxford University Press, 1936); Paul Ricoeur, "The Metaphorical Process," *Semeia* 4 (1975) 75–106; idem, *Interpretation Theory: Discourse and the Surplus of Meaning* (Fort Worth, Tex.: Texas Christian University Press, 1976); idem, *The Rule of Metaphor* (Toronto: University of Toronto Press, 1977); Sheldon Sacks, ed., *On Metaphor* (Chicago: University of Chicago Press, 1979); and Phillip Wheelwright, *Metaphor and Reality* (Bloomington, Ind.: Indiana University Press, 1962). For a recent application of metaphorical theory to the theology of the Book of Job, see Perdue, *Wisdom in Revolt*.

10. David Tracy emphasizes that "all major religions are grounded in certain root metaphors. . . . In a particular religion root metaphors form a cluster or network in which sustained metaphors both organize subsidiary metaphors and diffuse new ones. These networks describe the enigma and promise of the human situation and predescribe certain remedies for that situation" ("Metaphor and Religion: The Test Case of Christian Texts," Sacks, *On Metaphor*, 80).

(tenor and vehicle) within a sentence.[11] The tenor is the principal subject that is conveyed by a vehicle, or secondary subject.[12] Quite often the tenor, being somewhat enigmatic, is described by a vehicle that is better known. The vehicle serves as a lens through which to observe and then to attempt to describe and define the tenor. A new insight or a point of similarity between the two is seen as being true. And in the relationship between tenor and vehicle, meaning for the sentence is constructed. Yet it is not just the tenor that receives meaning and insight; the vehicle also may gain new understanding in this dynamic relationship.

Intrinsic to metaphors is the tension between the "is" and the "is not."[13] A subject (tenor) is something else, and yet at the same time it is not something else. There is sameness, and yet there is also difference. The proper response to a metaphor requires both "yes" and "no," thereby avoiding absolutism. Literalism accepts the "is" as real but does not allow for the "is not." When this tension between the two collapses, then the metaphor dies or is transformed into something else, either absurd or sterile.

In a more expanded, philosophical sense, metaphor is "as ultimate as speech itself, and speech as ultimate as thought," being "the instinctive and necessary act of the mind exploring reality and ordering experience."[14] Since language both describes and shapes reality, metaphor moves beyond factual description to participate in the very process of world building.[15] It functions as a semantic building block in the linguistic construction of reality.

THE METAPHORICAL PROCESS

Living metaphors, like humans, are not static and isolated. Rather, they exist in relationship with other words to inhabit meaning worlds of sentence, story, and life. They are not static, but active. Like living creatures, they are in process, dynamic, open, and take on an existence of their own. In addition to their grammatical and

---

11. Richards, *Philosophy of Rhetoric*, 96.

12. Wayne Booth, *A Rhetoric of Irony* (Chicago: University of Chicago Press, 1974) 22.

13. McFague, *Metaphorical Theology*, 18.

14. John Middleton Murry, *Countries of the Mind* (London: Oxford University Press, 1931) 1–2.

15. Nelson Goodman, in speaking of metaphor, argues: "Far from being a mere matter of ornament, it participates fully in the progress of knowledge: in replacing some stale 'natural' kinds with novel and illuminating categories, in contriving facts, in revising theory, and in bringing us new worlds" ("Metaphor as Moonlighting," Sacks, *On Metaphor*, 175).

philosophical character, metaphors work by taking an implied audience through a process that involves both the deconstruction of previous meaning and possibly even former worldviews to the construction of new and compelling visions. The stages in this process include the following.

The first stage is destabilization. In some measure, the metaphorical process begins with the absurd. This means that a vehicle portrays its tenor in a way that is blatantly false, if taken literally.[16] Nelson Goodman remarks:

> The oddity is that metaphorical truth is compatible with literal falsity; a sentence false when taken literally may be true when taken metaphorically, as in the case of "The joint is jumping" or "The lake is a sapphire."[17]

Paul Ricoeur argues that absurdity is a "strategy of discourse" that destroys the literal meaning of a statement and transforms it into a meaningful contradiction that provides for the possibility of new semantic insight.[18] The first shock, disorientation, is experienced by those who respond to the metaphor, for the ground of meaning is in process of being shifted from one level to another.

A second stage in the metaphorical process is mimesis. Through new and even contradictory associations brought to the tenor by its vehicle, the insight is gained that something in this relationship is true. This is the second shock, which Phillip Wheelwright calls the "shock of recognition."[19] In one respect, if not more, the tenor and its vehicle have fused, becoming one, but only for those creative moments of insight which lead to reflection. Through reflection, the audience may then come to the third stage in the metaphorical process, that of transformation and restabilization.

If the new metaphor is a compelling one, the audience may then be transformed. They experience a conversion in which their understanding of the subject is altered. A powerful metaphor may even re-create the meaning system of the audience, redescribing reality by shaping a new cosmology that provides instruction in the way to live within the new world.[20] If the metaphor becomes one of the

16. Ferré, "Metaphors, Models, and Religion," 330; Ricoeur, "The Metaphorical Process," 78–79; and idem, *The Rule of Metaphor*, 199.
17. Goodman, "Metaphor as Moonlighting," 175.
18. Ricoeur, "The Metaphorical Process," 77–78.
19. Wheelwright, *Metaphor and Reality*, 45f.
20. Ferré, "Metaphors, Models, and Religion," 331; and Ricoeur, "The Metaphorical Process," 75.

culture symbols shared by the audience, it provides a renewed vitality of understanding. Now disorientation is replaced by a nomos of meaning set within the context of a worldview that provides coherence and direction for the culture-producing society. Through the society's rituals of passage, new members may enter into this social reality and participate in its beliefs, values, and customs. A new world has been created, all by means of the linguistic construction of reality.

All of this is not to say that, even with the origination of new metaphors that aid in the linguistic construction of reality, tensions are removed or proscribed. Tensions occur in two areas: first, in the inherent contradictions between the tenor and its vehicle; and second, in the difficulties that inevitably emerge either within a new meaning system or one that has been significantly altered.[21] While it may seem ironic, these very tensions provide metaphors and the worlds they build with life-giving and life-sustaining energy.[22] When tensions are removed, especially by those who wish to misshape metaphor into literal and factual definitions, metaphors either die or become distorted, inflexible, and unyielding. Thus tenor merges with vehicle, not for moments of imagination and creative reflection, but as permanent and concrete distortions. This all too frequent occurrence of linguistic dogmatism is destructive to the reality systems in which root metaphors play an important role.

Related to the tensive character of metaphors is the recognition that ambiguity has an important part in the character of metaphor. Metaphors cannot possess "steno-meanings" that are accepted by all members of a culture. Inevitably, metaphors include a range of possible understandings grounded, at least in part, in individual experience and understanding.[23] A metaphor may not be given one clear, abiding definition. If this occurs, then the definition transforms it into something very different.

Metaphors, even those that become symbols that carry a culture's systems of meaning and values, are rarely immortal. Within any society, a metaphor may become so commonplace that its power to bear a culture's worldview is lost. No longer capable of transfor-

---

21. This is what Harries refers to as both collusion and collision ("Metaphor and Transcendence," Sacks, *On Metaphor*, 71f.).
22. Wheelwright, *Metaphor and Reality*, 45–69.
23. Ibid., 33.

mation, these stock metaphors die and new ones are required to reconstruct or redirect meaning systems.[24]

METAPHORICAL THEOLOGY: SALLIE McFAGUE

In this chapter, we have chosen to describe two similar approaches to theology, the work of contemporary theologian Sallie McFague and that of Phyllis Trible, a professor of Hebrew Bible. Of course, we also could have examined the works of these two scholars in the chapters on liberation theology and creation, since both of these features are also a part of their interpretative efforts. Even so, the distinctive features of their work include not only a concern with literary criticism and the nature of language but also a focus on the nature and function of metaphor in expressions of God-talk within a feminist perspective.

Metaphorical theory has been used by some theologians and biblical scholars who argue that religious language in general and linguistic representations of God in particular involve the important use of metaphors.[25] God becomes the tenor whose vehicles are to provide insight into the divine nature and character without falling into the trap of literal identity that leads to the creation of an idol. Yet, because male and female are made in the image of God, these metaphors for God also say a great deal about human beings and the social systems they construct. This reflects the fact that not only are tenors meaning receiving, they are also meaning giving. Thus, in using human terms to describe God, there is something significant being said in addition about human beings.[26]

Religious confessions of faith are judged by some theologians to be metaphorical models that convey meanings and values within a religious tradition.[27] Theologically speaking, these models should provide guidance for the life of faith and action without removing all degrees of tension and ambiguity that are a part of metaphorical language. It is when divine metaphors are taken literally that the

24. McFague, *Metaphorical Theology*, 41.
25. Barbour, *Myths, Models, and Paradigms.*
26. McFague, *Metaphorical Theology*, 38: "This is a very important point for religious models because the human images that are chosen as metaphors for God gain in stature and take on divine qualities by being placed in an interactive relationship with the divine."
27. McFague, *Metaphorical Theology*, 103; and Tracy, "Metaphor and Religion," 89.

creative tension between tenor and vehicle collapses, the two become one, and an idol is created.

Although she is a contemporary theologian, not a biblical scholar,
Sallie McFague's work still provides a very important example of
metaphorical theology that is suggestive for understanding the nature of language in Scripture and how one might go about the task of
writing Old Testament theology. In her work, she makes the significant move from the literary analysis of metaphor to the nature of
theological language within the framework of feminist hermeneutics that recognizes the power and abuses of language in shaping
reality.[28]

Drawing on many of the features of metaphor presented in the
preceding discussion, McFague asserts:

> We will not relinquish our idolatry in religious language unless we are
> freed from the myth that in order for images to be true they must be
> literal. Nor will we find religious language relevant unless we are freed
> from the myth that in order for images to be meaningful they must be
> traditional.[29]

McFague's work covers three related areas that will be described
in brief: the metaphorical character of the parables of Jesus and
other forms of Christian literature influenced by the parables; a
metaphorical model for doing contemporary theology; and the
presentation of alternative metaphors for God and the world that
challenge those that today, to a large extent, have become traditional and unconventional. While these old metaphors may not be
dead, they still wield a deadly power.[30]

PARABLES AS EXTENDED METAPHORS

McFague's book *Speaking in Parables* presents Jesus as the parable of God and interprets the parables spoken by Jesus as a model
for theological reflection. Parables, which are by nature and func-

---

28. In *Metaphorical Theology*, McFague describes her approach as presenting "a
post-Enlightenment, Protestant, feminist perspective which I would characterize
as skeptical, relativistic, prophetic, and iconoclastic" (p. x).

29. Ibid., 32.

30. In addition to *Metaphorical Theology* and *Models of God*, see McFague,
"Mother God"; idem, "Models of God for an Ecological Evolutionary Era: God as
Mother of the Universe," *Physics, Philosophy, and Theology: A Common Quest for
Understanding* (ed. Robert J. Russell et al.; Notre Dame, Ind.: Notre Dame
University Press, 1988) 249–71; and idem, "God as Mother," *Weaving the
Visions: New Patterns in Feminist Spirituality* (ed. Judith Plaskow and Carol
Christ; San Francisco: Harper & Row, 1989).

tion metaphorical, are the form, says McFague, that unites language, belief, and life.[31] Following her description of metaphor, McFague explains the triangular setting of parables, a literary form that she considers to be extended metaphors.[32] This setting, actually a hermeneutical model, involves narrator (Jesus), the aesthetic object (the narrative parable), and the effect (on the implied audience). For McFague, no text that creates meaning can exist outside this triangle, even though there is never one single and final interpretation. Through parable one may come to encounter the vision of their teller (in this case, Jesus), may hear the "voice" articulate, and may see in parabolic vision a self-attestation, although hidden and indirect. McFague calls this "the inverbalization of Jesus as the word." This vision of the world created by metaphor contrasts with the conventional, traditional world of the hearers.

The hearers are interpreted by parables in the responses they make. Whether aligning themselves with the old logic of conventional vision or with the new logic of grace shattering into existence, listeners are challenged to respond to those ultimate questions: what do you say? what will you do? For McFague, the parable itself is characterized by realism and strangeness, and, in this dynamic interaction, shock and disorientation turn the world upside down. Yet, through new vision that is the culmination as well as the stimulus for the process of coming to belief, the world is re-created and faith is born. Metaphors work, even as their narrative extensions work, because they are human life. Humans are living metaphor, for they too move through process to culmination.[33]

Thus parables contain the major features of metaphors. They are characterized by the tension between a conventional and a traditional understanding of reality and one that is radically different, iconoclastic, and challenging. Following disorientation, the audience sees the new interpretation as plausible, conventional understanding self-destructs, and a new world is born. Reality has thus been redescribed by the power of the metaphor. Yet, what has been assaulted and turned upside down is not only understandings of

31. McFague, *Speaking in Parables: A Study in Metaphor and Theology* (Philadelphia: Fortress, 1975) 3.
32. McFague argues that referring to a parable as a metaphor indicates that "the world of the parable itself includes both the ordinary and the transcendent in a complex interaction in which each illumines the other" (*Speaking in Parables*, 46).
33. See Stanley Hauerwas, "The Self as Story: A Reconsideration of the Relation of Religion and Morality from the Agent's Perspective," *Vision and Virtue* (Notre Dame, Ind.: Fides, 1974) 68–89.

God but also the entire socioeconomic reality in which people have dwelt securely.[34]

METAPHORICAL THEOLOGY

In *Metaphorical Theology*, McFague takes up the issue of moving from the imagistic language of metaphor to systematic thought for expressing contemporary Christian faith in an engaging and relevant fashion.[35] In doing so, she hopes to avoid the idolatry that unfortunately tends to accompany some theological language by making metaphors into literal dogma.

This process of movement to the conceptual formulation of theology occurs in what she refers to as a model. In looking at models in general, she notes four common things that they do. First, they provide a grid through which to look for similarity between the model and what is modeled. They seek out relationships and networks to explain what is less known by what is better known. Second, models make intelligible what is unintelligible, render in clear expression what is often unknown or obtuse. Third, models provide a lens for looking at reality by moving beyond themselves to ever expanding areas that call for explanation. Four, models work by depending on paradigms, that is, a common set of assumptions that direct interpretation.[36]

After appropriating these general features of models, McFague then moves into her own specific interests and argues that a metaphorical model, simply defined, is "a metaphor with staying power." That is, the metaphor shapes a comprehensive, ordering structure of meaning, a grid that helps in the organization of thoughts about a topic.[37] Thus a relational term for God (e.g., father or mother) provides a significant organizing model for understanding the nature of God, religion in general, and even reality itself.[38] And these models provide a guide to life. Conceptual language operates in these models to clarify the ambiguous nature of imagistic language. Yet one should recognize that conceptual language

---

34. McFague, *Metaphorical Theology*, 47.

35. McFague argues: "Theology begins with a root-metaphor and ends in an ordering, comprehensive system, but even the system, while different from the metaphors that found it, is or should be on a continuum with them" (*Metaphorical Theology*, 127).

36. McFague, *Metaphorical Theology*, 83–103.

37. McFague defines a metaphorical model as "a metaphor that has gained sufficient stability and scope so as to present a pattern for relatively comprehensive and coherent explanation" (*Models of God*, 34).

38. McFague, *Metaphorical Theology*, 23.

depends on images from which they draw their substance and strength. Thus models, for McFague, are both imagistic and conceptual.

Theologically conceived, faith for McFague is not belief in correctly stated doctrines but rather a process "more like a story than a doctrine," a position that aligns her with narrative theologians whose work will be discussed in the next chapter. Metaphorical theology, she contends, is intermediate theology that examines the ways in which the qualities of language, belief, and life come together in parables and in parable-like narratives of story and autobiography that are influenced by the parabolic tradition. However, she argues that any theology "influenced by the parables would be open-ended, tensive, secular, indirect, iconoclastic, and revolutionary."[39]

According to McFague, metaphorical theology stands between primary theology, that is the task of poets who create metaphors, and systematic presentation. Metaphorical theology sets forth both the imagistic, poetic character of theological language and conceptual formulation that stresses the clear articulation of beliefs in a coherent fashion. In order to engage in systematic theology, the theologian first should give attention to the parable or other types of narrative and the metaphors that are central to narrative configurations. Only after this intermediary theology is presented should the theologian set forth a systematic formulation that seeks to bring together a variety of models based on different metaphors into a coherent whole by centering on their relationship to one particular model or theme. Yet, for McFague, theology cannot be completely disembodied, that is, removed from its contextual setting and formulation in life. In its lifelike quality, narrative, of which parable . is but one expression, provides the revelatory form by which faith comes to exist.[40]

Like hermeneutics, metaphorical theology, explains McFague, does work with classic texts, beginning with Scripture, and exemplary theologies that are based on the classics to discover important metaphors, including both ignored and conventional ones. How-

39. Ibid., 48.

40. McFague argues that the truth of theological models should be evaluated by several criteria. These include consistency (the components need to fit together, while avoiding the idolatry of literalism), comprehensiveness (all of reality is described), the capability to cope with anomalies, the avoidance of absolutism, the capacity to illuminate or make sense of reality and experience, the ability to organize and point out analogies and patterns, and the power to address contemporary situations and faith. Simply put, valid models "make sense out of human experience" (*Metaphorical Theology*, 138–41).

ever, unlike hermeneutics, metaphorical theology, as she conceives it, does not concentrate primarily on discovering and then translating ancient metaphors into modern understanding. Instead, metaphorical theology shares with constructive theology the view that God language does not rely exclusively on the classics, as does hermeneutics; rather, it examines many other sources, including the sciences, literature, philosophy, and art, as well as Scripture and other Christian classics. In addition, metaphorical theology is concerned not only with the articulation of conceptual frameworks and clarity of expression but also with the richness of images. McFague argues that metaphorical theology is different from hermeneutics and constructive theology in that it is heuristic, that is, it seeks to "find out" through experimentation whether something is valid or true. Thus, while classical texts are examined along with a variety of other sources, heuristic, metaphorical theology is more open to experimentation, pluralism, and the power of images.[41]

Metaphorical theologians may not necessarily be engaged in the creation of new metaphors—this is the task of poets—but they must deform old and lifeless constructions that imprison and even deaden metaphors. According to McFague, metaphorical theology does not concern itself primarily with content but rather with the process of coming to belief in a Christian universe while at times despairing over the sinfulness of the present world.

NEW METAPHORS

In *Models of God*, McFague approaches the third area of her work: a heuristic presentation of new metaphors that will provoke and transform theological understanding in the postmodern period. By postmodern she means the contemporary period that has emerged after the end of an age dominated by the Enlightenment and its way of thinking. The postmodern period is a time in which there is a "greater appreciation of nature," a "chastened admiration for technology," an increased "recognition of the importance of language," a greater awareness of the importance of non-Christian religions, the "rise of the dispossessed" who have traditionally been those without status and power in the West, an "apocalyptic sensibility" characterized by the awareness of the dangers of nuclear holocaust and ecological disaster, and an appreciation for the "radi-

41. "Metaphorical theology is a kind of heuristic construction that in focusing on the imaginative construal of the God-world relationship, attempts to remythologize Christian faith through metaphors and models appropriate for an ecological, nuclear age" (*Models of God*, 40; see the discussion on pp. 36–40).

cal interdependence of life at all levels."[42] For McFague, these are the features that contemporary theology needs to address in a relevant and engaging way.

The problem for contemporary theology, she asserts, is that the traditional models have been grounded in patriarchal metaphors for God and the world. The dominant metaphor for God is the transcendent (absent) king who rules over his kingdom (the earth). Not only is this metaphorical model traditional and conventional, outdated and uninteresting, it has also become dangerous. It is dangerous because it promotes patriarchy, hierarchical relationships, and dualistic thinking (body/spirit, human/nonhuman, and male/female) and because it indicates that sovereign power, located in the hands of God or God's chosen, is the force that will promote justice and care for all (human and nonhuman) and will keep the world from chaos. This acknowledgment of the sovereignty of God leads to passivity and the lack of human responsibility for engaging in efforts designed to enhance well-being for all life.[43]

Recognizing then the power of language to construct or redescribe reality, McFague turns again to metaphorical theology and asks the evaluative question: are religious metaphors appropriate for our time? Theological language, based on new or rediscovered metaphors, needs to take a shape that will subvert patriarchy and hierarchy along with their inherent flaws and dangers and then create a vision that will lead to the assuming of responsibility to nurture and fulfill life in its various forms, all the while being open to newness and change.[44] The intent is not to demythologize religious language of its imagistic, poetic character by abstract conceptualization but rather to remythologize theological language in order that it may redescribe once more reality in a provocative and true manner and evoke transformation that is based on new understanding. Metaphorical models, however, dispense neither with conceptualization nor with imagistic language. Rather, the two exist in a symbiotic relation, each drawing strength and drawing clarity from the other.

McFague considers a variety of sources for new language. She argues that Scripture may be a classic text that endures by redescribing reality and allowing flexibility in interpretation. In searching for

---

42. McFague, *Models of God*, x.
43. "Language that supports hierarchical, dualistic, external, unchanging, atomistic, anthropocentric, and deterministic ways of understanding . . . is not appropriate for our time" (*Models of God*, 13).
44. McFague, *Models of God*, 32.

new metaphors, McFague looks to human liberation, not patriarchy, as the proper reformulation of the Christian paradigm. The
paradigm of Christian faith assaults conventional understandings
of power, includes rather than excludes, and is opposed to hierarchy
and triumphalism.[45] This paradigm is found in the parables and life
of Jesus in the Gospels and reemerges in a powerful way in liberation theology.

In her efforts to remythologize the gospel for our time, she proposes new or rediscovered metaphors: the world as the body of God,
and God as mother, lover, and friend. These metaphors clash
directly with the traditional Western model of God as a distant king
ruling over his earthly kingdom from afar, a monarchical model
promoting hierarchical and dualistic thinking that leads to oppression. The danger of this model is that it threatens life by positing
God's distance from the world, God's relationship to humans but
not the nonhuman world, and God's control of the world through
domination or benevolence.[46]

The world as God's body, argues McFague, promotes the ideas of
divine immanence, God's care for the physical (not just the spiritual) aspects of existence, human responsibility in that God's body
is in human hands, divine suffering as the world suffers, and sin as
both the refusal to be a part of the world and participation in actions
against the well-being of all life that is interdependent. Furthermore, the evolutionary and historical development of the world is a
process that is intrinsic to divine activity and not something that
God directs but is apart from.

McFague also proposes three metaphorical models for God:
mother, lover, and friend, all relational models that, for one thing,
keep the single model of the world as God's body from deteriorating
into pantheism. The metaphor of God as mother presents God as a
creator who is intimately concerned with and actively seeks the
well-being of life in all of its manifestations, while God as lover
presents God as a savior whose passion (love for the beloved and
suffering) is geared toward reconciliation between all life. God as
friend presents God as the sustainer who works with humans to
bring about healing to all the components of reality.[47] This does not
mean, for example, that God is defined as mother (or lover or
friend), or that McFague is attempting to set up a new hierarchy,

45. Ibid., 46.
46. Ibid., 65.
47. Ibid., 91–92.

only this time a maternal or feminine one. But it does mean that the image of mother is a relational term, like lover and friend, that allows us to consider what we do not know how to talk about.[48] Not coincidentally, these metaphors, she suggests, may replace the traditional trinitarian metaphors of Father, Son, and Holy Spirit or the more impersonal Creator, Savior, and Sustainer.

Throughout her writings, McFague emphasizes that metaphors are always indirect and tentative, although they do make assertions as well as judgments. They suggest that certain things about God may be true or provide some insight, but one should always acknowledge that any language about God is inadequate.

McFague's work illustrates how Old Testament theologians may approach the Bible, especially narratives or stories, in order to discover and understand significant theological metaphors and how they operate. Her work is especially useful for understanding Old Testament narratives that provide the form in which life, faith, and values find their unity. Her work also suggests that even the Old Testament theologian, once having assessed the metaphorical character of the narrative, may move to a systematic presentation of Israelite faith. However, this move should not eliminate the imagistic character of religious language.

METAPHORICAL THEOLOGY IN JEREMIAH

The Book of Jeremiah is rich in metaphors that are expressive of the major features of Israelite faith.[49] These include God, the nation, and the relationship between God and the nation. Of course, metaphorical theology is not linked necessarily to feminist hermeneutics. Since Phyllis Trible's work on feminine imagery in Jeremiah is presented in the following section, two metaphors used to portray Israel and Judah will be examined to illustrate how meta-

48. Ibid., 33. The danger in using relational language is sentimentality, individualism, and stereotyping that points to "traditional" male and female characteristics (e.g., women are by nature self-sacrificing and caring, while men are aggressive and assertive). In place of sentimentality, McFague stresses the importance and power of three types of love captured by the three metaphors: the love of parents, lovers, and friends. In place of individualism, McFague emphasizes that the divine lover's love is for the entirety of the cosmos, not simply one person or group or species, i.e., humanity. In place of stereotyping, McFague emphasizes that so-called male and female characteristics are learned through socialization rather than being intrinsic to gender differentiation.

49. See Daniel Bourguet's somewhat mechanical and unimaginative categorization of major metaphors in Jeremiah related to particular verbs: *Des métaphores de Jérémie* (Etudes Bibliques 9; Paris: J. Gabalda et Cie, 1987).

phorical theology would approach the interpretation of Jeremiah. These two metaphors are the linen loincloth (13:1-11) and the potter and the clay (18:1-12). Form-critically speaking, these two acts are narratives of symbolic actions of the prophet. Each is an auto-biographical, parable-like narrative with a metaphorical description of the chosen: Judah and Jerusalem.

THE LINEN LOINCLOTH

This narrative describes a symbolic action of the prophet and follows a traditional pattern: Yahweh commands the prophet to perform a symbolic act, the prophet who is the narrator describes his performance of the action, and then Yahweh interprets the meaning of the act within the context of a judgment oracle against Judah and Jerusalem. In 13:1-11, Yahweh tells Jeremiah to buy a linen waistcloth and to place it upon his loins. Jeremiah complies, and then Yahweh tells him to go to the river Euphrates and hide the loincloth in the cleft of a rock. Jeremiah again complies. Then Yahweh tells Jeremiah to return later to the place where he hid the loincloth. He does so, only to discover that the loincloth was ruined. Then Yahweh issues a judgment oracle: the "pride" of Judah and Jerusalem, that is, their glory which resided in their belonging to Yahweh, will become spoiled just like the loincloth.

Loincloths in ancient Israel were made either of leather (2 Kings 1:8) or of linen, as is the case in Jeremiah 13. This "girdle" was a wraparound and ordinarily not removed. Linen loincloths were worn by ordinary people as well as by priests who led the sacred worship of Yahweh (Ezek 44:17-18). The metaphor of Judah and Jerusalem as a loincloth suggests the closeness of their covenant relationship with Yahweh. The metaphorical description of Judah and Jerusalem as a linen loincloth that had become spoiled indicates the deterioration of the relationship between Yahweh and his chosen, due to their worship of other gods. Thus, in the judgment of Yahweh, the chosen, because of their religious apostasy, have become like a spoiled loincloth that is "good for nothing."

This narrative, centered in the metaphor of a linen loincloth, opposes a traditional and comfortable Israelite theology in which Judah, with its capital in Jerusalem, was the chosen of Yahweh. Indeed, Zion (=Jerusalem) was the City of God in which Yahweh took up special abode and then promised it divine protection. However, in this narrative, the theology of election is turned on its head. For Jeremiah, election is not without the requirements of responsibility and accountability. Election, for this narrative, is not an eternal choice that cannot be abrogated by the people's faithlessness. Thus the chosen are a rotten loincloth, an absurdity and yet something that may be very true. The metaphorical tension is between the plot of the tale and the conventional theology of election. Judah (Jerusalem) is and is not a rotten loincloth. Is there a similarity between the rotten loincloth and Judah's present situation? Jeremiah's audience must ask, "What will we do?" "What will we say?"

If this metaphorical tale is addressed to an exilic audience in captivity, disoriented by the destruction of Jerusalem and the exile to Babylon, then it moves them beyond absurdity and destabilization of the ground of religious faith to mimesis, that is, the correspondence between the metaphorical depiction and their own present condition. The implicit transformation that leads to new faith begins with the acceptance of their guilt and that of their fathers and mothers and is followed by the vow to turn again to Yahweh as their God. This is the narrative presentation of the potentiality of faith coming into being. In more conceptual terms, judgment is based on the theology of election that requires responsible faithfulness to Yahweh through the medium of covenant and law. Yet, as is typical in the Bible, this theology is presented in the language of narrative. The richness and power of the images should not be set aside. Metaphorical theology allows image and conception to coexist.

The Potter and the Clay

The second example of symbolic action centered in a metaphor is that of the potter and the clay in Jer 18:1-11. Once again, the narrative is structured into three movements: the divine command to the prophet, in this case the imperative to "go down to the potter's house"; the description of the action, specifically that of the potter's effort to shape a vessel that first fails and then succeeds; and the interpretation in the form of an "either/or" oracle calling for a decision that will lead to either life or death.

In this narrative of prophetic, symbolic action, the house of Israel (later Judah and Jerusalem, v. 11) is described metaphorically as a piece of clay in the hand of the potter, Yahweh. A potter is a common metaphor for God as creator in the formation of humanity and nations (see Gen 2:7 and Isa 29:16; 64:8). At first the clay vessel is not successfully shaped by the potter into a good and useful piece of crockery. In the second attempt, however, the potter succeeds in the effort to shape a vessel that is good and useful.

The parable traditionally has been interpreted to point to the radical sovereignty of God and to the predetermination of humans, nations, and the elect to a particular destiny. This parable may well have been used to explain the destruction and exile of first Israel and later Judah: it is God's radical, unquestionable freedom to shape the destiny of the chosen. One possible explanation of the destruction and exile is the argument that the failure of Israel was due ultimately to the failure of God. God failed Israel, possibly because of a lack of care or power. Another explanation suggested that Israel's inclination toward sin also is the fault of the creator of the nation who, in the forming of their very nature, bent them toward evil. Both explanations place the blame on God and reject moral responsibility. However, in an assault on this theology, Jeremiah in this prose tradition gives a very different interpretation.

The prophet is invited to reflect on this simple story of the potter, and then comes the revelation. Yahweh is the potter and Israel (later Judah and Jerusalem) is the clay. Israel is now the piece of clay in the hand of the divine potter. The clay is not simply a passive piece of unformed material whose destiny is shaped entirely by the potter. Should the potter fail in shaping the clay into a useful vessel, obviously a common result in pottery making, it cannot simply blame either the potter's lack of skill or the loose texture of the soil for the failure. In a rather stunning, even absurd interpretation, whether the potter succeeds or fails, depends in part on the "will" of the clay. Responsibility, grounded in covenant theology, is required of Israel.

In similar fashion to the narrative tale of Jeremiah 13, the theology of election, unbounded by moral and religious responsibility and possibly based on a belief in predestination that opens the door to such passivity, is rejected in favor of national accountability. A faithless and wicked nation may receive again divine favor, expressed by the theology of election, only by thoroughgoing repentance and a return to the requirements of covenant and law. Election and covenant theology are brought together in a symbiotic relationship. Thus two understandings of election are contrasted by this parabolic tale. The conventional one presents Israel as the chosen nation whose destiny is placed in the hands of God. Human freedom has no real place in this theology. But the second introduces human accountability by inserting the theology of covenant. Israel and now Judah are the elect, but their destiny at least in part depends on covenantal faithfulness. The parable of the potter and the clay has been radically transformed.

These two brief examples illustrate the metaphorical character of theological language in Jeremiah. The metaphors for Judah and Jerusalem operate within narratives that challenge traditional self-understanding and comfortable existence. These judgment-eliciting narratives shatter the audience's understanding of election and require them either to walk away in disgust or to enter into self-judgment leading to radical transformation.

RECAPTURING THE LANGUAGE OF ZION

RHETORICAL CRITICISM AND FEMINIST HERMENEUTICS

Whether they use literary or historical methods, or a combination of both, in their interpretative work, feminist biblical scholars point to the patriarchal character of much of the Old Testament and of much exegesis that represents a white-male perspective.[50] At the same time, this criticism of patriarchy in both the text and the scholarly tradition seeks to subvert or undermine sexist ideology at work in the text, in the scholarly tradition, and in their larger cultural ethos. There are several ways feminist scholars deal with patriarchy in the biblical text. One way is to use a "hermeneutics of suspicion," which, among other objectives, critically exposes sexist ideologies at work in the text, searches for the possible suppression of women's history, and seeks to recover forgotten stories of women in the biblical text and ancient Israel.

Some feminist scholars have worked mainly as historians to recover women's history in ancient Israel.[51] Thus, the approach to Old Testament theology takes on a decided history of religions character, that is, a wide variety of sources (archaeological, biblical, and other literary data) is assessed. Others have followed new and

---

50. For a discussion of feminist biblical interpretation, see Mary Ann Tolbert, ed., *The Bible and Feminist Hermeneutics* (Chico, Calif.: Scholars Press, 1983); Adela Collins, ed., *Feminist Perspectives on Biblical Scholarship* (Chico, Calif.: Scholars Press, 1985); Letty Russell, ed., *Feminist Interpretation of the Bible* (Philadelphia: Westminster, 1985); Cheryl Exum and Johanna Bos, eds., *Reasoning with the Foxes: Female Wit in a World of Male Power, Semeia* 42 (1988); and Trible, "Five Loaves and Two Fishes," 286–95.

51. See Athalya Brenner, *The Israelite Women* (Sheffield: *JSOT*, 1985); Phyllis Bird, "The Place of Women in the Israelite Cultus," *Ancient Israelite Religion* (ed. Patrick Miller et al.; Philadelphia: Fortress, 1987) 397–417; idem, "Images of Women in the Old Testament," *Religion and Sexism* (ed. Rosemary Ruether; New York: Simon & Schuster, 1974) 41–88; Jo Ann Hackett, "Women's Studies and the Hebrew Bible," *The Future of Biblical Studies* (ed. R. Friedman and H. Williamson; Atlanta: Scholars Press, 1987) 19–59; Carol Meyers, *Discovering Eve*; and Peggy Day, ed., *Gender and Difference in Ancient Israel* (Philadelphia: Fortress, 1989).

developing literary methods to subvert patriarchy in the Bible, give feminist readings to biblical texts, and rediscover or bring to the fore examples of women's stories.[52] Others bring together historical criticism, social-scientific analysis, and literary criticism in interpreting the Bible and ancient Israelite history from a feminist perspective.[53]

While arguing that it is too early to write a feminist biblical theology, Phyllis Trible has recently articulated a set of "overtures" that indicates what such a theology might begin to look like.[54] Her initial thoughts include the following three primary assumptions. First, this type of theology "might locate itself in reference to the classical discipline."[55] Mentioning the ongoing debate, she argues that feminist biblical theology would not be content with description but would be consciously constructive and hermeneutical. Using the metaphor of "pilgrim," she suggests that the Bible wanders through time and cannot be locked in the past. Second, she argues that this approach to biblical theology operates with the recognition that the Bible is not the property of any particular group; rather, it is owned by Jews and Christians, believing communities and scholarly academies, and the world. This approach "is neither essentially nor necessarily Christian." Third, Trible indicates that there would be, not a single method, but many; not one approach, but several.

With this basis firmly in place, Trible then suggests that feminist biblical theology would begin with the exegesis of texts, both familiar and neglected, always "mindful of androcentricity in Scripture and traditional biblical theology."[56] Passages that depict God

---

52. See e.g., Esther Fuchs, "The Literary Characterization of Mothers and Sexual Politics in the Hebrew Bible," Collins, *Feminist Perspectives on Biblical Scholarship*, 117–36; idem, "Who Is Hiding the Truth? Deceptive Women and Biblical Androcentrism," Collins, *Feminist Perspectives on Biblical Scholarship*, 137–44; Cheryl Exum, "'Mother in Israel,' A Familiar Figure Reconsidered," Russell, *Feminist Interpretation of the Bible*, 73–85; Toni Craven, "Women Who Lied for the Faith," *Justice and the Holy* (FS Walter Harrelson; ed. Douglas A. Knight and Peter Paris; Atlanta: Scholars Press, 1989); and Mieke Bal, ed., *Anti-Covenant: Counter-Reading Women's Lives in the Hebrew Bible* (JSOTSup 81; Sheffield: JSOT, 1989).

53. Claudia Camp, *Wisdom and the Feminine in the Book of Proverbs* (Sheffield: JSOT/Almond Press, 1985); A. L. Laffey, *An Introduction to the Old Testament: A Feminist Perspective* (Philadelphia: Fortress, 1988); and Phyllis Bird, "The Harlot as Heroine: Narrative Art and Social Presupposition in Three Old Testament Texts," *Narrative Research on the Hebrew Bible, Semeia* 46 (1989) 119–39.

54. Trible, "Five Loaves and Two Fishes," 289–95.

55. Ibid., 289.

56. Ibid., 289.

in feminine images would be addressed as well as neglected texts about women. The meaning of *rhm*, "womb" in the singular and "compassion" in the plural, as a metaphor for talking about God should be studied.

Trible then suggests that a feminist biblical theology would move into the area of "contours and content."[57] In contrast to other models, this approach would "focus upon the phenomenon of gender and sex in the articulation of faith."[58] Specifically stated, a feminist biblical theology would begin with Genesis 1–3 to interpret the "image of God male and female" within the mythical context of creation as over against history. Trible argues that the next step would be the investigation of the female not only in the Bible but also in related literature from the ancient Near East. Even Israelite "folk religion" would be studied, since women were often denied full participation in the Israelite cultus and thus with some men may have "forged an alternative Yahwism."[59]

Feminist biblical theology, according to Trible, would be especially construed to undermine idolatry, especially in noting that no one image or metaphor is used to speak of God and that no single articulation of the faith is normative. Also in the area of language, feminist biblical theology would probe into meanings of words and terms to explore a variety of meanings that are not traditional interpretations. The goal would be to "wrestle" with patriarchal language, even as Jacob struggled with God at the river Jabbok.

Finally, for Trible, feminist biblical theology "would also wrestle with models and meanings for authority." Authority would center in the reader, allowing for the reader to choose what is prescriptive in the text. In dialectic engagement with the text, the Bible might be seen as "authoritative, though not necessarily prescriptive."[60]

Recognizing these proposals as tentative, Trible emphasizes that the thrust of a feminist biblical theology not only would "explore the entire picture of gender and sex in all its diversity" but it would also "wrestle from the text a theology that subverts patriarchy."[61]

---

57. Ibid., 292.
58. Ibid., 292.
59. Ibid., 293. It is clear that Trible does not advocate writing a biblical theology that uses only the biblical text or that is limited simply to literature. Both the history of Israelite religion and social organization would make a contribution to her biblical theology.
60. Ibid., 294.
61. Ibid., 295.

RHETORICAL CRITICISM

The origins of rhetorical criticism are usually traced to James Muilenburg, although he himself acknowledged important predecessors, including especially Hermann Gunkel, Robert Lowth, and J. G. Herder.[62] The major task of rhetorical criticism is to define the limits of a literary unit (prose or poetry), uncover the component parts and structural patterns at work in its shape, and point out the literary techniques used in ordering its artistic composition. The focus is the literary work itself, not the mind of the audience or the understanding of the original audience. The argument is made that the artistry of the text renders its meaning. Artistic composition and the meaning of the text are inseparable.

The literary techniques that enable a unit to cohere and engage the imagination include anaphora (the repetition of a word or words at the beginning of successive clauses, lines, or strophes), refrains (words or phrases repeated at the end of strophes or other subunits), interweaving words or phrases *(mots crochets)* that blend together the entire unit or major subunit, inclusions (the repetition of the opening word or words at the close of the unit, thus marking its boundaries), and parallelism of members (strophes or lines within a poem that parallel in some fashion, although there is also a "seconding sequence" in the second part that extends, differs from, or in some fashion changes the idea in the first part).[63] Among the different kinds are especially synonymous parallelism and antithetical parallelism. Other features of artistic composition include onomatopoeia (use of words that imitate sounds), alliteration (the correspondence of sounds at the beginning of words), assonance (the correspondence of the sounds of accented vowels), and a variety of different structures for lines, paragraphs (narrative), and strophes (subunits of a poem that express normally one central idea), including chiasms (literally, an "x" formed by a pattern of lines: e.g., a, b, c, b1, a1) and acrostics (particularly alphabetic ones).

---

62. For an introduction to rhetorical criticism, see James Muilenburg, "Form Criticism and Beyond," *JBL* 88 (1969) 1–18; Norman Gottwald, "Poetry, Hebrew," *IDB* 3:829–38; Jared J. Jackson and Martin Kessler, eds., *Rhetorical Criticism: Essays in Honor of James Muilenburg* (Pittsburgh Theological Monograph Series 1; Pittsburg: Pickwick, 1974); and Toni Craven, *Artistry and Faith in the Book of Judith* (SBLDS 70; Chico, Calif.: Scholars Press, 1983) 11–46. Trible's forthcoming study of rhetorical criticism for the series Guides to Biblical Scholarship, to be published by Fortress, should be an important statement.

63. See especially James Kugel, *The Idea of Biblical Poetry* (New Haven: Yale University Press, 1981).

THE WEEPING RACHEL IN JEREMIAH

Trible's important work on the "weeping Rachel" in Jeremiah is found in her book *God and the Rhetoric of Sexuality*.[64] Drawing on rhetorical criticism and studies of metaphor by such scholars as Wheelwright and Ricoeur, Trible contends that the very nature of the Bible is hermeneutical, since it is "a pilgrim wandering through history to merge past and present." Her book is shaped by "feminist hermeneutics." By this she means, not an interpretation that only focuses on or is limited to women, but rather the recovery of neglected themes and counter literature that often lie dormant within the text. Yet it is not enough to awaken dormant texts to new life, for "feminism" is a "critique of culture in light of misogyny." This critique affects all issues of significant hermeneutical import that impact human existence in all of its vicissitudes: race, class, sexuality, ecology, and psychology.

To approach God language in the Bible, Trible points to four "clues" in the text: hermeneutical, dialectical, methodological, and topical. The hermeneutical clue is found by exploring the tension between God the lover and God the punisher. The variety of meanings and the different "hearings" indicate that biblical theology and hermeneutics eschew systematizing. The dialectical clue is found in the dynamic between the text and the world, as Scripture is engaged by issues of modern import: liberation theology, ecology, human sexuality, the black experience, and feminism. The methodological clue for Trible is rhetorical criticism that focuses on the totality of a text, stressing and discovering its organic unity. Through its literary crafting, the text comes to life and construes meaning. The rhetoric of the text also awakens the imagination, allowing the interpreter to enter its space and time. Finally, the topical clue is found in Gen 1:26-30. In the compelling language of metaphor, male and female are "the image of God." This means, argues Trible, that male and female are a definition for humanity, just as they are together a metaphor for God. According to Trible, Gen 1:26-30 provides the clue for understanding God in the Old Testament as one who is presented in both male and female images: father, king, husband, and warrior; but also pregnant woman (Isa 42:14), mother (Isa 66:13), midwife (Ps 22:9), and mistress (Ps 123:2).

In the remainder of the book, Trible works out two objectives. First, she examines feminine metaphors for God. For example, she

---

64. Phyllis Trible, *God and the Rhetoric of Sexuality* (Philadelphia: Fortress, 1977).

points to "womb" imagery in the Old Testament, noting that *rehem* in the singular means "womb" or "uterus" but in the plural expands to the abstraction of compassion, mercy, and love. Theologically conceived God is the one who creates humanity in the womb, prepares the organ for birth, participates in the birthing, receives the infant from the womb of the mother, and nurtures the person from birth through old age to the moment of death. Divine compassion is that of a mother who conceives and carries a child in her womb and is bonded to that life even after birth.

Second, Trible examines narratives that portray the relationships between male and female, including the eroticism of the love lyrics of the Song of Songs and narratives portraying women. For example, she concludes that the story of Ruth is a "human comedy" that provides "a theological interpretation of feminism: women working out their own salvation with fear and trembling, for it is God who works in them." The feminine image is a powerful and central one in biblical faith, says Trible, for it directs the reader to examine the goodness of creation, to explore the eroticism of Canticles, and to witness the struggle for life in the Book of Ruth.[65]

Trible's understanding of the metaphor of *rhm* provides important insight into the nature of God in Jeremiah. Divine compassion, normally extended to Jerusalem, is denied at the time of the invasion of the "foe from the north" (Jer 16:5), while the survivors of the Babylonian conquest are promised Yahweh's mercy and support (42:12; see 12:15; 30:18; 31:20; 33:26).

However, the best example of the theology of *rhm* is found in the poem of the "weeping Rachel" in 31:15-22. Trible refers to this poem as a drama of voices that "organize structure, fill content, and mold vision to create a new thing in the land (cf. v. 22b), and this new thing is the poem itself."[66] Using rhetorical criticism with accomplished skill, Trible sees the poem as having five strophes that form a chiasmus, with Ephraim's voice being at the center:

> Words of a *woman*: Rachel cries (v. 15)
> Words to a *woman*: Yahweh consoles (vv. 16-17)
> Words of a man: Ephraim confesses (vv. 18-19)
> Words of a *woman*: Yahweh contemplates (v. 20)
> Words to a *woman*: Jeremiah commands (vv. 21-22)[67]

---

65. Also see Phyllis Trible, *Texts of Terror* (Philadelphia: Fortress, 1985); and idem, "Five Loaves and Two Fishes," 279–85.
66. Trible, *God and the Rhetoric of Sexuality*, 40.
67. Ibid., 50.

It is woman and female images that surround and protect the man, in this case Ephraim, the Northern Kingdom.

According to Trible, the first strophe (v. 15) depicts a weeping mother, the matriarch Rachel, who long ago gave birth to Joseph and then to Benjamin (Gen 30:22-24; 35:16-20).[68] Now, Rachel is heard weeping in her tomb over the death of her children, that is, her descendants who have perished in the Assyrian (and perhaps also the Babylonian) holocaust and whose existence as a people is placed under great threat.

With the voice of Yahweh in vv. 16-17 (strophe II), Rachel is asked to refrain from lamentation, for soon her lost children will return from exile. She, Rachel, dominates the focus of this strophe, as it is her future, embodied in the returning exiles, that is assured by the divine voice.[69]

However, with the shift to the third strophe (vv. 18-19), attention is drawn to another voice, this time emanating from a male: Ephraim confessing his sins, turning back (repenting) to Yahweh, and pleading for restoration.

The final two strophes complete the pattern of concentric circles, thereby enfolding Ephraim within the protection of a poem replete with feminine images. Yahweh's voice emerges again in the fourth strophe (v. 20) and claims Ephraim as the child of special delight. Yahweh shares the mother's compassion *(rhm)* for the child, God's "womb trembles" for him.[70] For Trible, it is the voice of the divine mother now who loves her child, Ephraim. "As a result, the poem has moved from the desolate lamentation of Rachel to the redemptive compassion of God."[71]

With the fifth strophe (vv. 21-22), the enfolding of Ephraim is complete. Now it is the voice of Jeremiah that speaks words of redemption. The mood has changed from despair in the opening lines of Rachel's lamentation to hope in the prophetic call to return at the poem's conclusion. One other change occurs: the attention is now on virgin Israel, the daughter, not Ephraim, the son. This adds to the intention of the poem, suggests Trible, in surrounding the male with the female.[72] The last line is the climax of the poem. A much-debated line, Trible translates it: "For Yahweh has created a

---

68. Ibid., 40.
69. Ibid., 41.
70. Ibid., 45.
71. Ibid., 45.
72. Ibid., 46.

new thing in the land: female surrounds man." The new creation that Yahweh has brought into being is a new reality in which the virile male is surrounded and protected by the feminine: the weeping mother, Rachel, the divine mother, Yahweh, and the daughter, Israel, who surpasses the son. Indeed, for Trible, it is the poem itself that is the new reality.[73]

Not to be forgotten, argues Trible, is the importance of *rḥm* ("womb," "compassion") in the fourth strophe. This uterine metaphor, in Trible's interpretation, encompasses Ephraim, the chosen son, with the divine compassion of the Mother God. It is not only the female imagery of the poem but also the uterus that "nourishes, sustains, and redeems the male child Ephraim."[74]

The metaphor of God as mother, especially noted in the association of God with *rḥm*, is the theological portrait at the heart of this striking poem. Ephraim is sustained, not by military power and political treaty, but by the divine compassion of God. Indeed, it is Rachel, not Jacob, who surrounds poetically her grandchild and embraces him with her grief. It is the virgin daughter, Israel, who surpasses the son. The movement of this metaphorical poem is also parabolic: the images shatter conventional, male-dominated theology centering on the Divine Warrior and undermine the hubris of rulers and generals that leads them to depend on war and negotiations to bring well-being. Now, it is judgment time. It is left to the audience to reorient their theology and meaning system, or to turn away in disgust. But in the accepting of the reality redescribed by the metaphorical poem, Judah's entire theology and the social system that it undergirds would have to be transformed. The peaceable kingdom would replace active militarism, the strength of women would be affirmed and celebrated, the suppression and subordination of women would end, the patriarchal God would be replaced by a God who is and is not male and female, the children of exile (Israelites especially) would return and be embraced, and, most important, the reign of God would begin.

FEMINIST HERMENEUTICS AND
OLD TESTAMENT THEOLOGY: AN ASSESSMENT

The theologies of McFague and Trible point to one important, new journey on which Old Testament theology has embarked. They

73. Ibid., 50.
74. Ibid., 50.

are quick to remind us that the language of the text must be given primary consideration in any effort to set forth its theology. And they remind us of the importance of feminism in framing and seeking to answer theological questions. At least McFague allows that her own work is intermediary to a larger, systematic rendering. For her, metaphorical theology retains the imagistic character of theological language and yet also includes conceptualization. Both have recovered meanings of texts and theological expressions that have been encrusted by many layers of sexist readings. McFague reminds us of the radical theology of Jesus who subverted oppressive social and religious structures. Trible rediscovers the importance of "womb" imagery in Old Testament portraits of God. They both remind us that theological language may be idolatrous, if not critically assessed. They shatter the image of God as male by the use of the Bible's own language for deity. Sexist readings of texts that lead to a singular portrayal of Israel's God as male, for example, a Divine Warrior, are indeed undermined.

Indeed, most exciting about their work is that they offer a revolutionary way of speaking about God and of engaging in the theological enterprise. While McFague's metaphorical theology makes use of classic texts, including Scripture, her work proposes to set forth a way of speaking about God that is not simply limited to the re-presentation of biblical metaphors, even those neglected or suppressed. Neither is her work limited primarily to Scripture. Trible, however, is a Bible scholar who works with Scripture in order to reclaim or rediscover the full range of its variety of metaphors and then to address them to the contemporary scene. Their work suggests a radical reorientation of Old Testament theology that holds much promise.

In spite of the many valuable insights offered by these approaches, however, there are questions to ponder. First, why does each of these scholars often leap over the past two thousand years of biblical and theological interpretations as though they did not exist? Indeed, the very contexts in which the communities of believers now live are shaped in part by these interpretations. The reason for this avoidance may be the dominance of patriarchy, although certainly these centuries, like the Bible itself, contain instances where patriarchy is subverted. It is also interesting that McFague's metaphorical theology takes issue with theology as hermeneutics for primarily focusing on classical texts in order to transform the language of the past into an engaging formulation for the present. Yet, she still often looks to the past for at least part of her normative theology: a Christian paradigm largely exemplified by Jesus' parables and Jesus as the parable of God.[75]

Second, while not true of McFague, why does Trible not only ignore the form of the narratives, thereby disallowing generic conventions to appear, but also oppose a systematic formulation of Old Testament theology, a position that severely restricts dialogical correlation with the very issues of modern import she seeks to address? The result is a series of insightful and at times significant observations, but no constructive summary that allows for the full impact of her often provocative analysis either on biblical interpretation, Old Testament theology, or the contemporary culture.

This leads to a third question. What is the underlying structure of biblical feminism, that is, its shape, that allows constructive conversation with the modern world to occur? How are the conventional worlds of patriarchy and other forms of oppression typically subverted in the Bible? Feminism as represented by McFague and Trible needs to move into a more systematic form in order to present a clear and compelling theology, while at the same time maintaining a linkage with the imagistic character of metaphorical theology. Even McFague's contemporary metaphorical models are not always clarified individually, and the connections between the metaphorical models she proposes are not clearly delineated.

Fourth, while McFague does discuss Gadamer's hermeneutic, neither Trible nor she gives a detailed examination of the problem of distanciation. For Trible, the Bible is a "pilgrim" wandering through time that cannot be imprisoned by the past. Yet, how is the distance between ancient text and contemporary ethos overcome? Ancient audiences presumably had less difficulty entering into the linguistic world shaped by the biblical text than those of the contemporary period. This difficulty is more severe for Trible than for McFague, since the latter does not restrict her work to biblical texts. One of the advantages of historical criticism is that it provides for distanciation. In any theological enterprise, there needs to be a detailed explication of the world and community of the implied audiences of texts. In doing this, dialogical interaction with the narrative worlds of the Bible would be facilitated. Entering into these narrative worlds is no easy process and requires some hermeneutical effort that includes the interaction of texts and culture.

Finally, why is it that neither Trible nor McFague offers a reflective and critical analysis of the vision created by the text as inter-

75. See Sheila Greeve Davaney, "Review of *Models of God,*" *RSR* 16 (1990) 39.

preted through their respective lenses? Rather, both take disorienting texts or new feminist readings and use them to subvert patriarchal ones, to recover women's stories and feminine metaphors for God, and to move toward contemporary meaning. But neither engages in reflective criticism of her own approaches and findings. For example, McFague often admits her work is experimental, tentative, and suggestive, and certainly not closed or absolutist. Yet, a more consciously critical evaluation of the limitations and excesses of this approach needs to be articulated.

Finally, the potential of metaphor and rhetorical criticism for explicating the theology of Jeremiah is quite significant, particularly when the concern is not limited only to feminine images. Feminine metaphors are important in this prophetic book, but there are many other metaphors that provide an entrée into the understanding of the theology of Jeremiah. This work, carefully and rigorously carried through, might well prove very stimulating.[76]

76. See the study by Daniel Bourguet, *Des métaphores de Jérémie.*

PART FOUR

Old Testament Theology: Story and Imagination

CHAPTER 8

From History to Fiction:
Biblical Story
and Narrative Theology

One could not imagine two more different ways of doing Old Testament theology than those of George Ernest Wright, with whom we began this volume, and of Phyllis Trible, our last example: historical criticism grounded in positivism countered by the artistry of the text revealed by rhetorical criticism; the "objective" approach of the descriptive task in contrast to the existential concern of the modern interpreter; the recital of "the mighty acts of God" over against the contemporary issues of feminist hermeneutics; the theology of Yahweh as the Divine Warrior and the divine, compassionate Mother who is concerned with creation and sexuality; and most fundamental of all oppositions, history versus the text. Curiously, one important area where the two agree is a common abhorrence of any systematic presentation of biblical theology. One might well conclude that it is quite difficult, if not impossible, to find a basis for conversation between representatives of these two very different approaches.

Certainly those interested in creation and the literary nature of the text as the focus of Old Testament theology could and do have serious conversations. But what of history? Are we imprisoned in an ahistorical, postmodern *Zeitgeist* when theologizing will not permit the questions and methods of historical criticism? Are we necessarily faced with two very opposite disciplines: the history of Israelite religion and biblical theology? The collapse of history in much theological discourse of late does not signal necessarily the end of its contribution to Old Testament theology. It could well be that a new vitality of Old Testament theology may result from conversations that should occur between historians, literary specialists, and contemporary theologians about narrative and, as we shall see in the next chapter, imagination.

NARRATIVE THEOLOGY AND BIBLICAL STORY

The importance of narratives or stories in the Bible has led to another way of reconceiving Old Testament theology in more recent years. In contemporary theology and biblical scholarship, this approach is usually called narrative theology or theology of story, with the term narrative usually being equated with story.[1] Narratives, of course, may be historical, fictional, or a combination of both, but this theological approach usually interprets biblical narratives in much the same way that literary fiction is assessed, even when those narratives are considered to be "history-like" or "realistic." This raises the question of truth that has been the object of considerable debate. Can fiction, not grounded in history, be theologically true? And if so, what are the criteria for determining whether the claims of fiction are true?

Gabriel Fackre defines a story as "an account of characters and events moving over time and space, through conflict toward resolution."[2] Stories may be lifelike in describing the lives of individuals, or they may be communal in the sense that they describe the reality of groups of people. In the Bible, one doubts that any of the narratives were life stories of individuals; rather, what one has is a collection of communal narratives, even if individual characters play important roles. These narratives related the history and significant meanings of communities in Israelite society and history and expressed their traditions, values, and beliefs that shaped and sustained their identity and ethos. These narratives also shaped and sustained the identity of individuals who were members of these communities.

One may say that, in general, stories serve a variety of functions, including the presentation of a society's worldview, the expression of a community's understanding of human social organizations with their various customs, laws, and moral standards, and the providing of instruction for an individual's movement through the stages of life within a social context.[3] Stories not only are reflective of very important values and beliefs of communities and their participants but they also help to shape and define a community's or a

---

1. This approach to theology, which has developed rapidly since the 1970s, may be traced to H. Richard Niebuhr, who pointed to the early Christians' presentation of the faith as "the story of our life," *The Meaning of Revelation* (New York: Macmillan, 1941) 43–81.
2. Gabriel Fackre, "Narrative Theology: An Overview," *Int* 37 (1983) 341.
3. Kliever, *The Shattered Spectrum*, 153.

person's identity and way of living in the world. They shape the scattered and particular experiences of communities and individuals within a usually coherent narrative structure that construes meaning. Stories also are the repository for an individual's or a community's memory, enabling them to know who they are, what they believe and value, what they are to do, and from where they come and where they are going. Memory gives coherence to experience, establishes a connection between past and present, and enables the future to be anticipated.

Not only do stories carry the collective memory of what a community or an individual may see as most fundamentally real and true, they also have the power to summon people into the future of new beginning. Stories enable communities and individuals to anticipate the future in new and coherent forms. Through the imagination, stories allow experiences to be reorganized, connected in new ways, and structured into new configurations that reshape the past and open up the future to a variety of possibilities. Stories do not simply describe or even translate reality; they also redescribe and even create reality in new, vital, and provocative ways, thus enabling the audience to stand "betwixt and between" a past that through memory may impinge upon the present in ordinary or new and engaging ways and an indeterminate future that beckons with a variety of possibilities.

Stories may be disclosive in revealing to an audience new insight into meaning and existence. In certain cases, they may even possess the power to transform the world and those who choose to live within their time and space. This points to the last, but most significant function of stories: they are dwelling places at least for a period if not for a lifetime for those who choose to enter their narrative world.

Perhaps the attraction and the power of stories in part reside in their embodiment of important dimensions of human existence, including space, time, and action within an imaginative reality.[4] In part, their attraction and power may result from the possibility that they may reflect the structure of human consciousness, expressing the way humans pattern their thoughts, understand their emotions, and organize their experiences. In part, their attraction and power may reside in their ability to present or at least "re-present" a

4. See especially Stephen Crites, "The Narrative Quality of Experience," *JAAR* 39 (1971) 291–311; and idem, "The Spatial Dimensions of Narrative Truth Telling," *Scriptural Authority and Narrative Interpretation* (ed. Garrett Green; Philadelphia: Fortress, 1987) 97–118.

coherent and ordered world that provides meaning and guidance for existence. While one may regard a story as embodying that which is important and true, one may also step back to find that "telling a tale suggests a perspectival stance and confessional commitment without the necessary entailment of universal truth claims."[5]

NARRATIVE THEOLOGY

Theologies of story are divided into two broad areas. The first area, that of theology and literature, seeks to examine the interaction between religious belief and modern literature, while the second area, that of theology as literature, focuses on biblical stories and the narrative character of theology.[6] The second area is the one that is most directly important for biblical theology.[7]

Narrative theology is simply "discourse about God in the setting

---

5. Fackre, "Narrative Theology: An Overview," 341.

6. Kliever, *The Shattered Spectrum*, 157. Ronald Thiemann remarks: "Narrative highlights both a predominant literary category within the Bible and an appropriate theological category for interpreting the canon as a whole" (*Revelation and Theology: The Gospel as Narrated Promise* [Notre Dame, Ind.: University of Notre Dame Press, 1985] 83).

7. The scholarly literature is immense. Among the most important expressions of narrative theology are Hans Frei, *The Eclipse of Biblical Narrative: A Study in Eighteenth and Nineteenth Century Hermeneutics* (New Haven: Yale University Press, 1974); idem, *The Identity of Jesus Christ: The Hermeneutical Bases of Dogmatic Theology* (Philadelphia: Fortress, 1975); George Lindbeck, *The Nature of Doctrine: Religion and Theology in a Postliberal Age* (Philadelphia: Westminster, 1984); Paul Ricoeur, *Time and Narrative* (2 vols.; Chicago: University of Chicago Press, 1984, 1985); idem, "Biblical Hermeneutics," *Paul Ricoeur on Biblical Hermeneutics* (ed. John Dominic Crossan; *Semeia* 4 [1975], 29–146); idem, "The Narrative Function," 177–202; and *Essays on Biblical Interpretation* (ed. Lewis Mudge; Philadelphia: Fortress, 1980) 75–79; David Tracy, *Analogical Imagination* (New York: Crossroad, 1981; especially his analysis of the religious "classic"); Crites, "The Narrative Quality of Experience," and "The Spatial Dimensions of Narrative Truth Telling"; Michael Goldberg, *Theology and Narrative: A Critical Introduction* (Nashville: Abingdon, 1981, 1982); Green, *Scriptural Authority and Narrative Interpretation*; Stanley Hauerwas, *Vision and Virtue* (Notre Dame, Ind.: Fides, 1974); Stanley Hauerwas and L. Gregory Jones, eds., *Why Narrative?* (Grand Rapids: Eerdmans, 1989); A. E. Harvey, ed., *God Incarnate: Story and Belief* (London: SPCK, 1981); and George W. Stroup, *The Promise of Narrative Theology* (Atlanta: John Knox, 1981). According to Goldberg, narrative theologians generally subscribe to the following elements: the form of the biblical narrative reflects the structure of reality; the meaning of the story is of central importance; and the ethic expressed in and through the narrative is significant (*Theology and Narrative*, 155). Important overviews of narrative theology are provided by Goldberg, *Theology and Narrative*; Kliever, *The Shattered Spectrum*, 153–84; and George W. Stroup, "Theology of Narrative or Narrative Theology? A Response to *Why Narrative?*" *Today* 47 (1991) 424–32.

of story."[8] While there are distinctions between various approaches, there are several features common to narrative theology.[9] The most important affirmation is the general recognition of the fundamental importance of narrative as a subject of theological inquiry. Narrative is said to be indispensable in the presentation of God's action in history. Emphasizing that primary attention should be given to the biblical forms of literature, narrative theology is especially critical of systematic theology's primary dependence on philosophical paradigms to approach questions of truth, to conceptualize beliefs in discursive language, and to discuss the manner of revelation at the expense of ignoring the nature and character of narrative.[10]

BIBLICAL NARRATIVE AS "HISTORY-LIKE"

The major representative of the Yale school of narrative theology, Hans Frei has analyzed the problem that historical criticism has posed for the church in his volume *The Eclipse of Biblical Narrative*.[11] Frei portrays Christian reading of the Bible prior to the eighteenth century as "usually strongly realistic, i.e. at once literal and historical, and not only doctrinal or edifying." This "realistic" reading of Scripture was characterized by four major features. The Bible was read as describing real events and therefore presented what was literally true. Further, the stories of the Bible were shaped into the sequence of one long story, from the beginning (Genesis) to the end (Revelation). In addition, this story, argues Frei, was perceived to be the "real world" and included any and every age and reader. Precritical readers viewed their own lives as part of this grand drama that began at creation and would continue into the eschaton (i.e., from Genesis to Revelation). Finally, earlier biblical events could be seen as types or figures of later ones, thus providing a unified, continuous, interpretative whole.[12] All of these meant

8. Fackre, "Narrative Theology: An Overview," 343.
9. For a convenient and clear summary, see Fackre, "Narrative Theology: An Overview," 340–52.
10. Two important although distinctive "schools" of narrative theology have developed, one primarily associated with Yale (Hans Frei, Stanley Hauerwas, David Kelsey, and George Lindbeck) and the other largely identified with Chicago (Paul Ricoeur, David Tracy, and Julian Hartt). For a comparison of the two, see Gary Comstock, "Two Types of Narrative Theology," *JAAR* 55 (1987) 687–717.
11. See Frei, *The Eclipse of Biblical Narrative*; and idem, *The Identity of Jesus Christ*. For a careful and cogent critique, see James Duke, "Reading the Gospels Realistically: A Review of Hans Frei's 'Eclipse of Biblical Narrative' and 'Identity of Jesus Christ,'" *Encounter* 38 (1977) 296–306.
12. Similar is the view of George Lindbeck, who argues that the literary genre of the Bible is "an overarching story that has the specific literary features of realistic

then that there was not a serious hermeneutical gap between text and readers, for they had an immediate entrée into the real story that included all who believed it. While often revised, the story remained the true depiction of the world and possessed a disclosive power to reveal God, self, and the place of the individual within corporate life.[13]

With the rise of historical criticism, beginning with the Enlightenment, the connection between the literal meaning of the biblical stories and their reference to actual events began to break down. Truth began to be identified, not with the verbal interpretation of the story, but more so with whether the events of the story really happened. This meant that truth became associated with historical events outside the text itself. Distance between the narrative world and the "real," that is, historical, world began to develop and widen. Thus the "truth" of biblical narratives or their reality could be affirmed only by fitting them within either the framework of a modern perception of reality or history reconstructed by historical criticism. This meant that the truth of biblical narratives was based on whether they presented a moral lesson, eternal or universal belief, or historical fact. Instead of readers fitting within the biblical reality, now the biblical story had to be placed within their reality.

If narrative references to historical events were discovered to be false, then interpreters could argue that the message or spiritual meaning of the biblical stories could be true. This resulted, however, in the conviction that meaning, and therefore religious truth, should be detached from the story itself. Further, typology could no longer function as a valid hermeneutic, since there was no direct continuity between real events in the Bible and real events in later history. Historical-critical method also disconnected the sequences of the single story, turning the text into many disconnected fragments, although the critical history written by scholars produced the closest replacement for the precritical reading of the biblical story. Now truth became associated with historical events reconstructed by scholars and placed within a linear sequence of events, that is, a narrative history, and meaning was derived by reference to things outside the narrative itself. Since figurative interpretation as a hermeneutic was no longer valid, the theology of biblical concepts took its place. Thus biblical theology and historical criticism became very different interpretative enterprises.

---

narrative" (*The Nature of Doctrine*, 120–21).
13. See George Stroup, *The Promise of Narrative Theology*, 63–65.

The tragedy in this development, according to Frei, was that the "history-like" quality of biblical narrative was lost in the shuffle, while the Bible's reality and unity were seriously questioned. Even though scholars often spoke of the "realistic" and "history-like" nature of much of biblical narrative, the lack of reference to real events outside the story made it "untrue." Subsequently, a dichotomy was made between meaning and reference, that is, what the story says and what it is about. In effect, biblical narrative was denied a direct role in the presentation of theology and in the hermeneutical enterprise. Biblical narrative was "eclipsed."

Frei challenges this eclipse of biblical narrative and seeks to recover its important place in theology. His proposal is not the construction of a complete and detailed hermeneutic but one that will take the Bible seriously and adequately interpret it. He begins by arguing that the Bible contains "history-like," realistic narratives that should be read on their own terms and not evaluated as to whether they refer to real, historical events or present generalized moral lessons or universal truths.[14] These narratives do not separate meaning and reference (what the story says and what the story is about). The reference of the story (what the story is about) is internal to its literary form. The reference is not found outside the story either in events behind the text, in universal principles of faith, in religious experience, or in mythic archetypes; rather, it is found in the reality of action, space, time, characters, and movement within the narrative structure.

Frei also argues that the meaning of the story (what the story says) is also inseparable from its form. The location of meaning in realistic narrative is found within the structure or sequence of the story itself. He contends that the meaning of the realistic narratives of the Bible is autonomous, for they refer only to themselves, not to something outside themselves, including the beliefs or intent of the author or the audience. He states: "It is not going too far to say that the story is the meaning or, alternatively, that the meaning emerges from the story form, rather than being merely illustrated by it."[15] Meaning is narrated or "instantiated," and "this meaning through instantiation is not illustrated . . . but constituted through the mutual, specific determination of agents, speech, social context, and circumstances that form the indispensable narrative web."[16]

14. In Frei's assessment of the "history-like" character of biblical narratives, he is depending on Erich Auerbach, *Mimesis* (Garden City, N.Y.: Doubleday, 1957).
15. Frei, *The Eclipse of Biblical Narrative*, 280.
16. Ibid., 280.

For Frei and other narrative theologians, the affirmations of faith at the center of theology are best expressed by means of narrative.[17] Language creates the reality of authentic human life and is not simply descriptive of human experience. And it is important to attend to the form of language in which the reality of biblical faith is presented. Not only are the affirmations of biblical faith often grounded in events that are expressed in narratives, so are personal convictions of believers who encounter these texts. The hermeneutical task is to seek a convergence, that is, to place the readers' own stories within the biblical narrative in particular and then within the overarching story of the Christian faith. The biblical narrative invites readers to enter into the reality of its world that is linguistically created by its narrator. This new world becomes the framework in which they are to live out their lives.[18] They find their own narrative meaning and make sense of their own experiences primarily in and through the biblical narratives and the larger Christian story. For this to happen, these narratives must overcome, as it were, the readers' own worlds and replace these by the narrated reality.

Beyond the individual narrative stories, for example, the gospel story, Frei argues, there is the "overarching tale" of the Christian story, "a tale writ large" that embraces the faith narrative of Christianity from its inception onward.[19] Here the storyteller is neither a person nor a narrator of a scriptural narrative but rather is the community of faith. The meaning of this overarching tale is known to insiders, that is, to believers. It is a mistake to try to justify the faith apologetically by seeking to argue with and then persuade outsiders about the truth of the comprehensive story. Rather, the authenticity of the faith comes from living out the convictions expressed in the story in a liberated and liberating life that is "an appropriate response to God's actions toward us."[20] Thus there is a

---

17. Goldberg, *Theology and Narrative*, 34. In Frei's words, realistic narrative "simultaneously depicts and renders the reality (if any) of what it talks about" (*The Eclipse of Biblical Narrative*, 27).

18. See Lindbeck's discussion in *The Nature of Doctrine*, 117.

19. Lindbeck states that the genre of the entire Bible is "an overarching story that has the specific literary features of realistic narrative." Indeed, for Lindbeck, the function of this story is to render the character of God (*The Nature of Doctrine*, 120–21).

20. Comstock, "Two Types of Narrative Theology," 690. The description of the moral life in response to God's actions and revelation in and through narrative faith is especially developed in the work of Stanley Hauerwas.

pragmatic demonstration that the biblical story is true in authentic living that is an appropriate response to the story. In the Gospel narrative, Jesus' identity in the text converges with the encounter of the reader with the risen Christ. In general, it is the believer who encounters the risen Christ in the story and lives out a faithful response.

Narrative theology contends that it is wrong to attempt to abstract ideas from their narrative expression, without at the very least having first realized the importance of story for both understanding and expressing their significance. Frei represents the view of some narrative theologians in opposing the dependency of theology on abstract, speculative philosophies and the presentation of contemporary faith largely in discursive prose and systematic categories. Narrative, for Frei, is the unique, fundamental, and indispensable mode of discourse for the articulation of the faith. Believers explain the Christian faith by telling the story of Jesus Christ and their own life stories. The description and explanation of Christianity should be in terms of the language of biblical narratives and Christians' autobiographies, not in abstract philosophical categories and social-scientific laws.[21] The task of the narrative theologian is to determine whether doctrines, values, and morals are appropriate expressions of narrative faith.

In his hermeneutical work, Frei sets forth the "plain sense" interpretation of Scripture that for him means "the narrative depiction of the identity of Jesus Christ."[22] The interpreter should be bound by a minimum of theory as he or she poses two fundamental questions of the Gospels: Who is Jesus? and, What is he like? Frei notes that what we know about Jesus is "more nearly" fictional than historical. But modern preoccupation with historical questions and the identification of truth with literal meaning has led to the "eclipse" of other ways of reading biblical narratives that are important theologically. Even to call a narrative fictional or fiction-like is not to deny it by necessity the ring of truth. The "plain" or literal sense of a text is its narrative meaning, whether fictional or not. It may still be true.[23]

---

21. See Comstock, "Two Types of Narrative Theology," 690.
22. See Frei, *The Identity of Jesus Christ*; idem, "The 'Literal Reading' of Biblical Narrative in the Christian Tradition: Does It Stretch or Will It Break?" *The Bible and the Narrative Tradition* (ed. Frank McConnell; New York: Oxford University Press, 1986) 36–77; and Kathryn E. Tanner, "Theology and the Plain Sense," Green, *Scriptural Authority and Narrative Interpretation*, 59.
23. See Gary Comstock, "Truth or Meaning: Ricoeur versus Frei on Biblical

Narrative theology is compatible with the approach of biblical scholars who interpret the Bible by means of "close reading" methodology. Both give fundamental importance to the form and content of biblical narrative. Both are critical of the objectives of historical criticism in using biblical texts primarily to reconstruct the history and religion of Israel, for fragmenting biblical texts into minute pieces, and for speculative reconstructions of the development of biblical books. Finally, both are opposed to the use of abstract reason to set forth the systematic rendering of biblical and theological ideas at the expense of ignoring the form and at times the content of biblical narrative.

BIBLICAL STORY AND CLOSE READING

Many methodologies have developed in a variety of fields for interpreting and understanding stories (e.g., literature, psychology, sociology, philosophy, linguistics, and phenomenology). One of the important methodological moves from history to text is found in a variety of paradigms that have developed in the areas of literature and linguistics.[24] Perhaps the most influential of these in biblical studies is new criticism, sometimes called "close reading," a method that operates with three major assertions.[25] First, attention is to be placed on the biblical text as an object of beauty and meaning, not on the author. It is the text, not the one who wrote it, that is the focus of interpretation. This assertion of the nonreferential char-

Narrative," *JR* 66 (1986) 117–40; and Garrett Green, "'The Bible as . . .': Fictional Narrative and Scriptural Truth," *Scriptural Authority and Narrative Interpretation*, 79–86.

24. The literature in this area is vast. Among the more important treatments that have impacted biblical studies, see Wayne Booth, *The Rhetoric of Fiction* (Chicago: University of Chicago Press, 1961); Northrop Frye, *Anatomy of Criticism* (Princeton, N.J.: Princeton University Press, 1957); Frank Kermode, *The Genesis of Secrecy: On the Interpretation of Narrative* (Cambridge, Mass.: Harvard University Press, 1979); and Robert Scholes and Robert Kellogg, *The Nature of Narrative* (New York: Oxford University Press, 1966). Important literary treatments of biblical narrative include James Ackerman and Kenneth Gros-Louis, *Literary Interpretations of Biblical Narratives* (Nashville: Abingdon, 1974); Michael Fishbane, *Text and Texture* (New York: Schocken, 1979); J. P. Fokkelman, *Narrative Art in Genesis* (Assen: Van Gorcum, 1975); Jacob Licht, *Storytelling in the Bible* (Jerusalem: Magnes, 1978); and Meir Sternberg, *The Poetics of Biblical Narrative: Ideological Literature and the Drama of Reading* (Bloomington, Ind.: Indiana University Press, 1987).

25. See John Barton, *Reading the Old Testament: Method in Biblical Study* (Philadelphia: Westminster, 1984) 140–98.

acter of new criticism is of central importance. The text is not a means to get at an understanding of the identity, thought, and life of the author, or anything else outside the text itself. Meaning and reference are both internal to the text. This assertion flies directly in the face of the efforts of historical criticism and many ways of conceiving biblical theology.

Second, related to the above is the fact that new criticism eliminates the intentional fallacy by affirming that the biblical text, not the author, is the source and judge of the propriety of an interpretation. No importance is placed on the intention of the author, even if it could be determined, in discovering the meaning of the text.

Third, for some new critics, although not for all, meaning is a function of the position a text holds within a literary context. Texts have cultural fields of reference that impact their meaning. Nevertheless the specificity of a text's meaning, not widely diffused cultural values, is the focus of interpretation. A specific text is not read primarily to get at a larger cultural field, say, for example, Western literature. Rather, the search is for the specific meaning of a text that, in part, may be aided by reference to the larger semantic field and discourse of values existing in the surrounding culture. But it is the meaning of a text that comes from within its own narrative reality, not its location in some external field of discourse, that is of primary importance.

The literary questions of new critics address characterization, plot development, themes, motifs, mood, structure, point of view, and interaction of dialogue and narration within the biblical text. Repetition, especially of key words, is of important value in coming to the meaning inherent in the biblical text. Other techniques, including irony, satire, and flashbacks, are part and parcel of narrative art practiced in the Bible.

THE ART OF BIBLICAL NARRATIVE

Robert Alter approaches biblical interpretation by means of literary analysis, or what has been called "close reading," and in his very useful and important study provides a clear summary of the characteristic features of narrative in the Old Testament.[26] He con-

___

26. Robert Alter, *The Art of Biblical Narrative* (New York: Basic Books, 1981). He explains: "By literary analysis I mean the manifold varieties of minutely discriminating attention to the artful use of language, to the shifting play of ideas, conventions, tone, imagery, syntax, narrative viewpoint, compositional units, and

trasts his approach with historical criticism, which in his judgment is primarily "excavative" both in the use of archaeology and in the effort to recover original meanings, life situations, and diachronic developments of texts. While lamenting the excesses of this approach that have led to endless speculation, Alter notes that the interpreter is much indebted to the important discoveries of historical critics.

Alter explains that a literary approach focuses on the final form of biblical narrative and seeks to interpret it by understanding its significant artistic features.[27] These include sacred history and biblical prose fiction, biblical type-scenes and the uses of convention, narration and dialogue, repetition, characterization and the art of reticence, composite artistry, and narration and knowledge. This recognition of the artistry of the Hebrew Bible, Alter contends, is important, because literary criticism regards language, not as a literary embellishment of truths, beliefs, and ideas that are of primary importance, but as "an integral and dynamic component—an insistent dimension—of what is being narrated."[28] Thus Alter's objective is not only to describe the artistry of biblical literature in the effort to understand how and what a text means. He also seeks to teach one how to read biblical texts, not only to obtain entertainment and knowledge about the Bible, but also to derive insight into oneself and one's own narrative reality. Indeed, for Alter, biblical narrative has the ability to redescribe reality for those who, through informed and careful reading, are drawn into its world.

Alter begins with the broad discussion of the Hebrew Bible as both sacred history and prose fiction. While acknowledging that the Hebrew Bible in general is driven by the impulse to set forth the view of the God of Israel as the God of history, Alter nevertheless asserts "that prose fiction," or more specifically speaking, *"historicized* prose fiction," is the appropriate category for the narrative component of biblical literature.[29] Part of the justification of this approach is Alter's recognition that history is more similar to fiction than popularly assumed. Both narrative history and narrative fic-

---

much else; the kind of disciplined attention, in other words, which through a whole spectrum of critical approaches has illuminated, for example, the poetry of Dante, the plays of Shakespeare, the novels of Tolstoy" (pp. 12–13).

27. Alter states: "What we need to understand better is that the religious vision of the Bible is given depth and subtlety precisely by being conveyed through the most sophisticated resources of prose fiction" (*The Art of Biblical Narrative*, 22).

28. Ibid., 112.

29. Ibid., 24.

tion share a variety of strategies, techniques, and imaginative constructs, although the writer of fiction has more freedom to invent
the components of the story than the historian who must attend
carefully to historical data. Part of the justification is based on the
recognition that biblical authors used an impressive variety of literary artistry in creating the narrative story. They consciously used
their artistic freedom in shaping even inherited tradition in order to
give new form and even substance to the material. Alter suggests
that the Bible "interweaves" factual history with a variety of fictional lore: myth, legend, etiology, and so forth. Even the so-called
historical narratives about David, Alter contends, are not in the
strict sense historiography; rather, they are the "imaginative reenactment of history by a gifted writer who organizes his materials
along certain thematic biases and according to his own remarkable
intuition of the psychology of the characters."[30] The writer does so
by means of a variety of strategies and techniques, including the
invention of dialogue, interior monologue, and the ascribing of
feelings and motives to characters.

But what of the Bible as sacred history? Alter does not deny that
the Hebrew Bible is primarily concerned to set forth the actions of
God in history. Even so, biblical writers recognize two fundamental
tensions in their narrative portrayal of this divine activity. One is
the tension between the divine plan and the disorder of historical
events, and the other is the tension between divine will or providence and human freedom. For Alter, this twofold dialectic fundamentally shapes the thematic movement of biblical narratives.[31]
But even this (I would call it "theological") essence of the Bible as
sacred history does not preclude its narrative performance. Indeed,
for Alter prose fiction or historicized prose fiction, not narrative
history, is the primary literary means for the actualization of sacred
history.

Alter then proceeds to discuss major features of the artistry of
biblical narrative. The first feature is biblical type-scenes and the
uses of convention.[32] According to Alter, biblical type-scenes point,
not to the retelling of the same basic story with variations, as form
critics argue, but to narrative conventions that involve "a fixed
constellation of predetermined motifs."[33] Even variations or sup-

---

30. Ibid., 35. James Barr makes a similar point ("Some Thoughts on Narrative,
Myth and Incarnation," Harvey, *God Incarnate*, 14–23).
31. Alter, *The Art of Biblical Narrative*, 33.
32. Ibid., 47–62.
33. For example, hero stories often include the divine announcement of the hero's

pressions of these conventions may have import, while their repetition may recall other occurrences with their full range of theological and literary meaning. Significant meaning is found, then, not only in what is commonly repeated but also in the specific variations that occur in the different uses of the type-scene and its common conventions.

The art of biblical narration and dialogue is the next feature that Alter discusses.[34] He notes that in biblical narrative dialogue has a variety of functions: to reveal the relationship of characters to their actions, to express characters' thoughts, to convey what is happening and experienced, and to differentiate and define character. The most important dialogue usually occurs at the beginning of a story, for this often sets the mood, articulates the theme, and establishes the plot.

Alter's chapter on repetition demonstrates that this device is the primary way biblical narrative units are connected, the thematic argument develops, character is delineated, and plot unfolds.[35] He contends that repetition is the most important feature of the artistry of Hebrew narrative. Alter delineates between two types of repetition: the reiterative reoccurrence of words, themes, images, motifs, scenes, and so forth; and variational reoccurrence in which even the slightest change may provide significant insight into the meaning of a text.

Alter describes five types of "repetitive structuring and focuses in biblical narrative":

1. *Leitwort*—a "leading word" whose semantic meaning points to the meaning or theme of a narrative.
2. Motif—"a concrete image, sensory quality, action, or object" that is repeated throughout a narrative.
3. Theme—"an idea which is part of the value-system of the narrative . . . is made evident in some recurring pattern."
4. Sequence of actions—repeated actions that usually reach a climax or some other form of intensification with the final repetition.
5. Type-scene—a repeated scene characterized by the presence of conventions and recurrent themes.[36]

---

birth to his barren mother, the meeting between the hero and his betrothed at a well, the appearance of God to the hero in a field, the initiatory trial, the danger confronting the hero in the desert, the discovery of a well or other means of survival, and the testament of the dying hero (ibid., 47–62).

34. Ibid., 63–87.
35. Ibid., 88–113.
36. Ibid., 95–96.

In moving to the next feature of the artistry of biblical narrative, Alter explains that characterization and the art of reticence involve the biblical narrator in withholding key information necessary for making judgments about the intention and the virtue of characters. Characters in the Bible, for the most part, do not state explicitly their own reasons for actions.[37] Mystery, even ambiguity, are central to the biblical portrayal of characters whose complexity defies precise analysis and clear understanding.

It is at the end of the chapter on characterization that Alter reveals a major insight from which narrative theology may rightly proceed:

> The narrative art of the Bible, then, is more than an aesthetic enterprise, and learning to read its fine calibrations may bring us closer than the broad-gauge concepts of intellectual history and comparative religion to a structure of imagination in whose shadow we still stand.[38]

Through imagination, narrative worlds are constructed by storytellers who invite their implied audiences to enter and experience the mythic drama of biblical fiction. The art of reticence is one technique of biblical narrative that draws the reader into the story to make certain judgments, to "fill in the gaps," as it were, in order to arrive at a coherent meaning.

Michael Goldberg makes an important point that should be inserted at this juncture. This has to do with the narrative portrayal of God. In biblical narrative, God is either the implied narrator, speaking normally in the third person, or more commonly a character within the story itself. God is revealed in part through divine action and speech in time and space, although much of the ambiguity that is true of human characters also is true of God. The reader is drawn into the text and forced to make certain interpretative decisions even about God. This is due to the fact that the Bible does not set forth conceptual, systematic presentations of God, but most often "our ability to know God and his actions depends on our capacity to know how to identify him as an agent whose characteristic patterns of behavior find display within the context of some narrative."[39]

37. Thus, according to Alter, "we are compelled to get at character and motive . . . through a process of inference from fragmentary data, often with crucial pieces of narrative exposition strategically withheld, and this leads to multiple or sometimes even wavering perspectives on the characters" (ibid., 126).

38. Ibid., 130.

39. Michael Goldberg, "God, Acting and Narrative: Which Narrative? Which Action? Which God?" *JR* 68 (1988) 39. For a detailed discussion of the narrative

Alter's chapter on composite artistry takes up perhaps the most complicated issue facing the literary analysis of the Bible.[40] Historical criticism has pointed to the fragmentary, contradictory, and composite character of much biblical literature, arguing that a variety of sources and traditions has been woven together in a way that often defies coherence and logic. This view of the text stands in opposition to the efforts of the literary scholar to find artistry, coherence, and logic in biblical narratives.

In a controversial argument, Alter contends that biblical writers and redactors were as aware as are modern readers that narratives often do not always follow logic by presenting things in a coherent sequence. If this is correct, this means then that biblical authors and redactors had a different understanding of unity from that of their modern readers. On occasion, various versions of the same event or person are narrated (e.g., multiple creation stories, two of which are side by side) in order to provide something of a montage of varying perspectives that present and assess the complexities of human nature and historical action. Thus "composite artistry" may be an intentional technique.

Also important for understanding biblical narrative's artistry is Alter's chapter on "narration and knowledge." Here he explains that the reader learns from biblical narrative because of the "realism" of the presentation that points to experiences "not unlike our own," a point lying at the heart of Auerbach's *Mimesis* and Hans Frei's argument that biblical narrative is "history-like."[41] Yet the skilled writer of fiction is able to highlight and explore those critical moments that reveal the character of those who live out their lives within the context of the story. Further, the narrator may assume a role that Israelite theology disallowed, that is, identity with the voice of God. While the Bible denies that people may become divine, human writers through their omniscient narrators may adopt the all-knowing perspective and unlimited power of God. Thus the future may be revealed, miracles wrought, and inward knowledge obtained of the heart of characters involved in deception, disguises, and ambiguity. The implied audience may know significant information that is withheld from key characters even though it is important for moral decision making. For characters,

---

presentation of God, see Dale Patrick, *The Rendering of God in the Old Testament* (Overtures to Biblical Theology; Philadelphia: Fortress, 1981).
40. Alter, *The Art of Biblical Narrative*, 131–54.
41. See the discussion of Frei and Auerbach in the preceding section.

denouement comes at that revelatory moment when information and insight allow recognition and self-disclosure to occur. Yet most characters remain enigmatic, and actions do not always convey clear and unmistakable indications of propriety and virtue.[42]

Finally and most important for Alter, it is through fiction that readers are allowed entrance into the complexity of the interaction between human nature and divine intention, between the order of the divine plan and the disorder of historical events, and between providence and human freedom. It is the imagination that gives birth to fiction that mediates the complexity of this engagement, allowing the implied audience to experience and reflect on the realism of the text's world. And the story may well be disclosive of divine reality leading to the transformation of those who enter its reality.[43]

NARRATIVE THEOLOGY AND THE BOOK OF JEREMIAH

The application of "close reading" methodology to obtain a narrative theology of Jeremiah is a challenging process because of the rather complex composition of the book. Historical criticism has argued that Jeremiah is a collection of rather diverse sources or traditions that are neither carefully woven together nor placed within a clear narrative structure characterized by an obvious coherence and sequence.[44] However, the substantial presence of narrative, which enfolds many types of poetic and prose speeches, may prompt the use of the insights of close reading to read Jeremiah as story. The following is a start in this direction, providing an analysis of the section in the book most conducive to close reading: the so-called "passion" history (Jeremiah 37–44).

We begin with Fackre's definition of a narrative as "an account of characters and events moving over time and space, through conflict toward resolution."[45] The "passion" narrative is, in Auerbach's understanding, a "realistic" or "history-like" narrative, or to use Alter's term, "historicized prose fiction," although it is difficult to

---

42. For an examination of David as enigmatic character, see Leo G. Perdue, "'Is there anyone left of the house of Saul . . .?' Ambiguity and the Characterization of David in the Succession Narrative," *JSOT* 30 (1984) 67–84.

43. Arguing that form and content cannot be separated, Tracy contends that "the disclosive and transformative power and meaning of the story are grasped only in and through the narrative itself" (*Analogical Imagination*, 275).

44. See Perdue, "Jeremiah in Modern Research."

45. Fackre, "Narrative Theology: An Overview," 341.

separate fiction from history in general. This is without doubt the case with the narrative under consideration.

The "passion" story of Jeremiah narrates the prophet's actions and oracles from the time of the temporary lifting of the Babylonian siege (588 B.C.E.) to his exile in Egypt where he disappears from history (probably 570 B.C.E. or shortly before). The narrative traces sequentially, with little variation, the prophet's life from imprisonment during the siege of Jerusalem, to his liberation from prison by the Babylonians to dwell in Mizpah where Gedaliah presided over a provincial government, to his captivity and forced exile in Egypt with a remnant of Jewish survivors. In the "passion" narrative, as is the case elsewhere in the book, the life of Jeremiah is entwined with that of the nation, and indeed his own existence directly mirrors the fate of Judah during these most perilous times. His own passion reflects both the suffering of Judah and a struggling group of survivors in their efforts to survive and the pathos of God who brings judgment but also wills that a faithful remnant continue.

The narrative of the "passion" of Jeremiah is bracketed by two inclusios: the prominence of Baruch in the chapters immediately preceding and following (Jeremiah 36 and 45); and the reference to the Egyptian pharaoh (Hophra) at both the beginning of the narrative (Jer 37:5) and its conclusion (Jer 44:30). The contents of Jeremiah 36 and 45 are placed in the fourth year of Jehoiakim, and both mention that Baruch writes down the prophecies of Jeremiah at the prophet's dictation. The second inclusio frames the entire narrative within the reign of the Egyptian king Hophra (589–570 B.C.E.), to whom the pro-Egyptian party in Jerusalem and then the remnant under Johanan looked for aid and protection against Nebuchadrezzar. This is not fortuitous, for the narrative contrasts the Jews' repeated rejection of the offers of salvation by Yahweh with their vain efforts to obtain salvation from other sources, including false gods and a weak Egyptian king.

This tumultuous period of time for the life of Jeremiah is placed into three major sequences that occur in three different places: the siege and fall of Jerusalem (588–587 B.C.E.), the government of Gedaliah at Mizpah (587 B.C.E. to 582 B.C.E.?), and Jeremiah's forced exile in Egypt (582 B.C.E.? to 570 B.C.E.?). Following a general introduction in Jer 37:1-2 encapsulating in brief the theme of the entire narrative (the refusal of Zedekiah and the Jews to listen to Yahweh through his prophet), the narrative structure is set out according to these three sequences or acts, each having four to ten scenes:

1. The siege and fall of Jerusalem (37:3—40:6)
   Scene 1   Jeremiah's first oracle of judgment to Zedekiah (37:3-10)
   Scene 2   The imprisonment of Jeremiah (37:11-15)
   Scene 3   Jeremiah's second oracle of judgment to Zedekiah (37:16-21)
   Scene 4   Jeremiah imprisoned in the cistern (38:1-6)
   Scene 5   Ebed-melech rescues Jeremiah (38:7-13)
   Scene 6   Jeremiah's third oracle to Zedekiah: choice of life or death (38:14-28)
   Scene 7   Fall of Jerusalem (39:1-10)
   Scene 8   Nebuchadrezzar's protective order concerning Jeremiah (39:11-14)
   Scene 9   Jeremiah's oracle of salvation to Ebed-melech (39:15-18)
   Scene 10   Nebuzaradan's word to Jeremiah offering choice (40:1-6)
2. The collapse of the government of Gedaliah at Mizpah (40:7—41:8)
   Scene 11   Gedaliah's government at Mizpah (40:7-12)
   Scene 12   Johanan warns Gedaliah of an assassination plot (40:13-16)
   Scene 13   Ishmael assassinates Gedaliah (41:1-3)
   Scene 14   Ishmael murders pilgrims (41:4-8)
3. Forced exile in Egypt (41:9—44:30)
   Scene 15   Ishmael's flight to Ammon (41:9-10)
   Scene 16   Johanan's overtaking of Ishmael (41:11-18)
   Scene 17   Johanan seeks from Jeremiah a word of the Lord (42:1-6)
   Scene 18   Jeremiah's first oracle to the remnant: either/or (42:7-22)
   Scene 19   Rejection of Yahweh's word (43:1-7)
   Scene 20   Jeremiah's oracle of judgment against Egypt (43:8-13)
   Scene 21   Jeremiah's oracle of judgment against the Egyptian Jews (44:1-14)
   Scene 22   Defiance of the Egyptian Jews (44:15-19)
   Scene 23   Jeremiah's second oracle of judgment against the Egyptian Jews (44:20-30).

The narrator of this story is both omniscient, knowing, for example, what transpires in private conversations between king and prophet, and selective in what is told or not told. For example, is

Ishmael, a member of the royal family, driven by his desire for the throne of David in carrying out his murderous actions, or is he a misguided zealot who practices guerrilla warfare against Babylonian rule and Nebuchadrezzar's puppet governor in order to regain Jewish independence?

Ambiguity and mystery often surround the different characters in the narrative, even Jeremiah. Rarely is the reader given information by the narrator about the feelings, motives, and internal thoughts of characters. What is known about characters is derived from limited information provided by the narrator, their actions, and the various types of spoken discourse in which they are involved. God is also mysterious, for the reader is dependent on the speeches of the prophet for a perspective about Yahweh: characteristically, the "word of the Lord" comes to Jeremiah, who then declares it to the appropriate audience. While it is obvious in the view of the prophet that God is the Lord of history who causes in various ways important events to transpire, from the fall of Jerusalem to the predicted assassination of Hophra the king of Egypt, the mystery and even absence of God in the assassination of Gedaliah are puzzling. This narrative knows of no awe-inspiring miracles, no public visions, no dramatic theophanic appearances, not even dialogues between prophet and God. Because of mystery, ambiguity, and the sparsity of information, the reader is often forced to make certain judgments about the characters, including God.

The dominant feature of the "passion" narrative is the prominence of speeches and conversations: dialogues (especially, although not exclusively between Jeremiah and various people), the prophet's oracles of Yahweh (dominated by judgment speeches), two speeches from Babylonian officials that concern Jeremiah, one speech by Governor Gedaliah, and a disputation between Jeremiah and his opponents. These spoken discourses serve several functions: they explain and interpret what is happening, at least from the perspective of the speaker, they move the action forward, and they provide significant insight into the characters themselves, including God.

The dialogues between Jeremiah and various people most often are stimulated by the desire of the prophet's conversation partners to receive a word from Yahweh. This demonstrates that from the perspective of the other characters, most of them regard him as a true spokesperson for Yahweh. This is certainly the case for Zedekiah who three times directly or indirectly asks the prophet for a divine oracle: the first when the march of the Egyptian army led to the temporary lifting of the Babylonian siege, the second when the prophet had been imprisoned in the house of Jonathan the secretary, and the third after Ebed-melech had rescued Jeremiah from the cistern in the court of the guard. While Zedekiah apparently does not doubt the truthfulness of Jeremiah's words, even those that speak of the destruction of Jerusalem and his own exile to Babylon, he is seen as a weak, even vacillating man who lacks the courage to face down his pro-Egyptian advisers and officials who had pushed for and continued to sustain active resistance to the Babylonians. It is clear that Zedekiah fears for his own life. This threefold repetition of Zedekiah's desire for a word from the Lord through Jeremiah intensifies in the movement from an indirect request for a word of the Lord through emissaries to more direct and personal requests. An even more important intensification is demonstrated as the vacillating and fearful character of the king is progressively revealed. Finally, the content of the prophet's oracles to Zedekiah changes with each meeting, from the announcement of destruction of Jerusalem and the oracle that the king would be taken prisoner, to offering the king a choice between life (surrender to the Babylonians and both the city and he would be saved) and death (continued resistance will result in the destruction of Jerusalem and the captivity of the king).

Another dialogue, this one taking the form of disputation, occurs at the time of the decision of Johanan and the remnant to flee to Egypt for refuge or to stay in Judah. Desiring a word of the Lord from the prophet, they pledge that they will obey whatever directive is forthcoming from Yahweh. However, when they are told that Yahweh desires that they stay in Judah and receive divine blessing or face certain death by fleeing to Egypt, they accuse Jeremiah of lying. Thus the dialogue reveals the caprice and defiance of the remnant in the face of a prophetic word.

Two rather unusual speeches are made by Babylonians. The first is that of Nebuchadrezzar in which he issues a protective order concerning Jeremiah, following the fall of Jerusalem and the exile of its population. Nebuzaradan, the captain of Nebuchadrezzar's guard, and the one in charge of the deportation, is ordered to treat Jeremiah well and to do whatever the prophet asks. Neither the narrative nor the spoken discourse explains why Nebuchadrezzar is so concerned with Jeremiah's good treatment, but it is not idle speculation to suggest that Jeremiah's well-known pro-Babylonian stance and his counsel for king and populace to surrender may have bought the prophet the favor of the conquering king. The other speech by a Babylonian is even more intriguing. It comes from Nebuzaradan who releases Jeremiah from chains after the prophet

had been taken to Ramah with the other captives, prior to deportation to Babylon. In the speech, which was apparently referred to
as "the word that came to Jeremiah from the Lord," Nebuzaradan
tells Jeremiah that Yahweh was the one responsible for the evil
done to Jerusalem, because of their sinful disobedience. But as for
Jeremiah, the captain of the guard offers him the choice of coming
to Babylon under his protection, to go wherever he chooses, or to
remain in the land and stay with Gedaliah. What is astonishing is,
not so much the extension of grace to Jeremiah to choose where he
shall live, but that the captain of Nebuchadrezzar's guard speaks a
divine oracle as a believer in Yahweh!

Gedaliah utters the one other speech of significance, although he
makes no claim, nor does the narrator, that he has a word from
Yahweh, not an unimportant omission. This speech occurs sometime after Gedaliah had been appointed governor over Judah by
Nebuchadrezzar and after he had started to govern in Mizpah.
Various commanders of the Jewish military units still in the field
after the fall of Jerusalem went to Mizpah to meet with the new
governor. Sounding much like Jeremiah, Gedaliah encourages these
military troops to serve the Babylonians and their king and to dwell
in the land, that they may be blessed. He also admonishes them to
store up provisions and to dwell in the cities where they have taken
up residence. From this speech, coupled with the narrator's comments of the return of Jews from the Diaspora during this time, it
appears that Jeremiah's promise of well-being to a faithful, obedient
remnant is in the process of being realized. Of course, Ishmael's
assassination of the naive governor ended that dream.

Most important among the three types of spoken discourse are
the prophetic oracles, for they reveal not only important insight into
the prophet and interpret what is happening in the story, they also
provide the way the narrative seeks to render God. The oracles of
Jeremiah consist of three types: oracles of judgment (against nation
or person), an oracle of salvation (to Ebed-melech), and exhor-
tations that offer the choice of life or death. The oracles of the
prophet are arranged within the three narrative sequences as follows:

1. The siege and fall of Jerusalem (37:3—40:6)
   Scene 1   Jeremiah's first oracle to Zedekiah: judgment
              against Jerusalem (37:6-10)
   Scene 3   Jeremiah's second oracle to Zedekiah: judgment
              against the king (37:17)
   Scene 4   Jeremiah's reported admonition to the Jerusa-
              lem populace: defect to the Babylonians (38:2-3)

Scene 6   Jeremiah's third oracle to Zedekiah: choice of
life or death (38:17-18, 20-23)

Scene 9   Jeremiah's oracle of salvation to Ebed-melech
(39:15-18)

Scene 10   Nebuzaradan's word to Jeremiah: choose where
to live (40:2-5)

2. The government of Gedaliah at Mizpah (39:11—41:8)
3. Forced exile in Egypt (41:9—44:30)

Scene 18   Jeremiah's first oracle to the remnant: either/or
(42:9-22)

Scene 20   Jeremiah's oracle of judgment against Egypt
(43:8-13)

Scene 21   Jeremiah's oracle of judgment against the Egyptian Jews (44:2-14)

Scene 23   Jeremiah's second oracle of judgment against
the Egyptian Jews (44:20-30).

Of these ten prophetic oracles (nine by Jeremiah and one by
Nebuzaradan), five are oracles of judgment against a nation, city,
group, or individual (scenes 1, 3, 20, 21, and 23; the first two in the
narrative and the last three), one is an oracle of salvation (to Ebed-
melech, scene 9), and four are either/or speeches that offer the
audience the opportunity to choose life or death (scenes 4, 6, 10, 18;
the third, fourth, sixth, and seventh speeches). The first sequence,
occurring in Jerusalem, contains six speeches. The narrative begins
under the ominous cloud of judgment: first, the city of Jerusalem
will perish, in spite of the temporary lifting of the Babylonian siege
to meet the threat of an advancing Egyptian army; and second,
Zedekiah, the king, will be handed over to the king of Babylon.
However, the sentences of judgment that seem irrevocable are soft-
ened by two either/or speeches that offer the possibility of choosing
life. The first is a summary by pro-Egyptian officials of Jeremiah's
speech to the Jerusalem populace: defect to the Babylonians and
live or remain in the city and perish. The second, more important
example is in scene 6 where Zedekiah is offered a similar choice
between life and death: surrender to the Babylonians and the city
shall be spared, along with the royal house and the king himself; or
remain defiant, watch the city be destroyed, and become a prisoner
of the Babylonians. It is Yahweh himself who guarantees the promise of life, or so claims the prophet. There is a movement in this first
sequence, then, from what appears to be irreversible judgment to
the possibility of choosing life, even if the choice of life means
surrendering to the Babylonians. Zedekiah continues to fear the
pro-Egyptian officials, vacillates, and the opportunity for life passes

as the city falls to the Babylonians, Zedekiah watches the execution of his sons and officials, and he is blinded and then carried off into exile.

The fifth speech in this sequence involves a flashback to the court of the guard, prior to the fall of Jerusalem, after the prophet had been rescued from the cistern by Ebed-melech. Jeremiah is still a prisoner in the court of the guard, and he promises the Ethiopian salvation, the first and only salvation oracle in the entire "passion" narrative. While Jerusalem is to be destroyed, Yahweh will deliver the eunuch from both those he fears (presumably the pro-Egyptian officials angry over Jeremiah's rescue) and the Babylonian sack of the city. The reason for his courage in saving Jeremiah is his trust in Yahweh. Thus, the one man singled out for salvation because he has trusted in Yahweh is a black eunuch, presumably a pagan, from Ethiopia. But the promise came after the courageous rescue, not before. Hence, no obvious self-interest is displayed as a reason for the rescue.

The only other speech in the second sequence is the curious word of the Lord uttered to Jeremiah by Nebuzaradan. This captain of Nebuchadrezzar's guard offers the prophet the choice to go to Babylon under the captain's personal protection, to go wherever he may choose, or to remain in the land. If the prophet chooses the latter, Nebuzaradan tells him to remain with Gedaliah, presumably for protection. While not bearing quite the dramatic import of the same kind of "life or death" alternative offered earlier to the citizens of Jerusalem and to Zedekiah, nevertheless Jeremiah's life is at stake in the choice. And he chooses to remain in the land and to dwell at Mizpah with the new governor, appointed by Nebuchadrezzar to administer Judah.

The third act or sequence contains four speeches. The first is the offer of life or death to the surviving remnant led by the military commander Johanan. This is perhaps the most important instance in the entire narrative of the offer of "life or death": if Johanan and the remnant whom he delivered from the hands of the assassin, Ishmael, would remain in Judah, then Yahweh would bless them and save them from the king of Babylon. The language of "building up" and "planting" the remnant along with "deliver from the hand of" echoes major themes throughout the book, including the first chapter which serves as an overture to all that follows. On the other hand, if they decide to go to Egypt, then they will perish without survivor. This threat also echoes language that has been heard many times before in the book; for example, they will be "a horror, a curse, and a taunt." Unfortunately, the leaders and certain "insolent men" reject the admonition to remain in Judah, accusing Jeremiah of lying and Baruch of being behind a deceitful plot to deliver them over to the Babylonians either to perish or to be carried off into exile. Apparently Jeremiah's relationship of complicity with the Babylonians continued to evoke suspicion from the more militant zealots.

The last three speeches of the third sequence, exile in Egypt, and indeed of the entire "passion" story are judgment oracles, uttered by Jeremiah while in Egypt. The first is against Egypt, predicting the Babylonian conquest of the Egyptian kingdom; the second is uttered against the Jewish Diaspora in Egypt for their worship of other gods and idolatry; and the third continues the second, for it is also spoken against the Jewish Diaspora in Egypt for their defiant decision to continue to worship false gods, especially the Queen of Heaven. The sign that the latter judgment against the Jews in Egypt will be carried out will be the assassination of Pharaoh Hophra. The oracle against Egypt is designed to demonstrate the folly of the present Jews in Egypt in seeking out help from their neighbor to the south, even as their ancestors had done, to their peril. The two oracles against the Egyptian Jews compare their corruption and violation of the Torah to that of the Jews in Jerusalem and Judah who perished because of their disobedience. It is especially the case in the last two speeches that Jeremiah is the preacher of the law, who grounds judgment in the covenantal commandments.

What is interesting to note in the detailing of these speeches is the movement from what appears to be irreversible judgment (the destruction of the city of Jerusalem and the end of the house of David in the captivity of Zedekiah) to the possibility of the choosing of life by submitting to the Babylonians in the form of either/or decisions, to the one promise of salvation (Ebed-melech's life is spared), to the the either/or decisions offered to Jeremiah as to where he would live (presumably his chances would be better under Nebuzaradan's protection in Babylon) and then to Johanan and the surviving remnant, and finally to judgment once more, first against Egypt and second against the Jews of the Egyptian Diaspora. Thus the movement of the narrative is from disaster, to the possibility of salvation, to salvation, again to the possibility of salvation, and finally to disaster. The movement is from death, to life, to death. Rhetorically, judgment frames and encompasses the entire narrative. But in between judgment, there is the possibility of free decision to choose life, and there is that rare though important moment of salvation for one who chose to trust.

It is especially interesting and important to note the absence of any prophetic word about or to Gedaliah. This absence, of course, requires the reader to "fill in the gaps," a common requirement for reading Hebrew narrative. Perhaps the fault resides with Gedaliah. It is especially puzzling that the naive governor who refuses to believe that Ishmael would do him harm did not seek divine guidance from Jeremiah, who was in Mizpah. It appears that in the brief stint of his service as governor, peace, sufficient food, and the return of Jews from the Diaspora point to the promise of salvation from Yahweh, a promise earlier offered by Jeremiah in the Book of Consolation (Jeremiah 30–33). Certainly he sounds like Jeremiah in his counsel to the warriors to serve the Babylonians and in his urging that they settle down to a life of blessing. Yet with the assassination of the governor by a zealot who was a member of the royal family, Ishmael, this brief promise of Gedaliah's rule comes to an abrupt end. It is tragic that this grandson of Shaphan (the royal secretary who was perhaps the leading reformer during the reign of Josiah; see 2 Kings 22–23), and son of Ahikam (also a royal official involved in the reform who later saved Jeremiah's life; Jer. 7:26), died without the guidance of a prophetic word from the prophet so close to the reformers. Perhaps the fault, then, resides with Jeremiah, or ultimately with Yahweh himself, for the event is passed over in silence.

Most important, it is through prophetic speech (including the one from the lips of Nebuzaradan) that the rendering of God as character or active agent in the world takes place. The narrator refrains from speaking of Yahweh directly or even indirectly. The sole vehicle in this "passion" narrative for the rendering of God is the prophetic word. Indeed, it is through the spoken word of the prophet (and on one occasion a Babylonian captain of the guard) that Yahweh is presented as the primary agent who, through his vessel, the Babylonians, brings destruction to Jerusalem, delivers Zedekiah and his house over to the Babylonians, and promises a similar fate to faithless Jews who fled to Egypt for refuge. Yet, through the speeches of the prophet, Yahweh also offers the possibilities of grace and salvation, but on the condition that people respond in freedom and trust to that offer. The offer of salvation means submitting to the Babylonians and thus giving up dreams of national freedom and prominence. It also requires faithfulness to covenant and law and trust in Yahweh, while abandoning gods who offered well-being for the small price of worship. Most refused to accept these requirements, except possibly Gedaliah who fell victim, without divine aid, to an assassin. This absence of God and his prophet Jeremiah in the tragic death of Gedaliah raises the greatest question posed by the narrative: why did God abandon or refuse to aid this faithful grandson of the old reformer? The question is not answered, but it is a painful one. Finally, the God who offered to save a besieged Jerusalem and a vacillating king, even at the last moment, and the God who offers to a tiny contingency of survivors of the slaughter at Mizpah is implicitly the one who would in some fashion allow a new future for an as of yet unidentified faithful remnant, a divine will that goes beyond the limitations of covenant. The sign of this promise is the salvation provided to a black eunuch who trusted in Yahweh and acted courageously to save the prophet from death. This promise is narrated in the form of a flashback, for the city has already fallen. And because of the flashback strategy, presumably the reader would surmise correctly that the promise was fulfilled, for the city had been destroyed.

The "passion" narrative is also about the life and activity of Jeremiah. In this last and most dramatic phase of his prophetic ministry, there is the entwining of word and life. The word is proclaimed and rejected, and then judgment comes. The prophet is the victim who suffers for his preaching, yet he is rescued, only to face risk and to suffer once again. In his imprisonment, short-lived liberation, and new captivity he reflects the history of his people.

Jeremiah begins this last stage of his life in freedom, but he quickly loses it when he is accused of treason: he counseled surrender to the Babylonians, and he himself was mistakenly accused of trying to escape to the enemy. Imprisoned first in the house of Jonathan, the royal secretary, the prophet persuades King Zedekiah to remove him to the court of the guard, only to find himself cast into the mire of a cistern in the court of the guard because of accusations of treason against him by a pro-Egyptian entourage of royal officials. Rescued from the cistern by the eunuch Ebed-melech, whose action was supported by Zedekiah, Jeremiah returns to the court of the guard, where he remains until the fall of Jerusalem.

Once more the prophet is freed, this time at the command of Nebuchadrezzar himself, and the prophet goes to Mizpah, where Gedaliah has set up his Babylonian appointed government. The prophet refused the offer of Nebuzaradan, the captain of Nebuchadrezzar's guard, to accompany him to Babylon where he would provide the prophet protection. This refusal undoubtedly involved risk, since his reputation for being a Babylonian collaborator was widespread. The prophet then enters into a period of silence, saying nothing about Gedaliah or anything at all while in Mizpah.

Following the assassination of Gedaliah, Jeremiah apparently is among the surviving captives whom Ishmael attempts to take to Ammon. When the commander, Johanan, foils the escape attempt of Ishmael, Jeremiah is then taken to Egypt, in spite of his urging the military commander and the surviving remnant to remain in Judah. Finally, the prophet utters oracles of judgment against Egypt and the Egyptian Jews, oracles that presumably would come true, because of the fulfillment of the prophet's earlier oracles of judgment against Jerusalem and Zedekiah.

Jeremiah, then, from the content of his speeches, is one who lives within a reality that is controlled by the Lord of history. This world is one in which Yahweh offers humans the freedom to say yes or no to the possibilities of life lived within the requirements of obedience to Torah and trust in divine sovereignty. Within this reality, then, the prophet courageously reveals Yahweh's will, even when it means adhering to the unpopular, even dangerous position that survival is possible only under Babylonian suzerainty. He grounds his theology in the language world of Mosaic covenant and Torah and opposes the theology of promise and presence found in the royal traditions of Jerusalem as the sacred city, temple, and the house of David. Jeremiah's theology was not popular at any time, but it was particularly dangerous when the life of Jerusalem, monarchy, and state is under threat. The prophet lives a life of risk, then, because his life is constantly in peril. He also chooses to suffer the effects of the judgment he utters against his people. Chapters 37–44 do comprise, indeed, a "passion" story of Jeremiah, but there is no happy ending. The last word is judgment and destruction. But there is ever the hope that the same Yahweh who had offered the small group of survivors from Mizpah the opportunity to become the chosen people and who had mercy on a black eunuch who trusted in him would find others from whom to nurture a faithful remnant.

Ultimately, this story, the concluding one in the Jeremiah complex, except for a collection of oracles against the nations and a historical appendix (Jeremiah 52) largely taken from 2 Kings 24 and 25, is one of tragedy, both for the prophet and for Judah. The story ends with Jeremiah in forced captivity in Egypt with no apparent remnant of God's people to continue as the bearers of promise. It is clear that the Diaspora in Egypt has lost its opportunity to become that faithful remnant to continue as the people of God into the future, because of their infidelity and rejection of prophetic word and divine Torah. They have chosen death over life, faithlessness over trust, and the Queen of heaven over Yahweh, the God of their ancestors. Yet the future is indeterminate, still open to the gracious action of God, still capable of summoning a faithful remnant into the reality of new life. This hopeful anticipation of a new future depends, not on temple, sacred city, and monarchy, but only on a faithful remnant who would choose life through obedience to prophetic word and divine Torah. In the entire narrative, only one experiences divine redemption: a black eunuch, a pagan, from Ethiopia. Even so, this brief moment of salvation holds promise for some, as of yet unidentified remnant to realize the hope of an undetermined future.

CONCLUDING EVALUATION

What students of literature and narrative theologians have seen at work in biblical narratives and the "biblical story" is a theology of creative imagination as complex characters come to encounter God, the meaning of their own traditions, and themselves. It is through entrance into these imaginative worlds of biblical narrative that readers may experience that same encounter and achieve their own understanding of being and action in the world. By understanding the artistry of biblical narrative and by learning how to read these ancient, though compelling texts, the negative features of distanciation are overcome and the modern reader experiences the reality of the Bible's narrative world.[46]

Yet one should insist at this point that the distance between text and reader, largely due to historical separation and culture shock, does and should continue. Learning to read texts necessarily includes exegesis (defining Hebrew words, understanding social practices of the period, knowing the historical references to kings, battles, and countries, and so forth). Historical criticism makes readers in the contemporary world aware of the tremendous gulf that separates them from the narrative world constructed by biblical texts. The biblical world cannot be easily equated with the world of modernity, and efforts to characterize the narrative world of the Bible as "realistic" and "history-like" are occasionally naive. In the contemporary world, for example, asses do not talk, prophets do not ascend to heaven in whirlwinds, and holy war is a nightmare

---

46. Hans-Georg Gadamer, *Truth and Method* (New York: Seabury, 1975).

of terrorist insanity. Distanciation is a hermeneutical process in which, fully aware of the separation between the Bible's and one's own narrative worlds, one may enter that strange other world and understand and perhaps experience its reality. It may be that insight, even transformation, will occur, but so may revulsion and disbelief. Mimesis is not the only possibility. One may indeed return to naïveté, but only after the disconfirming and unsettling shock of the loss of innocence, a shock that is partially made possible through historical criticism.[47]

Frei has taught us that it is possible to maintain one's intellectual integrity and still affirm a text as theologically normative even if it is fiction and not history. Theological truth is not necessarily identified with history. This recognition breaks the stranglehold of positivistic exegesis that affirms that history and truth are synonymous. Biblical narrative at times "appeals to the imagination of its readers. It invites them to see the world differently—to see it as something different from the kind of world that it otherwise appears to be."[48]

This recognition of the importance of story for religious convictions does not necessarily negate the tasks of systematic theology, but it does require that theologians in undertaking the constructive task need to be attentive to the form and content of narrative.[49] Narrative is indeed important, but it should not be given a privileged, unique position that opposes constructive work that uses philosophy, psychology, discursive language, abstract thinking, historical interests, and systematic formulation.[50] Narrative should not be allowed to be autonomous; rather, it is a significant and important expression of faith at one level or order of understanding. Thus narrative theology stands somewhere between confession (the first order language of faith) and second order reflection in systematic theology.[51] Narratives are not the "Word of God" but rather the context or sphere in which the divine word may be heard and addressed among human words of story.[52]

A number of concerns need to be raised in reference to narrative

47. See the critique of Alter by R. N. Whybray, David Jobling, and Norman Habel in *JSOT* 27 (1983).
48. Green, "'The Bible as . . .': Fictional Narrative and Scriptural Truth," 92.
49. Goldberg, *Theology and Narrative*, 35.
50. See Tracy, *Analogical Imagination*.
51. Stroup, *The Promise of Narrative Theology*, 85.
52. Ibid., 241.

theology as represented by Frei's reading of biblical narrative.[53] First, how is it impossible to support the contention of the notion of "one story" for the Christian faith? The Bible has many stories, with very different understandings of reality. After all, there are four canonical Gospels, not to mention numerous noncanonical ones, each possessing a rich variety that cannot be harmonized into one story (although a heretic tried). Harmonization leads to an ignoring of the rich pluralism inherent, not only in the Christian tradition, but indeed within Scripture itself. Certainly, this recognition of pluralism in Scripture made possible by historical criticism cannot now simply be ignored by obfuscation.

Second, in addition to the sometimes naive view that biblical narrative is essentially "history-like," there is the complicated problem of genre which Frei does not address, although he often speaks of the narrative "form." There are many types of biblical narratives, many of which are not "history-like." What of poetry that does not tell a story? Or law? Or prophetic speech? Are these ignored, or forced into a "realistic" mode of narrative to make them fit? And what of the possibility that the Bible contains fiction that even ancient readers did not regard as "history-like" in a modern sense? What is especially needed is the recognition of the necessity of both historical criticism and narrative interpretation. Again, it is a questionable effort to attempt to resurrect a precritical reading after the emergence of a critical consciousness, even if we are entering a postmodern world. Even entrance into a postmodern world cannot pretend that the critical reason of the Enlightenment and its application to knowing and understanding did not exist. The questions of historical criticism cannot be simply ignored by pretending they are not valid. Both narrative theology and historical criticism have important contributions to make, and both are impoverished and at times appear perhaps a little foolish when not used together. Indeed, it is unfortunate that Frei's work takes on a decidedly "a-historical character, for his work leads to a polarization that is unnecessary and unfortunate."[54]

---

53. See Maurice Wills, "Scriptural Authority and Theological Construction: The Limitations of Narrative Interpretation," Green, *Scriptural Authority and Narrative Interpretation*, 42–58. Wills prefers to approach the Bible as a "classic" in the fashion of David Tracy *(Analogical Imagination)*.

54. See George Lindbeck's argument that both are needed ("The Story-shaped Church: Critical Exegesis and Theological Interpretation," Green, *Scriptural Authority and Narrative Interpretation*, 161–78).

Third, what of those who are not in the story, either because they have different stories (say, Hindus or Buddhists or Jews) or because they see the story as excluding them (feminists who reject the patriarchal character of much of the story)? Is it possible to approach these texts with a hermeneutic of suspicion? Where is the room for dialogue and mutual learning?

There is also the question of the role of readers. Contrary to Frei, the readers and their worlds play an important role in the process of interpretation. While pure subjectivity is an extreme to be avoided at all costs, it is not possible to argue that texts mean apart from the subjective knowing of interpreters who bring their identity, values, norms, and culture into play in the encounter of Scripture. The hermeneutical process, then, is not a monologue with only the text speaking but a dialogue between Scripture and interpreter.[55]

Narrative theology, as represented by Frei, also needs to address the question of the relationship of the reality of the story to the various realities at work in the contemporary world. In particular, what are the criteria available for the assessment of the truth of the reality presented by the story? Theologians should attempt to ascertain whether certain renderings of the faith, narrative included, are coherent and adequate. And they must make use of the discoveries of knowledge and insight from the sciences and the humanities, if they truly expect a correlation of one's experience with the faith in the present, and if they also anticipate receiving more from the public realm than the charge of sheer credulity. This means, then, that there is the need to move from the reality described by the story to the conceptual expression of theology that is conducive to critical theological reflection.

Finally, when applied to a book like Jeremiah, the artistry and theology of the text work together to create meaning that may be understood and even appropriated. However, how well this approach would work for the entire Book of Jeremiah is a serious question. Even a skilled literary critic like Alter would find this an imposing task.

55. See Duke, "Reading the Gospels Realistically," 305–6.

CHAPTER 9

From History to Imagination:
Between Memory
and Vision

One area emerging out of the discussions of metaphor and poetry and of narrative theology and biblical story that has stimulated another developing approach to biblical studies and contemporary hermeneutics is the theology of imagination.[1] Methodologically, efforts to define and characterize the important features of imagination are impacted by a variety of disciplines, including especially philosophy (epistemology in particular), linguistics, phenomenology, psychology, and literature.

DEFINING IMAGINATION

We begin with an effort to define and then describe imagination, a task that is both quite simple and, at the same time, extremely complex. Simply put, imagination is the capacity within the human

---

1. Among the more important studies are David J. Bryant, *Faith and the Play of Imagination: On the Role of Imagination in Religion* (Mercer, Ga.: Mercer University Press, 1989); Stephen Crites, "Unfinished Figure: On Theology and Imagination," *Unfinished . . .: Essays in Honor of Ray Hart* (ed. Mark C. Taylor; JAAR Thematic Studies; Chico, Calif.: Scholars Press, 1981) 172; Garrett Green, *Imagining God: Theology and the Religious Imagination* (San Francisco: Harper & Row, 1989); idem, "Myth, History, and Imagination: The Creation Narratives in Bible and Theology," *HBT* 12 (1990) 19–38; Ray Hart, *Unfinished Man and the Imagination* (New York: Herder & Herder, 1968); Julian Hartt, *Theological Method and Imagination* (New York: Seabury, 1977); Gordon Kaufman, *An Essay on Theological Method* (2d ed.; Missoula, Mont.: Scholars Press, 1979); idem, *The Theological Imagination: Constructing the Concept of God* (Philadelphia: Westminster, 1981); Ricoeur, "The Narrative Function," 177–202; Tracy, *Analogical Imagination*; Mary Warnock, *Imagination* (Berkeley and Los Angeles: University of California Press, 1976); and Amos Wilder, *Jesus' Parables and the War of Myths: Essays on Imagination in the Scripture* (Philadelphia: Fortress, 1985); idem, *Theopoetic: Theology and the Religious Imagination* (Philadelphia: Fortress, 1976).

mind to create basic images.[2] It is the power of the human psyche (conscious and unconscious) to form mental images, either immediately or indirectly derived from perception or sensation, that lead to the attainment of meaning.[3] In relationship to epistemology (experience, perception, and intuition) and cosmology (especially the construction and authentication of worldviews), imagination may range from a rather common ability to arrange and categorize experiences of sense perception to a more creative power to redescribe reality in highly unusual and provocative ways. In both of these ranges of meaning, imagination is the bridge between perception and thought or sensation and conception.[4]

The nature and character of imagination, at least as used in the following discussion, resists any equation with fantasy, that is, something unreal and therefore untrue. The common type of imagination operates within the limits of sense perceptions that are not distorted and the normal rules of rational analysis and correlation with experience. The more creative type of imagination, however, is less bound by convention and orthodoxy as the psyche seeks to invent or reinvent new realities that suggest or open up the possibility of the reorientation of human life and devotion.[5] The difference between the type of creative imagination that breaks away from the boundaries and conventions of traditional signification or images and sheer fantasy that is illusion and thus untrue is not easy to articulate. Critical analysis based on reason and correlation with experience are governing norms, and yet creative imagination by its very nature necessarily breaks out of the limitations of epistemological confinements to produce new bodies of knowledge derived from redescriptions of reality. Nonetheless, there are norms and criteria of evaluation that may be articulated, including tradition, reason, experience, coherence, compelling engagement, humaneness, and even results.

2. Warnock, *Imagination*, 10.

3. I draw on the definition of Stephen Crites, "Unfinished Figure: On Theology and Imagination," 155–184, although he argues that imagination involves only the power to form images not directly derived from perception or sensation.

4. Robert P. Scharlemann, "Transcendental and Poietic Imagination," *Morphologies of Faith* (ed. Mary Gerhart and Anthony C. Yu; AAR Studies in Religion 59; Atlanta: Scholars Press, 1990) 109–22.

5. Scharlemann calls these two types of imagination transcendental (what I call "common") and poietic (what I call "creative"): "Transcendental and Poietic Imagination." Other names are "reproductive" and "productive."

COMMON IMAGINATION

The beginning point is to describe a type of imagining that operates at several levels. This may be called common imagination. Common imagination may be largely differentiated from perception by recognizing that the former, in contrast to the latter, seeks to know or projects to exist something that is not subject to the immediate experience of a knowing mind. In one sense, this differentiation is an important one; in another sense, as will be seen, it is not broad enough in relating the imaginative activity to the nature and activity of perception. At a very basic level of perception, the imagination operates when the senses perceive an object, say, for example, the front of a house, and the mind projects that the house has rooms that are not immediately experienced. This projection may be based either on past experience (i.e., the person has been in the house before), or by the more general mental activity of classifying the object in the general category of "house," which ordinarily has rooms, and interpreting it as such. Thus, common or ordinary imagination completes the fragmentary data of the senses, since we cannot perceive the whole of an object at once. This activity of the imagination gives coherence to experiences, combines perceptions into integrated wholes, and places into relationships and categories things that are sensed and perceived. The totality of an object is not immediately available to the senses, and thus imagination is necessary to complete the picture. But at the same time, common imagination is directly related to sense perception.

This classification and interpretation of the object as a house is therefore a mental activity that is directly connected to immediate sense perception. Of course, if the house is merely the front of a building in a Hollywood set, with no rooms, a mistake in classification and interpretation has been made. Nevertheless, humans make their way in the world by using the imagination at this ordinary level to classify, organize, combine, and synthesize experiences, perceptions, and objects, interpret their significance and meaning, and then use these as the basis for decision making and action.

Another level of common or ordinary imagination is at work, however, when objects are projected by the mind to exist that are not perceived directly by the senses. For example, one may project the continued existence of a pleasant, public, Texas beach that faces out toward the Gulf of Mexico, either because of having had an enjoyable vacation there many years ago (thus through the activation of memory) or because of having seen pictures and read about the beach in a tourist brochure. One imagines the existence of the beach in the mind and may even experience pleasant feelings of association, and yet the beach is not immediately perceived by the senses. Again, there could be some distortion, either because the beach subsequent to the prior visit has been polluted by a nearby chemical plant or because the photos and description in the brochure tend to make the beach far more pleasant in appearance than it actually would be if perceived directly by one's own senses. In both cases, however, imagination is related to either direct (past experience) or indirect (the brochure) perception. In either case, the object of direct or indirect perception is "real" in the sense that the object is physically there.

In both of these levels of common imagination, then, the process operates according to conventional understandings of what is real and how perceptions and experiences may be organized, synthesized, and interpreted.

CREATIVE IMAGINATION

A second type of imagination at work in the human psyche is creative or artistic imagination. Here the features of freedom and originality come into various patterns of display. This type of imagination may be representational, that is, the psyche tries to produce or represent a mental image that as closely as possible accurately depicts an object not immediately perceived by the senses. For example, in representational or mimetic portrayals, an artist conceives in his or her mind an object and proceeds to construct it out of raw materials (paint, canvas, and brushes). Or a writer may attempt to portray with words, paper, pen, and ink a reality that "imitates life." This is the process that Alter and Frei describe in their view of biblical narrative as "history-like" or "historicized fiction."

A second level of creative imagination is even more constructive than the first. This level breaks with orthodox and conventional portrayals of images by giving them uncharacteristic features or by placing them in different alignments. Normally, this redescription of an object results from the intention either to redefine the usual understanding of an object to a more revolutionary desire to redescribe or even to invent a new reality. Thus a fresh or altered image may shatter existing meaning structures and lead to the creation of a new or different worldview. The artist or writer in this second level seeks to undermine the conventions of orthodoxy in order to usher into existence a new life-defining and life-orienting reality. This is the type of imagination that Ricoeur describes in his important work on metaphor. For him, metaphor has the ability to redefine reality and transform those who live within its world. While all levels of imagination may have disclosive power, that is, they signify or mean something as a result of interpretation, artistic imagination at this second level is imbued with the potentiality of transformative power.

The origins of the images in this transformative, unconventional portrayal of reality are debated, ranging from the human uncon-scious to the creative ability of the conscious mind to organize, synthesize, and interpret things in radically new and different ways. But since this second level of creative imagination is radical, even at times anarchic in its proposals, it is the subject of the highest degree of suspicion and should be the object of careful critical analysis. Most redescriptions of reality are rejected as too fantastic to accept or believe. However, this does not mean that in some sense they are not true or possible.

In both levels of creative imagination, the image or collection of images in the mind of the artist or writer is real, although in another sense the object (both the image in the mind and the finished piece of art) does not exist. It may be representational of something that is perceived by the senses, either in present or past perception or through logical extension into the future, or it may be unconven-tional in breaking with the norms of traditional orthodoxy. The image exists in the human psyche, but its reality or capacity for being true depends in large measure on the worldview or world-views operative for the image maker and those who contemplate the image.

RELIGIOUS IMAGINATION

Religious imagination is most like creative or artistic imagination in its two levels. It may function in its attempts to portray a com-monly accepted reality in images, symbols, words, liturgies, and artistic representations in ways that are conventional and tradi-tional, at least to the community in which the portrayals are made. In religions like Christianity that have a deity, the primary object for description, "God," is not attainable by ordinary sense per-ceptions. Thus, in its imagining of God, religious imagination operates in a way that is different from the levels of common imagi-nation and from the first level of creative imagination that tends to be representational or "realistic." In its depictions of God, religious imagination has to be totally constructive. The portrayal of God may be thought to be descriptive, in the sense that the task may be to consider as carefully as possible portrayals of God in existing art, narrative, and ritual, and then to imagine in one's mind what those portrayals seek to represent. However, this descriptive process is only the response to imaginative portrayals by others and not primary imagination. In this responsive role, the interpreter is depending on images presented by others who use their active imagination in the portrayal of God. This is what one might describe as a secondary use of the imagination, but not the primary function that creates or constructs images.

Religious imagination tends to be constructive in that images of God are created that are not based on sense perception, past, present, or presumably future. This does not mean that the activity of imagining God is not informed by a tradition that carries with it a worldview, since humans ordinarily inherit images that have been shaped over time by the community in which they participate as members. However, in the act of imagination, the mind may construct an image that replicates one already living in the tradition, may alter that image in various ways, or may even invent a new one that potentially could enter the tradition and thereby find for itself a continued existence beyond the mind of the one who constructed the image. In any case, the same features of imagination (organization, synthesis, and so on) are at work.

In addition to description (an act of secondary imagination), a second, typical way of imagining God is analogical. Whether primary or secondary imagination, God, who is not directly attainable by sense perception, may be imagined by reference to objects that are attainable to common perception. Thus, in the Bible, images of God from common social life are used: father, king, judge, man, warrior, mother, midwife, and so on. Creative imagination may be used in constructing images that bring together a variety of different objects into a new form. For example, this is at work in the mythical depictions of gods that combine animal and human forms and characteristics. From the common to the bizarre, the effort is made to imagine deity by analogy to objects that, at least in some form, are attainable to sense perception. Nevertheless the portrayal of God is still a constructive, nonreferential enterprise.

A third way of imagining God involves transcendental imagination in that one steps outside the normal boundaries of time, space, experience, and perception to give free reign to the exploration of the possible and even the impossible. It is in this unbounded domain of the imagination that the imagining of God may occur, and in this transcendent domain the imagined existence, nature, and character of God are explored. Transcendental imagination is at work when a spectator enters into the reality of an artwork or when a reader lives for a time within the narrative world of biblical story. It is the ability to conceive images of the nonactual that arguably is what is at stake for this type of religious imagination.

The origins of religious images of God are varied, ranging from the human conscious to the unconscious to various types of religious experience. Nevertheless, what images of God share is a common absence of deity, at least in terms of the senses perceiving directly the presence of a divine object in ordinary time and space. Images of God are brought to life by narrative, metaphor, works of art, creeds, and confessions, but each form struggles with the same difficulty: how to imagine for oneself as well as for others that which is not immediately subject to sense perception. Yet, on the contrary, each form also shares the common feature of the presence of God, at least in the experience of worship, devotion, contemplation, the orientation of life provided by a theological worldview, and the conscious and unconscious psyche, or, putting each of these together, in the imagination. It is arguably so that at the deepest level of religious experience the imagination is more important than either the conceptualization of images or ideas. For in the experience of the presence of God in devotion and commitment, one may argue for the actuality of the image, even though it is not present in the form of ordinary sense experience. But now the arguments for the actuality of the reality behind the image move largely into the areas of valuation. For example, a life committed to enhancing the well-being of others may be evoked as pointing, indirectly, to the authenticity of the reality behind the image. Or a "conversion" experience that leads to an affirmation of the love of others may result from an act of devotion or contemplation of the Holy. But, of course, there is always the risk that what one imagines as real is not.

SUMMARY OF LEVELS OF IMAGINATION

It is important to recognize that all types and levels of imagination share several common characteristics. First, the objects that are perceived or experienced and attainable to the imagination may be real, in that they are, have been, or will be attainable to the senses, either directly by the one doing the imagining or indirectly through the imagining of others. Images also may be unreal in that they are not directly or indirectly attainable to the senses but still exist in the mind; yet, in another sense they are real, only they exist in the world of the imagination and not in the world of sense perception. Second, imagination has the ability to organize, combine, and synthesize both past, present, and even anticipated perceptions and experiences into a coherent whole. Third, imagination is the power of distilling perceptions and experiences into a form that constitutes the basis of knowing and understanding objects. This invariably involves reductionism, for to some extent or in some way all experiences, perceptions, and objects are unique.

Fourth, imagination involves the ability to interpret experiences and perceptions and to explain what they signify and mean. There is no completed act of imagination that does not issue forth in interpretation. Fifth, imagination involves spatial dimensions, because the object imagined is present to the senses, is attainable through the recall of memory, is seen in the mind as existing or having existed even though it is not immediately present to the senses, or is existing in the mind as a projection into and thus from the future.

Related to the matter of space is a fifth feature: time. The objects perceived by imagination may exist in the past and thus are subject to recall by memory, in the present and directly or indirectly perceived and experienced, or in the future by means of logical extension, projection, or anticipation. Of course, things may be seen as existing either in only one temporal sphere or in two or even in all three.

A sixth feature of imagination at all levels and of all kinds has to do with the emotions. Images in the human psyche have the power to evoke feelings ranging from very mild sensations to extremely passionate emotions. These feelings may be pleasant or unpleasant, satisfying or unsatisfying.[6]

A seventh feature of imagination is its relationship to what might best be regarded as a tradition. Individuals normally participate in communities that are bound together by the same history, shared experiences, and a common commitment to certain values and beliefs that orient their actions. Traditions are the carriers and conveyors, then, of what may be broadly characterized as a worldview. The components of a worldview are varied, but they include images that usually present shared or similarly understood significations or meanings. Imagination, then, typically draws on these common images, although it is not necessarily the case that they will

6. Warnock, *Imagination*, 202. In this regard, Warnock speaks of the experience of "imaginative joy" in the creating of an image that is vivid, compelling, authentic.

be realistically re-presented in the human psyche. Imagination may involve critical reflection on these images and re-presenting them in new and even provocative ways. Even the worldview of the tradition may come under criticism, leading to the redescription of its reality or even the presentation of one that is radically new or different. Thus a destructuring activity is at work in the imagination when objects of perception and experience or even things that exist only in the human psyche of the participants in the community are broken apart, rearranged, or even discarded. The satisfaction felt from the experience of imagination is in forming a new or altered image within a different or transformed interpretative framework or world picture, a new creation that commands attention and possibly even allegiance.

Finally, imagination is at times related to perceptions and experiences of objects that are real, that is, they are subject to sense perception. But imagination also may involve images that are nonreferential, that is, they do not correspond to objects directly available to the senses. The one example we examined was God, although there are other nonreferential images not directly or indirectly related to sense perception (ranging from radically different life forms in science fiction to the concepts of immortality or eternity). But even in terms of things that are not available to the senses, it does not necessarily follow that they are unreal. The actuality of the image of God, we suggested, depends in large measure on whether it has the power to orient and direct existence in ways that are judged life-enhancing.

DISTORTION AND IMAGINATION

The major danger in the use of imagination comes from distortion, whether intentional or unintentional. Distortions may range from mistakes in the classification of experiences and perceptions to dangerous constructions that are demonic. The images in the mind of a psychotic are real to him or her, but even in their unreality they may produce destructive behavior. Hitler's worldview no doubt was real to him, and he convinced millions of the authenticity of what he saw in his own mind's eye. But the devastation that resulted from the dark time of the Third Reich gives one considerable pause. Whether one is dealing with the critical analysis of conceptions and ideas or with primordial images of religious experience, some considerable caution is necessary.

Prudence dictates that criteria of evaluation be used in assessing both the replications and the products of the imagination. Israel struggled with this process, for example, in attempting to establish criteria for evaluating prophetic visions. In regard to ordinary imagination, the process of evaluation is not necessarily difficult in identifying distortions, because one resorts to the canons of reason and empiricism. Have sense perceptions been distorted? Have they been accurately combined, classified, and synthesized by the imagination? Have the conceptions that clarify the interpretations of these experiences been convincingly and cogently articulated?

But when it comes to artistic imagination that goes beyond descriptive representation to new creation, then the task of critical assessment is all the more difficult but perhaps even more necessary. The canons of evaluation can only derive from what one thinks or believes are common human values. Are the products of the imagination life-enhancing or destructive? Are they liberating in their power to enable people to experience well-being and fulfillment or are they debilitating to the human spirit and eventuate in degradation and a loss of integrity? These are the ultimate questions that must address any image or worldview constructed by the imagination.

Two closing observations by scholars of imagination present a fitting conclusion to this brief discussion. First, Mary Warnock concludes her significant study of imagination by arguing:

> So imagination is necessary . . . to enable us to recognize things in the world as familiar, to take for granted features of the world which we need to take for granted and rely on, if we are to go about our ordinary business; but it is also necessary if we are to see the world as significant of something unfamiliar if we are ever to treat the objects of perception as symbolizing or suggesting things other than themselves.[7]

Second, for Amos Wilder, humans are more motivated by images than by ideas. The way we live our lives and the goals toward which we reach are grounded in the imaginative construal of reality and our place within it.[8]

IMAGINATION IN CONTEMPORARY THEOLOGY

Imagination, variously conceived and understood, has assumed an important place in theological inquiry among contemporary theologians. Some theologians have even made it into a major organizing principle for understanding how theology as a discipline

7. Ibid., 10.
8. Wilder, *Theopoetic.*

is conceived and carried out. Narrative theologians in particular have spoken about the importance of imagination in both the artistic creation of stories and their world of meaning by authors, redactors, and tradents, and in the interpretation of stories by audiences who seek to gain entrance into these worlds of meaning. Among the leading theologians in this important area are Gordon Kaufman, David Tracy, and, once more, Paul Ricoeur.

GORDON KAUFMAN

According to Kaufman,[9] attention to imagination begins by recognizing the historicity and linguisticality of human existence, both of which meet in the human imagination. With imagination humans construct a world in which to live (historicity), and the tools for this world construction are metaphors, symbols, concepts, and models (linguisticality). Historicality also derives from the recognition that the tradition of the culture in which we live informs our imagination (we share a common history and meaning system with others in our culture). Thus, each time imagination is put to work, we do not construct the world *de nouveau*, because we live in a world of meaning that is contained within our cultural tradition. We can and sometimes ought to reshape them, but these images still press themselves into our imaginations. And traditions are by nature at least partly linguistic, that is, they are conveyed by means of language as well as by artistic representation and dramatic performance. Thus humans are not only ontologically creatures of language, they also shape and transmit spoken and written traditions that reflect and shape a culture. This means that individual imagination is not an autonomous activity.

According to Kaufman, we construct our idea of God within the historical and linguistic context in which we exist.[10] In the engagement of and critical reflection on these traditions that carry a worldview, we do not necessarily bow the knee to their images as though they are and must be prescriptive. We may move beyond the merely

---

9. Gordon Kaufman, *An Essay on Theological Method*; and idem, *The Theological Imagination*. He never clearly defines imagination. Bryant, who provides a helpful introduction to Kaufman, suggests that he argues that imagination is both "the free activity of the human subject, who constructs and deconstructs images or concepts of the world and God in order to create an environment in which we can live humanly and humanely" and "the powers or activity by which the human subject projects meaning, using whatever tools and materials the past may make available" (*Faith and the Play of Imagination*, 2).

10. Kaufman, *The Theological Imagination*, 23.

representational by reconfiguring these images in new ways. Or we may even reject them and create fresh ones. But this traditioning process that is both historical and linguistic continues forward in space and time, because it occurs within the context of a community. Kaufman adds that in theological imagination one should draw on the linguistic resources of a contemporary culture that shares common features, not simply on the specific and limited resources of a particular religious community.

Imagination for Kaufman has to do with every kind of perception, including that connected with ordinary sensation. Through our heritage, we receive existing patterns for classifying and construing experience and data of the senses. But imagination is especially important in theology, contends Kaufman, for the objective is to construe something that is not directly experienced by the senses in the act of perception.

In beginning to speak of the image of God, Kaufman draws on his understanding that the role of imagination plays in creating images and synthesizing them into "a unified focus for attention, contemplation, devotion, or address," something we designate in Christianity as God.[11] For Kaufman, to affirm the role of imagination in theology requires the elimination of revelation as a consideration in methodology.[12] No longer is revelation in any form (whether a theophany at Mt. Sinai or an inspired Bible) the basis of theological method, since revelation presumes a reference to that which is objective and outside the human mind (Scripture, religious experience, history, and tradition). Theological concepts or doctrines are not referential, for the senses have no access to a transcendent deity. This simply means that God, or whatever we may mean when we say the word God, is not knowable by means of the human senses.[13] Rather, for Kaufman, theological concepts or doctrines are imaginative constructs, created in and by the human mind. These may be shaped into concepts that are shared and passed down. But Scripture, creeds, and confessions are themselves nothing more and nothing less than products of the imagination. Religious images, or images of God at least, are of a different order than concepts produced by the perceptions and experiences of objects in the world.[14]

11. Ibid., 22.
12. Ibid., 30–31.
13. Ibid., 21.
14. Ronald Thiemann argues that all conceptions are the products of imagination. He also argues that theology is both constructive and descriptive, especially when theology is attentive to narratives that construe reality, including God ("Reve-

God does not correspond to any precept (something perceived) or to any reality. Thus theology must be entirely constructive, not descriptive. Again, one may describe the image of God shaped in tradition, but this image itself is simply the result of another person's or group's constructive creation.

Kaufman draws two important conclusions from this nonreferential character of theological imagination. First, theology is intrinsically different from empirically grounded disciplines, since in its conceptions there is no precept that corresponds to the concept of God. Other disciplines are referential, that is, their images refer to things that are directly accessible to sense perception. Second, imagination, not revelation, is the proper basis for theological inquiry.

Theological thinking that is imaginative involves three distinct movements: it begins by constructing a concept of reality that becomes the context for experience. The worldview that one constructs is the result of the ability of the mind to integrate and synthesize the components of fragmented experiences and understandings into a whole. The cultural context in which one lives is important in this process of world construction through the imagination. Theological thinking then moves from this concept of the world to the creation of an idea of God that limits and relativizes this reality. For Christian theology, God becomes "the central focus of meaning" of this worldview. God is not a separate or isolated entity but rather "a constituent of and function of an overarching world view."[15] For Kaufman, in the Christian worldview God is both absolute and transcendent but also humane and immanent. The idea of God is the mind's greatest and most significant construct, since God is related to all other elements in the reality of imagination, is differentiated from them, and is the ground of them all.[16] Theology then returns to this constructed world, which is both historical and linguistic, and reconceives these elements in light of the concept of God who is "a focus or center for devotion and orientation."[17] God becomes the focus of orientation, summing up one's highest values and ideals and at the same time becoming the object of "devotion which can order and continuously transform individuals and societies toward fulfillment."[18]

---

lation and Imaginative Construction," *JR* 61 [1981] 242–63).

15. Kaufman, *The Theological Imagination*, 31–32.

16. Ibid., 22.

17. Ibid., 28–29, 32.

18. Ibid., 32.

As the object of devotion, both the absoluteness and the humaneness of God are significant, for the absoluteness points to the dependence of humans on that which is other, that which creates, sustains, and provides hope for salvation. At the same time, God's humaneness is indicated in terms of "God's concern for and active promotion of human well-being and fulfillment."[19] God acts to create, sustain, and bring to fulfillment human life in justice and love.[20] This world, in which God is the center and focus for human devotion and orientation, is the place in which humans in their imagination take up residence and dwell. This argument that God is a theological construct of the imagination does not mean that theology or the object of theological reflection is fantasy. For Kaufman, "life which comes to expression in love for and concern for other persons, and in the creation of communities of justice and freedom, is grounded in *actuality*, not merely fantasy."[21]

Faith, for Kaufman, is construing a reality with a center that humans never encounter directly by their senses. Imagination is therefore an essential feature of faith. Imagination is shaped in significant ways by the biblical witness to God's activity in history. Biblical genres have the capacity of redescribing reality in ways that engage human imagination, especially the imagination of those who live within a community of faith in which the Bible functions as Scripture. For Kaufman, this gives the Bible its power to stimulate the imagination and is the proper understanding of the authority of Scripture.

Theological imagination also involves envisioning new possibilities that do not yet exist, except perhaps in the mind's eye. Kaufman reasons:

> Unlike other animals, human beings have the power of imagination, the ability to envision possibilities which do not actually exist. This power to entertain the merely possible, the not-now-actual, and then to work to make these possibilities into actualities has enabled creation of the whole distinctively human world of culture and history; it has freed

19. Ibid., 39.
20. Kaufman summarizes by saying: "The Christian image/concept of God, as I have presented it here, is an imaginative construct which orients selves and communities so as to facilitate development toward loving and caring selfhood, and toward communities of openness, love, and freedom" (ibid., 48).
21. Ibid., 49. He adds: "Faith lives from a belief in, a confidence that, there is indeed a cosmic and vital movement—grounded in what is ultimately real— toward humaneness, that our being conscious and purposive and thirsting for love and freedom is no mere accident but is undergirded somehow in the very nature of things" (pp. 50–51).

humanity from being bound to the actual, the given, in the way all other animals are bound.[22]

Kaufman argues that the theologian is especially free to imagine different futures, both those that are grounded in the combination of experiences and understandings of past and present and those that disconnect from these experiences and understandings. And in the reconfiguration and redescription of reality, theological imagination may possess disclosive insight. What is real and authentic may be set forth and revealed, leading even to the possibility of transformation. These possibilities may summon one into the future.

Kaufman recognizes that there are imaginative constructions that are demonic. Subsequently, all such constructions require critical analysis and reflection. The criteria for evaluating the validity of theological constructions are not those of correspondence with or adequate description of the tradition of a particular religious group; rather, they are highly pragmatic and humanistic. The ultimate question for the validity of a theological construction of the imagination turns on whether it "orients selves and communities so as to facilitate development toward loving and caring selfhood, and toward communities of openness, love, and freedom."[23]

DAVID TRACY

David Tracy's *Analogical Imagination* is one of several books that, collectively, articulate three different kinds of theology: fundamental theology seeks to establish the intelligibility and credibility of foundational beliefs by reference to reasoning that is accessible to public criticism; systematic theology orders and clarifies these Christian beliefs; and practical theology is attentive to the application of Christian faith to ethics and devotion.[24] For Tracy, theology must address not only church, that is, as an internal process reflecting on and assessing tradition, but also the university and the larger society. Fundamental theology is in dialogue primarily with the academy or university, systematic theology with the church, and practical theology with society. Yet theology by its very nature is

---

22. Ibid., 60–61.
23. Ibid., 48.
24. See also David Tracy, *Blessed Rage for Order: The New Pluralism in Society* (Minneapolis: Winston/Seabury, 1975); idem, *Talking about God: Doing Theology in the Context of Modern Pluralism* (New York: Seabury, 1983); and idem, *Plurality and Ambiguity: Hermeneutics, Religion, Hope* (San Francisco: Harper & Row, 1987).

public discourse and thus must be evaluated and assessed by the norms of the culture and age to which it attempts to speak. Analogical imagination, Tracy's way of approaching systematic theology, seeks to move theology from the sphere of private preference to public examination, a task made especially difficult in but required by an age of pluralism.

Tracy's major contribution in his book *Analogical Imagination* is his understanding of the Christian "classic." For him, the classic not only possesses meaning at the point of origination but also transcends the limits of its own time and space to engage people in all generations, for it possesses a surplus of meaning that ever calls for and receives new interpretations. The classic is a piece of literature but it is also a work of art or an event that possesses ongoing, universal significance for the church and for the larger society. Classics define the values and thoughts of contemporary society and call forth and require by their very nature fresh interpretations. They are authoritative in shaping the values and beliefs of the church and the larger society, because they elicit new interpretations and possess the power not only to disclose reality but also to transform people by altering horizons of meaning and understanding. For Tracy then, systematic theology is hermeneutical, that is, the focus is on the interpretation of Christian classics, including the Bible, at the heart of the intellectual and cultural life of church and society.

The interpretation of the Bible as a classic of Western civilization must involve not simply historical criticism and sociological analysis, for these methods tend to lock Scripture in the past. Instead, these methods must be complemented by the literary-critical approaches of scholars like Ricoeur who open up Scripture to new meanings in the present. Hermeneutical method must allow the text to speak to the present, a process that requires the productive use of the imagination.

The Intersection of Narrative History and Narrative Fiction

Another important theologian who gives a significant place to the imagination is Paul Ricoeur.[25] His major objective is nothing less than an all-embracing narrative hermeneutics. But to set this forth, his work in the area of metaphor and imagination has been nothing

25. See Ricoeur, *Time and Narrative*; idem, "Biblical Hermeneutics," 29–146; idem, "The Narrative Function," 177–202; and Mudge, *Essays on Biblical Interpretation*, 75–79.

less than groundbreaking. At this point, I will limit my discussion to Ricoeur's understanding of imagination at work in narrative fiction and narrative theology. It is in this area that he builds an important bridge between history and fiction and their respective methods of historical criticism and literary study.

Ricoeur agrees with Hans Frei that the meaning of the biblical story of faith is known to a Christian audience and that apologetics should be avoided, but he disagrees with Frei over the matter of truth. Ricoeur argues not only that biblical narratives are concerned with the elaboration and presentation of truth but also that biblical stories are accessible to and make claims for a general public.[26]

The critical problem raised by Frei in his work in narrative theology is the question of meaning and reference. For Frei, stories mean by reference to their internal workings. The story is the meaning. They do not mean by reference to something that is external to their own narrative structures. The problem with historical criticism, according to Frei, is that the meaning and reference of narratives are related to something external. The external reference of course is critical history. For historical critics, something is not true if it cannot be identified with history. For literary critics, something does not have to be historical in order to be true. Thus we have some narrative theologians and literary critics arguing that the Bible should be interpreted according to the canons of fiction, while historical critics comb these narratives for data that may be associated with the history of Israel. For the latter, their narrative history replaces biblical narratives. These two approaches, even when they seek to incorporate elements from each other, represent very different strategies for biblical interpretation and biblical theology. Representatives of these two different approaches would not regard biblical narratives as history, but they disagree as to the proper objective of the interpretation of biblical texts: the writing of Israelite history (including the history of ideas) as opposed to assessing how and what individual biblical texts as literary fiction mean. They disagree over what is true: something that has happened historically as opposed to the validity of an idea or event by reference to the internal workings of narrative structure.

One way out of this apparent impasse is to recognize the important connections between historical narrative and narrative fiction and especially the role of imagination in shaping both types of

26. See Comstock, "Truth or Meaning," 117–40.

literature.[27] Perhaps the greatest help has been provided by Ricoeur in establishing rather important connections between narrative history and literary fiction that overcome significant opposition between the two strategies for biblical interpretation and biblical theology.[28] With increasing interest in narrative among contemporary theologians and Old Testament scholars, these insights appear all the more promising for important conversations about Old Testament theology.

Ricoeur's thesis, succinctly stated, is that narrative history and narrative fiction have something in common at the *level of sense*, that is, the form of the story. Although they differ at the *level of reference*, there is one important intersection. Historical narrative refers to events outside the narrative in ways that fictional narrative does not. "But both historical and fictional narratives have in common an intersecting reference, a reference to historicity, to the fundamental fact that we make our history and are historical beings."

Ricoeur argues that at the level of sense the structural unity of historical and fictional narratives is based on the concept of plot: events and experiences are sequenced and placed in clusters of related configuration. People react to events that reveal their character, and the results lead to climax and conclusion. Further, he argues that there is a dialectic between the histor (writer of history) and the documents used to construct the narrative history that approximates the dialectic between the storyteller and the received tradition used to construct fiction.

At the level of reference, however, the two (history and fiction) seem to be significantly different: history refers to that which is "true," while fiction refers to the imagined. Yet the seeming difference between the two may not be so great as one would think. First, history is more fictional than positivists would allow. As Hayden White demonstrates below, historians use their imagination in writing history and in the modes they choose to present their ex-

---

27. For a brief discussion of imagination, see A. R. Manser, "Imagination," *Encyclopedia of Philosophy* 4 (1967) 136–38. Manser stresses Kant's point that imagination is the ability to "form mental images, or other concepts not directly derived from sensation." Since the data of the senses are fragmentary and incomplete, imagination enables one to perceive the whole at once. Kant extended this understanding to argue that productive imagination combines human experiences into a single, connected whole, thereby making the world and human experience of the world coherent.

28. This summary is taken from Ricoeur, "The Narrative Function."

planations by formal arguments.[29] Second, Ricoeur contends that fiction tends to be more like history than at first thought. Borrowing from Aristotle and Auerbach, Ricoeur suggests that mimesis in fictional narrative imitates, not the actuality of events, but rather their logical structure. Like history, mimesis reenacts reality. Therefore fiction involves not reproductive but productive imagination, showing models for seeing things in new and compelling ways. Fiction does not tell us what reality is but prescribes a new and possibly even compelling reading of reality.

Third, Ricoeur suggests that history and fiction also intersect at the point of the historical nature of humanity. Not only do humans live in history, they are history. Their nature is radically historical, but that reality comes to expression only when they organize their experiences in the form of narrative. Thus, in narrative history, the attempt is made to describe the human world in ordinary discourse with the use of data and interpretation. By contrast, narrative fiction attempts to redescribe the human world, that is, to suspend conventional language and re-create the world according to the symbolic structures of literary fiction.

Ricoeur's essay shows the relationship between two kinds of narrative, history and fiction, and constructs the basis for dialogue between historical critics who write narrative history and literary scholars who assess the Bible as narrative fiction. This dialogue should include those who are interested in Old Testament theology. As we have seen, those who do Old Testament theology use widely different approaches, but certainly history, literature, including narrative fiction, and the imagination are major areas where interesting, even provocative conversation may occur.[30]

NARRATIVE HISTORY, LITERARY FICTION, AND IMAGINATION

When contemporary theology moves into the area of narrative and imagination, it provides significant opportunity for discussion

---

29. Hayden White, *Metahistory: The Historical Imagination in Nineteenth-Century Europe* (Baltimore: Johns Hopkins University Press, 1973). Also see his essay, "The Value of Narrativity in the Representation of Reality," *Critical Inquiry* 7 (1980) 5–27.

30. James Barr notes that biblical narrative is not simply a reporting of history, but at the same time it is not pure fiction. Indeed, biblical narrative's relation to history is "that of a spiral which runs back and forward across history, sometimes touching it or coinciding with it. Just how close it is to history, or just how far from it, is an interesting question: one that we should accept will never be solved" ("Some Thoughts on Narrative, Myth and Incarnation," Harvey, *God Incarnate*, 14).

with biblical study, not only in the form of newer methodological strategies, but also in the form of historical criticism that leads to the writing of Israelite history. A valuable approach that takes up narrative study and imagination in both history and fiction, as articulated by Ricoeur, is offered by Hayden White.[31] He points out that "imaginative reconstruction" has been a recognized feature of historiography since R. G. Collingwood.[32] According to Collingwood, the writing of history involves the process of reenactment or reconstruction of historical events in the imagination. This understanding of the role of imagination was combined with the fact that, epistemologically speaking, the positivistic notion of pure facts is considered impossible.

METAHISTORY AND IMAGINATION

White demonstrates in his study of nineteenth-century European histories that historians of various sorts used different literary techniques in their writings. He begins with the following definition of a historical work: "a verbal structure in the form of a narrative prose discourse that purports to be a model, or icon, of past structures and processes in the interest of explaining what they were by representing them."[33] This process of representation begins with perception, described by White as essentially a poetic act that is precritical. In this poetic act, "the historian both creates his objects of analysis and predetermines the modality of the conceptual strategies he will use to explain it."[34] For White, the system for classifying information involves four modes: metaphor, metonymy, synecdoche, and irony. The metaphorical mode perceives and classifies information in terms of similarity and difference between two things (e.g., "war is hell"), while the mode of metonymy works with a "part-to-whole" and "part-to-part" relationship that is reductive (e.g., "the roar of thunder"). This means that in the relationship between two things one element is reduced to function as a manifestation of the other; in other words, as a cause and an effect.

31. White, *Metahistory.*
32. R. G. Collingwood, *The Idea of History* (Oxford: Clarendon, 1946); also see John P. Hogan, "The Historical Imagination and the New Hermeneutic: Collingwood and Pannenberg," *The Pedagogy of God's Image: Essays on Symbol and the Religious Imagination* (ed. Robert Masson; Chico, Calif.: Scholars Press, 1983) 9–30.
33. White, *Metahistory*, 2.
34. Ibid., 31.

The mode of synecdoche classifies information in terms of an "object-to-whole" relationship that emphasizes their shared qualities (e.g., "he is all heart"). Finally, the mode of irony "is a self-conscious use of verbal self-negation." Irony, according to White, negates the literal level. Thus "he is all heart" becomes ironic when said sarcastically. These modes or tropes form, for White, the "deep structure of the historical imagination" that operates beneath any historical work. Historical imagination, thus, is the metahistorical feature inherent in all histories and attempts at history.

In examining the nature of history writing, most historians move beyond the mere chronicle to the telling of a story. Both the chronicle and the story "represent processes of selection and arrangement of data from the *unprocessed historical record* in the interest of rendering that record more comprehensible to an *audience* of a particular kind."[35] The chronicle is simply the selection and sequencing of events. A story moves beyond selecting and sequencing to shape a beginning, middle, and end of a narrative that uses plot, characterization, time, motifs, and themes. For White, the historian may adopt three kinds of strategy to explain what happened: explanation by emplotment, explanation by formal argument, and explanation by ideological implication.[36] Each of these three strategies involves different modes of articulation.

In the literary process of representation, historians approach "explanation by emplotment" by selecting one of four types of plot: romance, tragedy, comedy, and satire. Historians do not simply "tell it like it happened" but develop the events into a story that uses one of these four literary modes.[37] In romance, good triumphs over evil when the hero or his or her community is victorious over or liberated from the forces of nature and history that oppress or restrain. In satire, the hero or community is held captive by the world and its contingencies and is unable to overcome oppression exerted by the forces of nature and history. This is true even though they may think they have triumphed or gained a victory. Comedy functions between these two extremes of romance and satire. Here the hero or the community experiences or effectuates at least a reconciliation between good and evil. There remains the hope that good may eventually triumph. Finally, in tragedy the hero or the community may experience a modest triumph over the inhibiting

---

35. Ibid., 5.
36. Ibid., x.
37. Ibid., 7–11.

forces of nature and reality, but finally resigns to conditions as they are.

In addition, White contends that when historians engage in "explanation by formal argument" in the effort to tell "what it all adds up to," they use one of four paradigms also appropriated by fiction writers: formist, organicist, mechanistic, and contextualist. The formist paradigm stresses the unique features of historical data to describe their "variety, color, and vividness." These data are arranged by classes, genres, and characteristic features. The organicist paradigm, notes White, is an integrative effort to move from the microcosm of particular data to the macrocosmic character of reality. Data are placed within larger wholes which are seen as historical processes that move toward a goal.

The mechanistic paradigm indicates that causal laws lead to the outcomes of processes in history. Events are placed within a social and temporal context to speak of origins, developments, and consequences. History is often separated into distinguishable periods that move from one to the other in a connected chain of causes and events following timeless laws that lead to certain goals. Finally, the contextualist paradigm points to rules that, while not eternal and consequential, are relationships between people and events existing at particular times and places that are integrated into larger wholes. In "telling what happened," historians move back and forth between the "explanation by emplotment" and the "explanation by formal argument." They tell a story and provide an explanation.

Finally, the ideological approach to explanation by historians reflects one of four categories, according to White, which are also used by fiction writers: conservatism, liberalism, radicalism, and anarchism. Conservatism is an ideological stance that regards society and its culture as static and essentially good. While change may come about, it should follow a "natural rhythm." Progress may be valued, but it is to occur slowly within the framework of the current societal structure. Liberal ideology regards the societal structure and its culture as good, but appropriate changes should occur through a "social rhythm" that includes governmental policies and actions, education, and law. Progress toward an improving, even ideal society is greatly valued. Radicalism argues that the society and its culture are in need of significant transformation. The current order is flawed and must be completely changed in order to create a new and just societal structure. There is usually a sense of urgent imperative and the pressing need for imminent transformation. Finally, anarchist ideology considers the existing society and its culture to be completely evil and therefore must be totally destroyed. Often a community in the distant past is looked upon as the just, ideal society. This ideal society can and must be reinstituted through revolutionary upheaval.

Whether one agrees with the particulars of White's typology, grounded in the work of historians like Collingwood and literary scholars like Northrop Frye, his work is extremely suggestive in helping present thinking about both methodological approaches to narrative history and narrative fiction and the important role of imagination for each. In turn, this reflection suggests that history and literature have important common ground in carrying out their respective objectives in interpretation and in the usefulness of their approaches for doing Old Testament theology. Instead of seeing history and literature as opposites, White helps to make important connections between the two, especially in terms of how both use the imagination and plot similar strategies in the presentation of their stories. Indeed, Ricoeur and White remind us that it is the referential character of the two that is fundamentally different. Ultimately, it is up to the interpreter, including the Old Testament theologian, to decide whether to focus on the reconstructed history behind the text, the text itself, or the interplay between the two. But the methods and procedures do not represent irreconcilable opposites that impede serious conversation.

OLD TESTAMENT THEOLOGY AND IMAGINATION

Understanding the nature and role of religious imagination has become an important objective in the study of biblical narrative as well as poetry, especially metaphor. The realities of narrative and poem in Scripture have been shaped by the creative imagination of authors, redactors, and editors involved in the composing, redacting, and transmission of what is now the Old Testament canon. At the same time, these texts engage the imagination of hearers, readers, and interpreters by compelling them to move within the worlds of story. And in the hermeneutical enterprise, they potentially at least seek to shape a reality in which not only their original audiences were compelled to live but also later generations are summoned to exist. Thus the hermeneutic process as always involves both speaker (writer), text, and audience, united by, in this case, the exercise of the imagination. The promise of imagination for theology is significant, for it offers a way not only of accessing the linguistic and historical realities of the past but also of engaging these narrative and poetic worlds in the present. More than any other contemporary Old Testament scholar, Walter Brueggemann in his more mature reflection has articulated a theology of the imagination as a way of approaching, understanding, and appropriating Old Testament texts. He not only is an active participant in the preceding discussions of history, canon, narrative, fiction, and imagination but also sets forth a theology of imagination at work in Old Testament texts that takes these factors into consideration.[38]

Brueggemann seeks not only to do biblical theology but also to address the text to the contemporary situation. While he acknowledges that "the two are distinct tasks, they cannot be completely separated."[39] Indeed, historical interpretation and contemporary theological discussion are usually present in Brueggemann's work. How to make this move from ancient text to contemporary theology of course is one of the continuing, fundamental questions of biblical theology, and, for Brueggemann, the key is the imagination.

The essential methodological framework for Brueggemann's approach is set forth in two articles that provide clear summaries of his strategy for interpretation.[40] Brueggemann begins with two affirmations that have provided the impetus for Old Testament theology since the work of Johann Philipp Gabler. First, the Old Testament is a normative collection of texts that moves the interpreter beyond critical dissection and historical location to the sphere of contemporary hermeneutics in which the text addresses with authority the church in the present age. Scripture, for Brueggemann, is by nature a linguistic and historical text strongly rooted in the past. At the same time, it makes normative claims for the faith and practice of the believing community in the present, that is, for the historicality and linguisticality of the contemporary church. Sec-

38. In addition to Brueggemann, see the work of John Collins, *Apocalyptic Imagination: An Introduction to the Jewish Matrix of Christianity* (New York: Crossroad, 1984); and idem, "Is a Critical Biblical Theology Possible?" 1–17.

39. Walter Brueggemann, *Hopeful Imagination: Prophetic Voices in Exile* (Philadelphia: Fortress, 1986).

40. Brueggemann, "A Shape for Old Testament Theology, I: Structure Legitimation," *CBQ* 47 (1985) 28–46; and idem, "A Shape for Old Testament Theology, II: Embrace of Pain," *CBQ* 47 (1985) 395–415. These two essays, along with several others dealing with the strategies of biblical theology, are now found in *Old Testament Theology: Essays on Structure, Theme, and Text* (ed. Patrick D. Miller; Minneapolis: Fortress, 1992).

ond, "a theological statement is not concerned with how we got the text and what the text is. A theological statement is not concerned with *the process and character of the text,* but with *the process and character of the God* met in the text."[41]

To understand both the process of bringing together historical past and contemporary present and the "process and character of God" requires, for Brueggemann, recognizing the basic structure of Old Testament theology. Brueggemann contends that this structure consists of a bipolar or dialectical interplay of "structure legitimation" and the "embrace of pain." Both are at work in an Old Testament theology of imagination. On the one hand, the Old Testament imagines God by participating in the "common theology" of its world (thus, "structure legitimation"); yet on the other hand, the Old Testament struggles to be free from that common theology by imagining God as one who enters into the particularities of social interaction and conflict (i.e., the "embrace of pain"). Thus, Brueggemann proposes that the God of the Old Testament, like other ancient Near Eastern gods, is "above the fray," that is, transcends the everyday struggles of human life. At the same time, this same God participates "in the fray," that is, is present and active in Israel's historical experiences. These basic images of God as "above the fray" (i.e., transcendent and absolute) and "in the fray" (i.e., immanent and humane) correspond to the two fundamental polarities present in a Christian theology of imagination.

The "common theology" of the ancient Near East in which the Old Testament participates imagines a cosmic order ruled over and maintained by God that regulates nature, history, and social institutions. Indeed, social institutions, like law and conflict, are believed to be grounded in this cosmic order. This theology is a "contractual" one in which Israel is both bound to an absolute and transcendent God and is required to be a responsible party for fulfilling the legal requirements of covenant. This theology of "coherence and rationality" is fundamentally a theology of creation, for it imagines God as a transcendent ruler of heaven and earth who creates and sustains nature and history and asserts both sovereignty and providence as its fundamental understanding. The danger, of course, is that this theology of order, this "structure legitimation," may be abused to the point that it becomes a rationale for totalitarianism in which both God and representatives of God in public institutions so transcend everyday life that they rule by fiat and not

41. Brueggemann, "A Shape for Old Testament Theology, I," 30.

by compassion. If this happens, "creation theology becomes imperial propaganda and ideology" that legitimates the power and authority of a ruling elite, seeks to maintain the status quo of the present social arrangement, and removes dissension and the danger of anarchy quickly and at any price. In other words, creation theology faces the serious danger of becoming mere ideology.⁴²

In the Old Testament, what counters "structure legitimation" expressed primarily in creation theology is an antistructure, a theology of dissent, that originates by reason of its "embrace of pain." Since Israel's historical experience often did not correspond with articulation of order in this common theology, a theological crisis results. This crisis initiated by dissent is found in Israel's very beginnings in the time of the exodus, dissent that issued forth in a cry for liberation from suffering. Pain comes from alienation from God as well as disruption in creation, history, and social arrangement.⁴³ The features of this alternative theology of imagination include protest against a common theology that has become tyrannical, an assault on its order in the desire to transform it into a more humane system, and risk in daring to take on the power structure of divine rule and social institutions. The voices of this alternative theological portrayal are especially those of prophets, of psalmists who utter laments, and Job.

Brueggemann does not argue that the alternative pole of dissent, grounded in the "embrace of pain," negates the pole of "structure legitimation," although, like creative imagination in general, this alternative theology seeks to subvert conventional images of reality to shape a fresh and provocative one that transforms the community into a more humane and compassionate one. Indeed, it is the tension between the two poles that gives Old Testament theology its vitality. This is true, argues Brueggemann, for contemporary theology in which order and pain provide the necessary bipolarity for the presentation of faith.

PROPHETIC IMAGINATION

In a series of books over the past twenty years,⁴⁴ Brueggemann has set forth what he considers to be the important features of this

---

42. Ibid., 42.
43. Brueggemann, "A Shape for Old Testament Theology, II," 398.
44. Walter Brueggemann, *The Land* (Philadelphia: Fortress, 1977); *Living toward a Vision* (Philadelphia: United Church Press, 1982); *Hopeful Imagination; The Prophetic Imagination* (Philadelphia: Fortress, 1987); *Hope within History* (Atlanta: John Knox, 1987); *Power, Providence and Personality: Biblical Insight into Life and Ministry* (Louisville, Ky.: Westminster-John Knox, 1990); and *Interpretation and Obedience* (Minneapolis: Fortress, 1991).

dialectical structure of Old Testament theology. However, one book best illustrates Brueggemann's articulation of the process and content of this dialectic in Old Testament theology, *The Prophetic Imagination*, although others may supplement and further illustrate this work.

In this book, Brueggemann contends that prophetic imagination creates and evokes an alternative consciousness that stands in radical opposition to that of the consciousness of the dominant culture that has become tyrannical and oppressive. In its imagination, the dominant culture has constructed a view of the sovereignty and providence of God reflective of a postulated order in creation, history, and society that must be maintained at any cost (a "structure legitimation" that has become ideology). Prophetic imagination renders God as a participant in the pain of human life and as the agent of transformation in subverting tyranny and constructing a new corporate life that provides both order and stability and a caring response to human need.

Brueggemann takes as his paradigmatic case the tradition of Moses who "represents a radical break with the social reality of Pharaoh's Egypt." The prophetic consciousness of Moses is both critical and energizing. It radically assaults Egyptian society and religion, characterized by Brueggemann as the "religion of static triumphalism and the politics of oppression and exploitation." In destabilizing the mythology of Egypt, the social world of Pharaoh is thereby delegitimized. No longer supported by strong and oppressive gods, the power of the state collapses. The collapse is occasioned by the envisioning of a new and compelling social reality, grounded in the engagement of the "politics of justice and compassion" with a religion of divine freedom in which a gracious God decides to enter into human history to bring unexpected liberation to a suffering community of oppressed slaves. Out of this negation of a religion and society of tyrannical order, a productive social imagination creates a new vision of an alternative community that sanctions the dignity of human life grounded in freedom. Intimately related to authentic hope, the energy unleashed by an activated prophetic vision constructs a new society. And in the Song of Moses, to take one example, a liberated Israel issues a doxology, appropriately praising the enthronement of a gracious and free God who brought justice and freedom to a community of slaves.

The return in this dialectic, then, is to structure legitimation, the second pole of the dialectic, but the order that is reimagined and the God who rules over its corporate life become more concerned with and responsive to human pain. That is, the prophets imagine a new vision of order that is responsive to suffering humanity and the exploitation of those not in power and that seeks to compel a faithful community to enter into the vision's reality and to live it into being. In response to both the envisioning of engaging possibility and the realization of an alternative corporate life, the community enters into this new world and finally breaks forth into the unrestrained praise of God. God becomes the object of devotion but also of transformed social life.

For Brueggemann, discourse without a universe of human dwelling possesses neither sense nor meaning. Language, in the first case, lament, issues forth out of the real pain and hurt of human beings, most ignobly denied their dignity by the gods of order. Prophetic consciousness (imagination) rediscovers the formative symbols of a rich religious past, re-presents them in a way that engages present culture, and thereby articulates a new life-style of human community (vision) that issues into meaning for a community of victims whose pain is real and human-denying. Torah attempts to actualize the components of an alternative social reality that is grounded in the dialectical tension of the freedom and responsibility of both God and the human creature and consequently sets forth an authentic way of life for a historical people. Praise is the final culmination of the energizing power unleashed by prophetic vision and is uttered only by a people who have known the dehumanization of oppressive structures and have come to experience the exhilaration of the possibilities of freedom. Thus it is the interplay of prophetic imagination that enters into and is shaped by corporate memory within the context of a vital, living community that defines the process (criticism and energy) and shapes the content of prophetic vision. The goal is the reshaping of new corporate life, a vital and orderly structure that responds more humanely to human need. Theologically speaking, God is a sovereign, transcendent ruler of heaven and earth but also an immanent participant in the pain and disorder of human history.

THEOLOGICAL IMAGINATION IN JEREMIAH

Brueggemann's two-volume theological commentary on Jeremiah follows the same interpretative course outlined above.[45]

---

45. Brueggemann, *To Pluck Up, To Tear Down: A Commentary on the Book of Jeremiah 1–25*; and idem, *To Build, To Plant: A Commentary on Jeremiah 26–52.*

INTRODUCTION

Brueggemann contends that Jeremiah provides an alternative to a political analysis *(Realpolitik)* of Judah's situation within the history of ancient Near Eastern empires struggling for domination of the Fertile Crescent. This alternative is a theological interpretation of Judah's present and future that is expressed in both poetic reflection and didactic prose. The prophet's theological assessment breaks out of the limitations of imperial restraints to fashion a "new historical possibility" in which Judah's destiny is reshaped according to the sovereign intention of the God of the covenant.[46]

According to Brueggemann, this theological interpretation of Jeremiah is characterized by three features. First, Israel encounters God through the covenant that is grounded in the "memories and mandates of the Sinai traditions." Babylonia's claims to suzerainty are subordinated to the will of God who uses the imperial power for divine purposes. The covenant tradition present in Jeremiah is Deuteronomic in formulation and requires Israel's obedient and faithful response to God's instruction. Israel's response to God was to be shaped by the theology and teachings of the covenant. Faithlessness was met with the retributive justice of God's acting through the Babylonian conquerors.

The second feature of Jeremiah's theological interpretation, as seen by Brueggemann, is the "pathos of Yahweh." This means that God yearns to continue a relationship with an often disobedient and faithless people, a yearning that is in tension with the demands of covenant obligation. Thus the requirements of covenant are mediated through God's passion, a bold theological move that allows the prophet to articulate a future vision born of hopeful anticipation.[47]

The third element of Jeremiah's theological interpretation of Judah's situation, according to Brueggemann, is the prophetic critique of the "royal-temple ideology of Jerusalem." This ideology proposed that God's promises of covenant with the Davidic monarchy, his dwelling place in the temple, and the divine protection of Jerusalem against its enemies were irrevocable guarantees for all time. This ideology proposed that temple and monarchy were the vehicles for divine blessing and that opposition to its policies and practices was tantamount to rebellion against God. Jeremiah seeks to subvert this ideology by a theology that combines the memory of Sinai with

---

46. Brueggemann, *To Pluck Up, To Tear Down*, 2–3.
47. Ibid., 4–5.

divine pathos that moves beyond judgment to the formulation of a hopeful future based on divine grace.[48]

Brueggemann's reading of Jeremiah brings together historical criticism, social-scientific description, and literary analysis under the general rubric of imagination. He notes that by the use of metaphor and image the prophet invites a theological reading of Israel's situation that "summons the listener to reject the ideological discernment of the world by the royal-temple establishment."[49] Brueggemann explains that Jeremiah's proposal that rejects royal-temple ideology is "an imaginative construct, not a description of what is, nor a prediction of what will be." Instead, the linguistic world of the prophetic text

> invites the listener to participate in the proposed world so that one can imagine a terminated royal world while that world still exists, and one can receive in imaginative prospect a new community of covenant faith where none has yet emerged. The text leads the listener out beyond presently discerned reality to a new reality formed in the moment of speaking and hearing.[50]

This alternative consciousness or imaginative reality that is yet to be is opposed to the royal-temple ideology, also an imaginative construct. Jeremiah believes that God is actively at work to "create a new alternative community" that is to be characterized by a free and faithful response to divine guidance that issues in devotion to God and commitment to a just and compassionate community.[51]

COVENANT OBLIGATION

Jeremiah makes active use of collective memory, especially in the prose tradition, to recapture the theology and symbols of the Sinai covenant that shaped so dramatically the imagination of Israel. He also uses covenantal images articulated by Hosea, an earlier northern prophet, to describe Israel's relationship to God in the language of love, courtship, and marriage. In the early days of courtship, the people were like a young bride following God the husband faithfully in the wilderness time. But after entrance into Canaan, Israel became a faithless harlot seeking other lovers. Now it is judgment time in the form of the "foe from the north" (Jeremiah 4–10) who is coming to carry out God's punishment against a faithless people.

48. Ibid., 5–7.
49. Ibid., 16.
50. Ibid., 16.
51. Ibid., 17.

In his oracles of judgment, Jeremiah speaks of Israel's and Judah's irresponsible violation of covenant responsibility and its attendant history of salvation that included the exodus from Egypt, the wandering through the wilderness, and the gift of the land (Jer 2:6-7). In acts of religious and political apostasy, Israel has forsaken Yahweh to worship false gods and to align itself with foreign governments to ensure its political security (Jeremiah 2). Indeed, these violations lead to the prophet's *rîb* (lawsuit) in which Israel/Judah is indicted and found guilty (Jer 2:4-13).[52] Now, the northern enemy will come as God's instrument to destroy Jerusalem and bring to an end a false consciousness based on the ideology of kingship and temple.

For Brueggemann, this use of covenant theology comprises one of the important components of an alternative consciousness, a prophetic theology of imagination that seeks to subvert and then replace the ideology of kingship and temple that resulted in oppression and corruption.[53] The other is the pathos of God.

THE PATHOS OF GOD

The second important element of Jeremiah's theology of imagination is the pathos of God. God yearns to continue a relationship with Israel into the future, in spite of the violation of covenant and the destruction of Jerusalem. And God experiences in this divine pathos the pain of Israel's apostasy and the suffering caused by Babylonian holocaust. In Jeremiah, unlike any other biblical prophet, the pain of both prophet and people is captured in a series of laments situated within and following the oracles concerning the "foe from the north" in chapters 4–10 and in the "confessions" and related materials found in chapters 11–20.[54] Even Yahweh participates in lamentations that express divine grief over the approaching destruction of the chosen (12:7-13; 14:17-18).

Deriving perhaps from the early stage of Jeremiah's ministry, that is, before he came to Jerusalem in 609 B.C.E., the oracles of judgment in chapters 4–10 describe an unidentified enemy who will destroy Jerusalem and Judah. Jeremiah promises the possibility of redemption, if the inhabitants will engage in lamentation, confess their sins, and turn to Yahweh (see 4:7-8, 13-18; 6:26; 9:10-22).

52. Ibid., 32. Also see Brueggemann's discussion of covenant theology in Jer 11:1-17 (pp. 104–7).
53. E.g., ibid., 29.
54. See Brueggemann's discussions of these two sections (*To Pluck Up, To Tear Down*, 49–73, 82–103, 108–80).

The pathos of the prophet is graphically depicted during several interludes between the description of the havoc to be wrought by the northern enemy. Perhaps the most moving is found in 4:19-22 when the prophet, witnessing the destruction in his imagination, cries out:

> My anguish, my anguish! I writhe in pain!
>   Oh, the walls of my heart!
> My heart is beating wildly;
>   I cannot keep silent;
> for I hear the sound of the trumpet,
>   the alarm of war.

This description of the prophet's agony suffered as a result of approaching war is even more striking when one realizes that the line of separation between God and Jeremiah is often blurred. Perhaps more than with any other prophet, Jeremiah's identity at times merges with that of God. This suggests that the pain of the prophet over the impending doom of the nation also expresses the agony of God (cf. 8:18—9:3).

The people do finally lament (14:1-10, 19-22), but it is too late. Destruction has come:

> For a sound of wailing is heard from Zion:
>   "How we are ruined!
> We are utterly shamed,
>   because we have left the land,
>   because they have cast down our dwellings." (9:19)

The lamentation comes from those who now must go into exile as well as from those who are left behind to inhabit destroyed cities and to tend to ravaged fields.

The pain that Brueggemann considers to be the catalyst of prophetic vision is captured most vividly in Jeremiah's "confessions" (or laments), texts that are unique to prophetic literature. The confessions of the prophet are found scattered throughout chapters 11–20 and normally consist of two parts: the prophet's complaint and Yahweh's response. These laments probably originated in Jeremiah's struggles with the authorities following his coming to Jerusalem in 609 B.C.E. They are the response in part to the suffering the prophet endured for his opposition to the Jerusalem establishment who sought to silence the prophet (see 20:1-6 and 36-45). The recurring themes of these confessions include a description of the prophet's persecution by family and political enemies, his cry to

God for vengeance against his opponents, his questioning of divine justice and integrity, and his struggle with his call. God's responses indicate that the suffering of the prophet will only increase as the opposition to him increases, urge him to continue his prophetic role, and promise divine presence and redemption in the face of persecution. The confessions grow in intensity in their description of the dark night of the prophet's soul, until the last one has Jeremiah cursing his existence (20:14-18).

Of course, the pain expressed by Judah and its prophet, at least to this point, is not that of the oppressed who cry out for divine redemption. Judah's pain results from its obstinate refusal to follow the covenant, to practice justice, and to worship only Yahweh. Jeremiah's pain, which at times encompasses divine pathos, derives in part from witnessing in his imagination and then in historical reality the destruction of the nation and from his own failure to lead the people to repentance. In part, the prophet's pain also originates in his struggle with God, his call, and the conflict with family and national leaders. And Yahweh's response to national suffering is not the application of the balm of cheap grace; rather, it is an announcement of judgment that is not, as of yet, modified by the promise of a hopeful future. Jeremiah's pain will continue, alleviated only by the promise of divine presence and deliverance in times of trouble.

CRITIQUE OF IDEOLOGY

Both covenant obligation and divine pathos shape an alternative consciousness that is in opposition to the ideology of court and temple.[55] Prophetic vision, as assessed by Brueggemann, is evidenced in Jeremiah's radical criticism of Judah's corrupt society, especially its leadership, that has oppressed its own people. The abandonment of covenant and the violation of the Ten Commandments have led to social oppression and the worship of other gods (see especially the temple sermon in 7:1-15), while the indictment of the kings of Judah, ruling during Jeremiah's lifetime, rejects the David-Zion tradition and its emphasis on the eternal covenant between the house of David and Yahweh. Indeed, for Jeremiah, the Davidic kings were to establish justice, but they have time and again abandoned this mission and brought great suffering to their own people (21:11—23:8).

---

55. For a direct assault on this ideology, see Jer 7:1-15 (the temple sermon) and Jer 21:11—23:8 (oracles concerning the kings) and Brueggemann's discussion of each (*To Pluck Up, To Tear Down*, 74–78 and 181–200).

Brueggemann's understanding of the productive imagination at work in the visions of Jeremiah come into prominence in the Book of Consolation (Jeremiah 30–31) where the dreams for a new society are given concrete shape. This new community in which the heart of the faithful will be transformed in order to allow for the possibility of obedience fits quite nicely Brueggemann's alternative consciousness that shapes the formation of a new community whose faithfulness to covenant undermines the false consciousness of ideology and creates a world in which peace, justice, and love flourish.[56]

Perhaps it would be too much to expect the hermeneutic's culminating feature of praise to find a prominent place in the life of a prophet who experienced and envisioned so much tragedy. But a prophet from the Babylonian exile, known only as Second Isaiah (Isaiah 40–55), is perhaps the one who gives voice in grateful praise to Jeremiah's own hopes.

THE ROLE OF IMAGINATION IN HERMENEUTICS

Brueggemann contends that this theological reading of Jeremiah, in essence "a critique of ideology and a practice of liberated imagination," allows the text to have disclosive power for subsequent generations, including the present. In the theological assault on an ideology that seeks to maintain power through oppression and in the proposal for an alternative consciousness that is attuned to justice, compassion, and peace, one has the components essential for a modern theology of imagination. Indeed, Brueggemann suggests, by being attentive readers we may enter into the imaginative world of Jeremiah's prophetic vision and experience its potentiality and power for modern life. Then we too may shape our own theology of imagination that captures the essence of prophetic theology and brings it to expression in the contemporary world.[57]

CONCLUDING EVALUATION: THE PROMISE OF IMAGINATION

Brueggemann's analysis of the theology of prophetic imagination, especially in its application to the Book of Jeremiah, avoids a questionable abandonment of history as a significant component of biblical interpretation and Old Testament theology. His embrace of historical criticism and social-scientific analysis rejects a gnosticizing, ahistorical hermeneutic that, while grounded in texts, places

56. See Brueggemann, *To Build, To Plant*, 39–103.
57. Brueggemann, *To Pluck Up, To Tear Down*, 17.

little stock in the historical, everyday experiences of real people. While he asks and seeks to answer historical questions, he does not require that a text's authenticity and truth be determined solely by questions of locating it in a historical setting and especially in the life and thought of Jeremiah. His presentation of prophetic imagination also avoids the danger of psychological privatization in which interpretation and hermeneutics become the uncritical articulation of subjective fantasy and individual preference. In addition, Brueggemann's work also releases the stranglehold of a positivistic exegesis which silences the voice of the text for believing communities by locking a normative canon within an inescapable prison of the past. Finally, he emphasizes that the process and content of theological imagination leads to conceptualization in the articulation of the faith, to critical reflection on the authenticity and faithfulness of conceptualization, and to disciplined, committed obedience to the requirements of faith.[58]

Brueggemann overcomes these interpretative pitfalls in several ways. First, he emphasizes as important the role of memory in the life of the community of faith. Identity is in part shaped by the act of remembering those traditions of faith into which one enters and lives, at least for those enriching moments of critical understanding, devotion, ritual, and celebration. Tradition contains the myths, symbols, metaphors, and content for knowing, shaping, and interpreting Christian identity. Brueggemann reminds us of the role that memory plays in the experience and finally the articulation of Christian faith, a memory that is contained, at least in part, in a normative canon.

Second, Brueggemann's approach recognizes the important role of imagination in both the historical and the theological enterprise. Indeed, for Brueggemann the prophets as well as modern historians have used the imagination in recalling the events and symbols formative in the shaping of human life. Likewise, through the imagination those events and symbols may be reactualized in the life of the believing community in the present, particularly in the formation and development of an alternative consciousness that is at work in a liberated community. And it is through the power of imagination that the future may be envisioned so that the dreams of the alternative community, grounded in the justice and love of God, may be seen and realized through prophetic existence in the present. This requires to some extent an act of transcendent imagination on behalf of the interpreter who leaves his or her own time,

58. See Brueggemann, *Interpretation and Obedience*, 1.

space, and world and enters into the reality of prophetic imagination. It requires careful study and preparation, before entering
into the world of the text, in order to avoid the subjectivity of
private, uninformed interpretation. And it requires consent to the
affirmation that the books of Scripture, "like no others, will receive
our attention and will shape and govern our imagination."[59]

Third, privatization is avoided by Brueggemann's emphasis on
the corporate character of prophetic imagination. This theology of
imagination is shaped within the context of a historical community
and presents the possibility of the formation of a group of people
faithful to covenant. Privatization and individual preference are
also avoided by the existence of at least implicit criteria for evaluation. These criteria include the careful inquiry into theological
conceptualizations to ensure that ideological formulation is
avoided, the analysis of new formulations of theology to see whether they are capable of representing in authentic and convincing
ways the faith traditions of collective memory, and the more pragmatic evaluation of whether a theology enhances well-being, love,
justice, and peace.

A comprehensive Old Testament theology of imagination would
be most welcome. The methodology and approach have been elab-
orated by Brueggemann in numerous writings. Especially important
is the inclusion of historical criticism, social-scientific analysis, and
newer literary methodologies. Subsequently, this theology would
not polarize scholars and approaches but rather should allow for the
engagement of most of the work that students of the Old Testament
currently do. A theology of imagination applied to the entire Old
Testament could be quite stimulating and would open the door to
fruitful conversations with contemporary theologians who work in
the areas of imagination and narrative. In addition, conversations,
even theological ones, may be stimulated among Old Testament
scholars. History and historical questions would once again have an
important role in theological discussion, joining with other, more
recent methods to present a new and, it is hoped, compelling
presentation of biblical faith.

---

59. Ibid., 119. Brueggemann's position parallels Tracy's argument for analogical
imagination that centers hermeneutically on the classics, including Scripture: "The
classic text's fate is that only its constant reinterpretation by later finite, historical,
temporal beings who will risk asking it questions and listening, critically and
tactfully, to its responses can actualize the event of understanding beyond its
present fixation in a text" (Tracy, *Analogical Imagination*, 102).

SUMMARY
AND
CONCLUSIONS

CHAPTER 10

The Future of
Old Testament Theology

I should like to end this survey with several observations and assertions. First, it should be obvious by now that Old Testament theology is a vital discipline in the present. Its voices are many and disparate, they speak out of different methodologies and at times even conflicting epistemologies, but, nevertheless, they speak and should be heard. This variety of approaches and interpretations may be characterized as fragmentation, suggesting something of a negative image, or as diversity, implying a richness of insight that offers many opportunities for conversation. At times representatives of these approaches engage in dialogue with each other, but too often they either ignore or castigate each other. When conversation does not occur, there is a significant loss for the entire discipline.

Second, the primary question that stimulates all Old Testament theology is that of revelation and, issuing from revelation, the knowledge of God. And here is a major area of disagreement: do revelation and its correlate, the knowledge of God, reside behind the text in the narrative history written by historical critics; in the community (or social system) that produced at least a portion of the text; in the order and continuation of creation; in the dynamic interaction of canon and community; in the experience of the interpreter or the interpreter's group (e.g., women's experience); in the narrative world created by the vision of the text; or in the imagination of author, or narrator, or interpreter? This fundamental question resides behind all methodologies and theological constructions. It is impossible to believe that unanimity will ever be achieved by the securing of a single answer. This is one explanation for the diversity of Old Testament theology (not to mention contemporary theology), and it is highly doubtful that anything approaching a consensus of presentation and understanding will develop.

Third, this survey has been somewhat misleading in tracing only several major developments (liberation, creation, canon, feminism, story, and imagination) rather than stressing a more multidirectional sequence. Even so, what unites the development of these new approaches is their incorporation of the two fundamental features of human existence: historicality (including quite broadly questions and matters of cosmos) and linguisticality. To deny one in favor of the other or to privilege one while subordinating the other runs counter to what is fundamentally true about what it means to be human. Thus history and text belong together.

Fourth, all the various approaches to Old Testament theology since World War II have something of value to contribute. I suggest, however, that understanding the nature of imagination which creates narrative worlds of meaning, whether in history or fiction, provides the greatest potential for conversation between these developing ways of doing Old Testament theology and historical criticism. Narrative history and narrative fiction, as well as theology itself, involve the use of the imagination. And it is the imagination that offers the opportunity both for discourse between historians and literary scholars and for modern readers to enter into the world of the Bible.

Fifth, the shift to the theme of creation contains at least the recognition that part of the Old Testament cannot be subsumed under the theme of history in any of its understandings. The simplistic view of history and creation as mutually exclusive is properly discarded for any correct understanding of the Old Testament. Yet the tension between the two traditions may not be ignored, for it is present in the text itself. The Mighty Warrior of George Ernest Wright and the Mother Goddess of Phyllis Trible both are biblical portrayals of Israel's God. The question is whether one wishes to celebrate the pluralism or attempt to write a more integrative, even systematic, theology that puts these and other understandings of God into critical relationship, for each requires the other for a full explication.

Sixth, the last observation raises the question of whether one is content to describe or wishes to relate and then assess critically the various affirmations of the Old Testament text. For those who share a common passion for systematic presentation and ultimately constructive theology, these should not eliminate the plurality or too easily place into a hierarchic order theological traditions that are diverse. The world is created through conversation, not an inflexible order that leads to the suppression of pluralism, and this is true of the canon. Theology, to be creative and compelling, needs to retain that tensive quality at the heart of its being. Yet pluralism should not allow theology to enter into the quagmire of relativity and private preference.

Seventh, biblical theology should take into account that the Bible is at times a patriarchal book that has denied full humanity to women and other groups. There are ideologies present in Scripture. A descriptive approach cannot bring into question and then undermine texts, religious ideas, cultural forms, and social roles and institutions that are stereotypical of and demeaning to women and other oppressed groups. Whether the step is taken to use women's and other oppressed peoples' experience as a norm, as well as a source, for the evaluation of biblical theology is open to debate. But in moving toward a new Old Testament theology, a criteriology should be developed that includes their experiences as one consideration for constructive work. This is necessary for the correlation with human experience to operate as an evaluative criterion. Feminist and other liberation theologies provide a significant contribution to new efforts at the reconstruction of theological language.

Eighth, a comparison between narrative fiction and narrative history indicates that the two are not so radically different as may have been thought. Both make use of imagination in the presentation of plot, although fiction's imagination is productive, thus leaving to the narrator more license in the telling of the tale, while historical imagination is reproductive. Thus, for example, a biblical narrative like the Book of Ruth may be understood as fiction, while John Bright's *A History of Israel* attempts to be a narrative history that uses reproductive imagination. At the same time, both fiction and history may adopt the same four types of plot in their strategies of emplotment: romance, tragedy, comedy, and satire. However, even when one assesses the Book of Ruth according to literary methods that include Alter's close reading approach, one cannot ignore the culture that gives rise to the text and the changing contexts that have shaped it. Context contributes to meaning, indeed is inseparable from the process, just as assuredly as repetitions of words and motifs. To ignore these multiple contexts is to distort interpretation. Historical-critical method and social-scientific analysis of ancient culture provide access to these developing contexts. The search for the synchronic should not negate the equal importance of the diachronic in any new hermeneutic. Theology and culture are and must be inseparable.

Ninth, to take into serious consideration issues of text and language does not necessarily lead to an either/or decision for literary study as opposed to historical criticism. Historical criticism establishes the necessary distance between the biblical worlds and the modern reader. Distanciation is the critical and needed intersection between first and second naïveté. Yet, once distance is properly secured and narrative analysis takes place, the entrance into the linguistic worlds of the Bible may occur, leading to the intersection of life and faith. Further, Christian life is one of faith in the process of becoming. Narrative theology properly moves one away from the one-sided notion that faith is a system of correct doctrines to be believed to the view of faith as a journey in process that passes through a variety of collapsing and emerging worlds. And it is through the many entrances into the various worlds of the Bible, through conversation with other experiences of the biblical stories, and through interaction with culture past and present that the believer's faith is constructed, deconstructed, and reconstructed.

This does not mean that conceptualization of symbols, metaphors, and themes in the Old Testament should not take place, at least at the next level of theological discourse. This is a necessary step in order to do systematic theology in the contemporary period, but it is also necessary for biblical theologians, if indeed they wish to move beyond the enormous variety and nuances of literally thousands of texts and distill them into major understandings. Only then can these conceptions be scrutinized critically and ultimately used in constructive theological work in the present.

Finally, Old Testament theology in whatever form should address contemporary issues. The very questions that are posed to the text arise out of the contemporary world and the interpreter's community, either religious or secular, or both. To ignore these questions of contemporary meaning and still to do Old Testament theology is both impossible and self-deceptive.

CONSTRUCTING A PARADIGM
FOR OLD TESTAMENT THEOLOGY

Descriptive versus Constructive Presentation

Old Testament theology should be both descriptive and constructive. That is, it should attempt to reflect as accurately as possible the theology of the Old Testament texts but then move on to constructive work that attempts to relate the meaning of the text to the present. No biblical theology can by the very nature of the enterprise be purely descriptive, since the questions that are addressed to the text and the means of interpretation arise from the interpreter and his or her contemporary world. This does not mean that the interpreter may redescribe the content of biblical theology according to subjective whim. However, the questions addressed and the answers sought issue from the engagement of the modern interpreter, residing within a contemporary context of religious community and culture, with the biblical text, also shaped by its own religion and culture.

A constructive rendering of Old Testament theology begins with a recognition of the importance of Gadamer's articulation of distanciation and, second, naïveté. According to Gadamer, interpretation is a type of moral conversation with a classic text, a conversation that is shaped from the beginning by practical concerns about application that emerge from the interpreter's present culture and its questions. Hence systematic theology is the fusion of the whole of the past with the present; that is, if interpretation is successful, the vision of the contemporary culture fuses with the vision of the classic text. There is a fusion of the horizon emerging from the very practical questions we as human beings bring to the text with the horizon of the text itself. Yet the process for fusion of horizons is dialogical, for it involves both the questions and answers of cultural experience and the questions and answers of the Christian classics, including the Bible.

A constructive rendering of the material by necessity requires critical-reflective interaction. Once a systematic presentation and fusion of horizons occur, an evaluation must be given. This reflective, critical rendering allows for choices to be made, not on the premise of subjective preference but on the grounds of sound and clear criteria. These include the criteria of adequacy, coherence, and correlation with human experience. These criteria test the validity of the fusion of visions that emerge from the hermeneutical rendering of biblical theology. Of course, the systematization of the biblical traditions should not eliminate the pluralism inherent in the text. At the same time, pluralism should not be allowed to paralyze an intelligent rendering of the theology of the biblical traditions in a systematic form.

All of this means that biblical theologians must begin to make the effort to become more theologically literate. As biblical scholars who possess some sense of the importance of public discourse, we must learn to read texts that are not simply behind but also beyond the Bible. This means that we must attempt to become theologically literate in order to become familiar with the horizons of meaning that historical and modern cultures produce. Otherwise, the questions we bring to the text are highly subjective and unavoidably individualistic. And if we wish contemporary theologians to have access to and even use our material, we must assist them to do so, and not continue to hide behind the technical jargon of our complex disciplines. This does not mean that we should replace contemporary theology with a constructive biblical theology, but it is obvious that serious dialogue between the two groups would enrich them both.

A PARADIGM FOR OLD TESTAMENT THEOLOGY: A PROPOSAL

Is Old Testament theology a discipline that originates within theology or is it more a history of Israelite religion that sets forth the ideas, values, and beliefs of an ancient community? This has been the fundamental question for the past two centuries. But no major approach that has developed since World War II has cast its lot totally with one or the other of these two options. The goal of each new approach has been to allow Scripture to lead into contemporary hermeneutics, without completely sacrificing historical particularity.[1] To accomplish this overall goal, theological work on the Bible should proceed through no less than four successive stages.

The first stage of theological interpretation articulates the meaning that derives from understanding texts in their historical and cultural context. It is the fusion of the horizons of meaning of implied author, text, and implied audience within their historical and cultural context. This task is primarily descriptive and acknowledges the significant diversity and particularity that is present in the canon. This stage requires the activation of the imagination of the modern interpreter who follows the canons of exegetical interpretation in explaining the meaning of texts.

The second stage is conceptualization of the multiple images, ideas, and themes that leads to the systematic rendering of the multiple theologies of Old Testament texts within the dynamic matrix of creation and history. The nature and activity of God, the differing understandings of space and time in creation and history, and the nature and activity of humanity are conceptualized and then integrated into a systematic presentation. The unifying principle for this systematic presentation is the sovereignty and provi-

---

1. Ollenburger, "Biblical Theology: Situating the Discipline," 50.

dence of God who shapes and sustains in righteousness and compassion both cosmos and history and the humane and immanent deity who is present in the world. The meaning of human history derives in part from the meaning of creation. And the meaning of creation has to do with human history. Pluralism should not be eliminated, but through the evaluation of the multiple theologies of the biblical texts by accepted criteriology, an adequate, cogent, and coherent Old Testament theology should emerge.

The third stage is perhaps the most difficult, but it is important to recognize how biblical texts and their theologies have been construed within the history of interpretation. This process shapes the meaning of texts placed in new settings, and the ever-changing meaning of texts influences the modern interpreter and his or her contemporary setting.

Finally, in the fourth stage, hermeneutics requires critical reflection in order to correlate the theology of the Old Testament and past interpretations with horizons of meaning that derive from contemporary discourse involving theology, ethics, and issues of pressing concern. This necessitates serious conversation with contemporary theology and even with the interpreter's own theological tradition. It means that the context and identity of the interpreter need to be clearly articulated and set forth as acknowledged components in the conversation. It means that the text should enable believing communities to engage in theological reflection on their practical life. It also means that Old Testament theology should be critically evaluated in the light of modern hermeneutics, even as modern hermeneutics should be open to critical evaluation by Scripture and the history of its interpretation.

To abandon critical evaluation is to obstruct the possibility of dialogue between biblical, historical, and contemporary theologians. To abandon this responsibility also means that the Bible will contribute very little, if anything, to theological conversation in the present. It is as naive to think that contemporary theologians have the capacity to move unaided into biblical theology as it is to think that biblical theologians can address questions of modern import without assistance from contemporary theologians. This involves risk for biblical scholars, but so what? To borrow a phrase from Peter Berger: the plausibility of meaning systems "hangs together by the thin thread of conversation," in this case between contemporary and biblical theologians.[2]

2. Peter Berger, *The Sacred Canopy* (Garden City, N.Y.: Doubleday, 1969). See especially Berger's chapters on "Religion and World-Construction" and "Religion and World-Maintenance," pp. 3–51.

Index of

Modern Authors

309

Index of
Scripture References

OLD TESTAMENT

315

Apocryphal / Deuterocanical books